汉英双语教材
Chinese-English Bilingual Textbook

中国武术
CHINESE MARTIAL ARTS

主编 戴国斌 Chief Editor Dai Guobin
主译 陈丽江 Chief Translator Chen Lijiang

同济大学出版社
Tongji University Press

内 容 提 要

为适应中国武术国际交流与合作的需求,服务孔子学院的武术课程建设,提高来华学习武术留学生的教学质量,迫切需要适合中外武术学习者和爱好者的汉英对照教学读本。本书共十二章,阐述了中国武术文化的历史发展和整体概貌,介绍了少林罗汉十八手、太极拳、形意拳和八卦掌等著名拳种,以及七星剑、风魔棍和双节棍等代表性器械的学习要点和锻炼要求,还拓展性地介绍了马王堆导引术、五禽戏和武功整复术等流行养生术,以及民间体育南狮运动等内容。

全书配有大量图片,分步解析武术动作;同时设置学习计划、技术体验、文化体验和拓展阅读等内容,帮助读者深化学习理解,具有极强的针对性和实用性。

本书为汉英对照读本,适合来华学习武术的留学生作为习武教材使用,同时也适用于中外广大武术学习者和爱好者参考。

图书在版编目(CIP)数据

中国武术:汉英对照/戴国斌主编;陈丽江主译. —上海:同济大学出版社,2018.1
 ISBN 978-7-5608-7265-0

Ⅰ.①中… Ⅱ.①戴… ②陈… Ⅲ.①武术—中国—英、汉 Ⅳ.①G852

中国版本图书馆 CIP 数据核字(2017)第 190044 号

中国武术(汉英对照)

主编　戴国斌　　主译　陈丽江

责任编辑　戴如月　　责任校对　徐春莲　　封面设计　潘向蓁

出版发行	同济大学出版社　www.tongjipress.com.cn	
	(地址:上海市四平路1239号　邮编:200092　电话:021-65985622)	
经　销	全国各地新华书店	
排　版	南京月叶图文制作有限公司	
印　刷	启东市人民印刷有限公司	
开　本	787 mm×1092 mm　1/16	
印　张	26.75	
字　数	668 000	
版　次	2018年1月第1版　2018年1月第1次印刷	
书　号	ISBN 978-7-5608-7265-0	
定　价	98.00元	

本书若有印装质量问题,请向本社发行部调换　　版权所有　侵权必究

编 委 会

主　　　编　戴国斌
副 主 编　郭玉成
主　　　译　陈丽江
翻 译 人 员　熊前莉　卢爱华
编 译 委 员 会　（按姓氏笔画排序）
　　　　　　　　丁丽萍　王　三　王　震　李志明
　　　　　　　　陈　蓓　姜传银　韩丽云　谢业雷
　　　　　　　　蔡　纲　戴有祥

Editorial Committee

Chief Editor: Dai Guobin
Vice Chief Editor: Guo Yucheng
Chief Translator: Chen Lijiang
Translators: Xiong Qianli Lu Aihua
Author List: Ding Liping Wang San Wang Zhen
Li Zhiming Chen Bei Jiang Chuanyin
Han Liyun Xie Yelei Cai Gang
Dai Youxiang

前 言

武术是"武"之术。不论是甲骨文"持戈行军"之解还是楚庄王"止戈为武"之释，"武"的原义都是与军事相关的实践。经过数千年的演变发展，我们今天所见的武术不仅在运动方式上以散打形式继承了军事格斗方式，以套路形式演绎出更为理想、更为美化的动作技术系统，而且将武术运动的目的升华为"身心双修"，使武术运动成为中国人锻炼身体、平衡心性、熏陶精神、涵养道德的活动方式，将武术活动融入中国人的生活之中，使武术成为中华文化的组成部分。换言之，武术，作为中华民族传统体育运动之典范，积淀了中国人的文化创造和生存智慧，凝聚了中国人对天地人关系的理解，体现了中国人和平、包容的心境和优雅、自制的情趣，反映了中华文化强大的凝聚力、生命力和延续力。

近年来，武术在国际上越来越受到人们的关注。随着世界范围掀起的武术热，来华学习武术的留学生以及通过武术了解中国文化的国际友人逐年增多。为了适应武术国际交流与合作的需要，加快武术国际化进程，服务孔子学院（学堂）的武术课程建设，提高来华学习武术留学生的教学质量，本书在上海体育学院多年积累的留学生教学经验的基础上，依据"反映中国文化符号"的原则，编写了适合中外学生的武术教学内容。本书"武术概述"部分阐述了中国武术的历史发展和整体概貌；在具体武术类别上选择介绍了"少林罗汉十八手""太极拳""形意拳""八卦掌"等著名拳种、"七星剑""凤魔棍""双节棍"等代表性器械；还介绍了"马王堆导引术""五禽戏""武功整复术"等流行养生术，以凸显中国武术"外练筋骨皮，内练一口气"的锻炼要求；并选择介绍了"南狮"这一民间体育形式，以反映中国武术融入中国人生活，形成民间体育活动的历史。本书从六方面体现留学生武术教学的文化性、趣味性、养生性、技击性：导言板块，从源流发展与技术风格等方面简单介绍教学内容；学习体验板块，从动作说明、学习计划、技术体验、文化体验等层面深化留学生武术教学；总结板块，就如何学会练好武术、理解武术文化帮助留学生巩固学习效果；延伸学习板块，为留学生进一步学习武术提供具体的建议；思考与练习题板块，出示知识与技术的重点与难点，帮助留学生加深理解、体验学习内容，检查学习效果；参考文献板块，列举编写所引文献，为留学生深入学习提供帮助。

　　本书编写实行主编、主译负责制。编写人员大多为多年从事武术对外教育、具有丰富留学生武术教学经验的人员，英文译者大多为多年从事高等体育英语教学，具有武术翻译经历的人员。本书由戴国斌任主编，提出全书的编写体系、编写原则、编写要求并撰写前言，其中的中文稿由郭玉成一审，戴国斌二、三、终审，英文稿由陈丽江终审。具体分工如下：前言（戴国斌）、第一章武术概述（郭玉成）、第二章24式太极拳（戴有祥）、第三章形意拳（韩丽云）、第四章八卦掌（陈蓓）、第五章少林罗汉十八手（蔡纲）、第六章风魔棍（戴有祥）、第七章七星剑（丁丽萍）、第八章双节棍（姜传银）、第九章马王堆导引术（王震）、第十章五禽戏（谢业雷）、第十一章武功整复术（李志明）、第十二章南狮运动（王三）。段丽梅、刘启超担任秘书。

　　武术国际化面临众多跨文化沟通与传播问题，愿本书在弘扬中华民族优秀文化、造福人类健康、促进中国与世界文化交流的伟大事业中做出有益的工作。

编者
2017年11月

Preface

Wushu (known as Gung fu or Kungfu) is considered to be one of martial arts. "Wu" was originally the practice related to war, no matter it appeared with "marching with weapon carrying" in the Oracle, or said the King Chu Zhuangwang (? —591BC), "stopping the use of weapons and avoiding war is truly military". Today's wushu, not only adopts free combat to succeed the original military combat form, but uses Taolu (routines) to evolve it into a more ideal system of combat techniques. Wushu has been elevated to the cultivation of both body and mind, therefore, wushu becomes one mode of activities by which people build up their body, balance their states of mind, and cultivate their spirits and morals. Wushu activity has been integrated into Chinese daily life, making it one part of Chinese culture.

In recent years, wushu has obtained growing attention internationally. There is an annual increase of international students who come to China to study wushu or foreign friends who learn study Chinese culture by wushu. To satisfy the needs of international exchange and cooperation, quicken the steps of wushu internationalization, serve the wushu course construction of Confucius Institute (Confucius School) and improve the teaching quality for international students who learn wushu, we, based on the experience of studying and teaching abroad over the years, select the teaching content of wushu for international students following the principles that "the content should involve the important wushu schools and it can express the symbols of Chinese culture". Among them, it includes not only the general profile of Chinese wushu, but the famous quan styles such as Shaolin Arhat Eighteen Hands, Taijiquan, Xingyiquan and Baguazhang, etc.; the classical weapons involving Qixing Sword, Fengmo Cudgel-Play, Nunchakus. We also develop wushu in the direction of health building, Mawangdui Daoyin Exercise, Five-animal Exercise and Wushu Chiropractic, to name just a few. Moreover, Nanshi

(Southern Lion Exercise) is added in the book to express Chinese wushu's going into people's lives, thus to form the history of folk sport.

In addition, the book focuses on international students, trying to present its cultural and entertaining characteristics with health-building and fighting in wushu teaching from 6 aspects. In the chapter of introduction, we give a brief overview of wushu's history, styles and techniques; in the part of learning experience, the content involves movement instruction, learning plan, technique experience and cultural experience; in conclusion, we teach students how to practice wushu well and know wushu culture to solidify the students' learning effect; in extensive reading, we provide detailed suggestions for further study; in the part of questions and exercises, the key and difficult points of knowledge and techniques are picked out to deepen student's understanding toward wushu. In reference books, all literatures are listed out to help students find the sources.

The chief editor and chief translator assume the responsibility of the writing of the book. The Chinese writers are mainly those who teach wushu for foreigners over years and possess rich experience of wushu teaching for international students; while the English translators are those who teach English related to sport in higher institutes, with the rich experience of wushu translation accordingly. The initial reviewer for the Chinese part is Professor Guo Yucheng, the final reviewer is Professor Dai Guobin; while the reviewer for English part is Professor Chen Lijiang. The details are as followed: Preface (Dai Guobui), Chapter one (Guo Yucheng), Chapter Two (Dai Youxiang), Chapter Three (Han Liyun), Chapter Four (Chen Bei), Chapter Five (Cai Gang), Chapter Six (Dai Youxiang), Chapter Seven (Ding Liping), Chapter Eight (Jiang Chuanyin), Chapter Nine (Wang Zhen), Chapter Ten (Xie Yelei), Chapter Eleven (Li Zhiming) and Chapter Twelve (Wang San). Duan Limei and Li Qichao did some secretary work.

We hope this book will do some contribution to the great cause of promoting Chinese culture, benefiting human health and improving the international exchange between Chinese and world culture.

Chief Editor
November, 2017

目 录

中文部分

第一章　武术概述 ··· 3
　一、导言 ··· 3
　二、学习体验 ··· 3
　三、总结 ··· 8
　四、延伸学习 ··· 8
　五、思考题 ··· 9
　六、参考文献 ··· 9

第二章　24式太极拳 ·· 10
　一、导言 ·· 10
　二、学习体验 ·· 10
　三、总结 ·· 33
　四、延伸学习 ·· 33
　五、思考与练习题 ·· 33
　六、参考文献 ·· 33

第三章　形意拳（五行连环） ·· 34
　一、导言 ·· 34
　二、学习体验 ·· 34
　三、总结 ·· 38
　四、延伸学习 ·· 38
　五、思考与练习题 ·· 38
　六、参考文献 ·· 39

第四章　八卦掌（定势八掌） ·· 40
　一、导言 ·· 40

二、学习体验 ··· 40
　　三、总结 ··· 48
　　四、延伸学习 ··· 48
　　五、思考与练习题 ··· 48
　　六、参考文献 ··· 48

第五章　少林罗汉十八手 ··· 49
　　一、导言 ··· 49
　　二、学习体验 ··· 49
　　三、总结 ··· 57
　　四、延伸学习 ··· 57
　　五、思考题 ··· 58
　　六、参考文献 ··· 58

第六章　风魔棍 ··· 59
　　一、导言 ··· 59
　　二、学习体验 ··· 59
　　三、总结 ··· 67
　　四、延伸学习 ··· 68
　　五、思考与练习题 ··· 68
　　六、参考文献 ··· 68

第七章　七星剑 ··· 69
　　一、导言 ··· 69
　　二、学习体验 ··· 69
　　三、总结 ··· 81
　　四、延伸学习 ··· 81
　　五、思考与练习题 ··· 81
　　六、参考文献 ··· 82

第八章　双节棍 ··· 83
　　一、导言 ··· 83
　　二、学习体验 ··· 83
　　三、总结 ··· 93
　　四、延伸学习 ··· 93

五、思考与练习题 ·· 94
　　六、参考文献 ·· 94

第九章　马王堆导引术
　　一、导言 ·· 95
　　二、学习体验 ·· 95
　　三、总结 ·· 109
　　四、延伸学习 ·· 110
　　五、思考与练习题 ·· 110
　　六、参考文献 ·· 110

第十章　健身气功·五禽戏
　　一、导言 ·· 111
　　二、学习体验 ·· 111
　　三、总结 ·· 131
　　四、延伸学习 ·· 132
　　五、思考与练习题 ·· 132
　　六、参考文献 ·· 132

第十一章　武功整复术
　　一、导言 ·· 133
　　二、学习体验 ·· 133
　　三、总结 ·· 165
　　四、延伸学习 ·· 165
　　五、思考与练习题 ·· 166
　　六、参考文献 ·· 166

第十二章　南狮运动
　　一、南狮运动概述 ·· 167
　　二、学习体验 ·· 167
　　三、总结 ·· 172
　　四、延伸学习 ·· 172
　　五、思考与练习题 ·· 172
　　六、参考文献 ·· 172

英文部分

Chapter One   Introduction 175
    1 Introduction 175
    2 Learning experience 175
    3 Conclusion 184
    4 Extensive Reading 184
    5 Questions and Exercises 185
    6 References 185

Chapter Two   24-Form Taijiquan 186
    1 Introduction 186
    2 Learning experience 186
    3 Conclusion 216
    4 Extensive Reading 216
    5 Questions 217
    6 References 217

Chapter Three   Xingyiquan (Five-Element Link Fist-Play) 218
    1 Introduction 218
    2 Learning experience 218
    3 Conclusion 225
    4 Extensive reading 225
    5 Questions 225
    6 References 226

Chapter Four   Baguazhang (Eight-Diagram Palm-Play) 227
    1 Introduction 227
    2 Learning experience 227
    3 Conclusion 238
    4 Extensive reading 239
    5 Questions 239
    6 References 239

Chapter Five   Shaolin Arhat Eighteen Hands 240
    1 Introduction 240
    2 Learning experience 240

3	Conclusion	253
4	Extensive reading	254
5	Questions	254
6	References	254

Chapter Six   Fengmo Cudgel-Play ·················· 255
1	Introduction	255
2	Learning experience	255
3	Conclusion	267
4	Extensive Reading	268
5	Questions	268
6	References	268

Chapter Seven   Qixing Sword ·················· 269
1	Introduction	269
2	Learning experience	269
3	Conclusion	287
4	Extensive Reading	288
5	Questions	288
6	References	288

Chapter Eight   Nunchakus ·················· 289
1	Introduction	289
2	Learning experience	289
3	Conclusion	302
4	Extensive reading	302
5	Questions	302
6	References	303

Chapter Nine   Mawangdui Daoyin Exercise ·················· 304
1	Introduction	304
2	Learning experience	304
3	Conclusion	327
4	Extensive reading	327
5	Questions	327
6	References	328

Chapter Ten　Health Qigong · Wu Qin Xi …… 330
　1　Introduction …… 330
　2　Learning experience …… 330
　3　Conclusion …… 359
　4　Extensive reading …… 360
　5　Questions …… 360
　6　References …… 361

Chapter Eleven　Wushu Chiropractic …… 362
　1　Introduction …… 362
　2　Learning experience …… 362
　3　Conclusion …… 402
　4　Extensive reading …… 402
　5　Questions …… 403
　6　References …… 403

Chapter Twelve　Nanshi …… 405
　1　Introduction …… 405
　2　Learning experience …… 405
　3　Conclusion …… 412
　4　Extensive reading …… 412
　5　Questions …… 412
　6　Reference books …… 412

中文部分

第一章

武 术 概 述

一、导言

作为一种体育和文化,武术在中国传承了数千年,它既是中国人传统的健身方法,也是中国传统文化的载体。20 世纪以来,作为体育项目的武术,举办了世界武术锦标赛、亚运会武术比赛等赛事,在 2008 年北京奥运会期间还举办了"北京 2008 武术比赛"。根据国际武术联合会官方网站公布,武术已传播到全世界 147 个国家和地区。作为一项文化,武术已经融入了中国人的生活中,它不仅成为人们修身养性的手段,而且作为艺术形式,在娱人娱己的基础上成为中国文学和中国电影的一个特有类型。武术走向世界,不仅成为促进国际友人身心健康的手段,而且也成为国际友人了解中国文化的窗口。

二、学习体验

(一) 学习内容

1. 武术的概念与特性

(1) 武术的概念

武术是以中华文化为理论基础,以技击方法为基本内容,以套路、格斗、功法为主要运动形式的中国体育。

(2) 武术的特性

武术具有中国性、传统性、文化性、技击性、艺术性、体育性等特性。

① 中国性

"中国性"是武术之所以作为中国文化、中国体育项目存在的首要条件。武术的中国性,在形成和发展的过程中,独自创发,慢慢形成,并自成体系,与其他同类项目差异较大,并绵延数千年,在世界上有了独具特色的文化形态,以致"中国武术"成了中国的标志和符号、国外认识中国文化的一个窗口。

② 传统性

武术的传统性,是因为它的"传",在一代又一代武术人的传承中,武术经过了数千年的历史发展。武术的传统性,也因为它的"统",统是高度,武术反映了中华民族的内涵、特质和气势;统是标杆,武术形成了"源流有序、拳理明晰、风格独特、自成体系"的流派。

武术的传统性,还因它的时间性,它连接着过去,存活于现在,包蕴着未来,而具有强大的生命力。

③ 文化性

武术的文化性,是因为它是中华民族特有的身体文化。武术的文化性,不仅包含了中国人关于身体活动方式的想象,形成了千姿百态的拳种,而且凝聚着中国人对天地人关系的理解,体现了中国人和平、包容的心境和优雅、自制的情趣,蕴含着中华民族文化的内涵和气势,已成为我国文化软实力。

④ 技击性

技击性是武术的本质特征,决定了武术"防身自卫"之功能。武术的技击性,首先体现在与真实对手的散打运动中,以"击必中,中必摧"为标准;其次体现在与虚假对手的对练运动中,以逼真为追求;最后体现在与虚拟对手"搏击"的单练运动中,以"置身于一个充满战斗的场合里"为要求。

⑤ 艺术性

武术艺术性,首先体现在武术的元素美,它将武术的身体区分为"五体"(四肢与躯干),既要求"上下平衡、左右匀称、内外相称",也追求"斜中寓直、奇中寓正、正中含奇";它将武术的运动区分为动与静、起与落、快与慢、高与低、刚与柔、进与退、转与折、收与放、挺与含、虚与实、轻与重等运动状态,并通过互衬对比增强武术动作的艺术感染力。其次,武术的艺术性体现在形式美,它创造了多姿多彩的运动方式,不仅有直来直去的正面打也有"避正打斜"的走转式打,不仅有站着打还有倒地躺着打和站在桩上打,不仅有"放长击远"的远距离打还有贴身近战和"挨帮挤靠"的零距离打,不仅有身稳神清之打还有身形飘忽的醉态之打,不仅有手法密集的狂风暴雨式打还有行云流水的边走边打。最后,武术的艺术性体现在意蕴美,不仅以"静要有势、动要有韵"追求武术的神韵,而且也以动作表现战斗意境,传递中国人对人体运动美的理解,表达武术之美。

⑥ 体育性

体育性是武术特性中最易理解的特性。作为体育性的武术具有健身性,武术锻炼成为医生为患者康复开列的"运动处方"之一,成为许多中国人迈向健康之旅的"手杖",成为成千上万中老年人再造健美的"利器";作为体育性的武术具有竞技性,武术已形成较为完备的竞赛体系,国际性体育赛事就有世界武术锦标赛、世界杯散打比赛、世界青少年武术锦标赛、世界传统武术节、世界运动会武术比赛、世界传统运动会武术比赛、世界武搏运动会武术比赛和亚运会武术比赛等。

2. 武术的技术体系与内容

(1) 武术的技术体系

根据武术的运动形式,可将其技术体系分为套路运动、格斗运动及功法运动(图 1-1)。

套路运动,可分为徒手技术和器械技术两类,进一步区分为单练、对练和集体表演三类(其中包含了徒手与器械对练和徒手与器械集体表演)。

格斗运动,可分为体育范畴之外的实用格斗技术、体育范畴的竞技格斗技术,细分为长兵、短兵、散打、推手。

功法运动,可分为套路运动的"腰、腿、鼎、桩功"等基本功,格斗的拍打功等,以及传统的健身功、强身功、养生功等。

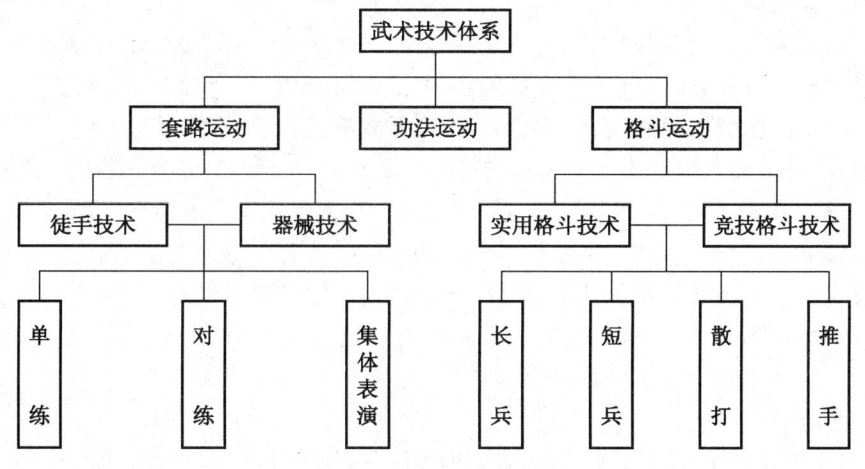

图 1-1　武术技术体系

（2）武术的技术内容

① 竞技武术

竞技武术的技术包括以长拳类、太极拳类、南拳类演练技术和散打、推手等格斗技术组成的技术体系。竞技武术有完善的竞赛体系，包括规定技术、教练员、运动员、裁判员和一定的竞赛形式。竞技武术是在传统武术基础上形成，具有体育的属性。

竞技武术套路运动全国锦标赛的竞赛内容，包括拳术（长拳、南拳、太极拳）、短器械（刀术、剑术、南刀、太极剑）、长器械（棍术、枪术、南棍）、对练（三人对练、二人对练）。

竞技武术套路（传统项目）竞赛内容，拳术包括形意拳、八卦掌、八极拳、通臂拳、劈挂拳、翻子拳、地躺拳、螳螂拳、鹰爪拳、象形拳、查拳、华拳、少林拳、南拳，以及陈式、杨式、武式、吴式、孙式和48式太极拳；器械包括南刀、醉剑、长穗剑、42式太极剑、男棍、朴刀（含大刀）、猴棍、双刀、双剑（含长穗双剑）、双钩、三节棍（含双节棍）、单鞭（含刀加鞭）、绳标（含流星锤）、传统太极器械（含刀、棍、剑、枪、大刀、拂尘）。

竞技武术格斗项目目前主要开展竞技武术散打和竞技推手。

② 武术拳种

根据国家体委1997年编纂的《中国武术史》记载："经过三年（1983—1986年）努力，初步查明流传各地的源流有序、拳理明晰、风格独特、自成体系的拳种129种"。

其主要拳种为：少林拳、心意六合拳、太极拳、形意拳、八卦掌、八极拳、劈挂拳、通臂拳、翻子拳、戳脚、红拳、查拳、华拳、八卦拳、三皇炮捶、六合拳、太祖拳、罗汉拳、拦手、秘宗拳、螳螂拳、猴拳、醉拳、五祖拳、地术拳法、洪家拳、咏春拳、佛家拳、蔡家拳、李家拳、莫家拳、达尊拳、龙尊拳、鹤拳、蔡李佛拳、孙膑拳、硬门拳、法门拳、字门拳、梅花拳、工力拳、花拳、岳氏连拳、绵拳、苌家拳、巫家拳、白眉拳、僧门拳、岳门拳、杜门拳、赵门拳、洪门拳、化门拳、慧门拳、余门拳、弹腿、七势、金狮拳、虎形、南枝拳、八拳、孙家拳、孙门拳、于门拳、王门拳、严门拳、空门拳、岳家拳、三十六路宋江拳、鱼门拳、杨家拳、梁家拳、精合拳、蹉脚门、石头拳、护身拳、指东拳、明堂拳、秘思拳、清拳、四通捶、顺手拳、水炮拳、佛汉拳、枪架拳、独门拳、豹虎拳、弓力拳、三义拳、信拳、二朗门拳、傅拳、鸳鸯拳、九拳、护符拳，等等。

其中,大多数拳种都有拳术、器械、功法等,自成一体。许多拳种都有不同的流派,并在新中国成立后,编创形成竞技性、健身性套路。以太极拳为例,太极拳是中国武术的一个拳种,起源于明末清初温县陈家沟,至今已有300多年的历史,在其发展和演变过程中逐步形成了以陈式、杨式、武式、吴式、孙式等为代表的太极拳流派。新中国成立后,为适应大众健身锻炼的需求及推动太极拳登上体育竞技舞台,国家体育运动委员会先后组织创编了24式简化太极拳和48式、88式等太极拳套路,以及42式太极拳竞赛套路和其他各式流派的太极拳竞赛套路。后为进一步在海内外推广太极拳,立足简单易学的原则又推出了8式、16式太极拳。这样,太极拳由最初重视武术之技击功能,逐渐转向以强身健体、辅助医疗和竞赛表演为走向的多元发展局面,尤其在增进健康和辅助医疗方面,正为世人做出越来越多的贡献。

③ 武术器械

武术的器械在各个拳种流派中都有,风格各异,除竞技武术中常用的刀、剑、棍、枪以外,还有短器械(鞭、鞭杆、钩、拐、锤、橛、匕首)、长器械(笔架叉、大刀、戈、戟、斧、钺、叉、三叉齿钉耙、镋、铲、狼牙棒)、双器械(铁筷子、峨嵋刺、铁梳子、鸡刀镰、月牙刺、马戟)、软器械(流星锤、绳镖、九节鞭、三节棍、龙头杆棒、飞锤、双飞过、四节说、杆子鞭),以及其他器械(判官笔、圈、天荷凤尾镩、狼筅),等等。

3. 武术的文化结构与类型

(1) 武术的文化结构

武术既是体育,也是文化。武术文化从广义上可以定义为:与武术相关的各种文化的总和,包括文化遗产中的武术、体育领域中的武术、影视中的武术、文学中的武术、学校教育中的武术等。从狭义角度看,则指源流有序、拳理明晰、风格独特、自成体系的传统武术拳种流派所蕴含的中国传统文化内涵,以及武德要求、传承制度等。

武术文化的结构分为物器技术层、制度习俗层、心理价值层三个层面。其中,物器技术层包括武术技术、武术器械、武术练功器具、场地、服装等,表现一种人与物的关系;制度习俗层包括武术组织方式、武术传承方式、武术教授方式、武术礼仪规范、武德内容、武术比赛方式等,是一种人与人的关系;心理价值层包括武术文化体现的民族性格、民族心理、民族情感等。一言以蔽之,技与术是外显层,礼与艺是中间层,道与理是核心层。

从武术文化的广义和狭义角度看,武术文化结构的中层为武术技术文化,以及传承和教育制度、武德要求等,内层为武术蕴含的中国传统文化精神和内涵等,属于狭义武术文化的范畴;外层为武术文化与其他文化融合所形成的武侠影视、武侠文学、武术舞剧等文化形态,属于广义武术的范畴。

(2) 武术的文化类型

作为一个相对独立的文化体系,武术文化的类型属于本土文化、大陆文化、大众文化、伦理文化等。其中,武术文化的本土性是相对于外来文化而言,在世界武技的文化之林中,唯有武术文化体系最庞大、内容最丰富,具有浓郁的民族特色和中国特色;武术文化的大陆性是指中国武术多姿多彩的拳种、异彩纷呈的流派与中国地域辽阔的大陆文化相关;武术文化的大众性是因其产生与发展一直以民间为主,进入体育行列的只是其中的一小部分;武术文化的伦理性是表明,武术不仅将人品作为入门考查的主要内容,而且也将武德作为武术训练的重要组成部分。

武术文化主要表现在文化的武术、教育的武术、艺术的武术、体育的武术四个方面。其中,文化的武术是中国武术在其发生发展中,融入中国传统哲学、引入中医理论、体现伦理关怀、散发兵家智慧、走进文学绘画书法音乐舞蹈戏剧等艺术领域,成为中国文化的全息影像和窗口;教育的武术:在夏代将战争技能作为学校教育的内容后,中国教育将"文武兼备"作为理想目标,中国武术将"德技双修"作为培养计划,武术成为修身养性的手段;艺术的武术:中国武术一直沿着"击""舞"两条道路发展,在以散打保持武术的"击"时,又以套路"舞"出了技击方式的千姿百态,增强了武术的艺术感染力,而使套路成为技击的艺术化形式;体育的武术:作为中国人有目的有计划的身体活动,现在已经成为一个体育项目,建立了较为完备的国内外竞赛体系,成为较为成熟的竞赛项目。

(二) 学习计划

本章内容2个课时,使学生了解中国武术概貌,掌握武术概念、特征、内容,以及武术文化的结构、类型和表现形态等。

(三) 文化体验

武术在中国传统文化中孕育形成,融合了中国哲学、医学、伦理、兵学、文学、绘画、书法、音乐、舞蹈、戏剧等文化要素,形成了独具特色的文化形态,成为中国传统文化中的一颗明珠。

武术融入了中国传统哲学的理论。古代武术拳家主动从传统哲学中汲取营养,自觉地以哲学说拳理,指导拳技理法,促进了武术理论的哲理化,使哲学融入拳理中。如太极拳以传统哲学中的太极之理说拳理,八卦掌以传统哲学中的八卦之理说拳理,形意拳以传统哲学中的五行之理说拳理。陈鑫《陈氏太极拳图说》云:"以阴阳开合运动周身者,教子孙以消磨饮食之法,理根太极,故名太极拳。"孙禄堂《八卦拳学》云:"是编为修身而作,取象于数理,立体于卦形,命名于拳术,谓之游身八卦连环掌。"以上说明了拳术与传统哲学的结合过程,是"集成拳术,复安易理。定八卦,合五行,加添招术,代代传流"。

武术技理中引入了中医的基本理论。武术与中医虽属不同学科,但都以认识人体生命活动规律,认识自然环境、药物作用、物理刺激、导引肢体对人体的影响等作为基础。中医依此探索施治之术,武术依此研制练武、用武的方法。如,跌打损伤疗法属中医骨伤科,武术中也有骨伤科方面的理论与技术,而且还有自己的独特治法,如以手法的拍点,通过穴位救治某些击伤处。《少林寺伤科妙方》就是武术伤科理论。武术与中医结合的典范是著名的"点穴"法,武术中的"穴位"有的就是中医的针灸穴位,武术的擒拿法是利用拿筋与拿穴的原理创编出来的。武术界有人使用"健身武术"这一概念,也是因为武术与中医结合的典范,"详推用意终何在,延年益寿不老春"便是武术健身的真实写照。

武术技击要求与中国兵法战略、战术如出一辙。如"知彼知己"是孙子兵法战术指导的总纲,武术技击也要求"知彼知己"。太极拳强调"人不知我,我独知人""以己粘人,必须知人"。郭云深论形意拳技击时说,应"心存谨慎,要知己知彼"。"致人而不致于人"是孙子兵法战术指导的立足点,明代武术家俞大猷的《剑经》中论述了许多棍法的实战技术,他总结说:"千言万语,不外乎致人而不致于人一句。"峨嵋拳创造出一套"不接手"的技击法,主张在与敌交手中以不接手为上策,认为防守容易被动,容易为人所制,因而"你打你的,我打我的"。"兵者诡道""示形于敌"是孙子致胜的主要手段。八卦掌在对敌中常常"或指下而用之上,或指左而用之右,或指此而打彼",形意拳主张"站左进右,站右进左,看正似斜,看斜似正",无不体现了"示形于敌""兵者诡道"的战术思想。"兵贵胜,不贵久"是孙子战术指导的基本要求,主张速战速决,反对打持久战。这与传统武术中"上打咽喉下打阴,遇敌先摘两盏灯"的"一招致敌"思想如出一辙。孙子提出了"兵之情主速"和"后人发,先人至",武术技击也要求快速进攻取胜。洪洞通背拳拳谚:"出手不见手,见手不算手",要求出手的速度快到对手看不见的程度。《少林交手要诀》要求"起落出手快如风,手出足起不见影"。"避实击虚"是孙子战术指导的突出环节,(清)张孔昭在《拳经拳法备要》中所说:"与人对敌时,总要攻击空处。空处何? 两肋、胸、腰与腋,并腿心腿腕是也。能攻处则敌人无所用力,自能百发百中,则所谓避实击虚之法也。"提出了避实击虚的战术原则。

武术与伦理的融合体现在"师徒传承"及"武德"要求上。如尊师重道、尚武崇德、见义勇为等等。武术与戏剧、武打、宗教等传统文化都有不可分割的关系。所以,武术文化是中国文化的浓缩体和载体,是中国文化活的见证。武术的文化性还表现在,武术已经融入中国人的生活中,成为中国人生活的一部分,大多数中国人都有剪不断的"武术情结"。有学者认为,武术是中国人的存在方式,武术包含有中国文化的全部"文化基因"。

三、总结

1. 武术是以中华文化为理论基础,以技击方法为基本内容,以套路、格斗、功法为主要运动形式的传统体育。
2. 武术具有中国性、传统性、文化性、技击性、艺术性、体育性等特性。
3. 武术的技术体系由套路运动、格斗运动和功法运动,以及竞技武术、武术拳种和器械组成。
4. 武术文化的结构有物器技术层、制度习俗层、心理价值层三个层面,武术的文化类型属于本土文化、大陆文化、伦理文化、大众文化,武术文化表现可概括为文化的武术、教育的武术、艺术的武术、体育的武术。

四、延伸学习

(一) 武术拳种流派的分类

武术的内容丰富多彩,历史上曾经有多种分类。按照拳理技法,分为内家与外家;按照地理空间,分为南派和北派;按照山川地域,分为少林派、武当派、峨眉派等;按照拳术风格,分为长拳类和短打类;按照江河流域,分为长江流域派、黄河流域派、珠江流域派等。

(二) 十八般武艺

明代将武术项目概括为"十八般武艺",《五杂俎》的记载为:一弓、二弩、三枪、四刀、五剑、六矛、七盾、八斧、九钺、十戟、十一鞭、十二锏、十三挝、十四殳、十五叉、十六钯头、十七棉绳套索、十八白打。

五、思考与练习题

1. 简述武术的概念。
2. 简述武术的特性。
3. 简述武术的技术体系。
4. 简述传统武术流派的分类。

六、参考文献

[1] 国家体委武术研究院编纂. 中国武术史[M]. 北京：人们体育出版社，1996，310-311.
[2] 全国体育院校教材委员会审定. 武术理论基础[M]. 北京：人民体育出版社，1997：27-28.
[3] 蔡龙云. 我对武术的看法[J]. 新体育，1957(2)：20-21.
[4] 邱丕相. 武术套路的美学特征与艺术性[J]. 上海体育学院学报，2004(2)：39-40.
[5] 戴国斌. 武术：身体的文化[M]. 北京：人民体育出版社，2011：405-441.
[6] 阮纪正. 武术：中国人的存在方式[J]. 开放时代，1996(3)：24-26.
[7] 郭玉成. 体育的武术与文化的武术[J]. 武术科学，2007(5)：1-3.

第二章

24 式太极拳

一、导言

太极拳是中国武术的一个重要拳种,具有陈式、杨式、吴式、武式、孙式等流派。新中国成立后,国家体育运动委员会先后创编了 24 式简化太极拳和 48 式、88 式等太极拳套路。其中,24 式太极拳,往返 4 趟,动作左右对称,全套 24 个动作包含了太极拳"掤、捋、挤、按、采、挒、肘、靠、进、退、顾、盼、定"等技法,是太极拳的入门套路。

二、学习体验

(一) 动作说明

1. 预备势。两脚并拢,身体自然站立,两手自然垂于大腿外侧;头项正直,口闭齿扣,胸腹放松;目平视前方(图 2-1)。

2. 起势。左脚向左分开,两脚平行同肩宽(图 2-2-1)。臂自然伸直,慢慢向前举;两手手心向下,举至同肩高(图 2-2-2,图 2-2-3)。两腿慢慢屈膝半蹲,同时屈肘坐腕两掌轻轻向下按至腹前(图 2-2-4)。

图 2-1 预备势

图 2-2-1 起势

图 2-2-2 起势

图 2-2-3　起势

图 2-2-4　起势

图 2-3-1　左野马分鬃

3. 左右野马分鬃，有 3 个动作。

（1）左野马分鬃。上体稍右转，右臂向外上划弧，左手心翻上（图 2-3-1）。上体稍左转，右臂屈肘平收，左臂屈抱于腹前，成右抱球；左脚收至右脚内侧成丁步（图 2-3-2）。上体保持，出左脚，两手臂相合（图 2-3-3）。左腿屈膝成左弓步，同时两掌前分后捋，目视左手的方向（图 2-3-4）。

图 2-3-2　左野马分鬃

图 2-3-3　左野马分鬃

图 2-3-4　左野马分鬃

（2）右野马分鬃。右腿屈膝，身体后坐，左脚尖勾起（图 2-3-5），身体左转，左脚尖外撇，左手心翻下外掤，右手心翻上（图 2-3-6）。上体稍左转，左腿屈膝半蹲收右脚成丁步左抱球（图 2-3-7）。上体保持，出右脚，两手臂稍合（图 2-3-8）。右腿屈膝成右弓步，同时两掌前分后捋，目视右手的方向（图 2-3-9）。

图 2-3-5　右野马分鬃　　　图 2-3-6　右野马分鬃　　　图 2-3-7　右野马分鬃

图 2-3-8　右野马分鬃　　　图 2-3-9　右野马分鬃

（3）左野马分鬃。动作同（1），见图 2-3-2—图 2-3-4。

4. 白鹤亮翅。上体左转正向，右脚跟上半步，同时两手在胸前屈臂抱球（图 2-4-1）。重心坐于右腿，上体右转，左手合于右腕处后上举（图 2-4-2）。上体回转正，左脚稍提起调整，成左脚虚步；同时右手分至右额前，掌心向内，左手按至左腿旁；眼平视前方（图 2-4-3）。

图 2-4-1　白鹤亮翅　　　图 2-4-2　白鹤亮翅　　　图 2-4-3　白鹤亮翅

5. 左右搂膝拗步, 有3个动作。

（1）左搂膝拗步。上体右转,右手至头偏左前下落(图2-5-1)。身体右转,右手下落至右胯侧向后方上举,左手随提转上摆(图2-5-2)。身体继续稍右转,右手向右上划弧落至右肩平;左脚收至右脚内侧成丁步;左手弧形下按于右肘内侧,目视右手(图2-5-3)。左脚向左侧出,同时,右臂屈肘,右手收于右耳侧(图2-5-4)。左腿屈膝成左弓步,左手经左膝前上方搂过,停于左腿外侧,掌心向下,指尖向前,右手经耳侧随转身向前推出(图2-5-5)。

图2-5-1　左搂膝拗步　　　图2-5-2　左搂膝拗步　　　图2-5-3　左搂膝拗步

图2-5-4　左搂膝拗步　　　图2-5-5　左搂膝拗步

（2）右搂膝拗步。右腿屈膝,重心后坐,左脚尖翘起(图2-5-6),上体左转,左脚稍外撇;同时左手向左侧划弧,右手随体转稍向上划弧(图2-5-7),重心移至左腿,右脚收至左脚内侧成丁步;同时,身体继续左转,左手手心朝上向左上划弧落至左肩平;右脚收至右脚内侧成丁步,右手弧形下按于左肘内侧,目视左手(图2-5-8)。右脚向右前方出步,同时,左臂屈肘,左手收于左耳侧(图2-5-9)。右腿屈膝成右弓步,同时,右手经右膝前上方搂过,停于右腿外侧,掌心向下,指尖向前,左手经耳侧随转身向前推出(图2-5-10)。

图 2-5-6 右搂膝拗步　　图 2-5-7 右搂膝拗步　　图 2-5-8 右搂膝拗步

图 2-5-9 右搂膝拗步　　图 2-5-10 右搂膝拗步

（3）左搂膝拗步。左腿屈膝，重心后坐，右脚尖翘起（图2-5-11）。上体右转，右脚稍外撇，身体重心往右腿移动；同时右手向右侧划弧，左手随体转稍向上划弧（图2-5-12）。身体继续稍右转，右手向右上划弧落至右肩平；左脚收至右脚内侧成丁步；左手弧形下按于右肘内侧，目视右手（图2-5-13）。左脚向左前方出，同时，右臂屈肘，右手收于右耳侧（图2-5-14）。左腿屈膝成左弓步，同时，左手经左膝前上方搂过，停于左腿外侧，掌心向下，指尖向前，右手经耳侧随转身向前推出（图2-5-15）。

图 2-5-11 左搂膝拗步　　图 2-5-12 左搂膝拗步　　图 2-5-13 左搂膝拗步

图 2-5-14　左搂膝拗步　　　　图 2-5-15　左搂膝拗步

6. 手挥琵琶。右脚向前收拢半步落于左脚后；右臂稍向前伸展（图 2-6-1）。重心移至右腿，上体右转，同时左手向前划弧摆动（图 2-6-2）。上体稍向左回转，左脚稍提起脚跟着地，成左虚步；两臂外旋屈肘合抱，右手与左肘相对，掌心向左，目视左手方向（图 2-6-3）。

图 2-6-1　手挥琵琶　　　　图 2-6-2　手挥琵琶　　　　图 2-6-3　手挥琵琶

7. 左右倒卷肱，有 4 个动作。

（1）右倒卷肱。上体稍右转，左手心翻上，右手旋外下落经右胯侧举（图 2-7-1）。左脚提起向后退一步后左转身体，同时，右臂屈肘，右手收至右耳侧；重心后移，成右虚步；右手推至体前，左手向后、向下划弧，收至左腰侧，手心向上；眼视右手方向（图 2-7-2）。

图 2-7-1　右倒卷肱　　　　图 2-7-2　右倒卷肱　　　　图 2-7-3　左倒卷肱

（2）左倒卷肱。上体稍左转，右手心翻上，左手旋外下落经左胯侧举（图2-7-3）。右脚提起向后退一步后右转身体，同时，左臂屈肘，左手收至左耳侧；重心后移，成左虚步；左手推至体前，右手向后、向下划弧，收至右腰侧，手心向上；眼视左手方向（图2-7-4）。

（3）右倒卷肱。上体稍右转，左手心翻上，右手旋外下落经右胯侧举（图2-7-5）。左脚提起向后退一步后左转身体，同时，右臂屈肘，右手收至右耳侧；重心后移，成右虚步；右手推至体前，左手向后、向下划弧，收至左腰侧，手心向上；眼视右手方向（图2-7-6）。

图2-7-4　左倒卷肱　　　图2-7-5　右倒卷肱　　　图2-7-6　右倒卷肱

（4）左倒卷肱。上体稍左转，右手心翻上，左手旋外下落经左胯侧举（图2-7-7）。右脚提起向后退一步后右转身体，同时，左臂屈肘，左手收至左耳侧；重心后移，成左虚步；左手推至体前，右手向后、向下划弧，收至右腰侧，手心向上；眼视左手方向（图2-7-8）。

图2-7-7　左倒卷肱　　　　　图2-7-8　左倒卷肱

8. 左揽雀尾。上体稍右转，右手向侧后上方划弧，左手在体前下落（图2-8-1），两手呈右抱球状，左脚收成丁步（图2-8-2）。上体左转，左脚向左前方迈步，两手臂随体转于胸前微合（图2-8-3），左腿屈膝前弓成弓步，同时，左臂屈肘，手心朝内向前平撑，右手捋按至右胯旁（图2-8-4）。

图 2-8-1　左揽雀尾

图 2-8-2　左揽雀尾

图 2-8-3　左揽雀尾

图 2-8-4　左揽雀尾

图 2-8-5　左揽雀尾

图 2-8-6　左揽雀尾

上体稍向左转,左手向左前方伸出,同时右臂外旋,向上、向前伸至左臂内侧,掌心向上(图 2-8-5)。身体右转、后坐,两手同时向下经腹前向右后方划弧捋至腹前(图 2-8-6)。上体稍右转,右手向右上划弧摆起,左手划弧至右胸侧(图 2-8-7),身体左转,右手随屈臂搭手于左腕内关处(图 2-8-8),左腿屈膝,身体重心前移成左弓步;右手推送左前臂向体前挤出,两臂撑圆(图 2-8-9)。

图 2-8-7　左揽雀尾

图 2-8-8　左揽雀尾

图 2-8-9　左揽雀尾

左手心翻下,右手前伸于两腕处交叉(图2-8-10),两手向外平滑开,与肩同宽(图2-8-11),屈右膝后坐,左脚尖勾起,两手随屈臂回收(图2-8-12),两手同高度回收至胸前一掌间隔时,下按于腹前(图2-8-13),重心前移成左弓步,两手前推至水平(图2-8-14)。

图 2-8-10　左揽雀尾　　　图 2-8-11　左揽雀尾　　　图 2-8-12　左揽雀尾

图 2-8-13　左揽雀尾　　　图 2-8-14　左揽雀尾

9. 右揽雀尾。 上体稍右转,右腿屈膝后坐(图2-9-1),上体继续右转,右手向右平划弧,左脚尖内扣(图2-9-2),身体重心移至左腿,右手向下划弧(图2-9-3),右腿回收成丁步,两手成抱球式(图2-9-4)。上体右转,右脚向右前方迈步,两手臂随体转于胸前微合(图2-9-5),右腿屈膝成弓步,同时,右臂屈肘,手心朝内向前平撑,左手捋按至右胯旁(图2-9-6)。

图 2-9-1　右揽雀尾　　　图 2-9-2　右揽雀尾　　　图 2-9-3　右揽雀尾

图 2-9-4　右揽雀尾　　　图 2-9-5　右揽雀尾　　　图 2-9-6　右揽雀尾

上体稍向右转,右手向右前方伸出,同时左臂外旋,向上、向前伸至右臂内侧,掌心向上(图 2-9-7)。上体左转,身体后坐,两手同时向下经腹前向右后方划弧捋至腹前(图 2-9-8)。上体稍左转,左手向左上划弧摆起,左手划弧至右胸侧(图 2-9-9),身体右转,左手随屈臂搭手于右腕内关处(图 2-9-10),右腿屈膝,身体重心前移成右弓步;左手推送右前臂向体前挤出,两臂撑圆(图 2-9-11)。

图 2-9-7　右揽雀尾　　　图 2-9-8　右揽雀尾　　　图 2-9-9　右揽雀尾

图 2-9-10　右揽雀尾　　　图 2-9-11　右揽雀尾

右手心翻下,左手前伸于两腕处交叉(图 2-9-12),两手向外平滑开,与肩同宽(图 2-9-13),屈右膝后坐,左脚尖勾起,两手随屈臂回收(图 2-9-14),两手同高度回收至胸前一掌间隔时,下按于腹前(图2-9-15),重心前移成右弓步,两手前推至水平(图2-9-16)。

图 2-9-12　右揽雀尾　　　图 2-9-13　右揽雀尾　　　图 2-9-14　右揽雀尾

图 2-9-15　右揽雀尾　　　图 2-9-16　右揽雀尾

10. 单鞭。上体稍左转,左腿屈膝后坐(图2-10-1),身体继续左转,左手心翻外后向左侧划弧,右手随体转在腹前划弧(图2-10-2),重心平移至右腿,右手向左上划弧经面颊移至右侧,手心朝内,左手下落(图2-10-3),右腿屈膝,左脚回收成丁步;右臂内旋,右手至右前方变成勾手,腕高与肩平,左手向下上划弧至左肘下,掌心向上;眼视勾手(图2-10-4)。上体稍左转,左脚向左前方迈步(图2-10-5),左腿屈膝,右腿前蹬成左弓步,同时,左手心旋外向前推按,目视左手前方(图2-10-6)。

图 2-10-1　单鞭　　　图 2-10-2　单鞭　　　图 2-10-3　单鞭

图 2-10-4 单鞭　　　图 2-10-5 单鞭　　　图 2-10-6 单鞭

11. 云手。身体重心后坐,左脚尖勾起(图 2-11-1),身体右转,左脚尖内扣,同时,右勾手变掌,左手向下划弧至右肘下(图 2-11-2)。上体稍左转,重心移至左腿,左手心朝内,向上划弧,右手下落划弧(图 2-11-3),右脚向左脚收并保持一脚宽距成小开立步,左手经头前向左划弧,过面颊后掌心渐渐向外翻转,右手向下、向左划弧(图 2-11-4)。

图 2-11-1 云手 　　　图 2-11-2 云手 　　　图 2-11-3 云手

图 2-11-4 云手 　　　图 2-11-5 云手 　　　图 2-11-6 云手

右手向左向上划弧,左手下按划弧(图2-11-5),身体稍右转,重心移至右腿,左脚向左横开一步,脚尖向前;右手心经面颊后掌心逐渐由内转向外,左手向下、向右划弧(图2-11-6)。上体稍左转,重心移至左腿,左手心朝内,向上划弧,右手下落划弧(图2-11-7),右脚向左脚收并保持一脚宽距成小开立步,左手经头前向左划弧,过面颊后掌心渐渐向外翻转,右手向下、向左划弧(图2-11-8)。

图2-11-7 云手　　　　图2-11-8 云手　　　　图2-11-9 云手

右手向左向上划弧,左手下按划弧(图2-11-9),身体稍右转,重心移至右腿,左脚向左横开一步,脚尖向前;右手心经面颊后掌心逐渐由内转向外,左手向下、向右划弧(图2-11-10)。上体稍左转,重心移至左腿,左手心朝内,向上划弧,右手下落划弧(图2-11-11),右脚向左脚收并保持一脚宽距成小开立步,左手经头前向左划弧,过面颊后掌心渐渐向外翻转,右手向下、向左划弧(图2-11-12)。

图2-11-10 云手　　　　图2-11-11 云手　　　　图2-11-12 云手

12. 单鞭。右手向左向上划弧,左手下按划弧(图2-12-1),身体稍右转,右手心经面颊后掌心逐渐由内转向外,左手向下、向右划弧(图2-12-2)。右腿屈膝支撑,左脚回收成丁步;右手变成勾手,左手向下上划弧至左肘下,掌心向上;目视勾手方向(图2-12-3)。

图 2-12-1 单鞭　　　图 2-12-2 单鞭　　　图 2-12-3 单鞭

上体稍左转,左脚向左前方迈步(图 2-12-4),左腿屈膝成左弓步,同时,左手心旋外向前推按,目视左手前方(2-12-5)。

图 2-12-4 单鞭　　　图 2-12-5 单鞭　　　图 2-13-1 高探马

13. 高探马。后脚向前收拢半步;右手勾手变掌,两手翻心转向上目视右手方向(图 2-13-1)。上体稍左转,左脚稍提起落步移成左虚步;右手经耳侧向前推出;左臂屈收至腹前,掌心向上目视右手方向(图 2-13-2)。

图 2-13-2 高探马　　　图 2-14-1 右蹬脚　　　图 2-14-2 右蹬脚

14. 右蹬脚。上体稍左转,左脚向左前方迈出,脚跟着地;左手稍向后收,左手经右手背上方向前穿出,两手交叉,左掌心斜向上,右掌心斜向下(图2-14-1)。两臂内旋,两手心翻外分手(图2-14-2),重心移至左腿屈膝半蹲,右脚收至左腿内侧,两手继续划弧下分(图2-14-3),左腿直立支撑,右腿屈膝上提,同时,两手下手腕处交叉,右手在外,两掌心皆转向内,收于胸前合抱(图2-14-4)。两手手心翻外撑开,右足跟用力慢慢向右前上方蹬出,膝关节伸直,右腿与右臂上下相对,目视右手方向(图2-14-5)。

图2-14-3 右蹬脚　　　　图2-14-4 右蹬脚　　　　图2-14-5 右蹬脚

15. 双峰贯耳。身体右转,右小腿屈膝回收,左手心朝上向体前划弧,与右手并行(图2-15-1)。左腿屈膝,右脚出步,同时,两手下落于要两侧(图2-15-2)。右屈膝前弓成右弓步;两手变拳拳经两腰侧向后、向外、向前上划弧摆至头前,两臂半屈成钳形,两拳相对,同头宽,拳眼斜向下(图2-15-3)。

图2-15-1 双峰贯耳　　　　图2-15-2 双峰贯耳　　　　图2-15-3 双峰贯耳

16. 转身左蹬脚。重心后移至左腿,右脚尖勾起(图2-16-1),上体左转,两拳变掌(图2-16-2)。重心右移,两手向下划弧(图2-16-3)。右腿直立,左腿收并后屈膝上提,两臂交叉合抱于胸前,左手在外,两手心皆向内(图2-16-4)。上体微左转,两手手心翻外撑开,左跟用力慢慢向左前上方蹬出,膝关节伸直,左腿与左臂上下相对,目视左手方向(图2-16-5)。

图2-16-1　转身左蹬脚　　　图2-16-2　转身左蹬脚　　　图2-16-3　转身左蹬脚

图2-16-4　转身左蹬脚　　　图2-16-5　转身左蹬脚

17. 左下势独立。左腿屈收于右腿内侧，右手成勾，左手平摆至右肘处，掌心向右（图2-17-1）。上体不动，左腿向左侧落步（图2-17-2），身体左转，髋部下沉成左仆步，同时左掌贴身向下沿左腿内侧向左穿掌，虎口朝上（图2-17-3），重心移向左腿成左弓步；左手前穿并向上挑起，右勾手内旋，勾尖朝上，置于身后（图2-17-4）。上体左转，重心前移，左手心翻下，右手成掌向下、向上挑（图2-17-5），左腿直立，右腿屈膝提起成左独立步；左手下落按于左胯旁，右掌继续向上挑起，掌心向左，高于眼平，右臂半屈成弧（图2-17-6）。

图2-17-1　左下势独立　　　图2-17-2　左下势独立　　　图2-17-3　左下势独立

图 2-17-4　左下势独立　　　图 2-17-5　左下势独立　　　图 2-17-6　左下势独立

18. 右下势独立。右脚落于左脚右前方，脚前掌着地（图 2-18-1），上体左转，左脚以脚掌为轴随之扭转，左手变勾手向上提举于身体左侧，高与肩平，右手划弧摆至左肩前，掌心向左（图 2-18-2）。

图 2-18-1　右下势独立　　　图 2-18-2　右下势独立　　　图 2-18-3　右下势独立

右脚向右侧出步，髋部下沉成右仆步，同时右掌贴身向下沿右腿内侧向右穿掌，虎口朝上（图 2-18-3）。重心移向右腿成右弓步，右手前穿并向上挑起，左勾手内旋，勾尖朝上，置于身后（图 2-18-4）。上体右转，重心前移，右手心翻下，左手成掌向下、向上挑（图 2-18-5），右腿直立，左腿屈膝提起成右独立步；右手下落按于右胯旁，左掌继续向上挑起，掌心向右，高于眼平，左臂半屈成弧（图 2-18-6）。

图 2-18-4　右下势独立　　　图 2-18-5　右下势独立　　　图 2-18-6　右下势独立

19. 左右穿梭,有 2 个动作。

(1) 右穿梭。上体左转,左脚向左前方落步,脚尖外撇,左手心翻下(图 2-19-1),左腿屈膝支撑,右腿收并左脚内侧成丁步,右手心翻上,两手呈左抱球状(图 2-19-2)。上体右转,右脚向右前方出步;右手向前上方划弧举起,左手下落于左腰侧(图 2-19-3),左腿蹬转,右腿屈膝成右弓步,同时,右臂翻转上举,架于右额前上方,左手前推(图 2-19-4)。

图 2-19-1　右穿梭　　　图 2-19-2　右穿梭　　　图 2-19-3　右穿梭

图 2-19-4　右穿梭　　　图 2-19-5　左穿梭

(2) 左穿梭。重心稍后移,右脚尖翘起后落地重心移至右腿,左手心翻上(图 2-19-5),左脚收成丁步,两手在右肋前上下相抱成抱球(图 2-19-6)。上体右转,左脚向左前方出步;左手向前上方划弧举起,右手下落于右腰侧(图 2-19-7),右腿蹬转,左腿屈膝成左弓步,同时,左臂翻转上举,架于左额前上方,右手前推(图 2-19-8)。

图 2-19-6　左穿梭　　　图 2-19-7　左穿梭　　　图 2-19-8　左穿梭

20. 海底针。左臂下落,右臂回收,右脚向前收拢半步,随之重心后移,右腿屈坐(图2-20-1)。上体右转,提左膝,左手向右划弧下落至左膝上方,掌心向下,指尖斜向右,右手屈臂提抽至耳侧,掌心向左,指尖向前(图2-20-2),左脚前落成左虚步,上体左转向前俯身,右手向前下方斜插,左手经膝前划弧搂过,按至左大腿侧,目视前下方(图2-20-3)。

图 2-20-1 海底针　　　　图 2-20-2 海底针　　　　图 2-20-3 海底针

21. 闪通臂。上体右转,左脚出步,右上提内旋,手心斜向外上,左手上举,指尖贴近右腕内侧(图2-21-1)。左腿屈膝成左弓步,上体稍右转,左手随提转向左侧推出,右手撑于头侧上方,掌心斜向上,目视左手方向(图2-21-2)。

图 2-21-1 闪通臂　　　　图 2-21-2 闪通臂

22. 转身搬拦拳。重心后移,右腿屈膝(图2-22-1);左脚尖内扣,身体右转,重心逐步移至左腿,同时,右手摆至体右侧,左手摆至头左侧,掌心均向外(图2-22-2);左腿屈膝支撑,上体继续右转,右手变拳收于腹前,右腿屈膝回收(图2-22-3);右脚稍上提,左手经胸前下按,右臂屈肘,右拳上摆(图2-22-4),上体稍右转,右脚向前出步,同时,右拳以肘为轴向前翻拳,力达拳背,左手回收于左胯旁(图2-22-5),右脚尖外撇,重心前移,右臂内旋,拳心向下(图2-22-6),上体右转,重心前移,右拳向右划弧至体侧,拳心向下,左臂外撑后随体转向前划弧,手心朝下,左腿屈膝回收(图2-22-7),左脚向前上步,左臂稍外旋,使左掌虎口朝上拦击,右拳翻转收至腰间,拳心向上(图2-22-8),上体左转,重心前移成左弓步,右拳向前打出,拳眼向上,左手回收掌指附于右前臂内侧,掌心向右(图2-22-9)。

图 2-22-1 转身搬拦拳

图 2-22-2 转身搬拦拳

图 2-22-3 转身搬拦拳

图 2-22-4 转身搬拦拳

图 2-22-5 转身搬拦拳

图 2-22-6 转身搬拦拳

图 2-22-7 转身搬拦拳

图 2-22-8 转身搬拦拳

图 2-22-9 转身搬拦拳

23. 如封似闭。 左手心翻转向上，从右前臂下向前穿出（图 2-23-1），右拳变掌，翻转朝上，左手前伸（图 2-23-2），左右掌左右平分同肩宽，手心朝上（图 2-23-3）。重心后移，左脚尖勾起，两臂屈收后引（图 2-23-4），两手收至胸前，内旋手臂，使手心朝下按于腹前（图 2-23-5）。重心前移成左弓步；两手前推上翘至水平后前推（图 2-23-6）。

图 2-23-1　如封似闭 　　图 2-23-2　如封似闭 　　图 2-23-3　如封似闭

图 2-23-4　如封似闭 　　图 2-23-5　如封似闭 　　图 2-23-6　如封似闭

24. 十字手。身体后坐,左脚尖勾起(图 2-24-1),上体右转,左脚尖内扣,右手向右平划弧(图 2-24-2),上体右转,右脚外撇;同时,右手继续划弧至右侧(图 2-24-3)。

两手臂下落,两手腕在腹前交叉,右手在外;手心皆向上。右脚蹬地收右脚于左脚边,同肩宽;同时两手上举于胸前,手心朝内(图 2-24-4)。

图 2-24-1　十字手 　　图 2-24-2　十字手 　　图 2-24-3　十字手

图 2-24-4　十字手　　　　图 2-25-1　收势　　　　图 2-25-2　收势

25. 收势。两臂内旋,两手翻转向下(图 2-25-1),两臂左右平分开(图 2-25-2)。两腿直立,同时两手臂下按于两胯旁(图 2-25-3),两手自然下垂,目视前方(图 2-25-4)。左脚轻轻收回,恢复成预备姿势,保持目视方向(图 2-25-5)。

图 2-25-3　收势　　　　图 2-25-4　收势　　　　图 2-25-5　收势

(二) 学习计划

项目	内　容
前期准备	1. 太极拳手法(体验太极拳动作的松、柔、慢、圆) 2. 太极拳步伐(体验太极拳迈步与重心变化) 3. 太极拳桩法(体验身体状态与心理调整)
学习进度	1. 学会动作路线 (1) 起式—野马分鬃—白鹤亮翅 (2) 搂膝拗步—手挥琵琶 (3) 倒卷肱—左右揽雀尾 (4) 单鞭—云手—单鞭 (5) 高探马—右蹬腿—双峰贯耳—左蹬腿 (6) 右下势独立—左下势独立 (7) 穿梭—海底针—闪通臂 (8) 转身搬拦捶—如封似闭—十字手—收式 2. 体验太极拳运动风格

（三）技术体验

内容	要求
心静体松	"心静"是太极拳锻炼时力争排除杂念，思想集中，呼吸平和； "体松"不是全身松懈疲塌，而是在保持身体姿势正确的基础上，有意识地让全身关节、肌肉等达到最大限度的放松状态
虚实分明	太极拳锻炼中，要分清虚实；下肢主要支撑体重的腿为"实"，辅助支撑或移动换步的腿为"虚"；上肢体现动作主要内容的手臂为"实"，辅助配合的手臂为"虚"。在太极拳锻炼中要注意虚实变化
圆活连贯	"圆活"是太极拳的重要运动规律。讲究动作路线走圆呈弧，肢体形态保持圆弧状；以确保身体不僵滞，动作衔接自然流畅。 "连贯"不仅有肢体以腰为枢纽的"节节贯穿"，有下肢以腰带胯、以胯带膝、以膝带足的连贯，有上肢以腰带背、以背带肩、以肩带肘、以肘带手的连贯；而且有动作与动作之间的衔接，即"势势相连"
呼吸自然	呼吸方法有自然呼吸（平时多数人的无意识呼吸）、腹式顺呼吸、腹式逆呼吸。太极拳的呼吸自然是在有意识运用腹式呼吸的基础上，逐步纯熟，达到自然呼吸的地步

（四）文化体验

• 太极

受《周易·系辞传》的启发，宋代哲学家周敦颐在《太极图说》中阐释了其宇宙观：无极而生太极，太极而生阳，动极而静。静极复动，一动一静，互为其根；分阴分阳，两仪立焉。

太极拳含蓄内敛、连绵不断、以柔克刚、急缓相间、行云流水的拳术风格使习练者的意、气、形、神逐渐趋于圆融一体的至高境界，而其对于武德修养的要求也使得习练者在增强体质的同时提高自身素养，提升人与自然、人与社会的融洽与和谐。

• 阴阳

阴阳，源自古代中国的自然观，是古人对自然界中各种对立又相联现象的哲学概括，如天地、日月、昼夜、寒暑、男女、上下等。

太极拳技击法皆遵循阴阳之理，以"引化合发"为主要技击过程。技击中，由听劲感知对方来力大小及方向，"顺其势而改其路"，将来力引化掉，再借力发力。

太极拳的特点是："以柔克刚，以静待动，以圆化直，以小胜大，以弱胜强。"

• 太极十三势歌

十三总势莫轻视，命意源头在腰际。变换虚实需留意，气遍身躯不稍滞。
静中触动动尤静，因敌变化示神奇。势势存心揆用意，得来不觉费功夫。
刻刻留心在腰间，腹内松静气腾然。尾闾中正神贯顶，满身轻利顶头悬。
仔细留心向推求，屈伸开合听自由。入门引路需口授，功夫无息法自修。
若言体用何为准，意气君来骨肉臣。详推用意终何在，益寿延年不老春。
歌兮歌兮百四十，字字真切义无遗。若不向此推求去，枉费工夫贻叹息。

三、总结

（一）24 式太极拳是太极拳的入门套路。
（二）在熟悉动作路线后,要体会太极拳的松、柔、慢要求。
（三）在心静体松、呼吸自然的基础上,进一步体验虚实分明、圆活连贯。

四、延伸学习

学会 24 式太极拳后,你可在进一步提高太极拳运动风格上延伸学习,也可将新的套路作为延伸学习的内容,如 48 式太极拳、42 式太极剑等,还可以陈式、杨式、吴式、武式、孙式等流派太极拳的学习拓展对太极拳的理解。

五、思考与练习题

1. 太极拳的四个主要手法掤、捋、挤、按对应的动作是什么?
2. 如何做到呼吸自然?
3. 如何理解太极拳的慢,做到慢的最佳途径是什么?

六、参考文献

[1] 邱丕相.中国武术教程(上册)[M].北京:人民体育出版社,2004.
[2] 全国体育学院教材编写组.武术—体育学院普修通用教材[M].北京:人民体育出版社,1989.
[3] 唐豪,顾留馨.太极拳研究[M].北京:人民体育出版社,1964.
[4] 武冬.24 式太极拳入门与提高[M].太原:山西科学技术出版社,2001.

第三章

形意拳(五行连环)

一、导言

形意拳发源于山西,广泛流传于山西、河北、河南三地。它以三体式为基础桩法,以五行拳(劈、崩、钻、炮、横)和十二形拳(龙、虎、猴、马、鸡、鹞、燕、蛇、鼍、骀、鹰、熊)为基本拳法,其单练套路有五行连环、杂式锤、八式拳等,对练套路有三手炮、五花炮、安身炮等。

二、学习体验

(一) 动作说明

1. 预备式。 身体直立,两臂自然下垂,两脚并拢,目视前下方(图3-1)。

2. 进步劈拳。 身体方向不变,左脚前进一步,两脚脚跟前后相对,相距约两脚长,两腿屈膝,重心偏于右腿;同时两拳由腹上前后变掌,左掌前伸,肘部微屈,掌心向前下方,五指分开,掌心内含,高与胸齐,右掌后撤落于腹前,拇指根节紧靠肚脐,手腕向下塌,眼看左掌食指(图3-2)。

3. 进步右崩拳。 身体左转,两掌变拳握紧,然后左脚前进一步,右脚随之跟步,重心仍在右腿;前脚跟与后脚跟相对,两脚距离约20～30厘米;同时,右拳顺着左臂方向直向前打出,拳眼向上,拳面微向前倾,左拳撤至腰部左侧,拳心向上,目视右拳(图3-3)。

图3-1　预备式　　　　图3-2　进步劈掌(侧面)　　　　图3-3　进步右崩拳

要点：左脚前进落地与右拳打出时要整齐一致，抬脚不要过高，身体要平稳，腰要塌住。

4. 退步左崩拳（青龙出水）。 右脚后撤半步，左脚撤至右脚后方，同时左拳同时向前冲出（拳眼向上），右拳撤至腰部右侧（拳心向上），目视左拳（图3-4）。

5. 顺步右崩拳（黑虎出洞）。 右脚向前一步，左脚跟进半步；同时右拳顺着右脚方向冲出（拳眼向上，高与胸平），左拳撤至腰部左侧（拳心向上），目视右拳（图3-5）。

图 3-4　退步左崩拳　　　图 3-5　顺步右崩拳　　　图 3-6　撤步分臂

6. 退步抱拳（白鹤亮翅）。 身体左转，左脚向左后方撤半步，同时右臂屈肘，右拳贴近腹部由上向下插，拳心向上，左拳置于右拳下方，拳心向下（图3-6），两臂同时向上摆起（右拳左掌），经头部前上方分开，再由两侧下落划一立圆，收到腹前，右拳落在左掌心内；上体稍右转，同时右脚撤到左脚前方；目视前方（图3-7）。

7. 进步炮拳。 右脚向右斜前方迈进一步，左脚向前跟进半步；同时右拳经胸前向上翻转上架，停于头部右上方，左掌变拳向前打出，目视左拳（图3-8）。

8. 退步左劈掌。 右拳拳心向上体前下落，左拳收回左腰侧，右脚随之向后撤一步，目视右拳（图3-9）。左拳经右前臂上方前伸变掌翻转前按，右拳变掌下按至腹前，目视左掌（图3-10）。

图 3-7　退步抱拳　　　图 3-8　进步炮拳　　　图 3-9　退步落拳

9. 拗步右钻拳。 身体稍向右转，左掌变拳屈收胸前，拳心均向上（图3-11），左脚收回，紧靠在右脚踝关节处后前进一步,右脚随之跟进半步,同时左拳经胸前按拳右拳顺左前臂上方钻出,高与鼻尖平,左小臂内旋撤至腹部偏左,拳心向下,目视右拳(图3-12)。

图 3-10　左劈右按(侧面)　　　图 3-11　上步按拳　　　图 3-12　跟步钻拳

10. 跳步双劈掌(狸猫上树)。 两手不动,左脚向前垫半步,同时后腿屈膝抬脚,脚尖斜勾(图3-13);右脚脚跟用力向前下踩落地,左脚随之跟进半步,脚跟离地,成右脚横、左脚顺的交叉半蹲姿势;同时,左拳变掌顺右臂内侧上伸向前、向上劈,前手高不过口,右拳变掌撤至腹前,目视左掌食指尖(图3-14)。

图 3-13　提膝垫步　　　图 3-14　盖步劈掌　　　图 3-15　进步右崩拳

11. 进步右崩拳。 两掌变拳,右脚向前垫步,左脚向前进一步,右脚随之跟进半步;同时右拳顺左臂直向前打出,拳眼向上,左拳撤至左腰侧(拳心向上),目视右拳(图3-15)。

12. 回身式(狸猫倒上树)。 左脚尖内扣,以右脚掌为轴,身体由右侧向右后转180°,同时右拳屈肘收回右腰侧(拳心向上),重心偏于左脚,目视右前方水平位置;重心移至左腿,右腿向上提起,脚尖上勾,同时,右拳由胸前经下颌向上、向前钻出,高与鼻尖齐平(图3-16);右脚脚跟离地,左膝与右膝窝抵紧,左拳顺着右臂内侧上伸、向前向下劈,前手高不过口,右拳变掌撤至腹前,眼看左掌食指尖(图3-17)。

图 3-16　提膝钻拳　　图 3-17　盖步劈掌　　图 3-18　退步冲拳　　图 3-19　退步分臂拳

13. 收式。两掌变拳，右脚向后撤回半步，左脚再撤至右脚后方，两腿交叉，左脚顺，右脚横，左脚跟微离地面，仍成交叉半坐盘式；左脚后撤时，左拳向前打出，右拳收回腰部右侧，拳心向上，目视左拳（图 3-18）；右脚收回靠拢左脚，身体轻缓起立，两手垂于身体两侧（图 3-19）。

（二）学习计划

	学习目标	学习内容
前期准备	形意拳基本桩法	三体式
	形意拳步伐	进步、退步、跟步、撤步、垫步、磨胫步、摆步、扣步、盖步、倒插步、换步、顺步、拗步、跳步、纵跳步、纵步、跃步、并步、跟步
学习进度	学习五行连环拳套路	劈拳 崩拳 钻拳 炮拳 横拳 五行连环拳

（三）技术体验

内容	要　　求
动作规范	1. 三体式 2. 动作路线和架势 3. 动作熟练
外三合	1. 肩与髋合 2. 肘与膝合 3. 手与足合
内三合	1. 心与意合 2. 意与气合 3. 气与力合
运动风格	内外结合形成一个完整统一体 紧凑、协调、沉稳、完整 三尖相对、三节相随 朴实明快

（四）文化体验

- **形意拳五行生克原理**

　　五行拳即"劈、崩、钻、炮、横"。

　　劈拳之形似斧,属金;崩拳之形似箭,属木;钻拳之形似电,属水;炮拳之形似炮,属火;横拳之形似弹,属土;横拳为五拳之母,因万物土中生,土是万物的根本,所以横拳称为母拳。

　　五行拳遵循"五行相生相克"的原理,五行拳之间的相生关系是:"劈拳变钻拳,钻拳变崩拳,崩拳变炮拳,炮拳变横拳,横拳变劈拳",五拳之间的相克关系是:"劈拳破崩拳,崩拳破横拳,横拳破钻拳,钻拳破炮拳,炮拳破劈拳"。

- **形意拳的"内外兼修""术道并重"**

　　"内"指人体内脏器官、大脑意识,"外"指由骨骼肌收缩引起的肢体动作;"内"指人体,"外"则是指人体以外的"天"。"术"指技术、方法,"道"指武术锻炼应遵循的规律。

　　形意拳把人体自身看作一个小"宇宙",把外界环境看作一个大"宇宙",通过修炼追求大、小"宇宙"和谐统一,以达到"天人合一"。

- **形意拳三体式**

　　三体势是形意拳的主要桩法,不仅是形意拳各种套路的起势和收势,而且也是形意拳的基础身体姿势。

　　三体势体现了形意拳的太极、两仪、三节、四梢、五行、六合、七星、八字及八要、九数等要领,既为入门必修,也是高层功夫所必须,有"万法出于三体势"之说。

三、总结

　　（一）形意拳入门以练习三体势为基础,三体式是形意拳运动的基本身体姿势。

　　（二）五行连环拳是形意拳的基础套路,是对"劈、崩、钻、炮、横"五行母拳的训练。

　　（三）学习五行连环拳首先追求动作路线、动作规格的正确,其次追求"六合",最后要体现形意拳的运动风格。

　　（四）形意拳不仅要求桩步稳固,而且强调裹劲、抱劲、争劲等。

四、延伸学习

　　学会五行连环拳后不仅可借此提高运动中内外三合程度,体现形意拳运动风格的基础,而且也可将"十二形"作为延伸学习的内容。形意拳的"十二形"取自于龙、虎、猴、马、鼍、鸡、燕、鹞、蛇、鹰、熊等十二种动物的特殊技能,以形取意,意自形生。

五、思考与练习题

1. 形意拳为什么要加强对内外三合的练习?

2. 形意拳的练习为什么要注重两肘不离肋、两手不离心？
3. 如何理解"松胸实腹，气沉丹田"？

六、参考文献

李德印. 形意拳术[M]. 北京：人民体育出版，1981.

第四章

八卦掌(定势八掌)

一、导言

八卦掌创始于董海川,是中国武术流传很广的拳种之一,其运动特点是"沿圈走转,随走换势,身捷步灵,势势相连,行步平稳,摆扣清晰,纵横交错,协调圆活"。本套为"定势八掌",由"按、托、撞、合、撑、抱、立、推"八个单势转掌所构成,是八卦掌的初级套路。

二、学习体验

(一)动作说明

1. 预备势。面南沿圈站立,两脚并拢,两手自然垂于大腿外侧;头项正直,口闭齿扣,胸腹放松;目平视前方(图 4-1)。

2. 按掌(下沉掌),有左右 2 势。

(1) 左势。两掌臂外旋,掌心向上,经身体两侧向上托起,肘部微屈,双手略高于肩;目视前方(图 4-2-1);两掌屈肘,掌心向下,指尖相对,沿体前下落于小腹前;同时,两腿屈膝略蹲;目平视前方(图 4-2-2)。

图 4-1 预备势　　　图 4-2-1 按掌　　　图 4-2-2 按掌

接上动,两掌不变,上体左转,面对左侧圆心,重心移至右腿;同时,左脚贴右脚内踝向前迈一步,脚面绷直,脚掌虚接地面,脚尖顺直;目视左侧圆心(图 4-2-3)。重心前移至左腿,屈左膝,右脚贴左脚内踝向前迈一步,脚面绷直,脚掌虚接地面,脚尖微扣;上体两掌不变;目视圆心(图4-2-4)。两脚依次交替沿圈走转至起势处(图4-2-5—图4-2-7)。

图 4-2-3　按掌　　　图 4-2-4　按掌(侧)　　　图 4-2-5　按掌

图 4-2-6　按掌　　　图 4-2-7　按掌　　　图 4-2-8　按掌

(2) 右势。接上势,行至左脚在前(图4-2-7),右脚向前迈一步至左脚前扣步,面对圆心,两掌不变,目视圆心(图4-2-9)。以腰带肩,以肩带臂,两掌于腹前自左向前向右划平弧,掌心向下,置于腹右侧处,重心移至右腿,目视两掌(图4-2-10),上体左转,重心前移至左腿,右脚向前沿圈摆步,脚尖顺直,上体及两臂随转腰右拧对圆心;目平视(图4-2-11)。沿圈走转,成按掌右势。

图 4-2-9　按掌　　　图 4-2-10　按掌　　　图 4-2-11　按掌

3. 托掌(大鹏展翅),有左右2势。

(1) 右势。接上势,左脚向前迈一步至右脚前扣步,两掌臂外旋,指尖斜向上,由腹前托起,交叉于胸前;目视两掌(图4-3-1)。重心前移至左腿,同时向前迈一步成摆步,两掌由额前向身体两侧伸展开,肘略下垂,掌心向上,略高于肩成托掌,上体向右转面向圆心;目平视,沿圈走转(图4-3-2)。

图4-3-1 托掌　　　　图4-3-2 托掌　　　　图4-3-3 托掌

（2）左势。接上势,左脚向前迈一步至右脚前扣步,两腿屈膝成夹马式,同时两臂内合交叉,掌心向上置于胸前上方;目视两掌(图4-3-3)。上体右转,重心移至左腿,右腿转向右后方上步外摆,脚尖顺直成平马步;同时,两臂内旋,两掌翻转向下按于膝两侧,五指相对,掌心斜向外;目视圆心(图4-3-4)。重心右移,左脚向右前方上一步,脚尖略外展,同时两臂外旋,两掌翻转由身体两侧向上托起,掌心向上,略高于肩;上体不变唯腰左拧,面向圆心;沿圈走转(图4-3-5)。

图4-3-4 托掌　　　　图4-3-5 托掌　　　　图4-4-1 撞掌

4. 撞掌（双撞掌）,有左右2势。

（1）左势。接上势,两臂屈肘旋腕,经两肩前向前推撞,两掌心向外,拇指向下,指尖相对,两臂圆撑,高与胸齐;上体与两腿不变,沿圈走转一周至左脚在前时换下势;目视两掌(图4-4-1)。

（2）右势。接上势,右脚上步至左脚前扣步,左脚不变,两腿屈膝相抱成平马势,面对圆心;两掌不变,目视两掌(图4-4-2)。重心移至右腿,上体略左转,左腿随上体左转向左后方摆步;同时右掌经左肘下穿出,两掌臂相交,左掌在上,右掌在下,两臂交叉上举于胸前,目视左掌(图4-4-3)。右脚经左脚内侧踝向前上一步,上体略向右拧转,同时,两掌随右拧身旋臂转腕向前撞掌,拇指向下,掌心朝向圆心,高与胸平;沿圈走转一周至右脚在前时换下势;目视两掌(图4-4-4)。

图 4-4-2 撞掌

图 4-4-3 撞掌

图 4-4-4 撞掌

5. 合掌（白猿献桃），有左右 2 势。

（1）右势。接上势，两臂屈肘旋腕，由上向下经腰两侧向前合腕推出，两掌根相并，拇指朝上，掌心向外朝向圆心，高与腹平；沿圈走转一周至右脚在前时换下势（图 4-5-1）。

（2）左势。接上势，左脚向右前方迈一步至右脚前扣步，两腿屈膝相抱成夹马式；上体与两掌不变，目视两掌（图 4-5-2）。上体右转，重心置于右腿，右脚向右迈半步，同时两掌置于左胯前；目视两掌（图 4-5-3）。左脚向右前方上一步，右脚不变成拗步，上体略左转；同时，两掌合腕向前朝圆心推出，掌根相并，拇指朝上，掌心朝向圆心，高与胸腹平，目视两掌。沿圈走转一周至左脚在前时换下势（图 4-5-4）。

图 4-5-1 合掌　　图 4-5-2 合掌　　图 4-5-3 合掌

图 4-5-4 合掌　　图 4-6-1 撑掌　　图 4-6-2 撑掌

6. 撑掌（阴阳掌），有左右 2 势。

（1）左势。接上势，上体不变"略"向左转；同右臂内旋，屈肘横掌向右前方推出，拇指朝下，掌心向前，高与头平，同时左臂内旋，左掌沿左腰侧向身后磨肋掖出，掌心向后，高与胯平；目视圆心，沿圈走转一周至左脚在前时换下势（图 4-6-1）。

(2) 右势。接上势,右脚向前上步至左脚前扣步,左脚不变,两腿屈膝相抱成夹马式,面对圆心;两掌不变;目平视(图4-6-2)。上体左转,左脚向左后方摆步,脚尖顺直,右脚不变,两腿屈膝成半马步;同时,左掌向左前方撩出,拇指向下,掌心向前,高与胸齐,右臂内旋右掌由上向下置于体右侧后,五指向下,掌心向后;目视左掌(图4-6-3)。右脚向前迈一步,同时,右掌臂外旋自左臂下向前穿出,掌心向上,高与眉齐,左掌旋腕转臂屈肘回抽置于右肘内侧上方,掌心向上;目视右掌(图4-6-4)。上体略右转,左臂内旋,左掌心向前拇指向下,屈肘向前推出,高与头齐,右臂随之内旋,右掌沿右腰侧向身后磨肋掖出,掌心向后,高与胯齐;目视圆心,沿圈走转一周至右脚在前时换下势(图4-6-5)。

图4-6-3 撑掌　　图4-6-4 撑掌　　图4-6-5 撑掌

7. 抱掌(狮子张口),有左右2势。

(1) 右势。接上势,右臂屈肘外旋,右掌自体后方向圆心伸出,掌心向上,高与肩平;左掌屈肘外旋置于头左侧前上方,掌心斜向下,与右掌掌心相对,目视右掌,沿圈走转一周至右脚在前时换下势(图4-7-1)。

(2) 左势。接上势,左脚上前一步,至右脚前扣步,两腿屈膝相抱成夹马式,上体与两掌不变,面对圆心;目视右掌(图4-7-2)。上体右转,右脚随转身向右后方上步外摆,脚尖外展;同时,左臂外旋,自右臂下向左侧前方穿出,掌心向上,高与肩齐,右臂内旋,掌心拧转向上,置于头右侧前方;目视左掌(图4-7-3)。左脚上一步至右脚前扣步;同时,上体向右仰面翻身,两掌不变,目视左掌(图4-7-4)。上体右转,右脚向右后方撤一步,左脚不变,成横裆步;两掌小臂内旋,自体前向下向右撩带,掌心均向下置于小腹左前下方;目视双掌(图4-7-5)。上体略左转,左脚向右上一步至右脚前,脚尖略扣,右脚前顺,成剪子步;同时,左掌小臂外旋,向左前方托出,掌心向上,高与肩平,右掌旋臂转腕由下向上、向前推出,置于头右侧前上方,掌心斜向下,与左掌心相对;目视左掌,沿圈走转一周至左脚在前时换下势(图4-7-6)。

图4-7-1 抱掌　　图4-7-2 抱掌　　图4-7-3 抱掌

图 4-7-4　抱掌

图 4-7-5　抱掌

图 4-7-6　抱掌

8. 立掌(指天插地),有左右 2 势。

（1）左势。接上势,左掌小臂保持外旋,沿身体左侧上穿,五指向上,掌心向内,置头侧后上方;同时,右掌小臂外旋下插,置于左胯旁,指尖向下,掌心向外;目视圆心,沿圈走转一周至左脚在前时换下势(图 4-8-1)。

（2）右势。接上势,上体两掌不变,右脚向前方上一步至左脚前扣步,成夹马式,面向圆心;目平视(图 4-8-2)。上体左转,左脚向左前方外摆上半步,脚尖顺直;同时,两掌小臂外旋,左掌由上下落,右掌由下上穿于体前相交,右掌指尖向上,掌心向里,沿右臂内侧上穿,置于头右侧后上方;左掌指尖向下,掌心向外,沿外侧下插置于右胯旁;目视圆心(图4-8-3)。上体两掌不变;沿圈走转一周至右脚在前时换下势(图 4-8-4)。

图 4-8-1　立掌

图 4-8-2　立掌

图 4-8-3　立掌

图 4-8-4　立掌

9. 推掌(青龙探抓),有左右 2 势。

（1）右势。接上势,右掌小臂微屈内旋下落,指尖向上,掌心向内,高与眉齐;同时左臂内旋上提,屈肘置于右肘内侧下方,指尖向上,掌心斜向外;目视右掌,沿圈走转一周至右脚在前时换下势(图 4-9-1)。

（2）左势。接上势,左脚向前迈一步至右脚前扣步,两腿屈膝相抱成夹马式,面向圆心;目视右掌(图 4-9-2)。重心左移,上体右转,右脚向右前方外摆上半步,两腿屈膝成夹马步;同时右掌小臂内旋圆撑置于右前方,指尖斜向上,掌心向前,高与肩齐;左掌小臂外旋,掌心向上,经右臂下向体右侧穿出,置于右腋下外侧;目视左掌(图4-9-3)。左脚上前一步,右脚不变,两腿屈膝成剪子步;左掌继续前穿至高与头齐时,右掌屈肘旋腕回抽置于左小臂内侧上,两掌心均向上;目视左掌(图4-9-4)。上体左转,左脚向前上一步;同时,两掌随上体左转旋臂转腕向左推按,左掌在前,五指向上,掌心向外,高与眉齐,右掌屈肘置于左肘内侧下方,五指向上,掌心向外;目视左掌(图4-9-5,图4-9-6),沿圈走转一周至左脚在前时换下势。

图4-9-1 推掌　　　图4-9-2 推掌　　　图4-9-3 推掌

图4-9-4 推掌　　　图4-9-5 推掌　　　图4-9-6 推掌

10. 收势。

接上势,右脚向前上步至左脚前扣步与左脚并步,左脚不变唯脚尖外摆顺直,两腿直立;同时,两臂外旋由两侧上举,掌心向上,高与眉齐,目平视(图4-10-1)。两掌内旋屈肘,两掌心下按,五指相对(图4-10-2),沿体前下落置于大腿外侧,目平视(图4-10-3)。

图4-10-1 收势　　　图4-10-2 收势　　　图4-10-3 收势

(二) 学习计划

项目	内 容
前期准备	1. 柔韧性练习 2. 八卦掌基本步法
学习进度	1. 按掌(下沉掌) 2. 托掌(大鹏展翅) 3. 撞掌(双撞掌) 4. 合掌(白猿献桃) 5. 撑掌(阴阳掌) 6. 抱掌(狮子张口) 7. 立掌(指天插地) 8. 推掌(青龙探抓)、收势

(三) 技术体验

类型	内容	要求
身体规范	一意五劲	"一意",步若蹚泥; "五劲",从起步到落步要有"蹚、踢、摩、探、踩"五种劲法
	三空三扣	"三空",掌心空,脚心空,胸心空; "三扣",两肩扣,手心脚心扣,牙齿扣
	三圆三顶	"三圆",脊背团圆,臀部敛圆,虎口张圆; "三顶",头顶天,舌顶颚,掌顶前
	四坠四敏	"四坠",肩坠腰,腰坠胯,胯坠膝,膝坠脚; "四敏",眼敏,手敏,身敏,步敏
	十要三病	"十要",意识引导动作;先采用自然呼吸,后掌握腹式呼吸;腰、臂、手、颈拧转对圆心;塌腰坐腕;提肛敛臀;裹肘拧臂;垂肩垂肘;掤撑整力;关节放松;上下顺遂,动作协调。 "三病",不可憋气,不可僵化,不可轻浮。
动格运风	三形三势	"三形","行走如龙,动转若猴,换势似鹰"; "三势","行步若蹚泥,两臂似拧绳,走转如推磨"

(四) 文化体验

- **蹚泥步**

八卦掌的蹚泥步要求"一意五劲"。"一意"指"步若蹚泥",要感觉脚周围泥水的粘力、脚底的粘吸、脚跟的粘拖、脚左右的粘附、脚前的粘阻、脚背的粘压;"五劲"指从起步到落步要有"蹚、踢、摩、探、踩"五种劲法,脚掌要有"蹚劲"、脚背和小腿胫骨夹角处向前的"踢劲"、迈步两胫的"摩劲"、落地瞬间的"探劲"和"踩劲"。

- **八卦**

八卦是中国古代的一套有象征意义的符号,它以"—"代表阳、"--"代表阴,用两种这样的符号,按照大自然的阴阳变化平行组合。组成八种不同形式,叫做八卦。每一卦形代表一定的事物。乾代表天,坤代表地,坎代表水,离代表火,震代表雷,艮代表山,巽代表风,兑代表泽。八卦互相搭配又得到六十四卦用来象征各种自然现象和人事现象。

三、总结

(一)以"沿圈走转,随走换势"的八卦掌首先要练好蹚泥步,要在沿圈走转中体验步履均匀、摆扣分明,体验其中的"一意五劲"。

(二)本套为八卦掌的初级套路,要学会"按、托、撞、合、撑、抱、立、推"八个单势转掌方法。

(三)在熟悉动作路线后,要进一步体验八卦掌的"三空三扣""三圆三顶""四坠四敏",以"十要"避免"三病"。

(四)在运动中,要不断体验八卦掌的"三形三势"运动风格。

四、延伸学习

学会"定势八掌"后,可继续学习"八卦连环掌""游身八卦掌""阴阳八卦掌"等套路,进一步学习"八卦剑""八卦刀""子午鸳鸯钺"等器械套路和"八卦掌对练""八卦六十四拆手"等对练套路。

五、思考与练习题

1. 如何走好"蹚泥步"?
2. 八卦掌的呼吸同时要结合下肢步法的运用,怎样做到动静全在呼吸之间?
3. 本套八个单势可以采取单势反复练习和八势连贯练习两种练习方法,熟练单势动作以后可以尝试进行八势连贯练习。

六、参考文献

[1] 全国体育院校教材委员会. 中国武术教程[M]. 北京:人民体育出版社,2004.
[2] 中国武术系列规定套路编写组. 八卦掌[M]. 北京:北京体育大学出版社,1998.

第五章

少林罗汉十八手

一、导言

"少林罗汉十八手"是少林拳的基础套路,由往来两段、24个动作、18种技击方法(6种拳法、2种掌法、1种肘法、4种腿法、5种拿法)组成,具有朴实、简洁、古拙之特点。

二、学习体验

(一)动作说明

1. 准备动作,有2个动作。

(1)预备式。两腿伸直并拢,两臂垂于身体两侧,两手五指并拢贴靠于腿外侧,身躯正直,两目平视(图5-1-1)。

(2)并步抱拳。两手握拳,屈肘收抱于两腰侧,拳心朝上,拳轮贴身,眼视左侧(图5-1-2)。

图 5-1-1　准备动作

图 5-1-2　准备动作

图 5-2-1　弓步掤手推掌

第一段

2. 弓步掤手推掌。两腿屈膝稍蹲,左脚向左侧跨出;左拳变掌,从左腰侧向左上方屈肘绕环抄起,伸向右肩前,掌指朝上,拇指张开;眼视左掌(图5-2-1);左掌外旋掤抓后变拳,拳心朝上,屈肘收抱于左腰侧;右拳变掌,从右腰侧向前直臂推出;同时,右腿挺膝蹬直,左腿屈膝半蹲,成左弓步;眼视右掌前方(图5-2-2)。

3. 虚步推掌。重心后移,右腿屈膝半蹲,左脚收回半步以脚尖虚点地面,成左虚步;同时,右掌变拳收抱于右腰侧,左拳变掌向前推出,眼向左掌前方注视(图5-3)。

4. 弓步掳手挎肘。 左脚向前踏实,左臂内旋,拇指张开朝下;右掌直臂伸向身后下方,拳心朝前;眼视左掌(图5-4-1)。左臂外旋使掌心朝上,握拳屈肘收抱于左腰侧;同时,右脚向前跨步,屈膝半蹲成马步,右拳随身转动从身后直臂向下、屈肘向身前绕环挎起,拳面朝上,拳眼朝右,高与眉齐;头向右转,眼向右侧前方注视(图5-4-2正、反)。

图5-2-2 弓步掳手推掌　　图5-3 虚步推掌　　图5-4-1 弓步掳手挎肘

图5-4-2 弓步掳手挎肘(正)　　图5-4-2 弓步掳手挎肘(反)　　图5-5 马步架打冲拳

5. 马步架打冲拳。 右脚尖外展,身体右转,左脚随身转动向前跨步,两腿屈膝半蹲成马步;右拳随之臂内旋从身前向右侧上方屈肘上架,左拳从左腰侧向左侧冲出,拳心朝下;眼向左拳前方注视(图5-5)。

6. 弓步架打冲拳。 左脚尖外展,身体左转,成左弓步;同时,左拳变掌,从身前屈肘上架,右拳屈肘经右腰侧向前冲出,拳心朝下;眼向右拳前方注视(图5-6)。

图5-6 弓步架打冲拳　　图5-7-1 弓步绾肘　　图5-7-2 弓步绾肘

7. 弓步缩肘。左掌从上向下向右拳背拍打,握住右腕,身体右转,右拳和左掌一起屈肘收于右肋下方,贴近身躯,眼视左掌(图5-7-1)。右脚向前上步,成右弓步;同时右肘向上提起,从上向前、向下绕环压下;眼视右肘(图5-7-2)。

图5-8-1　翻身马步磕打　　图5-8-2　翻身马步磕打　　图5-9-1　马步托掌冲拳

8. 翻身马步磕打。身体直立,右脚离地屈膝提起(图5-8-1);左脚蹬地跳起,身体右转,右脚落在左脚起跳前的步位,左脚随之落在左侧,两腿屈膝半蹲成马步;同时,左掌松开右拳,由右臂上面顺肘关节绕向肘下翻转成掌心朝上;右拳则从左臂里面向上、经额前向前直臂磕打,拳心朝上,眼视右拳(图5-8-2)。

9. 马步托掌冲拳。右拳从左掌上面抽回,屈肘收抱于右腰侧,左掌贴着右臂下面向前直臂伸出,臂内旋,拇指张开,虎口朝上,掌心朝前;眼视左掌(图5-9-1)。右拳从右腰侧向前直臂冲出,拳心朝下;同时,左掌屈肘收于右肩前,拇指仍张开,掌心朝右,掌指朝上;眼视右拳(图5-9-2)。

图5-9-2　马步托掌冲拳　　图5-10-1　弓步格挡冲拳　　图5-10-2　弓步格挡冲拳

10. 弓步格挡冲拳。右拳屈肘收抱于右腰侧,左掌变拳,臂外旋,向左绕行格挡;同时,左脚尖外展,身体左转,成左弓箭步;眼视左拳(图5-10-1)。右脚向前上步,成右弓步;同时,左拳屈肘收抱于左腰侧,右拳向前直臂冲出,拳心朝下;眼视右拳前方(图5-10-2)。

11. 弓步格挡冲拳。右臂内旋使拳眼朝下,从前向下、经腹前屈肘向左胸部弧形绕环,以前臂挠骨一侧向上经面前向右绕行格挡,拳面朝上;眼视右拳(图5-11-1)。左脚向前上步,成左弓步;同时,右拳屈肘收抱于右腰侧。左拳则向前冲出,拳心朝下,眼视左拳前方(图5-11-2)。

图 5-11-1　弓步格挡冲拳　　图 5-11-2　弓步格挡冲拳　　图 5-12-1　挂腿勾踢

12. 挂腿勾踢。重心前移，左腿微屈，右脚离地在身后屈膝提起，脚尖朝下；左拳变立掌，右拳变掌从右腰侧直臂向下、向后、向上经头顶上方向前弧形绕环至左掌腕上，两掌上下交叉，(图5-12-1)；两掌从胸前直臂向下、向左右两侧分开平举，左掌指尖朝上，掌心朝前，右掌变勾手，勾尖朝下；同时，右脚脚尖勾翘，从身后向左前斜方摆腿勾挂踢起，在右脚踢经正前方地面时，以脚跟擦击地面；眼视前方(图5-12-2)。

13. 缠腕马步冲拳。右腿屈膝，右勾手变掌，从右侧直臂向下、由腹前屈肘向左、向上弧形绕环抄至胸前，掌心朝外，掌指朝上，拇指张开；同时，左掌从左侧屈肘向上、向右、由脸前向下弧形绕环按握右掌腕部；眼视右掌(图5-13-1)。右掌臂外旋转腕绕至掌心朝上时变拳屈肘收抱于右腰前，左手握住右腕臂随之收抱；同时，身体右转，右脚向左脚侧旁踏脚震步，左脚屈提于右腿后；眼视右拳(图5-13-2)。左脚向左侧落步，成马步；同时，右拳收向右腰侧，左手松开右腕变拳，向左侧方冲出，拳心朝下；眼视左拳前方(图5-13-3)。

图 5-12-2　挂腿勾踢　　图 5-13-1　缠腕马步冲拳　　图 5-13-2　缠腕马步冲拳

14. 伏身后扫腿。左脚跟外展，左腿屈膝全蹲，右腿伸直在右侧铺下，右脚尖里扣；同时，两拳变掌，随身体右转右摆向右下方扶地；眼视右脚(图5-14-1)；右脚趁摆臂探身之势直腿从右向后贴地扫转半周，眼随右脚而视(图5-14-2)。

图 5-13-3　缠腕马步冲拳　　图 5-14-1　伏身后扫腿　　图 5-14-2　伏身后扫腿

第二段

15. 翻身弓步劈砸。 身体重心向右移动,右脚跟里转使脚尖朝向右前方,身体右转,右腿屈膝、左腿伸直成右弓步;同时,两掌变拳,右掌随身转动,经右膝前向身后绕行反臂斜举,拳眼朝下,左掌变拳随身转动,直臂举至身前,拳心朝下;眼视左拳(图5-15-1)。左拳臂内旋使拳眼朝下,从身前直臂向上、向后弧形绕环劈砸,拳眼变为朝上;右拳则随之从身后直臂向下、向前弧形绕环摆动,拳眼朝上;在两臂绕环的同时,身体左转;眼视左拳(图5-15-2)。身体继续左转,成左弓步;同时,两拳继续向后弧形绕环抢臂劈砸;左拳抢臂劈砸至身前后屈肘收抱于左腰侧,右拳抢臂劈砸至身前,拳眼朝上;眼视右拳前方(图5-15-3)。

图5-15-1 翻身弓步劈砸　　图5-15-2 翻身弓步劈砸　　图5-15-3 翻身弓步劈砸

16. 冲拳弹腿踢击。 右拳臂外旋使拳心朝上,屈肘收抱于右腰侧;左拳随之从左腰侧向前直臂平冲,拳心朝下;同时,重心前移,左腿微屈,右腿弹腿,眼视前方(图5-16)。

17. 腾身二起飞脚。 右脚向前落步起跳,左脚向前摆腿;同时,左拳变掌,掌心朝下,向额前上方摆起;右拳变掌,从右腰侧直臂向下、向前弧形绕环摆动,以掌背向上甩击左掌心;眼视前方(图5-17-1)。右脚绷直向前踢出,脚尖朝前;右掌向前击拍右脚脚面,左掌向左侧平举;眼视右脚(图5-17-2)。身体下降,左脚落地(图5-17-3)。

图5-16 冲拳弹腿踢击

18. 弓步切按举掌。 右脚向身后落步,身体右转,成右弓步;同时,右臂外旋直臂向下、由右腿外侧向后弧形绕环摆动向上举起,左掌向上弧形绕环,至头前上方后向下切按于右膝内侧掌心朝下;眼视左前方(图5-18正、反)。

图5-17-1 腾身二起飞脚　　图5-17-2 腾身二起飞脚　　图5-17-3 腾身二起飞脚

图 5-18　弓步切按举掌（正）　　图 5-18　弓步切按举掌（反）　　图 5-19-1　偷步绕臂沉肘

19. 偷步绕臂沉肘。重心左移，成马步；右掌从上向左下抓左肩，左掌变拳，臂外旋，经腹前、向左弧形绕行摆动，肘微屈，拳心朝上；眼视左拳（图 5-19-1）。左拳继续向上绕环举起，拳心朝右；重心继续前移，右腿向身后插步；右掌握肩不变，眼看左拳（图 5-19-2）。重心继续前移，左脚向左侧横跨一步，两腿屈膝成马步；同时，左拳随身躯转动使拳心转朝身后，在身前外侧屈肘用上臂骨向下沉压，小臂垂直，拳与眉齐高；眼视左前方（图 5-19-3）。

图 5-19-2　偷步绕臂沉肘　　图 5-19-3　偷步绕臂沉肘　　图 5-20-1　弓步架打冲拳

20. 弓步架打冲拳。身体左转，右脚跟外转，右腿伸直，左腿屈膝，成左弓步；左拳屈肘收于右肩前，拳轮贴身，拳心朝左；右掌变拳，从左上臂的下面屈肘向前、向上绕行架起，拳眼朝下（图 5-20-1）。重心后移，身体右转，两腿屈膝成马步；同时，右臂屈肘架拳于右肩上方，拳面朝左，拳心朝上；左拳即从右肩前向左侧方冲出，拳心朝下；眼视左拳前方（图 5-20-2）。

图 5-20-2　弓步架打冲拳　　图 5-21　弓步架打顶肘　　图 5-22　并步习搂手磕打

21. 弓步架打顶肘。 左脚尖、右脚跟外展，身体左转，成左弓步；同时，左拳变掌从身前向额前上方屈肘环举上架；右拳屈肘向下、经右肩前向左腋前移动，臂内旋使拳心朝下，肘尖向前顶出；眼视前方（图5-21）。

22. 并步习搂手磕打。 左腿直起，右脚向前并步；同时，左掌从上屈肘向右肘尖前搂按，掌心朝下；右拳则以肘关节为轴，从左腋处向上、向前弧形绕环直臂磕打，拳心朝上；在右拳向前磕打时，左掌随势使掌心翻转朝上托住右肘；眼视右拳前方（图5-22）。

23. 托掌马步冲拳。 身躯微向后仰闪，左掌顺着右臂下面直臂向前伸出，臂内旋使虎口朝上，向前上分托起；同时，右拳从左掌上面抽回，屈肘收抱于右腰侧，拳心朝上；右脚随之提膝，眼视左掌（图5-23-1）。右脚向前落步，身躯左转，两腿屈膝半蹲成马步；同时，左掌屈肘架掌于左肩上方，右拳向右侧方冲出，拳心朝下；眼视右拳前方（图5-23-2）。

图5-23-1 托掌马步冲拳　　图5-23-2 托掌马步冲拳　　图5-24-1 分掌弓步双推

24. 分掌弓步双推。 右腿直立，左腿屈膝；同时右拳变掌直臂上举后与左掌一起向后、向下弧形绕环转动，掌心相对（图5-24-1）。两掌一起分由两侧屈肘向前、向上弧形绕环转动，向两耳侧挑起，掌指朝后身躯顺势微向后仰（图5-24-2）。左脚向前落步，成左弓步；两掌一起向前直臂平伸推出；眼视两掌前方（图5-24-3）。

图5-24-2 分掌弓步双推　　图5-24-3 分掌弓步双推　　图5-25-1 虚步护身掌

25. 虚步护身掌。 重心前移，左腿稍向上站起，右脚离地屈膝提起以脚面勾扣于左脚后面的膝弯处；同时，两掌臂外旋使掌心朝上，分从两侧直臂向下、向后弧形绕环摆动（图5-25-1）。右脚向身体右侧方落步，重心右移，成左虚步；同时，两掌从后向上绕环，至绕过头部高度时继续向前绕环，至身前时左掌平举，肘微屈，右掌屈肘附于左肘近侧；眼视左掌前方（图5-25-2）。

图 5-25-2　虚步护身掌　　　图 5-26　并步抱拳　　　图 5-27　收势

结束动作

26. 并步抱拳。 右脚跟里转,两腿直起,左脚随之向右脚并步靠拢;与此同时,两掌变拳屈肘收抱于两腰侧,眼视左侧(图 5-26)。

27. 收势。 两拳变掌直臂下垂,头向右转正,恢复到立正姿势(图 5-27)。

(二) 学习计划

项目	内　容
前期准备	1. 具备一定的柔韧、协调和力量素质; 2. 掌握武术基本手型、步型、手法、步法
学习进度	1. 学会动作路线(本套 18 个动作,分 8 次课学习。其中,6 次新授,2 次复习); 2. 掌握各个动作的规格要求; 3. 提高整套动作的演练水平; 4. 体验各个动作的技击用法

(三) 技术体验

内容	要　求
动作规格	1. 手型规范:拳要紧、掌要并拢挺伸、勾要屈腕捏拢; 2. 步型规范:重心稳实,互变迅疾、扎实灵动; 3. 身型规范:顶头竖项、挺胸塌腰、收腹敛臀、躯干中正; 4. 手法、腿法规范:方法正确、路线清楚、力点准确
技击用法	1. 技击用法是以退、转、闪、躲、缩等避开对方之攻招,同时又巧妙和合理地实施进攻之法; 2. 知晓每一动作的攻与防,如"冲拳"要有寸劲,准确击打对方脸部和胸腹部;"缠手"以小指一侧掌缘击拿对方腕关节;"切掌"以掌锋劈砍对方小腿胫骨、脚背或踝关节;"钩挂腿"用小腿的摆踢力量,勾挑对方踝关节近处;"扫荡腿"用脚后跟部位,扫荡对方腿部;"鸳鸯腿"以虚实攻击对方裆、腹部和下颏。"分掌"为防护头、脸部位被攻击;"架拳"是防对方的劈打;"托掌"是化解对方击打。 3. 在教师指导下,通过"拆手""喂手"等方法,深入理解动作的攻防含义,不断体会动作的攻防用法。
运动意向	1. 劲力顺达:检查动作的"用力顺达,发力完整,力点准确",体验"眼随手到,手到步到,上下相随"的运动状态; 2. 节奏恰当:体验动作的节奏,力争体现"动静分明、快慢结合、起伏转折、缓急有度"; 3. 形神兼备:理解"眼无神,拳无魂"之拳谚,体验精神贯注、置身战斗场合的精神状态

（四）文化体验

• **抱拳礼**

相见礼,源于周代以前,是中华民族特有的传统礼仪。抱拳礼是武术界礼仪中常见的一种行礼方式,其姿势为,并步站立,头正,身直,目视受礼者,左掌右拳在胸前环抱,高与胸齐,拳、掌与胸间距离为20~30厘米。面容举止自然大方。

1. 以左掌表示德、智、体、美四育齐备,象征高尚情操、有武德之意;屈左手拇指表示不自大、不骄傲、不以老大自居;右拳表示勇猛习武,左掌掩右拳相抱,表示"以理服人、武不犯禁"来约束勇武本意。

2. 左掌右拳两臂撑圆抱于胸前,手有五指为"五湖",分四个区间为"四海",即平时所讲"五湖四海",过去讲"五湖四海皆兄弟"(泛指五洲四洋)表示天下武林是一家,谦虚团结、以武会友之意。

3. 左掌为文,右拳为武,表示文武兼学,虚心渴望求知,恭候师友或前辈指教。

4. 两手抱于胸前微外翻,是向对方展示在交手前没拿暗器,表示清白、不失光明磊落,而致以上演绎而成现在的抱拳礼。

• **长拳二十四要**

长拳二十四要细分为"四击、八法、十二形"。

1. 四击:踢、打、摔、拿四种击法。拳术套路的组成,一般都以技击动作为中心,整套动作的主要部分离不开四击的法则。

2. 八法:手、眼、身法、步,精神、气、力、功八种方法总称。具体要求是:"拳(手)似流星眼似电;腰(身法)如蛇行步赛粘;精神充沛气宜沉;力要顺达功宜纯。"即练功要求做到手捷快,眼明锐,身灵活,步稳固,精充沛,气下沉,力顺达,功纯青。

3. 十二形:指动、静、起、落、站、立、转、折、轻、重、快、慢等十二种运动形态,要求做到:"动如涛、静如岳、起如猿、落如鹊、站如松、立如鹤、转如轮、折如弓、轻如叶、重如铁、快如风、慢如鹰。"

三、总结

（一）少林罗汉十八手,是少林拳的基础套路,也是武术的基础套路。

（二）在熟悉动作路线后,要不断检查动作规范。

（三）在动作规范基础上,体验动作的技击用法,体现少林拳的运动风格,提高武德修养,理解武术文化和中国文化。

四、延伸学习

（一）学会少林罗汉十八手的动作路线之后,要反复纠错,提高动作的规范性。

（二）学会少林罗汉十八手套路后,要注意攻防动作与呼吸的配合,做到以气催力,气、力、形合为一体,力争练出"武术的味道"。

（三）学会少林罗汉十八手套路后，可从"动作节奏、形神兼备"等方面提高演练的感染力。

（四）熟练掌握少林罗汉十八手单练套路后，可进一步选择对练套路进行学习。

五、思考与练习题

1. 如何在套路演练中体现"形神兼备"的技术要求。
2. 思考少林罗汉十八手每一动的攻防含义和实战用法。

六、参考文献

［1］蔡龙云.少林寺拳棒禅宗［M］.杭州:浙江科学技术出版社,1983.
［2］全国体育院校教材委员会.中国武术教程（上）［M］.北京:人民体育出版社,2004.

第六章

风 魔 棍

一、导言

"风魔棍"是"少林七十二秘笈之一",是武术棍术基本套路之一。该套有三十种棍法,强调梢与把的混用,要求"上必有下、左必有右"的呼应与配合,讲究棍势如风、劈打快速有力。

二、学习体验

(一)动作说明

预备势

1. 并步持棍。 面东而立,两腿并拢站立,右手虎口握棍贴于右腿并拢,左手五指并拢贴靠于左外侧,棍根竖直触地,眼睛平视前方(图 6-1)。

2. 虚步捧棍。 左腿屈膝,右脚后退一步成左弓步,右手捋着棍杆上移于右肩前。满握棍杆,左手握棍,两手虎口均朝棍梢,两手使棍根离地向前举起(图 6-2-1)。身体重心后移,右腿屈膝半蹲,成左虚步;同时,左手直臂使棍把向前举至水平部位,眼视棍把前方(图 6-2-2)。

图 6-1 并步持棍

图 6-2-1 虚步捧棍

图 6-2-2 虚步捧棍

第一段

3. 弓步撂棍。 重心前移,右脚向前上步,成右弓步;右手满握直臂使棍梢沿身体右侧向上、向后下斜伸,手心朝上;左手握住棍把,体前屈肘,眼视前方(图 6-3-1)。上动不停,左手使棍把从前向左、向后下弧形绕环摆动屈肘收抱于左腰侧,手心靠身,右手使棍梢从后向右、向前上斜行弧形绕环摆动,直臂螺握用棍梢向前擂打,手心斜朝左上,虎口朝前,眼视棍梢(图6-3-2)。

4. 弓步戳棍。两手一起将棍抽回,右手握位不变,屈肘收于胸前,手心朝上,左手稍让棍把向后穿出握于棍把前,屈肘拉于腰后;同时两腿站起,左腿伸直,右腿屈膝;眼视棍梢(图6-4-1);上动微停,右脚向前落步,成右弓步;同时,两手一起将棍梢向前上方斜伸戳出,右手握位不变,臂伸直,左臂屈肘满握收抱于左腰侧,手心靠身;眼视棍梢(图6-4-2)。

棍 法

棍为无刃的兵器,素有"百兵之首"之称。棍有棍梢、棍身、棍把三部分组成,可"劈、摔、抡、扫、撩"等远击,也可"点、崩、戳、扎、盖"等近击,还可"架、格、拨"等防御。

图6-3-1 弓步擂棍

图6-3-2 弓步擂棍

图6-4-1 弓步戳棍

图6-4-2 弓步戳棍

5. 挟棍靠打。右手持棍握位不变,直臂使棍梢向左、向下、贴近地面向右弧形搅动,继之使棍梢从前下方向右、向后弧形绕环摆动,至后方时屈肘将棍向右肩上方举起;同时,左手将棍把从左腰侧向左肩上方举起,使棍把从后向左、向前弧形绕环摆动,肘臂随势向前伸直,手微松使棍把穿出;在棍梢绕至后方、棍把绕至前方的时候,两腿站起,左脚随着棍把向前上步(图6-5-1);

上动不停,右手持棍屈肘向上、由头顶上

换 手

换手也称"倒手",将原先握于棍把的手倒换至棍梢,或是将原先握于棍梢前面的手倒换至棍把。

其中,一手倒换,另一手不变,为单换手;两手相互易位倒换,则称双换手。

换手的动作必须快速,给人出其不意之感。

方向左、向下绕至左肩前,将棍杆从右肩越过头顶移至左肩;同时,右脚离地在身后屈膝提起,眼视棍梢(图6-5-2);上动不停,身体右转,右脚向前落步,成右弓步;同时,左手屈肘收于右腋下使棍把从前向右、向后弧形绕环平摆;右手直臂使棍梢从身体左侧由后向左、向前下方弧形绕环摆动,用棍梢向前下方斜打;左手满握,手心朝上;身体左侧由右手螺握,手心朝下;眼视棍梢(图6-5-3)。

图 6-5-1 挟棍靠打

图 6-5-2 挟棍靠打

图 6-5-3 挟棍靠打

6. 换手横把。左手放开棍杆,右手持棍屈肘收于右腰侧将棍抽回,左手换握右手前棍梢,两手心朝下,眼视前方(图6-6-1);上动未停,右手继续将棍向后抽,左手顺势前握;随即右手使棍把从后直臂向右、向前下方弧形绕环,用棍把向前横击;同时,左手使棍梢从前屈肘向左、向后弧形绕环,收抱于左肋,眼视棍把(图6-6-2)。

图 6-6-1 换手横把

图 6-6-2 换手横把

7. 挑把撩棍。右手持棍屈肘向上收于右耳侧、使棍把从前向上、向后弧形绕环,用棍把向上挑起、虎口朝下,左手持棍直臂向下伸出,使棍梢从后向下、向前弧形绕环,虎口朝上;同时,左腿伸直,右腿提膝,眼向前方注视(图6-7-1);上动不停,右脚落步成右弓步;同时,左手使棍头向下、向前弧形绕环,用棍梢向前下撩击,眼视棍梢(图6-7-2)。

图 6-7-1 挑把撩棍

图 6-7-2 挑把撩棍

8. 弓步盖把。 左手微松，右手持棍顺着棍把的方向直臂斜上举，随而移抱棍梢方接着左手满握屈肘收抱于左腰侧，手心靠身，虎口朝前；同时，右手从上直臂向前使棍把向上、向前弧形绕环，而向前上方劈盖，手心朝下，虎口朝左；眼视棍把（图6-8）。

图 6-8　弓步盖把

9. 换手剪棍。 左手直臂向前伸出，右手松把后正握持棍屈肘收至右耳侧，两手均为满握，虎口均朝后，眼视前方（图6-9-1）；上动不停，左手持棍使棍梢从前向左、向后弧形绕环摆动，屈肘收抱于左肋处，手心靠身，同时，右手持棍直臂右后垂下，使棍把从后向下、向右、向前弧形绕环，向前下方剪击，眼视棍把（图6-9-2）。

图 6-9-1　换手剪棍　　　　图 6-9-2　换手剪棍

10. 弓步擓棍。 两手持棍，使棍梢从前贴近地面向右、向后弧形绕环摆动；左手肘微屈平举胸前，手心朝下；右手臂外旋斜伸右腿后侧，手心朝右；眼视前方（图6-10-1）；上动不停，左手持棍使棍根从前向左、向后下弧形绕环摆动屈肘收抱于左腰侧，手心靠身；右手持棍使棍梢从后向右、向前上斜行弧形绕环摆动，用棍梢向前擓打，手心斜朝左上；眼视棍梢（图6-10-2）。

图 6-10-1　弓步擓棍　　　　图 6-10-2　弓步擓棍

11. 撸挂扎棍。 两腿站起，身躯左转；同时，两手持棍使棍梢向上高出头部，眼视棍梢（图6-11-1）；上动不停，右手持棍由身前向下、向右摆臂使棍头从上向身前、向下、向右、向后弧形绕环摆动，用棍梢向右腿外侧下方撸棍格挂，右臂屈肘收至右腰侧，左手由左腰侧向左、向前摆动使棍根从后向左、向前上弧形绕环，肘屈平举于胸前，虎口朝后；同时，左脚跟外展，身体右转，右脚离地提膝，眼视前方（图6-11-2）；上动不停，右脚向前落步，右手直臂使棍头贴近地面从后向右、

图 6-11-1　撸挂扎棍

向前弧形绕环摆动,左手屈肘使棍根从前向左、向后弧形绕环收于左肋;随后,右腿屈膝成右弓步;右手松握,左手直臂前伸将棍向前下方扎出使右手握于左手前;身躯前探,眼视棍梢前端(图6-11-3)。

图 6-11-2　撸挂扎棍

图 6-11-3　撸挂扎棍

12. 拖棍架梁。右脚向后退步,身体右转,两手换握成左手在前,右手在后,同时向后拖拉抽回屈肘收向右腰侧,两膝下蹲腿屈,重心偏右,眼视棍梢前端(图6-12-1);上动不停,左脚迈过右脚向右侧跨跳,右脚蹬地跳起,拖棍后退(图6-12-2);上动不停,右脚向右落步,两腿屈膝下蹲,重心偏右;两手将棍横于腹前(图6-12-3);上动不停,左脚尖和右脚跟一起外展,身体左转成左弓箭步;同时,右手握位稍向里移,两手直臂上举将棍从身前向头顶上方架起,左手手心朝后,右手手心朝前;眼视前方(图6-12-4)。

图 6-12-1　拖棍架梁

图 6-12-2　拖棍架梁

图 6-12-3　拖棍架梁

图 6-12-4　拖棍架梁

第二段

13. 换手剪棍。重心前移,并步于左脚旁;同时,右手向里滑动易握,左手随之放开棍杆,用右手臂外旋使棍根从右向前、棍头从左向后在头顶上方盘旋,随即将棍杆由右耳侧降下;此时,左手由头顶上方前伸握住于右手前,左手手心朝右,右手手心朝左(图6-13-1);上动不停,左脚向后退步,成右弓箭步;同时,左手持棍使棍根从前向左、向后弧形绕环摆动,屈肘收抱于左肋处,手心靠身;右手则持棍由右肩上向后下方斜伸,使棍头从后向下、向右、向前贴近地面弧形绕环,用棍梢向前下方剪击,螺握,手心斜朝左上;眼视棍稍前端(图 6-13-2)。

图 6-13-1　换手剪棍　　　　图 6-13-2　换手剪棍

14. 虚步盖把。重心前移,左脚向前上步以脚尖点地成左虚步;同时,左手持棍臂内旋离左胁向左肩外翻起,顺着棍根的方向后上斜举,将棍向后上抽提,右手顺左手抽棍之势让棍上提,握住棍杆第二握位;随后,右手持棍向下、向后弧形绕环屈肘收抱于右腰侧,钳握,手背靠身,虎口朝下;与此同时,左手从上向前使棍根向上、向前弧形绕环,用棍把向前上方劈盖,顺势将手易于棍杆第三握位,钳握,虎口朝上,手心朝右,肘环屈;眼视棍把(图 6-14)。

图 6-14　虚步盖把

15. 弓步捣把。右手直臂后伸,左手屈肘收向胸前,将棍向后平抽收回;同时,右腿直立,左膝屈提,眼视前下方(图 6-15-1);上动不停,左脚向前落步,成左弓步;同时,左手前伸,右手屈肘收向左胸前,两手持棍用棍根向前下捣击;两手虎口均朝上,左手手心朝右,右手手心朝左;眼视棍把前端(图 6-15-2)。

图 6-15-1　弓步捣把　　　　图 6-15-2　弓步捣把

16. 上步剪棍。右手持棍顺棍头方向直臂伸出,将棍向后抽拉,左手让棍后抽顺势握住棍把,右脚随之前上步,成右弓箭步;同时,左手持棍满握,使棍根从前向左、向后弧形绕环摆动,屈肘收抱于左肋处,右手持棍,直臂向右后下垂,使棍头从后向下、贴近地面向右、向前弧形绕环摆动,用棍梢向前下方剪击,手心斜朝左上;眼视棍梢(图 6-16)。

17. 蹲身搅扫。两手持棍微向后带,右手持棍肘微屈使

图 6-16　上步剪棍

棍梢在前从下向右、向上、向左、向下搅一半径两尺左右的圆环；在棍头搅向左侧时，身躯微向左转，左腿屈膝，在棍梢搅向下方时，身躯微向右转，左手持棍收抱至左肋处，眼视棍梢（图6-17）。

18. 闪身卷拿。 紧接前动，右手臂外旋使手心向上与左手一起将棍微向后带，使棍梢在前从下向右、向上搅动，完成半个圆环后；向左搅动时，右手臂内旋，转动腕关节使棍头向左、向下弧形卷绕拿棍，手心翻转朝下；左手则持棍随棍头的卷绕使棍根在后自然搅动，在卷绕拿棍的同时，身微左转，右腿伸直，重心偏左，眼视棍梢（图6-18）。

图6-17　蹲身搅扫　　　　　　　图6-18　闪身卷拿

19. 挑掤下搪。 重心右移，右腿屈膝，身躯微向右转；右手持棍外旋，用棍梢从下微向左、向上、向右弧形绕环挑起崩棍，屈肘手心斜朝上；左手持棍内旋，向下移于左髋处，手心靠身；眼视棍梢（图6-19-1）；上动微停，左手持棍后抽，右手向棍梢方向易握，身躯右转，右脚退步，成左弓箭步；在右脚退步，同时，右手持棍屈肘收于左胸前，左手松握让棍根向后下伸出后向棍中易握后使棍把从后向左、向前弧形绕环，用棍把向前下方拦搪；左手手心朝右，右手手心朝左，虎口均朝上；眼视棍把（图6-19-2）。

图6-19-1　挑掤下搪　　　　　　图6-19-2　挑掤下搪

20. 并步搅棍。 两手持棍，右手向后经右肩直臂向下斜伸，左手向后屈肘收至左肩前，同时将棍梢伸向后方斜下举；两腿站起，右脚以脚掌碾地为轴，身体左转180°，左脚离地后向右脚靠拢并步；同时眼视棍梢（图6-20-1）；上动不停，右手使棍梢从下向右、向上弧形绕环搅动，右臂顺势屈肘，左手使棍根从上向南、向下弧形绕环搅动，左臂顺势伸屈；同时，身体右转，两腿屈膝微蹲，眼视正前方（图6-20-2）。

图 6-20-1　并步　　　　　图 6-20-2　并步

21．**跳步腾身**。紧接前动,两手持棍继续使棍梢从上向左绕环搅动;同时,两脚蹬地跳起,身体腾空(图 6-21)。

22．**虚步盖把**。身体右转,右脚先落地,脚尖外展,左脚随之前落落步以脚尖虚点,两腿屈膝成左虚步;同时,右手持棍臂外旋屈肘收抱于右腰侧,手背靠身,虎口朝下;左手持棍使棍根向上、向前劈盖,眼视棍把(参看图 6-14)。

23．**弓步捣把**。与第二段第三动"弓步捣把"相同(参看图 6-15-1、6-15-2)。

图 6-21　跳步腾身

24．**上步剪棍**。与第二段第四动"上步剪棍"相同(图 6-16)。

25．**弓步擂棍**。与第一段第八动"弓步捆棍"相同(参看图 6-10-1、图 6-10-2)。

26．**撸挂扎棍**。与第一段第九动"撸挂扎棍"相同(参看图 6-11-1—图 6-11-3)。

27．**拖棍架梁**。与第一段第十动"拖棍架梁"相同(参看图 6-12-1—图 6-12-4)。

28．**收势**。右脚向前与左脚并步,立正直立,同时,两手持棍,由前向下直臂收至右腿外侧,左手由后向上屈肘举至额前上方,将棍收于身体右侧垂直,棍根柱地,棍头朝上(图 6-22-1);左手放开棍梢,五指并拢由身前落下直臂收至左腿外侧,手心贴靠腿侧,掌指朝下;右手钳握,拇指靠身;两肘均微屈,眼向前方注视,持棍立正姿势站好(图 6-22-2)。

图 6-22-1　收势　　　　　图 6-22-2　收势

(二) 学习计划

项目	内　容
前期准备	1. 基本棍法：掌握基本握棍方法，把位互换，舞花，以及一些基本的劈棍，崩棍，扎棍等。 2. 基本动作：掌握基本步型：弓步，马步，仆步，虚步，以及结合步型完成的简单棍法。
学习进度	第一次课：1. 预备式，2. 虚步捧棍 　　　　　第一段：1. 弓步擂棍　2. 弓步戳棍 第二次课：第一段：3. 挟棍靠打　4. 换手横把　5. 挑把撩棍　6. 弓步盖把 第三次课：第一段：7. 换手剪棍　8. 弓步擂棍　9. 橹挂扎棍　10. 拖棍架梁 第四次课：第二段：1. 换手剪棍　2. 虚步盖把　3. 弓步捣把　4. 上步剪棍 第五次课：第二段：5. 蹲身搅扫　6. 闪身卷拿　7. 挑掤下搪　8. 并步搅棍 第六次课：第二段：9. 跳步腾身　10. 虚步盖把　11. 弓步捣把　12. 上步剪棍 第七次课：第二段：13. 弓步擂棍　14. 橹挂扎棍　15. 拖棍架梁　16. 收势 第八次课：复习提高

(三) 技术体验

内　容	要　　求
动作规范	动作规范是掌握棍术的第一步，要做到动作外形到位，以及动作路线正确
棍术技术用法	棍术关键在于棍法，要求握把正确、灵活转换、力点准确
棍术演练水平	棍术的演练要体现"棍打一大片"的气势，以及横平、竖直的要求。 风魔棍是一套传统的基础性棍术，动作朴实，简单明了，演练的水平主要体现在动作规范和棍法准确

(四) 文化体验

• **棍打一大片**

　　棍，攻击范围大于刀、枪，作为一种兵器，其作用和威力是不可忽视的。棍法快速勇猛，舞动如飞，练起来呼呼生风，握把灵活，常双手或单手抡棍，攻击面积很大，故有"棍打一大片"之说。

• **少林十三棍僧**

　　隋末唐初，隋将王世充拥兵东都称帝，唐武德三年(620年)，李世民统领诸路军马前往征讨王世充，初战失利时，驻守柏谷庄的少林武僧志操、惠锡、昙宗等十三名武僧因不满王仁则侵占少林寺封地，便"率众以拒伪师"。昙宗等十三武僧夜间攻入郑兵大营，生擒王仁则，献于李世民，为秦王统一全国立下了汗马功劳。

三、总结

　　(一) 风魔棍是少林拳基础套路，也是武术棍术基础套路。
　　(二) 从握把入手，加强棍法的学习。

（三）利用身体动作体现棍术力点及"棍打一大片"风格。

四、延伸学习

（一）掌握风魔棍动作路线后，不断领会其中的握把和换把方法，体会身棍合一。
（二）熟练掌握风魔棍套路后，可学习长拳类棍术，以及棍术竞赛套路。

五、思考与练习题

1. 风魔棍的握把是固定的还是灵活的？
2. 如何发挥棍的击打力量？
3. 如何理解"棍打一大片"这句话？

六、参考文献

［1］蔡龙云.少林寺拳棒禅宗［M］.杭州：浙江科学技术出版社，1983.
［2］全国体育院校教材委员会.中国武术教程（上）［M］.北京：人民体育出版社，2004年.

第七章

七 星 剑

一、导言

七星剑,是武术剑术的基础套路之一。该套动作规整、优美大方,属于工架剑套路。

二、学习体验

(一) 动作说明

1. 预备动作,有2个动作。

(1) 预备势。面南站立,左手反握剑柄,右手成剑指贴靠右腿,眼视前方(图7-1-1)。

(2) 提膝抱剑。右脚向前上步,成右弓步,右手剑指自右腰侧向前平伸指出,目视剑指(图7-1-2);右腿伸直站立,左腿提膝,双手屈抱于胸前,目视剑尖(图7-1-3)。

图 7-1-1　预备势　　　图 7-1-2　提膝抱剑　　　图 7-1-3　提膝抱剑

第一段

2. 提膝独立前刺。右手握剑向前直刺,左剑指屈肘收于右肩前,目视剑尖(图7-2)。

3. 左右撩削举腿架剑。右手持剑,右臂内旋,在身体右侧使剑尖从前向上、向后、向下、向前绕行一周撩起,手心朝上(图7-3-1)。右手持剑在身体左侧,使剑尖从前向上、向左后绕行,剑刃向后下削,手心朝右,眼视左侧(图7-3-2)。右手持剑使剑尖向下、向前绕行,右臂上举将剑架于头上方;同时,右脚跟里转,身体右转;左腿向左侧蹬腿;左手剑指向左前指,目视剑指(图7-3-3)。

图 7-2　提膝独立前刺　　　　图 7-3-1　左右撩削举腿架剑

图 7-3-2　左右撩削举腿架剑（正）　　图 7-3-2　左右撩削举腿架剑（反）　　图 7-3-3　左右撩削举腿架剑

4. 弓步后劈剑。右手持剑向下沉臂，左臂向上、向右绕行附于右肩前；同时，左腿提膝，目视剑尖（图 7-4-1）。左脚向左落步，成左弓步；右手持剑从下向左，向上回环、向右后平劈；左手剑指从右肩前向下、向左弧形绕行平举，目视剑身（图 7-4-2）。

5. 提膝独立抱剑。右手持剑向下、向右撩剑；左腿伸直，身体从左向后转，左手剑指架于头上，右腿提膝，右手屈肘将剑收于胸前，目视右侧（正东）（图 7-5）。

图 7-4-1　弓步后劈剑　　　　图 7-4-2　弓步后劈剑　　　　图 7-5　提膝独立抱剑

6. 马步抱剑弓步下刺。右脚向右侧落步，成马步；同时，右手持剑将剑柄下沉于腹前，使剑尖斜朝右上方高与头齐，左手剑指随下沉附于右腕里面，目视剑尖（图 7-6-1）。略停后，右脚尖外展，成右弓步；同时，右手持剑向前下方直刺，左手剑指向后上方直臂斜伸举起；目视剑尖（图 7-6-2）。

图 7-6-1　马步抱剑弓步下刺（正）　　图 7-6-1　马步抱剑弓步下刺（反）　　图 7-6-2　马步抱剑弓步下刺

7. 上步回身劈剑。左脚向前上步，右手持剑臂外旋后从前向上、贴左侧向后、向下绕行削剑；同时，左剑指从后直臂向下、屈肘向前弧形绕行至右腋下；眼随剑身（图 7-7-1）。右手持剑继续用剑刃向下、向前、向上抡臂绕行举起，身体右转，右脚向身后退步，左手剑指不变（图 7-7-2）。身体右转，右手持剑由头向前下劈砍，左手剑指向下、向后弧形绕行举起，目视前下方（图 7-7-3）。

图 7-7-1　上步回身劈剑　　　图 7-7-2　上步回身劈剑　　　图 7-7-3　上步回身劈剑

8. 挽花马步提剑。身体左转，右臂内旋使剑尖向下、由左腿外侧向后弧形绕行抄挂，左剑指附于右腕上面，目视剑尖（图 7-8-1）。右手持剑向上绕行，随身体起立右转而将剑柄落至胸前，左手剑指附于右腕不变；同时，左脚向后退步，左腿屈膝；眼随剑尖（图 7-8-2）。右手持剑使剑尖从前向下、由右腿外侧向后、向上绕行挽花（图 7-8-3）。右手持剑向下、由右腿外侧向后弧形绕行提起，剑尖下垂，臂平举；左手剑指随势屈肘收于右肩前；右脚向后退步，成马步，同时，眼视剑柄（图 7-8-4）。左手剑指向左指出，目视剑指（图 7-8-5）。

图 7-8-1　挽花马步提剑　　　图 7-8-2　挽花马步提剑　　　图 7-8-3　挽花马步提剑

图 7-8-4　挽花马步提剑　　图 7-8-5　挽花马步提剑　　图 7-9-1　左右挂剑歇步上架

9. 左右挂剑歇步上架。 右手持剑使剑尖从下由身前向左、向上、向右绕行抄挂于头前；左手剑指在剑尖绕行至上方时屈肘附于右腕上面；同时，身体右转，左腿伸直，目视剑尖（图7-9-1）。右手持剑使剑尖由右腿外侧向后、向上、向前绕行抄挂于头上；左手剑指在剑尖绕行至下方时屈肘附于右肩下；在剑尖向上、向前绕行时左脚向前上步成左弓步，眼随剑尖（图7-9-2）。右手持剑使剑由左腿外侧屈肘向后、向上、向前绕行抄挂于头前，左手剑指在剑尖绕行至后方时屈肘附于右腕上；在剑尖向上、向前绕行的同时右脚向前上步（图7-9-3）。右手持剑使剑尖由右腿外侧向后、向上、向前绕行抄挂于头上；同时，身躯右转向南，两腿屈膝成左歇步；左手剑指在剑尖绕行至下方时屈肘收至右肩前，在剑尖绕行至前方成歇步时直臂向前下方斜伸下指，目视剑指（图7-9-4）。

图 7-9-2　左右挂剑歇步上架　　图 7-9-3　左右挂剑歇步上架　　图 7-9-4　左右挂剑歇步上架

第二段

10. 跳步回身刺剑。 两腿直起，右脚掌碾地，身体后转（至正西）；右手持剑随身转动，在头顶上平云绕行一周半后外旋下落；左手剑指随身转动，向左后上方直臂举起（图7-10-1）。重心前移，左脚向前移步蹬地跳起（图7-10-2）；同时，右手持剑向后、向上向前绕行；身躯随之从右向后旋转；左手剑指在剑尖向后绕行时从上向前绕行，在剑尖向上、向前绕行时则向下、向后绕行（图7-10-3）在空中，右手持剑使剑尖向下、向后绕行，左手剑指向上、向前绕行；同时，身体右后旋转至北方时，右脚先落地，左脚后落地，成马步；至此，右手持剑平刺，目视剑尖（图7-10-4）。

图 7-10-1　跳步回身刺剑　　图 7-10-2　跳步回身刺剑　　图 7-10-3　跳步回身刺剑

图 7-10-4　跳步回身刺剑　　图 7-11-1　翻身虚步点剑　　图 7-11-2　翻身虚步点剑

11. 翻身虚步点剑。两腿直起,右脚从身后向左插步,右手持剑向左绕行至左肩前,左手剑指向下、由腹前屈肘绕至右腋下;目视剑身(图 7-11-1)。身体从右向后上翻转;右手持剑向下、向右提起,左手剑指随身绕行(图 7-11-2)。身躯直起半面右转,身稍前倾,成右虚步,右手持剑向西、向下绕行点击,左手剑指随之向上斜举,目视剑尖(图 7-11-3)。

图 7-11-3　翻身虚步点剑　　图 7-12-1　马步切剑　　图 7-12-2　马步切剑

12. 马步切剑。右手持剑使剑尖由左腿外侧向下、向后绕行挽花,左手剑指从上向前附于右腕上面(图 7-12-1)。右手持剑使剑尖从后向上、向前、向下绕行挽花,左手剑指附于右腕(图 7-12-2)。右手持剑使剑尖由右腿外侧向后、向上绕行挽花,左手剑指附于右腕,同时,身体重心前移,左脚向前摆起,右脚蹬地跳起,身体腾空(图 7-12-3)。左脚向前落地,身体左转(向南),右脚在身体右侧落地,成马步;同时,右手持剑用剑刃中端向右腿外侧下切,剑身横平,剑尖朝向身前;左手剑指屈肘举起,目视剑身(图 7-12-4)。

图 7-12-3　马步切剑　　　图 7-12-4　马步切剑　　　图 7-13-1　挽花弓步劈剑

13. 挽花弓步劈剑。右手持剑内旋使剑尖摆向左侧、由左向上、向右绕行挽花,左手剑指附于右腕;同时,身躯右转(向西),重心移于左腿,成右虚步,目视剑尖(图7-13-1)。右手持剑使剑尖向下刁把绕行(图7-13-2)。重心前移,右脚踏实,左脚向前上步,成左弓步;同时,右手持剑使剑尖由右腿外侧向后、向上绕行挽花,向前平劈;左手剑指收于右肩前,目视剑身(图7-13-3)。

图 7-13-2　挽花弓步劈剑　　图 7-13-3　挽花弓步劈剑　　图 7-14-1　探海平衡下刺剑

14. 探海平衡下刺剑。右脚向左脚靠拢并步,重心右移,左脚以脚尖虚点地面;同时,右手持剑使剑尖在前向上翘起高与头齐,左手剑指伸向右腕,目视剑身(图7-14-1)。上动微停,右腿伸直站立,左腿伸直向后举起,左脚脚面绷平,脚尖朝后;右手持剑向前下方直刺,左手剑指向下、由左腿外侧向后、向上举于头顶上方,目视剑尖(图7-14-2)。

图 7-14-2　探海平衡下刺剑　　图 7-15-1　回身弓步横击　　图 7-15-2　回身弓步横击

15. 回身弓步横击。身躯俯下,左脚落于右脚旁,左手剑指附于右腕(图7-15-1)。右脚向身后退步,身体后转(朝向东方),成右弓步;同时,右手持剑随身转动向正东前下方斜摆横击;左手剑指斜伸于左后上方,目视剑尖(图7-15-2)。

16. 提膝独立举剑。右腿直起，左脚前移；右手持剑使剑尖从前向上、由右肩外侧向后、向下、向前直臂绕行一周挽花；同时，左手剑指从后向下、由左腿外侧向前屈肘弧形绕行，附于右肩前，眼随剑尖（图7-16-1）。右脚跟外转，身躯从左向后转（朝向西方），左腿屈膝提起，右手持剑向上举起，左手剑指在转身提膝之后向前平伸指出，目视剑指（图7-16-2）。

图7-16-1　提膝独立举剑　　图7-16-2　提膝独立举剑　　图7-17-1　叉步下势推剑

17. 叉步下势推剑。左脚向前落步，右脚在身后屈膝提起；右手持剑使剑尖向身后下沉，左剑指收于右肩前（图7-17-1）。右手持剑将剑柄从上向左、由左肩前向下、向右腰侧绕行收住，剑尖横向身躯前方；左手剑指向下、向左、屈肘向上绕行举于头顶上方；同时，右脚向西摆起，左脚蹬地跳起伸向右腿后面，身体腾空，目视身体右侧下方（图7-17-2）。右脚先落地，右腿屈膝半蹲，左脚从右腿后面插步，同时，右手持剑向左下方斜伸推铲，目视剑身（图7-17-3）。

图7-17-2　叉步下势推剑　　图7-17-3　叉步下势推剑　　图7-18-1　虚步抱剑

第三段

18. 虚步抱剑。右腿直起，左脚向东迈步，右脚由左脚前向东迈步；同时，右手持剑使剑尖摆向身躯右侧，将剑从右向前平摆绕行；左手剑指附于右腕，眼随剑身（图7-18-1）。左脚向东再迈一步，身向左转；同时，右手持剑随身转动向东平摆绕行，将剑柄屈肘收近腰前，剑尖斜向前上方稍高过头；左手剑指附于右腕；重心后移，右腿屈膝，左脚尖前点，成左虚步，目视剑尖(图 7-18-2)。

图 7-18-2　虚步抱剑　　　图 7-19　弓步前上刺剑　　　图 7-20　仆步扫剑

19. 弓步前上刺剑。左脚向前上步,屈膝成左弓步;右手持剑与左手剑指一起用剑尖向前上方直刺,剑尖高与头齐,目视剑尖(图 7-19)。

20. 仆步扫剑。身体右转,成右仆步,同时,右手持剑用剑刃向右、向后下方斜扫摆,左手剑指举于左侧斜上方,目视剑身(图 7-20)。

21. 挽花歇步反撩。两腿站起,左脚跟外转,身躯右转,右脚回收半步,两腿稍作屈膝;同时,右手持剑将剑柄向胸前提起,左手剑指附于右腕;目视剑柄(图 7-21-1)。右手持剑使剑尖由右腿外侧向后、向上绕行挽花(图 7-21-2)。右脚向后退步,身体右转(向北),左脚从身后插步,两腿屈膝成左歇步;同时,右手持剑向西、向下、向东、向上反撩,左剑指收于右肩前;目视剑尖(图 7-21-3)。

图 7-21-1　挽花歇步反撩　　　图 7-21-2　挽花歇步反撩　　　图 7-21-3　挽花歇步反撩

22. 退步直刺。身体直起左转(向西),右脚向后退步,成左弓步;右手持剑使剑尖从上向下经腰向前刺出,左手剑指附于右肩;目视剑尖(图 7-22)。

23. 提膝独立劈剑。左脚向后退步,右手持剑使剑下绕行,左手剑指随势移向右腕,眼随剑尖(图 7-23-1)。右手持剑使剑尖由下从左侧向后绕行抄挂,臂内旋将剑柄向上经左肩前提起,用剑刃向前劈砍;左手剑指收至右肩前;同时,左腿伸直站立,右腿屈膝提起;目视剑身(图 7-23-2)。

图 7-22　退步直刺　　　图 7-23-1　提膝独立劈剑　　　图 7-23-2　提膝独立劈剑

24. 虚步抱剑。 左腿屈膝，右脚向后落步，右腿伸直；右手持剑使剑向上竖起，左手剑指移至右腕（图 7-24-1）。左脚尖里扣，身体后转，重心后移，成右虚步；右手持剑与左手剑指一起随身转动，将剑柄稍下沉与腰平齐；眼随剑身（图 7-24-2）。

图 7-24-1　虚步抱剑　　　图 7-24-2　虚步抱剑　　　图 7-25-1　马步提剑

25. 马步提剑。 左脚向前上步，身体右转，两腿屈膝成马步；同时，右手持剑将剑柄向下、向右弧形绕行提起，剑尖下垂；左手剑指随势收于右肩前，目视剑柄（图 7-25-1）。左手剑指向左平伸指出，目视剑指（图 7-25-2）。

图 7-25-2　马步提剑　　　图 7-26-1　回身前点虚步提剑　　　图 7-26-2　回身前点虚步提剑

26. 回身前点虚步提剑。 右手持剑在体前向左挂剑，同时右脚从身后向左插步，左手剑指上举，身躯从右向后转；眼随剑尖（图 7-26-1）。身体向右后转，右手持剑随转体向右挂剑（图 7-26-2）。右手持剑向左前点，左手剑指从上向前附于右腕，目视剑尖（图 7-26-3）。右手持剑将剑柄向下、由右腿外侧向后抽回，提于身后，剑尖朝前斜下垂（图 7-26-4）；同时，重心后移，成左虚步；左手剑指向前平伸指出，目视剑指（图 7-26-5）。

图 7-26-3　回身前点虚步提剑　　图 7-26-4　回身前点虚步提剑　　图 7-26-5　回身前点虚步提剑

第四段

27. 点步上刺。右脚向前上步，左脚随之向前上步以脚尖点地；同时，右手持剑使剑柄经过右腰侧，用剑尖由身前直臂向上穿刺，左手剑指收于右肩前，目视剑尖（图 7-27）。

28. 歇步下斩。右手持剑使剑尖向左绕行、将剑柄收至腹前，左手剑指向下、向左、向上弧形绕行斜举，眼视前下方（图 7-28-1）。两腿屈膝全蹲成歇步，右手持剑用剑刃向前下方斜摆横斩，左手剑指斜举于左后上方，目视剑身（图 7-28-2）。

 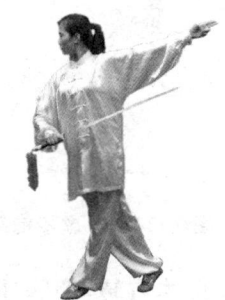 

图 7-27　点步上刺　　　　图 7-28-1　歇步下斩　　　　图 7-28-2　歇步下斩

29. 提膝独立抱剑。两腿直起，左腿直立，右腿提膝；同时，右手持剑将剑柄向上提至左耳侧，剑尖斜朝前下方；左手剑指附于右腕，目视前下方（图 7-29）。

30. 前跃歇步下切。右脚向前落步，右手持剑使剑尖向下、由右腿外侧向后、向上、向左绕行转动，左手剑指顺势收至右肩前；在剑尖向上绕行的同时，左脚向前跃进，右脚蹬地跳起从身后伸向左侧，身体腾空（图 7-30-1）。左脚先落地，右脚随之在左侧落地，成歇步；同时，右手持剑在身前向左切下，左手剑指趁势伸向右腋下；身前俯，头左转，目视剑尖（图 7-30-2）。

图 7-29　提膝独立抱剑　　图 7-30-1　前跃歇步下切　　图 7-30-2　前跃歇步下切

31. 翻身弓步劈剑。右手持剑将剑柄向右拉开，左手剑指向左拉开；同时，两腿站起，成右插步（图7-31-1）。身体右转向后（西），右脚上半步，成右弓步；右手持剑随身翻转，从上向前劈剑；左剑指从左后向上举于头顶；目视剑身（图7-31-2）。

图7-31-1 翻身弓步劈剑　　　图7-31-2 翻身弓步劈剑

32. 提膝独立直刺。右手持剑使剑由右腿外侧向后、向上、向前挽花一周后，屈肘将剑柄收向右腰后；左手剑指附于右腕；同时，右脚尖外展，左脚向前移进半步，成左歇步；目视右侧后方（图7-32-1）。身体左转，左脚向前（西）上步，左腿伸直站立，右腿屈膝提起；同时，右手持剑用剑尖向前刺出，左手剑指由身前向左后平摆绕行，目视剑尖（图7-32-2）。

图7-32-1 提膝独立直刺　　　图7-32-2 提膝独立直刺

结束动作

33. 并步持剑。左脚跟里转，身体左转，右脚向西侧落，成右弓步；同时，右手持剑将剑柄向头顶上方提起，左剑指扶剑柄，目视剑柄（图7-33-1）。身体右转成右仆步，左手反手将剑柄接握、向上提起，右手变剑指穿向右侧，眼随右剑指（图7-33-2）。两腿直起，左脚向右脚靠拢并步，右手剑指向上亮指，举于头顶上方，左手持剑落于身体左侧，目视左侧（图7-33-3）。

图7-33-1 并步持剑　　图7-33-2 并步持剑　　图7-33-3 并步持剑

34. 收势。右手剑指从上向右、向下弧形绕行下垂，变掌贴靠于右腿侧；两肘自然微屈，头转正，目视正前方，同起势（图 7-1-1）。

（二）学习计划

项目	内　容
前期准备	1. 具备一定的柔韧、协调和力量基础； 2. 掌握武术的基本步型和步法； 3. 了解剑的结构； 4. 学会剑术基本技法动作（劈剑、刺剑、点剑、挂剑、撩剑、挽花等）
学习进度	1. 学会动作路线（本套共 34 个动作，每次课学习 4 个动作，约需 10 次课、20 学时）； 2. 提高动作规范性

（三）技术体验

内容	要　求
形健骨遒	七星剑是工架剑，要求功架工整。因此，掌握基本步型、步法、平衡等动作，是练好七星剑的基本要求和必备条件
击刺得法	七星剑的剑法有"刺、点、撩、劈、截、崩、架、斩、挂、云"等，要了解各种剑法的力点。如刺与点的力点在剑尖；撩与劈则力达剑身前部；截剑须臂与剑成一直线；崩剑动作要点是要沉腕使剑尖猛向前上崩起；架剑要剑高过头，力达剑身；斩剑是平剑向左或右横出，高度在头与肩之间，力达剑身；挂剑要注意立圆、贴身挂出；云剑要平剑在头顶或头前上方平圆绕环。
身械协调	在动作中，要将身体动作与剑的动作紧密配合，使身体运动的劲力达于剑之锋刃。例如，剑指与剑的配合、剑法与步法的配合（剑引步随、步行剑随）、身法与剑法的配合（身动剑随、剑行身随）等

（四）文化体验

• **兵剑与武术剑**

作为"百兵之君"，兵剑以两种方式作战：一是与盾配合直接投身作战。二是作为备用武器。

中国武术在兵剑锋之"刺"和刃之"斩"（击）的基础上，将剑的认识深化为"三锋四刃"，不仅建构了不同方法的技术系统，而且形成了"工行醉绵"演练体式。

• **剑器轻清**

剑有两面刃，故持剑时不能触身，因此剑术的技法，如点、崩、截、绞等都十分注重敏捷、轻巧、准确，力点多在剑尖或剑前端。剑术演练时，在轻快的行步、潇洒的腾跃、闪展的避让等过程中，剑术劲力的运使多柔中带刚，以在敏捷的出击、纵横的劈刺中力透剑器的某一部位，刚柔相推发挥剑器轻清之特点。

• **工架剑重骨**

"工架剑"是一招一势，形健筋遒，端庄势整，犹如中国书法的楷书。因此，要求剑术的动作势式具有"骨法",即通过骨骼的变化体现出架式的匀称,骨架的结体布局讲究中和。主张"先仪骨体,后尽精神,有肤有血,有力有筋",其形方能"方中矩,圆中规"。

- **递接剑、持剑礼**

  递接剑礼

  1. 双手递剑礼:并步站立,身体自然直立,双手掌心向上掌指向前,捧住护手平举于体前,剑身垂直,剑刃朝左右,目视接剑者。

  2. 单手递剑礼:并步站立,身体自然直立,左手靠近护手处,虎口向上握剑柄,目视递剑者。

  持剑礼

  并步站立,左手持剑,屈臂抬起,使剑身贴前臂外侧斜横于胸前;右手成掌,以掌外沿附于左手食指根节,高与胸齐。两手与胸间距离为20～30厘米。

三、总结

(一) 七星剑是武术器械中剑术的基础套路,因此包含了武术剑术的基本剑法,如刺剑、挂剑、斩剑、撩剑、云剑、点剑、劈剑等。

(二) 七星剑属于工架剑,需要以"规范的功架"和"清晰的剑法"作为基础,在一招一式体现其端庄势整之风。

(三) 练习七星剑,需在"剑指与剑的配合、剑法与步法的配合、身法与剑法的配合"中不断体验身械协调,力争在一招一势中以"形断意连、势断气连"体现剑术之"气势连贯"。

(四) 学习七星剑,体现"剑器轻清"的演练特征,了解"好剑轻死、励精图志、宁折不弯"的文化精神。

四、延伸学习

(一) 学会七星剑动作路线之后,反复纠错,不断提高动作的规范性。

(二) 学会七星剑套路后,可从"身械协调""气势连贯"等方面提高演练的感染力。

(三) 学会七星剑套路后,可进一步学习另一套工架剑术(盘龙剑),也可以选择三合对剑作为进一步学习的内容。

五、思考与练习题

1. 了解剑术工行醉绵的演练体式。
2. 思考七星剑的运动特点。
3. 思考剑术演练风格与中国传统文化的关系。

六、参考文献

[1] 蔡龙云. 剑术[M]. 南昌：江西人民出版社，1982.
[2] 戴国斌. 剑的文化传记[J]. 体育与科学，2009(5)：11-13.
[3] 全国体育院校教材委员会. 中国武术教程(上)[M]. 北京：人民体育出版社，2004.

第八章 双节棍

一、导言

传说双节棍由宋太祖赵匡胤所创,用来扫击敌军马脚、破甲兵或硬兵器。后来这种兵器由南传至菲律宾,由东传至日本,并经李小龙带上银幕,而广为流传,成为美国警察的防身物。如今,双节棍运动不仅融刀枪剑棍九节鞭等武术动作,而且也吸收现代时尚音乐和舞蹈元素,成为搏击与表演相结合的时尚运动、防身与健身相结合的大众武术健身活动,具有"轻灵威猛、刚柔有度、动静有法、自由无限"特点。

> **双节棍结构**
>
> 由 A 棍、B 棍和中间链条构成,A,B 棍的长度大约为 30 厘米,中间链条的长度大约为 12 厘米。棍分为远棍端和近棍端,靠近中间链条的为近棍段,远离中间链条的为远棍端。

二、学习体验

(一) 动作说明

1. 基本姿势。两脚前后开立,双脚全脚掌着地,左右距离 10～15 厘米。持棍手与前支撑脚方向保持一致,握住 A 棍近端,抬头挺胸,两眼平视(图 8-1)。

2. 流星赶月。以肘关节为轴,右手由内向下、向前上、再向外向后、向下向前运动,使 B 棍成大八字形里圆舞花状(图 8-2-1—图 8-2-3)。

图 8-1 预备势

图 8-2-1 流星赶月

图 8-2-2 流星赶月

图 8-2-3 流星赶月

3. 左右逢源。 右臂伸直或微屈,以腕关节为轴,由内向下、向前上、再向外向后、向下向前上运动,使 B 棍成小八字形立圆舞花(图 8-3-1—图 8-3-6)。

图 8-3-1 左右逢源

图 8-3-2 左右逢源

图 8-3-3 左右逢源

图 8-3-4 左右逢源

图 8-3-5 左右逢源

图 8-3-6 左右逢源

4. 毒蛇吐信。 手握 A 棍的近棍端,将 B 棍夹于腋下;右脚蹬地转髋,送肩摧肘,将 B 棍向前弹射而出,犹如毒蛇吐信;将 B 棍顺势向下向后回收至腋下,准备第二次进攻(图 8-4-1—图 8-4-4)。

图 8-4-1 毒蛇吐信

图 8-4-2 毒蛇吐信

图 8-4-3 毒蛇吐信

图 8-4-4 毒蛇吐信

5. 毒蛇出洞。 右手握 A 棍近棍端,拇指与食指、中指夹住 B 棍近棍端;蹬地转腰摧肩送肘,将棍向前射出,以 B 棍远棍端为着力点,点射目标点;回收时,顺势将 B 棍夹于腋下(图 8-5-1—图 8-5-3)。

图 8-5-1 毒蛇出洞

图 8-5-2 毒蛇出洞

图 8-5-3　毒蛇出洞　　　图 8-6-1　腰部变向　　　图 8-6-2　腰部变向

6. 腰部变向。右手握 A 棍于肩上，向左斜前方劈击，力量向斜前方，顺势向左后方回带，以躯干阻挡，回弹后将 B 棍收于右腋下（图 8-6-1—图 8-6-4）。

图 8-6-3　腰部变向　　　图 8-6-4　腰部变向　　　图 8-7-1　臂部变向

7. 臂部变向。（右手握棍于肩上，以肘关节为轴，向前下方劈棍，至上臂时反弹回至肩上握棍，以此反复练习。左手方法同右手）（图 8-7-1—图 8-7-4）

图 8-7-2　臂部变向　　　图 8-7-3　臂部变向　　　图 8-7-4　臂部变向

8. 腿部变向。右手持 A 棍于肩上，向左前方劈击的同时左腿提膝，以小腿阻击双节棍的链条部分，使 B 棍顺势反弹于大腿部（图 8-8-1—图 8-8-3）。

图 8-8-1　腿部变向　　　图 8-8-2　腿部变向　　　图 8-8-3　腿部变向

9. 转身变向。右手握 A 棍向后绕环，左脚在前，右脚在后。在 B 棍向前上运行时，向右后转身，变成向前绕环，右脚在前，左脚在后（图 8-9-1—图 8-9-4）。

图 8-9-1　转身变向　　　图 8-9-2　转身变向　　　图 8-9-3　转身变向

图 8-9-4　转身变向　　　图 8-10-1　背后换棍　　　图 8-10-2　背后换棍

10. 背后换棍。右手握 A 棍近端，从左下方向右后平扫至身后，左手在身后握住 B 棍近端（图 8-10-1—图 8-10-3）。

图 8-10-3　背后换棍　　　图 8-11-1　胸前换棍　　　图 8-11-2　胸前换棍

11. 胸前换棍。 右手握 A 棍近端，做上下劈棍；当棍下劈于地面垂直时，左手从胸前换握 A 棍近端（图 8-11-1、图 8-11-2）。

12. 腋下换棍。 右手握 A 棍近端，将 B 棍由下向上向后摆动至右上臂时，左手迅速至右腋下抓住 B 棍的近棍端；反手同正手（图 8-12-1—图 8-12-3）。

图 8-12-1　腋下换棍　　　图 8-12-2　腋下换棍　　　图 8-12-3　腋下换棍

13. 正手正舞花。 右手握 A 棍近端，向左下方摆动，至 B 棍向右上方运行时，右手抛开 A 棍，让链条绕着右手背滑动，然后右手顺势反抓 B 棍近端（图 8-13-1—图 8-13-4）。

图 8-13-1　正手正舞花　　　图 8-13-2　正手正舞花　　　图 8-13-3　正手正舞花

图 8-13-4　正手正舞花　　　图 8-14-1　反手正舞花　　　图 8-14-2　反手正舞花

14. 反手正舞花。右手反握 A 棍,向右后方摆动,当 B 棍至右后上方时,右手抛开 A 棍,让链条绕着右手背滑动,然后右手顺势正抓 B 棍近端(图 8-14-1—图 8-14-3)。

图 8-14-3　反手正舞花　　　图 8-15-1　正手反舞花　　　图 8-15-2　正手反舞花

15. 正手反舞花。右手正握 A 棍近端,向前上方摆动,当 B 棍运行至右下方时,右手抛开 A 棍,让链条绕着右手背滑动,然后右手顺势反抓 B 棍近端(图 8-15-1—图 8-15-4)。

图 8-15-3　正手反舞花　　　图 8-15-4　正手反舞花　　　图 8-16-1　反手反舞花

16. 反手反舞花。右手反握 A 棍,由下向前上方摆动,当运行至后下方时,用右手臂推送棍至左后下方,右手抛开 A 棍,让链条绕着右手背滑动,然后右手顺势正抓 B 棍近端(图 8-16-1—图 8-16-5)。

图8-16-2 反手反舞花

图8-16-3 反手反舞花

图8-16-4 反手反舞花

图8-16-5 反手反舞花

图8-17-1 胸前正平舞花

图8-17-2 胸前正平舞花

17. 胸前正平舞花。右手反握A棍近端,由体右侧向体左侧水平摆动一圈后,抛开A棍,让链条绕着右手背滑动,然后右手顺势正抓B棍近端(图8-17-1—图8-17-4)。

图8-17-3 胸前正平舞花

图8-17-4 胸前正平舞花

图8-18-1 胸前反平舞花

18. 胸前反平舞花。右手正握A棍近端,由体左侧向体右侧水平摆动一圈后抛开A棍,让链条绕着右手背滑动,然后右手顺势反抓B棍近端(图8-18-1—图8-18-4)。

  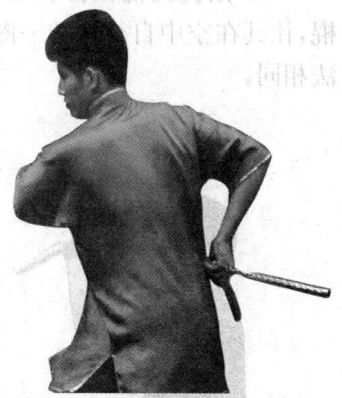

图 8-18-2　胸前反平舞花　　　图 8-18-3　胸前反平舞花　　　图 8-18-4　胸前反平舞花

19. 侧面抛接棍。 右手握 A 棍近端，向左手臂腋下摆动，至后上方运行时，抛开 A 棍，让其在空中自行运转一圈后，用左手抓握 B 棍近端（图 8-19-1—图 8-19-4）。另一侧方法相同。

图 8-19-1　侧面抛接棍　　　　　图 8-19-2　侧面抛接棍

图 8-19-3　侧面抛接棍　　　　　图 8-19-4　侧面抛接棍

20. 后抛接棍。右手握 A 棍近端，由上向下向右腋下摆动，至后上方运行时，抛开 A 棍，让其在空中自行运转一圈后，用右手抓握 B 棍近端（图 8-20-1—图 8-20-6）。另一侧方法相同。

图 8-20-1　后抛接棍 　　　图 8-20-2　后抛接棍 　　　图 8-20-3　后抛接棍

图 8-20-4　后抛接棍 　　　图 8-20-5　后抛接棍 　　　图 8-20-6　后抛接棍

21. 收棍。当棍运行至最远点时，顺势回收棍，让棍回荡时，右手用食指和中指抓住回荡的棍的近端（图 8-21-1—图 8-21-3）。

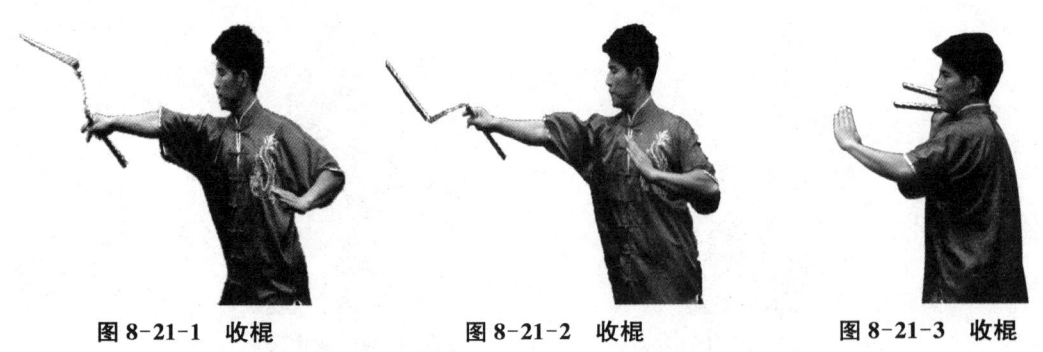

图 8-21-1　收棍　　　图 8-21-2　收棍　　　图 8-21-3　收棍

(二) 学习计划

项目	内　　容
前期准备	1. 具有较好的协调能力。 2. 掌握武术基本功和简单的器械套路
学习进度	1. 第一阶段,首先学会前4个基本技术(2个课时)。 2. 第二阶段,在掌握4个基本技术的基础上学会换手,达到左右手都能练习的目的(2个课时)。 3. 第三阶段,学会变向动作,达到在移动中练习动作的目的(2个课时)。 4. 第四阶段,学会舞花动作,达到棍花飞舞,见棍不见人境界(8个课时)。 5. 第五阶段,学会抛接动作,使舞花和抛接有机结合,在身法和步法的配合下,体验棍随身动、遍地生花的高升境界(2个课时)

(三) 技术体验

内容	要　　求
动作规范	1. 学会动作的运行路线。 2. 掌握动作的发力要领和发力部位。 3. 要求动作舒展,身械协调,动迅静定
技击用法	1. 以棍顶端点击对方的眼睛或面部,如毒蛇吐信、毒蛇出洞等。 2. 以棍远端击打对方的要害部位,如腰部变向中的前劈棍等。 3. 以棍的中间链条绞杀对方的颈部或其它关节部位
演练水平	1. 在熟练掌握技术动作基础上,不断加快动作速度。 2. 在提高动作速度后,注意动作演练的节奏,做到快慢相间,动迅静定。 3. 在提高动作速度后,体验动作力度(以腰为发力点,手腕要放松)。 4. 在提高动作力度后,体验"棍随手动,眼随棍转"的身械协调和动作的精神饱满之要求

三、总结

- 以上动作是双节棍基本动作,是进一步练习各种组合动作的基础。
- 首先应学会动作路线与自我保护方法,力争不伤及自己、不出现掉棍现象。
- 在学习各种动作时,要放松手腕,在放慢速度熟悉动作路线后,体验动作力点、动作节奏,理解动作的技击用法,最终体验中国武术"身械合一""眼随手动""步随身行"的要求,力争做到"身械协调合一"。

四、延伸学习

- 学会单个动作后,可换手练习,力争左右手都能灵活舞动双节棍。
- 学会单个动作后,也可以通过模拟技击训练(击打沙袋、树干等)深化对动作技击的理解。
- 学会单个动作后,还可以学习成套动作(如段位制双节棍套路),以提高单个动作的连贯能力。

五、思考与练习题

1. 练习双节棍的目的和意义？
2. 如何克服练习双节棍的畏惧心理？
3. 如何提高双节棍的演练水平？

六、参考文献

［1］国家体育总局武术研究院．中国武术段位制系列教程——双节棍［M］．北京：高等教育出版社，2009（9）．
［2］双节棍教学网——中国双节棍教学中文网［http://www.lz1980.com/］．
［3］鱼宏映，马野．国内双节棍运动的发展现状研究［J］．体育科技文献通报，2011（2）：89-104．

第九章 马王堆导引术

一、导言

"健身气功·马王堆导引术"是中国健身气功协会向海内外正式推广的健身气功项目。它是由上海体育学院组织专家依据湖南长沙考古发掘出土的马王堆《导引图》的动作原型，结合健身气功的基础理论以及现代健身的要求，编创的健身气功新功法。

二、学习体验

(一) 动作说明

1. 起势。两脚并步站立，头正颈直，下颌微收，含胸拔背；两臂自然下垂，周身中正；唇齿轻叩，舌抵上腭；目视前方（图9-1-1）。托掌时百会穴上领，身体保持中正安舒，托掌高度与肚脐齐高（图9-1-2）。托掌时意念劳宫穴，目视前下方（图9-1-3）。按掌时意注神阙穴，脚趾微抓地，目视前方（图9-1-4）。

功理作用——引导清气上行，浊气下降；改善练习者手足末端的气血循环，起到温煦手足的作用。

2. 第一式挽弓。用胸廓完成开合拉气，开吸合呼，目视前下方（图9-2-1，图9-2-2）。伸臂时意注体内气机延（手太阴肺

图9-1-1 起势

图9-1-2 起势

图9-1-3 起势

图9-1-4 起势

经)走向,从胸中(中府穴,前正中线旁开6寸,平第1肋间隙处),经肘窝(尺泽穴,在肘横纹中,肱二头肌腱桡侧凹陷处)贯注拇指端(少商穴,拇指桡侧指甲角旁0.1寸)(图9-2-3)。前伸手掌高度与眼眉齐平,目视前手掌;后拉手掌高度跟中府穴位置齐平。

图 9-2-1　挽弓　　　　　图 9-2-2　挽弓　　　　　图 9-2-3　挽弓

功理作用——扩胸展肩提髋,可以有效刺激内脏及拉伸颈肩部肌肉,有利于颈、肩部运动不适的预防与调治。本式动作配合呼吸吐纳,有利于祛除胸闷、气喘等身体不适。

手太阴肺经

流注线:起于中府(在胸外侧部,云门下1寸,平第一肋间隙处,距前正中线6寸),终于少商(在手拇指末节桡侧,距指甲角0.1寸)。

循行:肺手太阴之脉,起于中焦,下络大肠,还循胃口,上膈属肺。从肺系,横出腋下,下循臑内,行少阴、心主之前,下肘中,臂内上骨下廉,入寸口,上鱼,循鱼际,出大指之端。其支者,从腕后直出次指内廉,出其端。

穴位:中府、云门、天府、侠白、尺泽、孔最、列缺、经渠、太渊、鱼际、少商左右各11个穴位。

口诀:手太阴肺十一穴,中府云门天府诀,侠白尺泽孔最存,列缺经渠太渊涉,鱼际少商如韭叶。

---

3. 第二式引背。提踵拱背时,两臂以食指为轴内旋,两食指之间距离与本人鼻翼等宽,目视两手食指。拱背时,意念从食指端(商阳穴,食指桡侧指甲角旁0.1寸)经肘外侧(曲池穴,屈肘成直角,在肘横纹外侧端与肱骨外上髁连线中点)到鼻翼两侧(迎香穴,位于鼻翼外缘中点旁,当鼻唇沟中间)(图9-3-1)。前伸勾手弓背时,两手腕之间距离与本人鼻翼等宽。目视两手腕。弓背时,意念从食指端(商阳穴,食指桡侧指甲角旁0.1寸)经肘外侧(曲池穴)到鼻翼两侧(迎香穴)(图9-3-2)。按掌远眺时,两手食指微上翘(图9-3-3)。

功理作用——抻臂拱背,使腕、肩、背部肌肉得到充分牵拉,有利于改善手指、腕、肩、背部运动不适。牵拉两胁,配合近观远望,有利于眼睛不适的预防和调治。

图 9-3-1 引　　　　图 9-3-2 引　　　　图 9-3-3 引

手阳明大肠经

流注线：此一经起于商阳（在食指末节桡侧，距指甲角 0.1 寸），终于迎香（在面部鼻唇沟内的上段，横平鼻翼中部，口禾髎穴外上方 1 寸处）。

循行：大肠手阳明之脉，起于大指次之端，循指上廉，出合谷两骨之间，上入两筋之中，循臂上廉，入肘外廉，上臑外前廉，上肩，出髃骨之前廉，上出于柱骨之会上，下入缺盆，络肺，下膈，属大肠。其支者，从缺盆上颈，贯颊，入下齿中；还出夹口，交人中，左之右，右之左，上夹鼻孔。

穴位：商阳（井）、二间（荥）、三间（输）、合谷（原）、阳溪（经）、偏历（络）、温溜、下廉、上廉、手三里、曲池（合）、肘髎、手五里、臂臑、肩髃、巨骨、天鼎、扶突、禾髎、迎香左右各 20 个穴位。

口诀：手阳明穴起商阳，二间三间合谷藏，阳溪偏历温溜长，下廉上廉手三里，曲池肘髎五里近，臂臑肩髃巨骨当，天鼎扶突禾髎接，鼻旁五分号迎香。

---

4. 第三式凫浴。 摆臂至体侧后方时，上手与头齐高，侧方位顶胯，目视侧前方（图 9-4-1）；旋腰后视过程中，屈膝时膝盖不要超过脚尖（图 9-4-2）。两臂下落时，意念从面部（承泣穴，位于面部，瞳孔直下，当眼球与眶下缘之间）经腹侧（天枢穴，脐中旁开 2 寸）、胫骨外侧（足三里穴，外膝眼下三寸，胫骨外侧约一横指处）至脚趾端（厉兑穴，在足第 2 趾末节外侧，距趾甲角 0.1 寸）（图 9-4-3）。

图 9-4-1 凫　　　　图 9-4-2 凫　　　　图 9-4-3 凫浴

功理作用——通过左右摆臂和转体，有利于减少腰部脂肪的堆积。顶胯摆臂旋腰，有利于肩、腰部运动不适的预防和调治。

> **足阳明胃经**
>
> 流注线：起于头维（在头侧部，当额角发际上0.5寸，头正中线旁4.5寸）、承泣（在面部，瞳孔直下，当眼球与眶下缘之间），终于厉兑（在足第2趾末节外侧，距趾甲角0.1寸）。
>
> 循行：胃足阳明之脉，起于鼻，交頞中，旁约太阳之脉，下循鼻外，入上齿中，还出挟口，环唇，下交承浆，却循颐后下廉，出大迎，循颊车，上耳前，过客主人，循发际，至额颅。其支者：从大迎前，下人迎，循喉咙，入缺盆，下膈，属胃，络脾。其直者：从缺盆下乳内廉，下夹脐，入气街中。其支者：起于胃口，下循腹里，下至气街中而合。以下髀关，抵伏兔，下膝髌中，下循胫外廉，下足跗，入中趾内间。其支者，下膝三寸而别，下入中趾外间。其直者：别跗上，入大趾间，出其端。
>
> 穴位：承泣、四白、巨髎、地仓、大迎、颊车、下关、头维、人迎、水突、气舍、缺盆、气户、库房、屋翳、膺窗、乳中、乳根、不容、承满、梁门、关门、太乙、滑肉门、天枢、外陵、大巨、水道、归来、气冲、髀关、伏兔、阴市、梁丘、犊鼻、足三里、上巨虚、条口、下巨虚、丰隆、解溪、冲阳、陷谷、内庭、厉兑，左右各45个腧穴。
>
> 口诀：四十五穴足阳明，头维下关颊车停，承泣四白巨髎经，地仓大迎对人迎，水突气舍连缺盆，气户库房屋翳屯，膺窗乳中延乳根，不容承满梁门起，关门太乙滑肉门，天枢外陵大巨存，水道归来气冲次，髀关伏兔走阴市，梁丘犊鼻足三里，上巨虚连条口位，下巨虚跳上丰隆，解溪冲阳陷谷中，内庭厉兑经穴终。

5. 第四式龙登。下蹲幅度以脚跟不离地面为准，根据自身年龄及柔韧性状况，可选择全蹲或半蹲（图9-5-1）。两手上举时，意念从大趾（隐白穴，在足大趾末节内侧，距趾甲角0.1寸）上行，经膝关节内侧（阴陵泉穴，胫骨内侧髁后下方凹陷处）至腋下（大包穴，在侧胸部，腋中线上，当第6肋间隙处）（图9-5-2）。手掌外展提踵下看时，保持重心平衡，全身尽量伸展（图9-5-3）。

图9-5-1　龙登　　　图9-5-2　龙登　　　图9-5-3　龙登

功理作用——两臂撑展，有利于祛除胸闷、气郁、气喘等身体不适。提踵而立可拉长足底肌肉、韧带，提高人体平衡能力。伸展屈蹲，有利于改善颈、肩、腰、腿部运动不适。

> ### 足太阴脾经
>
> 流注线:起于隐白(足大趾内侧趾甲角旁0.1寸的爪甲根部),终于大包(在侧胸部腋中在线,当第6肋间隙处;侧卧举臂,在腋下6寸,腋中在线取穴)。
>
> 循行:脾足太阴之脉,起于大指之端,循指内侧白肉际,过核骨后,上内踝前廉,上踹内,循胫骨后,交出厥阴之前,上膝股内前廉,入腹,属脾,络胃,上膈,夹咽,连舌本散舌下。其支者,复从胃,别上膈,注心中(脾之大络,名曰大包,出渊腋下三寸,布胸胁)。
>
> 穴位:隐白、大都、太白、公孙、商丘、三阴交、漏谷、地机、阴陵泉、血海、箕门、冲门、府舍、腹结、大横、腹哀、食窦、天溪溪、胸乡、周荣、大包,共21穴,左右合42穴。
>
> 口诀:二十一穴脾中州,隐白在足大趾头,大都太白公孙盛,商丘三阴交可求,漏谷地机阴陵泉,血海箕门冲门开,府舍腹结大横排,腹哀食窦连天溪,胸乡周荣大包随。

6. 第五式鸟伸。侧摆臂时,意念从腋下(极泉穴,腋窝正中,腋动脉搏动处)经肘(少海穴,屈肘,当肘横纹内侧端与肱骨内上髁连线的中点处。屈肘,当肘横纹内侧端与肱骨内上髁连线的中点处)至小指端(少冲穴,位于左右手部,小指指甲下缘,靠无名指侧的边缘上)(图9-6-1)。再摆臂时,注意身体由屈蹲经顶髋、展腹、扩胸、伸颈,向前俯身,背部与地面平行(图9-6-2)。下颚向内回收,由腰椎、胸椎、颈椎节节蠕动伸展,双手随动作前摆下按;随即抬头目视前方,头颈与脊柱的运动要协调一致(图9-6-3)。

图9-6-1 鸟伸

图9-6-2 鸟伸

图9-6-3 鸟伸

功理作用——展臂前伸,有利于改善颈、肩部运动不适的预防与调治。蠕动脊柱,有利于腰背部运动不适的预防与调治。

> ### 手少阴心经
>
> 流注线:起于极泉(在腋窝顶点,腋动脉搏动处),终于少冲(在小指末节桡侧,距指甲角0.1寸)。
>
> 循行:心手少阴之脉,起于心中,出属心系,下膈,络小肠。

其支者：从心系，上夹咽，系目系。其直者：复从心系，却上肺，下出腋下，下循臑内后廉，行太阴、心主之后，下肘内，循臂内后廉，抵掌后锐骨之端，入掌内后廉，循小指之内，出其端。《灵枢·经脉》

穴位：极泉、青灵、少海（合穴）、灵道（经穴）、通里（络穴）、阴郄（郄穴）神门（输穴、原穴）、少府（荥穴）、少冲（井穴），共九穴，左右合18穴。

口诀：九穴午时手少阴，极泉青灵少海深，灵道通里阴郄遂，神门少府少冲寻。

7. 第六式引腹。两臂内旋外展时，注意腹部放松，同时左右顶髋（图9-7-1）。两手上撑时的上手小指对准肩部后侧（臑俞穴，位于人体的肩部，当腋后纹头直上，肩胛冈下缘凹陷中），下手拇指对准臀部（环跳穴，侧卧屈股，股骨大转子最凸点与骶管裂孔连线的外1/3与中1/3交点处）（图9-7-2）。两手撑按时，意念从小指端（少泽穴，小指尺侧指甲角旁0.1寸）经肘关节内侧（小海穴，位于人体的肘内侧，当尺骨鹰嘴与肱骨内上髁之间凹陷处）至耳前（听宫穴，位于面部，耳屏前，下颌骨髁状突的后方，张口时呈凹陷处）。

图9-7-1 引腹　　　　图9-7-2 引腹

功理作用——两臂内旋外展，有利于肩、肘、手部运动不适的预防与调治。手臂动作配合髋关节的扭动，可刺激内脏，有利于消化不良、腹部胀气等身体不适的预防与调治。

手太阳小肠经

流注线：此一经起于少泽（在手小指末节尺侧，距甲根角0.1寸），终于听宫（在面部，耳屏前，下颌骨髁状突的后方，张口时呈凹陷处）。

循行：小肠手太阳之脉，起于小指之端，循手外侧上腕，出踝中，直上循臂骨下廉，出肘内侧两骨之间，上循臑外后廉出肩解，绕肩胛，交肩上，入缺盆，络心，循咽下膈，抵胃，属小肠。其支者：从缺盆循颈，上颊，至目锐眦，却入耳中。其支者：别颊上抵鼻，至目内眦（斜络于颧）。

穴位：少泽、前谷、后溪、腕骨、阳谷、养老、支正、小海、肩贞、臑俞、天宗、秉风、曲垣、肩外俞、肩中俞、天窗、天容、颧髎、听宫，共19穴，左右合38穴。

口诀：手太阳穴一十九，少泽前谷后溪薮，腕谷阳谷养老绳，支正小海外辅肘，肩贞臑俞接天宗，髎外秉风曲垣首，肩外俞连肩中俞，天窗乃与天容偶，锐骨之端上颧髎，听宫耳前珠上走。

8. 第七式鸱(chī)视。两臂前摆屈肘摩肋(图9-8-1)。踢脚时，两臂伸展，掌心向外(图9-8-2)。勾脚尖时，头微用力前探，目视前上方，意念从头经后背、腘窝(委中穴，腘横纹中点，当股二头肌腱与半腱肌肌腱的中间)至脚趾端(至阴穴，足小趾外侧趾甲角旁0.1寸)(图9-8-3)。

图9-8-1　鸱视

图9-8-2　鸱视

图9-8-3　鸱视

功理作用——抻臂拔肩，头颈前探，有利于颈、肩部运动不适的预防与调治。上步抬腿踢脚，可改善身体平衡能力，有利于下肢运动不适的预防与调治。上举臂，下勾脚，有利于足膀胱经脉的循行。

足太阳膀胱经

流注线：起于睛明（在面部，目内眦角上方凹陷处），终于至阴（在足小趾末节外侧，距趾甲角0.1寸）。

循行：膀胱足太阳之脉，起于目内眦，上额，交巅。其支者：从巅至耳上角。其支者：从巅入络脑，还出别下项，循肩髆内，夹脊抵腰中，入循膂，络肾，属膀胱。其支者：从腰中，下夹脊，贯臀，入腘中。其支者：从髆内左右别下贯胛，夹脊内，过髀枢，循髀外后廉下合腘中，以下贯踹内，出外踝之后，循京骨至小指外侧。

穴位：睛明、攒竹、眉冲、曲差、五处、承光、通天、络却、玉枕、天柱、大杼、风门、肺俞、厥阴俞、心俞、督俞、膈俞、肝俞、胆俞、脾俞、胃俞、三焦俞、肾俞、气海俞、大肠俞、关元俞、小肠俞、膀胱俞、中膂俞、白环俞、上髎、次髎、中髎、下髎、会阳、承扶、殷门、浮郄、委阳、委中、附分、魄户、膏肓俞、神堂、譩嘻、膈关、魂门、阳纲、意舍、胃仓、肓门、志室、胞肓、秩边、合阳、承筋、承山、飞扬、跗阳、昆仑、仆参、申脉、金门、京骨、束骨、足通谷、至阴，共67穴，左右合134穴。

口诀:足太阳经六十七,睛明目内红肉藏,攒竹眉冲与曲差,五处上寸半承光,通天络却玉枕昂,天柱后际大筋外,大杼背部第二行,风门肺俞厥阴俞,心俞督俞膈俞强,肝胆脾胃俱挨次,三焦肾气海大肠,关元小肠到膀胱,中脊白环仔细量,自从大杼至白环,各各节外寸半长,上髎次髎中复下,一空二空腰踝当,会阳阴尾骨外取,附分侠脊第三行,魄户膏肓与神堂,谚嘻膈关魂门九,阳纲意舍仍胃仓,肓门志室胞肓续,二十椎下秩边场,承扶臀横纹中央,殷门扶郄到委阳,委中合阳承筋是,承山飞扬踝跗阳,昆仑仆参连申脉,金门京骨束骨忙,通谷至阴小指旁。

9. **第八式引腰**。摩运带脉前,两手拇指食指相接,抚于腹前(图9-9-1)。抵腰前推时,四指需用力;下颚内收,目视前方(图9-9-2)。转腰提肩方向与头转的方向要一致。前俯时,头部不要低垂(图9-9-3)。两手上提时,意念从脚底(涌泉穴,位于足前部凹陷处第2、3趾趾缝纹头端与足跟连线的前三分之一处)经膝关节内侧(阴谷穴,位于腘窝内侧,屈膝时,当半腱肌肌腱与半膜肌肌腱之间)至锁骨下沿(俞府穴,位于胸部,当锁骨下缘,前正中线旁开2寸)。

图 9-9-1 引腰

图 9-9-2 引腰

图 9-9-3 引腰

功理作用——前俯后仰,侧屈扭转,可以充分锻炼腰背肌,有利于腰部运动不适的预防与调治。在前俯的过程中拧转颈项,不仅可以加大牵拉腰背肌的效果,而且有利于颈部和背部运动不适的预防与调治。

足少阴肾经

流注线:起于涌泉(在足底部,卷足时足前部凹陷处,约当第2、3趾趾缝纹头端与足跟联机的前1/3与后2/3交点上),终于俞府(在胸部,当锁骨下缘,前正中线旁开2寸)。

循行:肾足少阴之脉,起于小指之下,邪走足心,出于然谷之下,循内踝之后,别入跟中,以上踹内,出腘内廉,上股内后廉,贯脊属肾,络膀胱。其直者,从肾上贯肝,膈,入肺中,循喉咙,夹舌本。其支者,从肺出,络心,注胸中。

穴位：涌泉、然谷、太溪、大钟、水泉、照海、复溜、交信、筑宾、阴谷、横骨、大赫、气穴、四满、中注、肓俞、商曲、石关、阴都、通谷、幽门、步廊、神封、灵墟、神藏、彧中、俞府，共 27 穴，左右合 54 穴。

口诀：足少阴穴二十七，涌泉然谷太溪溢，大钟水泉通照海，复溜交信筑宾实，阴谷膝内跗骨后，以上从足走至膝，横骨大赫联气穴，四满中注肓俞脐，商曲石关阴都密，通谷幽门寸半辟，折量腹上分十一，步廊神封膺灵墟，神藏彧中俞府毕。

10. 第九式雁飞。两臂先侧平举（图 9-10-1），再一手上举，一手下落，两臂与地面成 45 度夹角（图 9-10-2）。屈蹲时膝盖不要超过脚尖（图 9-10-3）。转头下视时，意念从胸内（天池穴，在胸部，当第四肋间隙，乳头外 1 寸，前正中线旁开 5 寸）经肘横纹中（曲泽穴，在肘横纹中，当肱二头肌腱的尺侧缘）至中指端（中冲穴，手中指末节尖端中央）（图 9-10-4）。

功理作用——身体左右倾斜，可以较好地调理全身气血运行，有平气血、宁心神的功效。

图 9-10-1　雁飞

图 9-10-2　雁飞

图 9-10-3　雁飞

图 9-10-4　雁飞

手厥阴心包经

流注线：此一经起于天池（在胸部，当第四肋间隙，乳头外 1 寸，前正中线旁开 5 寸），终于中冲（在手中指末节尖端中央）。

循行：心主手厥阴心包络之脉，起于胸中，出属心包络，下膈，历络三焦。其支者，循胸出胁，下腋三寸，上抵腋下，循臑内，行太阴、少阴之间，入肘中，下臂，行两筋之间，入掌中，循中指，出其端。其支者，别掌中，循小指次指出其端。

穴位：天池、天泉、曲泽、郄门、间使、内关、大陵、劳宫、中冲。共九穴。

口诀：九穴心包手厥阴，天池天泉曲泽深，郄门间使内关对，大陵劳宫中冲侵。

11. 第十式鹤舞。前后摆臂，与肩同高（图9-11-1）。下按转身，按掌至肚脐高度，双手如按在漂浮在水面的球（图9-11-2）。收掌先收肩、次收肘、再收手（图9-11-3）。推按时，目视后手，感知无名指胀为度，意念从无名指指端（关冲穴，在手无名指末节尺侧，距指甲根角0.1寸处），经肘外侧（天井穴，在上臂外侧，屈肘时，肘尖直上1寸凹陷处）贯注至头面部（丝竹空穴，在眉梢凹陷处）（图9-11-4）。

功理作用——两手臂前后摆动，躯干的扭转可有效促进全身气血的运行，有利于颈、肩、背、腰运动不适的预防与调治。

图9-11-1 鹤舞

图9-11-2 鹤舞

图9-11-3 鹤舞

图9-11-4 鹤舞

手少阳三焦经

流注线：起于关冲（在手环指末节尺侧，距指甲角0.1寸），终于耳门（在面部，当眉梢凹陷处）。

循行：三焦手少阳之脉，起于小指次指之端，上出两指之间，循手表腕，出臂外两骨之间，上贯肘，循臑外上肩，而交出足少阳之后，入缺盆，布膻中，散络心包下膈，遍属三焦。其支者，从膻中，上出缺盆，上项，系耳后，直上出上角，以屈下颊至。其支者，从耳后入耳中，出走耳前，过客主人，前交颊，至目锐眦。

穴位：关冲、液门、中渚、阳池、外关、支沟、会宗、三阳络、四渎、天井、清冷渊、消泺、臑会、肩髎、天髎、天牖、翳风、瘈脉、颅息、角孙、耳门、耳和髎、丝竹空，本经一侧23穴，左右两侧共46穴。

口诀：二十三穴手少阳，关冲液门中渚旁，阳池外关支沟正，会宗三阳四渎长，天井清冷渊消泺，臑会肩髎天髎堂，天牖翳风瘈脉青，颅息角孙丝竹空，和髎耳门听有常。

12. 第十一式仰呼。两臂上举，掌心相对，如举能量之球，祥和之气（图9-12-1）。两臂分落至水平，颈部肌肉放松，头好似枕在脖子上，同时翘臀（图9-12-2）。手翻掌下落摩运时，意念从头面部（瞳子髎穴，位于面部，目外眦旁，当眶外侧缘处）经身体外侧（环跳穴，侧卧屈股，股骨大转子最凸点与骶管裂孔连线的外1/3与中1/3交点处）至脚趾端（足窍阴穴，人体第4趾末节外侧，距趾甲角0.1寸）（图9-12-3）。

图 9-12-1　仰呼　　　　　图 9-12-2　仰呼　　　　　图 9-12-3　仰呼

功理作用——举臂外展，阔胸呼气，可祛除气喘、胸闷等身体不适，并有利于颈、肩部的不适的预防和调治。立足可发展小腿后肌群力量，拉长足底肌肉、韧带，提高人体平衡能力。

> **足少阳胆经**
>
> 流注线：起于瞳子髎（在面部，目外眦旁，当眶外侧缘处），终于足窍阴（在第4趾末节外侧，距趾甲角0.1寸）。
>
> 循行：胆足少阳之脉，起于目锐眦，上抵头角，下耳后，循颈，行手少阳之前，至肩上，却交出手少阳之后，入缺盆。其支者，从耳后入耳中，出走耳前至目锐眦后。其支者，别锐眦，下大迎，合于手少阳，抵于，下加颊车，下颈，合缺盆，以下胸中，贯膈，络肝，属胆，循胁里，出气街，绕毛际，横入髀厌中。其直者，从缺盆下腋，循胸，过季胁，下合髀厌中。以下循髀阳，出膝外廉，下外辅骨之前，直下抵绝骨之端，下出外踝之前，循足跗上，入小指次指之间。其支者，别跗上，入大指之间，循大指歧骨内，出其端，还贯爪甲，出三毛。
>
> 穴位：瞳子髎、听会、上关、颔厌、悬颅、悬厘、曲鬓、率谷、天冲、浮白、头窍阴、完骨、本神、阳白、头临泣、目窗、正营、承灵、脑空、风池、肩井、渊液、辄筋、日月、京门、带脉、五枢、维道、居髎、环跳、风市、中渎、膝阳关、阳陵泉、阳交、外丘、光明、阳辅、悬钟、丘墟、足临泣、地五会、侠溪、足窍阴，共44穴，左右合88穴。
>
> 口诀一：少阳足经瞳子胶，四十四穴行逍遥；听会上关颔厌集，悬颅悬厘曲鬓翘；率谷天冲浮白次，窍阴完骨本神邀；阳白头临目窗僻，正营承灵脑空摇；风池肩井渊腋部，辄筋日月京门镖；带脉五枢维道续，居胶环跳风市招；中渎阳关阳陵泉，阳交外丘光明宵；阳辅悬钟丘墟外，足临地五会侠溪；第四趾外窍阴毕。
>
> 口诀二：瞳子听会上关缘，颔厌悬颅悬厘饶，曲鬓率谷天冲斜，浮白窍阴完骨认，本神阳白头临泣，目窗正营承灵后，脑空风池肩井峰，渊腋辄筋日月下，京门带脉五枢真，维道居髎环跳陷，风市中渎膝阳关，阳陵阳交外丘踝，光明阳辅悬钟高，丘墟临泣地五会，会下一寸侠溪接，何处欲觅足窍阴？小趾次趾外侧边。

13. 第十二式折阴。上步举手时，尽量拉伸躯干，上下手有对撑感，下手面与后臀面齐平（图9-13-1）。上臂旋落后（图9-13-2），经体侧平举（图9-13-3），向前拢气（图9-13-4），向下抱气（图9-13-5），再向上捧气（图9-13-6）。双手沿下肢内侧上行时，意念从脚趾端（大敦穴，位于足大指末节外侧，距趾甲角0.1寸）经膝关节（曲泉穴，位于人体的膝内侧，屈膝，当膝关穴节内侧端，股骨内侧髁的后缘，半腱肌、半膜肌止端的前缘凹陷处）至腹侧（期门穴，位于胸部，当乳头直下，第6肋间隙，前正中线旁开4寸）。

图9-13-1 折阴　　　图9-13-2 折阴　　　图9-13-3 折阴

图9-13-4 折阴　　　图9-13-5 折阴　　　图9-13-6 折阴

功理作用——手臂伸举旋落，有利于肩部运动不适的预防与调治。折叠前俯，可以有效刺激内脏，并有利于脊柱各关节运动不适的预防与调治。

足厥阴肝经

流注线：此经起于大敦（足大趾末节外侧，距趾甲角0.1寸），终于期门（在胸部，当乳头直下，第六肋间隙，前正中线旁开4寸）。

循行：肝足厥阴之脉，起于大指从毛之际，上循足跗上廉，去内踝一寸，上踝八寸，交出太阴之后，上腘内廉，循股阴，入毛中，环阴器，抵小腹，夹胃，属肝，络胆，上贯膈，布胁肋，循喉咙之后，上入颃颡，连目系，上出额，与目系下颊里，环唇内。其支者，复从肝别贯膈，上注肺。

穴位：大敦、行间、太冲、中封、蠡沟、中都、膝关、曲泉、阴包、足五里、阴廉、急脉、章门、期门，左右各14穴。

口诀一：足大趾端名大敦，行间大趾缝中存，太冲本节后二寸，踝前一寸号中封，蠡沟踝上五寸是，中都踝上七寸中，膝关阴陵后一寸，曲泉屈膝尽横纹，阴包膝上方四寸，气冲三寸下五里，阴廉冲下只二寸，急脉阴旁二寸半，章门平脐季胁端，乳下两肋取期门。

口诀二：一十四穴足厥阴，大郭行间太冲侵；中封蠡沟中都近，膝关曲泉阴包临；五里阴廉急脉穴，章门常对期门深。

14. 收势。两掌体前合拢时,身体重心随动微移(图 9-14-1)。两掌心依次对照胸部(膻中穴,在体前正中线,两乳头连线之中点)(图 9-14-2)、上腹部(中脘穴,位于人体上腹部,前正中线上,当脐中上 4 寸)(图 9-14-3)、下腹部(神阙穴,位于人体的腹中部,脐中央)(图 9-14-4)。下按时,意念涌泉穴(图 9-14-5)。

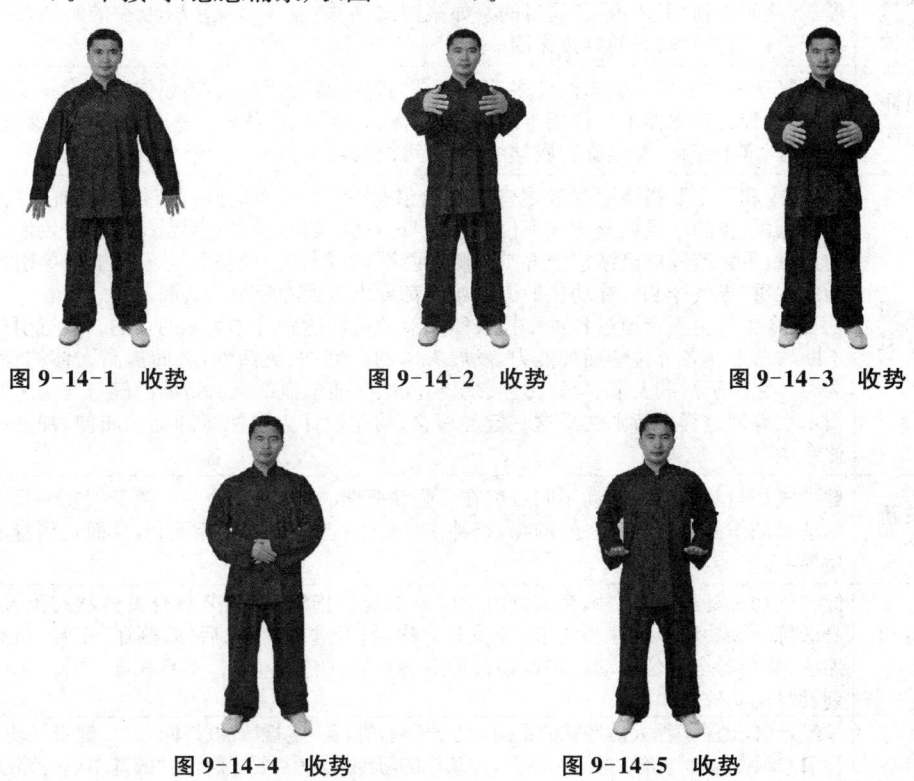

图 9-14-1 收势　　　图 9-14-2 收势　　　图 9-14-3 收势

图 9-14-4 收势　　　图 9-14-5 收势

功理作用——引气归元,静养心神。意念涌泉,平和气息。

(二) 学习计划

项目	内　容
前期准备	1. 了解健身气功的发展简史。 2. 知晓马王堆导引术的来历。 3. 学习养生调息操。 4. 学习人体主要经络的起至点及走向
学习进度	1. 学习顺序 (1) 学习掌握基本动作规格; (2) 熟练掌握呼吸和动作配合; (3) 逐步掌握意识和动作合一,注重演练神韵。 2. 教学安排,本课程分 5 次课学完,每次三节,每节 45 分钟。 (1) 基本动作的学习; (2) 完整套路的练习; (3) 熟练功法套路; (4) 体悟动作和意识的整合; (5) 考核技术动作

（三）技术体验

内容	要　求
抻筋拔骨 松紧交替	抻筋拔骨可以更大范围的牵拉人体各部位的肌腱、韧带等结缔组织，配合松紧交替的运动形式，从而达到"引体令柔"的目的。如第四式动作"龙登"，在手臂上举的时候，压掌提踵，对于身体筋骨有较好的抻拔作用
旋转屈伸 舒缓圆活	健身气功·马王堆导引术的许多动作都是通过四肢、躯干的旋转屈伸达到牵拉刺激脏腑的作用，这种旋转屈伸不仅作用于内脏，对身体各关节也有益处。整套功法柔和缓慢，动作舒展大方、富于变化，并多旋转屈伸的练习，可以为习练者营造出惬意的练功意境
导气令和 引体令柔	"导气令和"，主要指调顺呼吸之气以配合肢体运动，从而达到调节体内气血运行的目的。细、匀、深、长的呼吸调整方式不仅能帮助身体处于舒适自然的状态，还可有效增加横隔肌的力量，更大范围的刺激按摩五脏六腑，促使气血顺畅。健身气功·马王堆导引术练习开始就注重"导气令和"，在功法锻炼的始终都要求做到呼吸细、匀、深、长。 "引体令柔"，主要指通过各种牵拉肢体关节的运动达到身体柔顺的目的。通过引体的动作不断改善人体各部位的屈伸能力，发展人体的柔韧性、灵活性，进而提高人体的稳定性、耐久力。它对于滑利关节、松解粘连、疏导经脉、畅通气血都有所帮助。健身气功·马王堆导引术在编创过程中特别注重这一健身理念，动作设计大多注意到旋转屈伸、抻筋拔骨，"引体令柔"
吐故纳新 身心合一	健身气功与其他体育运动不同点就在于强调呼吸，注重身心合一。健身气功·马王堆导引术整套动作都要求呼吸自然顺畅，精神内守，意念与肢体动作相配合，从而达到身心合一的境界
全身运动 内外合一	健身气功·马王堆导引术在编创时就以整体观为指导，从调节自身整体状态出发，注重全身锻炼。该功法以脊柱为纽带，带动上下肢、躯干进行前俯、后仰、侧屈、扭转、折叠、开合、缩放、提落等全方位运动。在运动过程中，始终强调精神内守，形意相随，内外合一，从而达到健身的功效
循经导引 形意相随	循经导引，就是遵循人体经脉的走向，配合呼吸，进行一定规律的肢体运动。健身气功·马王堆导引术动作编排与经络理论相结合，在动作的习练过程中，要了解经脉的基本运行路线，便于掌握动作要领。如"第一式 挽弓"，通过胸廓开合，调节胸中之肺气，在转体伸臂的过程中，意念引导肺气沿手太阴肺经的方向运行。 形意相随，就是在功法的习练过程中，意念活动与形体动作相互配合，它是循经导引的关键因素。
定向疏导 畅通经脉	定向疏导就是运用意念与肢体的配合，按照经脉气血的运行方向进行疏导的方法。健身气功·马王堆导引术通过肢体导引与意念的相互配合，突出强调了疏通经脉是此功法的健身理念

（四）文化体验

表9-1　马王堆导引术与手太阴-足太阴循行起止点

功法名称	挽弓	引背	凫浴	龙登
手太阴足太阴	手太阴肺经	手阳明大肠经	足阳明胃经	足太阴脾经
起点	中府	商阳	承泣	隐白
位置	肋一，中六寸	食指内	眼下	大趾内
走向	胸→手	手→头	头→足	足→腹
终点	少商	迎香	厉兑	大包
位置	拇指内	鼻外	二趾外	肋六，腋中线

表 9-2　马王堆导引术与手少阴～足少阴循行起止点

功法名称	鸟伸	引腹	鸥视	引腰
手少阴-足太阴	手少阴心经	手太阳小肠经	足太阳膀胱经	足少阴肾经
起点	极泉	少泽	睛明	涌泉
位置	腋窝	小指外	眼内	足心
走向	胸→手	手→头	头→足	足→腹
终点	少冲	听宫	至阴	俞府
位置	小指内	耳前	小趾外	锁骨下,中二寸

表 9-3　马王堆导引术与手厥阴～足厥阴循行起止点

功法名称	雁飞	鹤舞	仰呼	折阴
手厥阴-足厥阴	手厥阴心包经	手少阳三焦经	足少阳胆经	足厥阴肝经
起点	天池	关冲	瞳子髎	大敦
位置	四肋间,乳头外一寸	无名指外	眼外	大趾外
走向	胸→手	手→头	头→足	足→腹
终点	中冲	丝竹空	足窍阴	期门
位置	中指尖	眉外	四趾外	乳下,六肋间

三、总结

1. 健身气功·马王堆导引术是"引体令柔"的导引术。

2. 健身气功·马王堆导引术的动作,还要配合十二经络循行路径,进行身、心、息三调的导引训练。

3. 健身气功·马王堆导引术的经络循行路径是,由胸走手、由手走头、由头走足、由足回胸腹的循行,而将十二经络分成太阴-阳明、少阴-太阳、厥阴-少阳三个循行系统进行教学(图 9-15)。

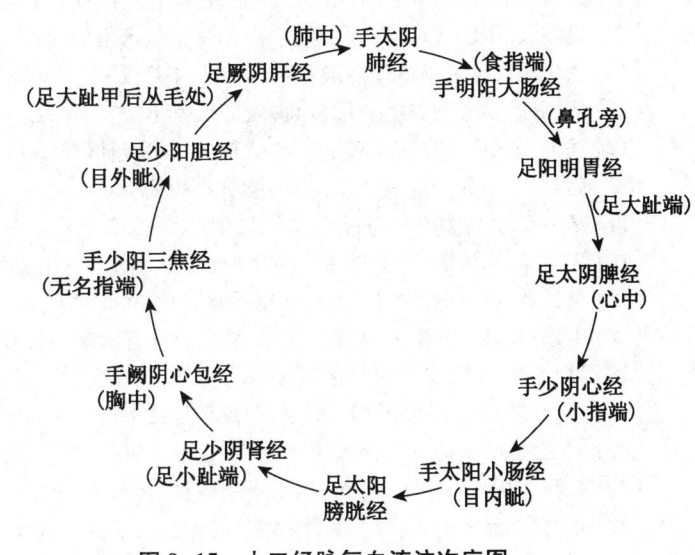

图 9-15　十二经脉气血流注次序图

四、延伸学习

健身气功是中国政府推出的健身体育项目，它动作优美、内涵丰富、易学易练，非常适合大众普及推广的优秀体育项目。学会健身气功马王堆导引术者，还可以继续学习其他8种健身气功功法。

五、思考与练习题

1. 马王堆导引术动作与经脉照应的关系是什么？
2. 马王堆导引术的习练技术特点有哪些？
3. 如何练好马王堆导引术？

六、参考文献

[1] 陈撄宁. 道教与养生[M]. 北京：华文出版社，2000.
[2] 国家体育总局健身气功管理中心. 健身气功·马王堆导引术[M]. 北京：人民体育出版社，2010.
[3] 国家体育总局健身气功管理中心. 健身气功社会指导员培训教材[M]. 北京：人民体育出版社，2007.
[4] 侯良. 尘封的文明[M]. 湖南：湖南人民出版社，2002.
[5] 焦国瑞. 气功养生学概要[M]. 北京：人民体育出版社，1984.
[6] 李远国. 道教气功养生学[M]. 四川：四川省社会科学院出版社，1988.
[7] 李志庸. 中国气功史[M]. 河南：河南科学技术出版社，1988.
[8] 刘天君. 气功入静之门[M]. 北京：人民体育出版社，1995.
[9] 马济人. 中国气功学[M]. 陕西：陕西科学技术出版社，1988.
[10] 马王堆汉墓帛书整理小组. 导引图·马王堆汉墓帛书[M]. 北京：文物出版社，1979.
[11] 潘雨廷. 易学与养生[M]. 上海：复旦大学出版社，2001.
[12] 沈寿. 导引养生图说[M]. 北京：人民体育出版社，1992.
[13] 施杞. 中国养生全书[M]. 上海：学林出版社，1990.
[14] 汤一介. 道学精华[M]. 北京：北京出版社，1996.
[15] 王卜雄，周世荣. 中国气功学术发展史[M]. 湖南：湖南科学技术出版社，1989.
[16] 吴长新. 招帝王养生法[M]. 北京：团结出版社，2000.
[17] 吴志超. 导引养生史论稿[M]. 北京：北京体育大学出版社，1996.
[18] 萧兵，叶舒宪. 老子的文化解读[M]. 湖北：湖北人民出版社，1993.
[19] 杨力. 周易与中医学[M]. 北京：北京科学技术出版社，1997.
[20] 虞定海，吴京梅. 中国传统保健体育[M]. 上海：上海科学技术出版，1990.
[21] 张和. 中国气功学[M]. 北京：五洲出版社，1984.
[22] 张君房. 云笈七签[M]. 蒋力生等校注. 北京：华夏出版社，1996.
[23] 周稔丰，李自然. 气功康复养生精要[M]. 天津：天津科学技术出版社，1987.
[24] 周一谋. 马王堆医书考注[M]. 天津：天津科学技术出版社，1998.

第十章 健身气功·五禽戏

一、导言

五禽戏是东汉名医华佗根据虎、鹿、熊、猿、鸟的活动特点,结合古代导引吐纳之术以及人体脏腑、经络和气血等理论而编成的仿生类功法。"健身气功·五禽戏"是上海体育学院根据时代特征和科学健身的理念,结合历史记载的华佗五禽戏动作素材而编创。

二、学习体验

(一) 动作说明

1. 预备式(起势调息)

动作一:两脚并拢,两腿自然伸直;两手自然垂于体侧;胸腹放松,头项正直,下颌微收,舌抵上腭;目视前方(图 10-1-1)。

动作二:左脚向左平开一步,稍宽于肩,两膝微曲,松静站立;调息数次,意守丹田(图 10-1-2)。

动作三:肘微曲,两臂在体前向上、向前平托,与胸部(膻中穴)同高(图 10-1-3)。

动作四:两肘下垂外展,小臂内旋两掌向内翻转,并缓慢下按于腹前;目视前方(图 10-1-4)。

重复三、四动作两遍后,两手自然垂于体侧(图 10-1-5)。

图 10-1-1 预备式

图 10-1-2 预备式

图 10-1-3 预备式

图 10-1-4　预备式　　　　　图 10-1-5　预备式

动作要点——两臂上提下按，意在两掌劳宫穴，动作柔和、均匀、连贯。动作与呼吸配合，两臂上提时吸气，下按时呼气。

意念运用——在两掌的劳宫穴有热感或者两臂有上抬重物的感觉。引气经中丹田（膻中穴），再下沉至下丹田（气海穴）。

功理与作用——排除杂念，诱导入静，调和气息，宁心安神。吐故纳新，升清降浊，调理气机。

2. 虎戏。有虎举、虎扑两式。动作要做到刚中有柔、柔中生刚、外刚内柔、刚柔相济，神发于目，虎视眈眈；威生于爪，伸缩有力，神威并重，气势凌人。要体现虎的威猛，具有动如雷霆无阻挡、静如泰山不可摇的气势。

（1）虎举。动作一：接上式，两手掌心向下，十指撑开，再弯曲成虎爪状；目视两掌（图10-2-1）。动作二：两手外旋，由小指先弯曲，其余四指依次弯曲握拳，两拳沿体前缓慢上提（图10-2-2），至肩前时，十指撑开，举至头上方再弯曲成虎爪状，目视两掌（图10-2-3）。动作三：两掌外旋握拳，拳心相对，目视两拳。动作四：两拳下拉至肩前时，变掌下按（图10-2-4）；沿体前下落至腹前，十指撑开，掌心向下，目视两掌（图10-2-5）。

动作一至三重复四遍后，两手自然垂于体侧，目视前方（图10-2-6）。

图 10-2-1　虎举　　　　图 10-2-2　虎举　　　　图 10-2-3　虎举

图10-2-4 虎举　　　　　图10-2-5 虎举　　　　　图10-2-6 虎举

动作要点——十指撑开、弯曲成"虎爪"和外旋握拳,三个环节均要贯注劲力;两掌向上如托举重物,提胸收腹,充分拔长躯体;两掌下落如拉双环,含胸松腹,气沉丹田;两掌上举时吸气,下落时呼气。

意念——撑掌握指,意念放在虎爪上,劲达指尖,劳宫穴含空;上举时犹如提重物,翻举至头上方有拨云观日之意,也有托天驻地之意,体现天地人合一境界。

功理与作用——两掌举起,吸入清气,两掌下按,呼出浊气;一升一降,疏通三焦气机,调理三焦功能;掌成"虎爪"变拳,可增强握力,改善上肢远端关节的血液循环。

(2)虎扑。动作一,接上式,两手握空拳,沿身体两侧上提至肩前上方(图10-2-7)。

动作二,两手向上、向前划弧,十指弯曲成"虎爪",掌心向下;同时上体前俯,挺胸塌腰;目视前方(图10-2-8、图10-2-8侧)。

图10-2-7 虎扑　　　　　图10-2-8 虎扑　　　　　图10-2-8 侧

动作三,两腿屈膝半蹲,收腹含胸;同时,两手向下划弧至两膝侧,掌心向下,目视前下方(图10-2-9)。随后,两腿伸腿,送髋,挺腹,后仰;同时,两掌握空拳,沿体侧向上提至胸侧;目视前上方(图10-2-10、图10-2-10侧)。

图 10-2-9　虎扑　　　　图 10-2-10　虎扑　　　　图 10-2-10　侧

动作四，左腿自然提起，两手上举（图 10-2-11）。左腿向前迈出一步，脚跟着地；右脚外摆约 45 度，重心移至右腿屈膝下蹲，成左虚步；同时上体前倾，两拳变"虎爪"向前、向下扑至膝前两侧，含胸收腹，掌心向下；目视前下方（图 10-2-12）。随后上体抬起，左脚收回，开步站立；两手自然下落于体侧；目视前方（图 10-2-13）。

图 10-2-11　虎扑　　　　图 10-2-12　虎扑　　　　图 10-2-13　虎扑

动作六至八，同动作一至四，唯左右相反（图 10-2-14—图 10-2-20）。

图 10-2-14　虎扑　　　　图 10-2-15　虎扑　　　　图 10-2-16　虎扑

图 10-2-17　虎扑

图 10-2-18　虎扑

图 10-2-19　虎扑

动作一至八重复一遍后，两掌向身体侧前方举起，与胸同高，掌心向上，目视前方（图 10-2-21）。两臂屈肘，两掌内合下按，自然垂于体侧，目视前方（图 10-2-22）。

图 10-2-20　虎扑

图 10-2-21　虎扑

图 10-2-22　虎扑

动作要点——上体前俯，两手尽力向前伸，而臀部向后引，充分拉伸脊柱；屈膝敛臀下蹲、收腹含胸要与伸膝、送髋、挺腹、后仰动作过程连贯，使脊柱形成有折叠到展开的蠕动，两掌下按上提要与之配合协调；虚步下扑时，速度均匀，落点成刚，柔中寓刚，配合深呼气，气沉丹田，以气催劲，劲达指尖，表现出虎的威猛；中老年习练者、体弱者以及膝关节与腰椎不适者，可根据个人具体情况适当减小动作幅度。

意念——两臂尽量前伸，臀部后坐，使腰身有对拉拔伸之意。目视前方，虎视眈眈盯着猎物；下扑时试想有猎物在脚下；上提、前伸、下扑带动躯干脊柱蠕动，整个过程犹如古人在摇转辘轳，意走任督两脉。

功理与作用——虎扑动作形成了脊柱的前后伸展折叠运动，尤其是引腰前伸，增加了脊柱各关节的柔韧性和伸展度，可使脊柱保持正常的生理弧度；脊柱运动能增强腰部肌肉力量，对常见的腰部疾病，如腰肌劳损，习惯性腰扭伤等症有防治作用；督脉行于背部正中，任脉行于腹部正中。脊柱的前后伸张折叠，牵动任、督两脉，起动调理引腰、疏通经络、活跃气血的作用。

3. 鹿戏，有**鹿抵**、**鹿奔**两式。习练"鹿戏"，要体现鹿喜挺身眺望、好角抵、善奔走特点，而动作轻盈舒展、神态安闲雅静、运转尾闾通任督两脉。

(1) 鹿抵。动作一,接上式,两腿微屈,身体重心移至右腿,左腿经右腿内侧向左前方约45°迈步,脚跟着地;同时,身体稍右转;两掌握空拳,向右侧摆起,拳心向下,高与肩平;目随手动,视右拳(图10-3-1)。动作二,身体重心前移;左腿屈膝。脚尖外展约90°落平踏实;右脚蹬伸踏实;同时,身体左转,两掌成"鹿角",左臂向左划弧,掌心向外,指尖朝左,左臂弯曲外展平伸,左肘收抵靠至左腰侧;右臂举至头前,向左后方伸抵,掌心向外,指尖朝后,目视右脚跟(图10-3-2)。随后,身体右转,左脚收回,开步站立;同时两手向上、向右、向下划弧,两"鹿角"至肩前握空拳,下落于体前;目视前方(图10-3-3)。动作三、四,同动作一、二,唯左右相反(图10-3-4至图10-3-6)。动作五至八,同动作一至四。动作一至八重复一遍。

图10-3-1 鹿抵　　图10-3-2 鹿抵　　图10-3-3 鹿抵

图10-3-4 鹿抵　　图10-3-5 鹿抵　　图10-3-6 鹿抵

动作要点——抬腿上步以及回收要轻灵圆活;腰部侧屈拧转,侧屈的一侧腰部要压紧,另一侧腰部则借助上举手臂后伸,得到充分牵拉;后脚脚跟要蹬实,固定下肢位置,加大腰、腹部的拧转幅度,运转尾闾;动作可配合呼吸,两掌向上划弧摆动时吸气,向后伸抵时呼气;上摆至肩前时吸气,转身下落时呼气。

意念——目视脚跟时,意在尾闾;要有两鹿抵角嬉戏意境,象形取意。

功理与作用——腰部的侧屈拧转,使整个脊椎充分旋转,可增强腰部的肌肉力量,也可防治腰部的脂肪沉积;目视后脚脚跟,加大腰部在拧转时的侧屈程度,可防治腰椎、胸椎、颈椎小关节紊乱等症;中医认为,"腰为肾之府"。尾闾运转,可起到强腰补肾、强筋健骨的功效。

(2) 鹿奔。动作一,接上式,左脚提膝抬腿向前跨一步,屈膝,右腿伸直成左弓步;同时，两手握空拳，向上、向前划弧至体前，屈腕，高与肩平，与肩同宽，拳心向下；目视前方（图 10-3-7）。动作二，身体重心后移；左膝伸直，全脚掌着地；右腿屈膝后坐；低头，含胸，弓背，收腹，敛臀；同时，两臂内旋前伸，掌背相对，拳变"鹿角"（图 10-3-8、图 10-3-8 侧）。动作三，身体重心前移，上体抬起；右腿伸直，左腿屈膝，成左弓步；松肩沉肘，两臂外旋，"鹿角"变空拳，高与肩平，拳心向下；目视前方（图 10-3-9）。动作四，左脚收回，开步直立；两拳变掌，回落于体侧；目视前方（图 10-3-10）。动作五至八，同动作一至动作四，唯左右相反（图 10-3-11 至图 10-3-14）。重复动作一至八一遍后，两掌向身体侧前方举起，与胸同高，掌心向上；目视前方（图 10-3-15）。屈肘，两掌内合下按，自然垂于体侧；目视前方（图 10-3-16）。

图 10-3-7　鹿奔　　　图 10-3-8　鹿奔　　　图 10-3-8　侧面

图 10-3-9　鹿奔　　　图 10-3-10　鹿奔　　　图 10-3-11　鹿奔

图 10-3-12　鹿奔　　　图 10-3-13　鹿奔　　　图 10-3-14　鹿奔

图 10-3-15　鹿奔　　　　　图 10-3-16　鹿奔

　　动作要点——提腿前跨要有弧度，落步轻灵，体现鹿的安舒神态。身体后坐时，两臂前伸，胸部内含，背部形成"横弓"状；头前伸，背后拱，腹收缩，臀内敛，形成"竖弓"状，使腰、背部得到充分伸展和拔长。动作可配合呼吸。上提抬腿时吸气，落步成弓步时呼气；身体后坐时，配合吸气。重心前移时，配合呼气。

　　意念——模仿鹿在奔跑，高抬腿，跨大步落小步，轻巧灵活。前伸后拱，"横、竖"两张弓，意在开大椎，凸命门。

　　功理与作用——两臂内旋前伸，肩、背部肌肉得到牵拉，对颈肩综合症、肩关节周围炎等症有防治作用；躯干弓背收腹，能矫正脊柱畸形，增强腰、背部肌肉力量。向前落步时，气充丹田。身体重心后坐时，气运命门，加强了人的先天与后天之气的交流。尤其是重心后坐，整条脊柱后弯，内夹尾闾，后凸命门，打开大椎，意在疏通督脉经气，具有振奋全身阳气的作用。

　　4. 熊戏，有熊运、熊晃两式，要表现出熊憨厚沉稳、松静自然的神态，在外观笨重拖沓中蕴含沉稳、灵敏，运势外阴内阳，外动内静，外刚内柔，以意领气，气沉丹田。

　　（1）熊运。动作一，接上式，两掌握空拳成"熊掌"，拳眼相对，垂于下腹部；目视前下方（图10-4-1）。动作二，以腰、腹为轴，上体做顺时针摇晃；同时，两拳随之沿右肋部、上腹部、左肋部下腹部划圆；目随上体摇晃环视（图10-4-2至图10-4-5）。

图 10-4-1　熊运　　　　　图 10-4-2　熊运　　　　　图 10-4-3　熊运

图 10-4-4　熊运　　　　　图 10-4-5　熊运　　　　　图 10-4-6　熊运

动作三、四，同动作一、二。动作五至八，同动作一至四，唯左右相反，上体做逆时针摇晃，两拳随之划圆（图 10-4-6 至图 10-4-9）。做完最后一动，两拳变掌下落，自然垂于体侧，目视前方（图 10-4-10）。

图 10-4-7　熊运　　　　　图 10-4-8　熊运　　　　　图 10-4-9　熊运

动作要点——两掌划圆应随腰、腹部的摇晃而被动牵动，要协调自然。两掌划圆是外导，腰、腹摇晃为内引，意念内气在腹部丹田运气。动作可配合呼气，身体上提时吸气，身体前俯时呼气。

意念——试想自己是钟表分针，按照顺逆时针做圆运动。外导内引，意助脾胃运化。

功理与作用——活动腰部关节和肌肉，可防治腰肌劳损及软组织损伤。腰腹转动，两掌划圆，引导内气运行，可加强脾、胃的运化功能。运用腰、腹摇晃，对消化器官进行体内按摩，可防治消化不良、腹胀纳呆、便秘腹泻等症。

（2）熊晃。动作一，接上式。身体重心右移；左髋上提，牵动左脚离地，微屈左膝；两掌握空拳成"熊掌"；目视左前方（图 10-4-11）。动作二，身体重心前移；左脚向左前方（约45°）落地，全脚掌踏实，脚尖向前，右脚伸直；身体右转，左臂内旋前靠，左拳摆至左膝前上方，拳心朝左；右拳摆至体后，拳心朝后；目视左前方（图 10-4-12）。动作三，身体左转，重心后坐；右腿屈膝，左腿伸直；拧腰晃肩，带动两臂前后弧形摆动；右拳摆至左膝前上方，拳心朝右；左拳摆至体后，拳心朝后；目视左前方（图 10-4-13）。

图 10-4-10　熊运

图 10-4-11　熊晃

图 10-4-12　熊晃

动作四,身体右转,重心前移;左腿屈膝,右腿伸直;同时,左臂内旋前靠,左拳摆至左膝前上方,拳心朝左;右拳摆至体后,拳心朝后;目视左前方(图 10-4-14)。动作五至动作八,同动作一至四,唯左右相反(图 10-4-15 至图 10-4-18)。

图 10-4-13　熊晃

图 10-4-14　熊晃

图 10-4-15　熊晃

图 10-4-16　熊晃

图 10-4-17　熊晃

图 10-4-18　熊晃

重复一至八动一遍后,左脚上步,开步站立;同时,两手自然垂于体侧(图 10-4-19)。两掌向身体侧前方举起,与胸同高,掌心向上;目视前方(图 10-4-20)。屈肘,两掌内合下按,自然垂于体侧;目视前方(图 10-4-21)。

图 10-4-19　熊晃　　　　　图 10-4-20　熊晃　　　　　图 10-4-21　熊晃

动作要点——用腰侧肌群收缩来牵动大腿上提,按提髋、起腿、屈膝的先后顺序提腿。两脚前移,横向间距稍宽于肩,随身体重心前移,全脚掌踏实,使震动感传至髋关节处,体现熊步的沉稳厚实。

意念——提髋沉肩,意在挤压两肋。行步模仿熊步,左右摇晃,意在腰裆换劲。

功理与作用——身体左右晃动,意在两肋,调理肝脾。提髋行走,加上落步的微震,可增强髋关节周围肌肉的力量,提高平衡能力,有助于防治老年人下肢无力、髋关节损伤、膝痛等症。

5. 猿戏,有猿提、猿摘两式,在模仿猿之机智、灵敏、善纵攀中,外练肢体的敏捷,内练精神的宁静。

(1) 猿提。动作一,接上式,两掌在体前,手指伸直分开(图10-5-1),再屈腕撮拢捏紧成"猿钩"(图10-5-2)。动作二,两掌上提至胸,两肩上耸,收腹提肛;同时,脚跟提起,头向左转;目随头动,视身体左侧(图10-5-3、图10-5-3侧)。

图 10-5-1　猿提　　　　　图 10-5-2　猿提　　　　　图 10-5-3　猿提

动作三,头转正,两肩下沉,松腹落肛,脚跟着地;"猿钩"变掌,掌心向下;目视前方(图10-5-4)。动作四,两掌沿体前下按落于体侧;目视前方(图10-5-5)。动作五至八,同动作一至动作四,唯头向右转(图10-5-6至图10-5-10)。重复一至八动作一遍。

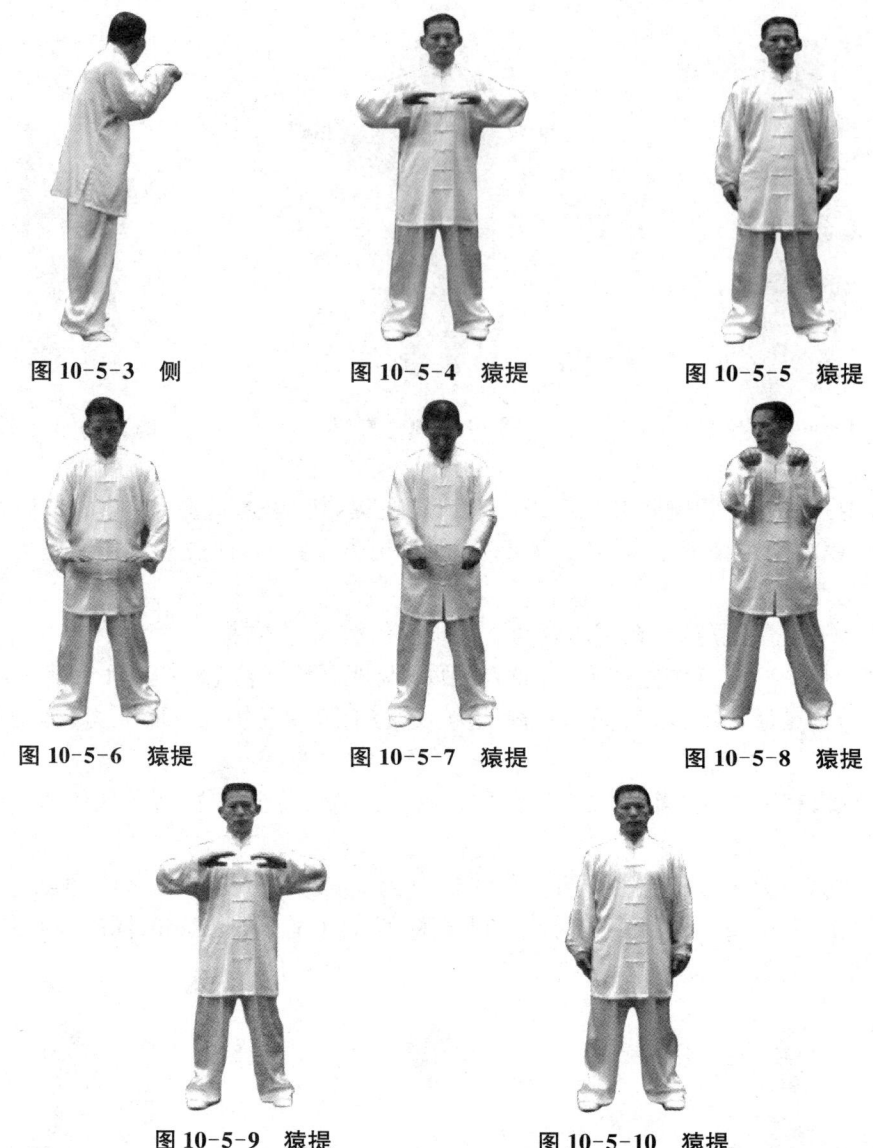

图 10-5-3 侧　　　图 10-5-4 猿提　　　图 10-5-5 猿提

图 10-5-6 猿提　　　图 10-5-7 猿提　　　图 10-5-8 猿提

图 10-5-9 猿提　　　图 10-5-10 猿提

动作要点——掌指撮拢变钩，速度稍快。按耸肩、收腹、提肛、脚跟离地、转头的顺序，上提重心。耸肩、缩胸、屈肘、提腕要充分。动作可配合提肛呼吸。两掌上提吸气时，稍用意提起会阴部；下按呼气时，放下会阴部。

意念——站立时犹如站立的猴子，机警的左右观望。耸肩、夹肘、含胸，意在挤压按摩心脏。

功理与作用——"猿钩"的快速变化，意在增强神经—肌肉反应的灵敏性。两掌上提时，缩颈，耸肩，团胸吸气，挤压胸腔和颈部血管；两掌下按时，伸颈，沉肩，松腹，扩大胸腔体积，可增强呼吸，按摩心脏，改善脑部供血。可预防肩颈疾病。提踵直立，可增强腿部力量，提高平衡能力。

（2）猿摘。动作一，接上式，左脚向左后方退步，脚尖点地，右腿屈膝，重心落于右腿；同时，左臂屈肘，左掌成"猿钩"收至左腰侧；右掌向右前方自然摆起，掌心向下（图10-5-11）。

动作二，身体重心后移；左脚踏实，屈膝下蹲，右脚收至左脚内侧，脚尖点地，成右丁步；同时，右掌向下经腹前向左上方划弧至头左侧，掌心对太阳穴；目先随右掌动，再转头注视右前上方（图10-5-12）。动作三，右掌内旋，掌心向下，沿体侧下按至左髋侧；目视右掌（图10-5-13）。右脚向右前方迈出一大步，左腿蹬伸，身体重心前移；右腿伸直，左脚脚尖点地；同时，右掌经体前向右上方划弧，举至右上侧变"猿钩"，稍高于肩；左掌向前、向上伸举，屈腕撮钩，成采摘势，目视左掌（图10-5-14）。

图10-5-11 猿摘

图10-5-12 猿摘

图10-5-13 猿摘

动作四，身体重心后移；左掌由"猿钩"变成"握固"；右手变掌，自然回落于体侧，虎口朝前（图10-5-15）。随后，左腿屈膝下蹲，右脚收至左脚内侧，脚尖点地，成右丁步；同时，左臂屈肘收至左耳旁，掌指分开，掌心向上，成托桃状；右掌经体前向左划弧至左肘下捧托；目视左掌（图10-5-16）。动作五至八，同动作一至四，唯左右相反（图10-5-17至图10-5-22）。

图10-5-14 猿摘

图10-5-15 猿摘

图10-5-16 猿摘

图10-5-17 猿摘

图10-5-18 猿摘

图10-5-19 猿摘

图 10-5-20 猿摘

图 10-5-21 猿摘

图 10-5-22 猿摘

重复一至八动一遍后,左脚向左横开一步,两腿直立;同时,两手自然垂于体侧(图 10-5-23)。两掌向身体侧前方举起,与胸同高,掌心向上;目视前方(图 10-5-24)。屈肘,两掌内合下按,自然垂于体侧;目视前方(图 10-5-25)。

图 10-5-23 猿摘

图 10-5-24 猿摘

图 10-5-25 猿摘

动作要点——眼要随上肢动作变化左顾右盼,表现出猿猴眼神的灵敏。屈膝下蹲时,全身呈收缩状。蹬腿迈步,向上采摘,肢体要充分展开。采摘时变"猿钩",手指撮拢快而敏捷;变握固后,成托桃状时,掌指要及时分开。动作以神似为主,重在体会其意境,不可太夸张。

意念——前摆采气,气注太阳穴。体现猴子从发现树上桃子,攀枝采摘,回收得意的意境,意想整个动作过程的变化细节。

功理与作用——眼神的左顾右盼,有利于颈部运动,促进脑部的血液循环。可预防肩颈椎疾病。动作的多样性体现了神经系统和肢体动作的协调性,模拟猿猴在采摘桃果时愉悦的心情,可减轻大脑神经系统的紧张度,对神经紧张和精神忧郁等症有防治作用。

6. 鸟戏,取形于鹤,有鸟伸、鸟飞两式,在表现鹤的昂然挺拔与悠然自得神韵,模仿鹤翅飞翔、抑扬开合中,活跃周身经络,灵活四肢关节。

(1) 鸟伸。动作一,接上式,两腿微屈下蹲,两掌在腹前相叠(图 10-6-1)。动作二,两掌向上举至头前上方,掌心向下,指尖向前;身体微前倾、提肩、缩颈、挺胸、塌腰;目视前下方(图 10-6-2、图 10-6-2 侧)。动作三,两腿微屈下蹲;同时,两掌相叠下按至腹前;目视两掌(图 10-6-3)。

图 10-6-1　鸟伸　　　　图 10-6-2　鸟伸　　　　图 10-6-2　侧

动作四，身体重心右移；右腿蹬直，左腿伸直向后抬起；同时，两掌左右分开，掌成"鸟翅"，向体侧后方摆起，掌心向上；抬头，伸颈，挺胸，塌腰；目视前方（图10-6-4、图10-6-4侧）。动作五至八，同动作一至动作四，唯左右相反（图10-6-5至图10-6-8）。

图 10-6-3　鸟伸　　　　图 10-6-4　鸟伸　　　　图 10-6-4　侧

图 10-6-5　鸟伸　　　　图 10-6-6　鸟伸　　　　图 10-6-7　鸟伸

图 10-6-8　鸟伸　　　　图 10-6-9　鸟伸

重复一至八动一遍后,左脚下落,两脚开步站立,两手自然垂于体侧;目视前方(图10-6-9)。

动作要点——两掌在体前相叠,上下位置可任选,以舒适自然为宜。注意动作的松紧变化。掌上举时,颈、肩、臀部紧缩;下落时,两腿微屈,颈、肩、臀部松沉。两臂后摆时,身体向上拔伸,并形成向后反弓状。

意念——两掌相叠上举,意想为百会与尾间相合。两臂后摆,头颈前伸,试想自己是一只欲飞的仙鹤。

功理与作用——两掌上举吸气,扩大胸腔;两手下按,气沉丹田,呼出浊气,可加强肺的吐故纳新功能,增加肺活量,改善慢性支气管炎、肺气肿、肩颈等病的症状。两掌上举,作用于大椎和尾间,督脉得到牵动;两掌后摆,身体成反弓状,任脉得到拉伸。这种松紧交替的练习方法,可增强疏通任、督两脉经气的作用。

(2)鸟飞。接上式,两掌成"鸟翅"合于腹前,掌心相对;目视前下方(图10-6-10)。动作一,右腿伸直独立,左腿屈膝提起,小腿自然下垂,脚尖朝下;同时,两掌成展翅状,在体侧平举向上,稍高于肩,掌心向下;目视前方(图10-6-11)。动作二,左脚下落在右脚旁,脚尖着地,两腿微屈;同时,两掌合于腹前,掌心相对;目视前下方(图10-6-12)。动作三,右腿伸直独立,左脚屈膝提起,小腿自然下垂,脚尖朝下;同时,两掌经体侧,向上举至头顶上方,掌背相对,指尖向上;目视前方(图10-6-13)。

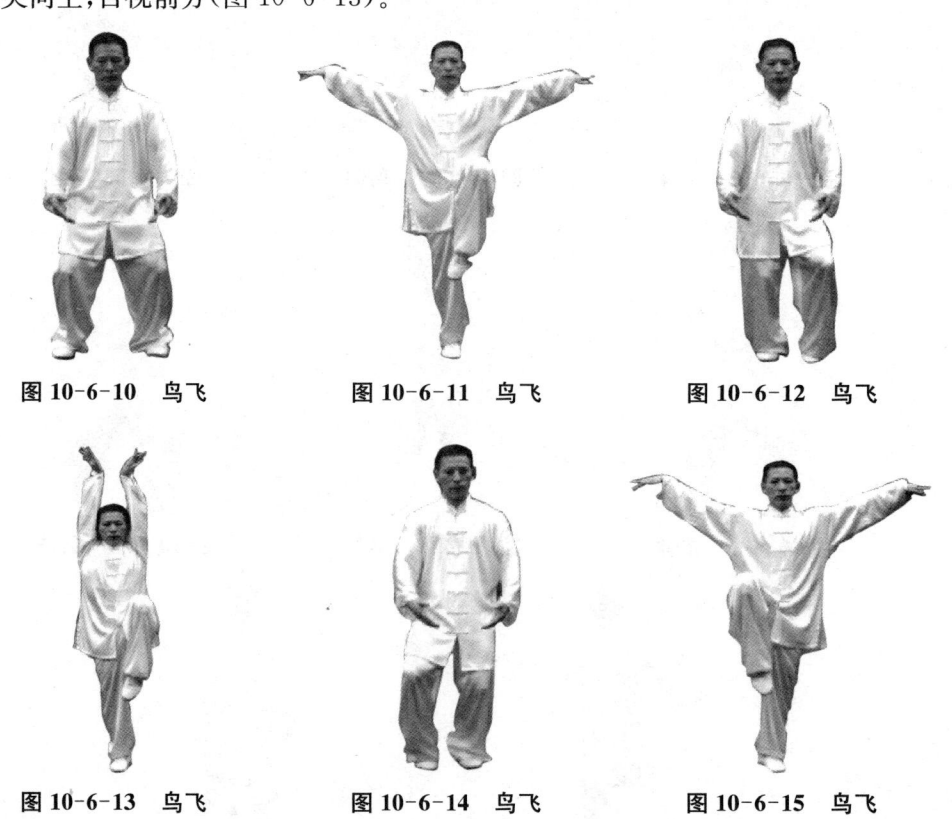

图 10-6-10 鸟飞　　　　图 10-6-11 鸟飞　　　　图 10-6-12 鸟飞

图 10-6-13 鸟飞　　　　图 10-6-14 鸟飞　　　　图 10-6-15 鸟飞

动作四,左脚下落在右脚旁,全脚掌着地,两腿微屈;同时,两掌合于腹前,掌心相对;目视前下方(图10-6-14)。动作五至八,同动作一至动作四,唯左右相反(图10-6-15至图

10-6-18)。重复一至八动一遍后,两掌向身体侧前方举起,与胸同高,掌心向上;目视前方(图 10-6-19)。屈肘,两掌内合下按,自然垂于体侧;目视前方(图 10-6-20)。

图 10-6-16　鸟飞　　　　图 10-6-17　鸟飞　　　　图 10-6-18　鸟飞

图 10-6-19　鸟飞　　　　图 10-6-20　鸟飞

动作要点——两臂侧举,动作舒展,幅度要大,尽量展开胸部两侧;两臂下落内合,尽量挤压胸部两侧。手脚变化配合协调,同起同落。动作可配合呼吸,两掌上提时吸气,下落时呼气。

意念——提膝过腰,两臂上举,意在提肛收腹,目视远方,有助保持平衡。鸟翅的拇指、食指、小指领劲,配之吸气,身体有轻灵欲飞的感觉;落地轻点,犹如蜻蜓点水。

功理与作用——两臂的上下运动可改变胸腔空寂,若配合呼吸运动可起到按摩心肺作用。增强血氧交换能力。预防肩肘腕指关节疾病。拇指、食指的上翘紧绷,意在刺激手太阴肺经,加强肺经经气的流通,提高心肺功能。提膝独立,可提高人体平衡能力。预防跌滑摔伤。

7. 收势(引气归元)。动作一,两掌经体侧上举至头顶上方,掌心向下(图 10-7-1)。动作二,两掌指尖相对,沿体前缓慢下按至腹前;目视前方(图 10-7-2)。重复一、二动两遍。动作三,两手缓慢在体前划平弧,掌心相对,高与脐平;目视前方(图 10-7-3)。动作四,两手在腹前合拢,虎口交叉,叠掌;眼微闭静养,调匀呼吸,意守丹田(图 10-7-4)。

图 10-7-1　收势　　　　图 10-7-2　收势　　　　图 10-7-3　收势

动作五，数分钟后，两眼慢慢睁开，两手合掌，在胸前搓擦至热（图 10-7-5）。动作六，掌贴面部，上、下擦摩，浴面 3~5 遍（图 10-7-6）。动作七，两掌向后沿头顶、耳后、胸前下落，自然垂于体侧；目视前方（图 10-7-7）。动作八，左脚提起向右脚并拢，前脚掌先着地，随之全脚踏实，恢复成预备势；目视前方（图 10-7-8）。

图 10-7-4　收势　　　　图 10-7-5　收势　　　　图 10-7-6　收势

图 10-7-7　收势　　　　图 10-7-8　收势

动作要点——两掌由上向下按时，身体各部位要随之放松，直达脚底涌泉穴。两掌腹前划平弧动作，衔接要自然、圆活，有向前收拢物体之势，意将气息合抱引入丹田。

意念——两臂上捧，意在掌心，有捧气上升的感觉。合抱下按时，意贯百会经中丹田、下丹田，至涌泉穴。最后一次气息引入下丹田。

功理与作用——引气归元就是使气息逐渐平和,意将练功时所得体内、外之气,导引归入丹田,起到和气血、通经脉、理脏腑的功效。通过搓手、浴面,恢复常态,收功。

(二) 学习计划

表 10-1　学习步骤

项目	内　容
前期准备	1. 学会五禽戏手型与手法、步型与步法以及辅助基本功。 2. 学习养生调息操
学习进度	1. 效仿虎、鹿、熊、猿、鸟,模仿五禽动作,经粗化动作到细化动作、精化动作阶段,掌握动作规范,以达到调身目的。 2. 呼吸与动作配合,以达到调息目的。 3. 形神意气合一,形神兼备,内外合一,以达到调神目的

(三) 技术体验

表 10-2　五禽戏技术体验

内　容	要　求
动作规范	动作到位,合乎规范,特别是动作的起落、高低、轻重、缓急、虚实要分辨清楚,不僵不滞,柔和灵活
呼吸与动作配合	习练健身气功·五禽戏时,呼吸和动作的配合有以下规律:起吸落呼、开吸合呼、先吸后呼、蓄吸发呼。其主要呼吸方式有自然呼吸、腹式呼吸、提肛呼吸等,可根据姿势变化或劲力要求而选用。如起势调息,上捧为吸气,下按为呼气;熊运,自右而上为吸气,向左而下为呼气,采用腹式呼吸;猿提,两臂上提、提踵转头时,为吸气,下落为呼气,采用提肛呼吸法
身心和谐	习练健身气功·五禽戏,必须把握好"形、神、意、气"四个环节,要实现"形、神、意、气的合一",要将"练功时的'形'、神态与神韵、意念与意境、呼吸"高度统一。 "形",是练功时的姿势。形正气顺,意宁神聚。要根据动作名称含义,做出与之相适应的动作造型,动作到位,合乎规范,努力做到"演虎象虎"、"学熊象熊"。"神",即神态、神韵。习练时应做到"惟神似守"。只有掌握五禽的神态,进行玩耍、游戏的意境,神韵方能显现出来,动作形象才能逼真。"意"即意念、意境。习练每戏时,逐步进入五禽的意境,模仿不同动物的不同动作。模仿虎在扑猎,鹿在奔跑,熊在散步,猿在攀爬,鸟在飞翔。意随形动,气随意行,达到意、气、形合一。"气",是指练功时对呼吸的锻炼,也称调息。先学动作,明其含义,调整呼吸,动作与呼吸、意识、神韵的结合,理解动作内涵和意境,从而达到"形神兼备,内外合一"。
运动意境	虎戏要仿效虎的威猛气势,虎视眈眈,体现虎之威猛。 鹿戏要仿效鹿的轻捷舒展,自由奔放,体现鹿之安舒。 熊戏要仿效熊的憨厚刚直,步履沉稳,体现熊之沉稳。 猿戏要仿效猿的灵活敏捷,轻松活泼,体现猿之灵巧。 鸟戏要仿效鹤的昂首挺立,轻盈潇洒,体现鸟之轻捷。

(四) 文化体验

- **基本手型**

虎爪:五指张开,虎口撑圆,第一、二指关节弯曲内扣。

鹿角：拇指伸直，食指、小指伸直，中指、无名指弯曲内扣。
熊掌：拇指压在食指指端上，其余四指并拢弯曲，虎口撑圆。
猿钩：五指指腹捏拢，屈腕。
鸟翅：五指伸直，拇指、食指、小指上翘，无名指、中指并拢下压。
握固：拇指抵掐无名指根节内侧，其余四指屈拢收于掌心。

- **三调合一**

三调是调身、调息、调心的合称。三调合一是通过练功把形体、呼吸、意念紧密结合起来，达到一种身心合一的状态。三调合一是气功锻炼的基本基本境界。

五劳

是指肝、心、脾、肺、肾五脏的劳损，亦指五种因劳累过度而致的人体损伤。《素问·宣明五气篇》认为，"久视伤血，久卧伤气，久坐伤肉，久立伤骨，久行伤筋，是谓五劳"，提示气功学练者应注意劳逸结合。

- **呼吸法**

顺腹式呼吸。吸气时，腹肌放松，膈肌随之下降，腹壁逐渐隆起；呼气时，腹肌收缩，腹壁回缩或稍内凹，膈肌也随之上升还原。如五禽戏起势调息。

逆腹式呼吸。吸气时，腹肌收缩，腹壁回缩或稍内凹，膈肌随之收缩下降，使腹腔容积变小；呼气时，腹肌放松，腹壁隆起，膈肌上升还原，腹腔容积变大。如五禽戏熊运。

提肛呼吸。把提肛动作和呼吸配合起来的练习方法。吸气时有意识地收缩肛门及会阴部的肌肉，呼气时放松肛门及会阴部的肌肉。如猿提动作即运用此法。

表 10-3　健身气功常用穴位表

身体部位	穴 名	所属经脉	分 布 位 置
头	百 会	督 脉	头顶正中，两耳尖连线中点
	印 堂	经外奇穴	两眉头连线中点，正对鼻尖
	太 阳	经外奇穴	眉梢与目外眦之间向后约1寸凹陷处
	人 中	督 脉	上唇人中沟上 1/3 处
	承 浆	任 脉	下唇沟正中凹陷处
颈	玉 枕	足太阳膀胱经	枕外粗隆上缘外侧
	风 池	足少阳胆经	头颈后两侧发际凹陷处
	天 柱	足太阳膀胱经	平哑门旁开1.3寸斜方肌外缘凹陷中
背腰胸	大 椎	督 脉	第七颈椎棘突下凹陷处
	命 门	督 脉	第二腰椎棘突下凹陷处
	肾 俞	足太阳膀胱经	命门旁开1.5寸
	膻 中	任 脉	两乳头连线中点

(续表)

身体部位	穴名	所属经脉	分布位置
腹	中脘	任脉	脐上4寸
	神阙	任脉	肚脐中
	气海	任脉	肚脐下1.5寸
	关元	任脉	肚脐下3寸处
裆髋	会阴	任脉	前居二阴连线中点
肩	肩井	手阳明大肠经	肩端,平举肩时前上方凹陷处
臂	曲池	手阳明大肠经	肘弯横纹桡侧端凹陷处
	内关	手厥阴心胞经	仰掌腕横纹上2寸
	劳宫	手厥阴心包经	握拳,中指尖所点处
手腿	足三里	足阳明胃经	膝下3寸,胫骨前嵴外侧
	承山	足太阳膀胱经	腓肠肌腹下出现尖端凹陷处
	委中	足太阳膀胱经	膝后窝横纹中央
	三阴交	足三阴经上	内踝尖上3寸,胫骨内侧后缘处
足	太溪	足少阴肾经	内踝后,跟骨上凹陷中
	太冲	足厥阴肝经	足第一、二跖骨结合部之前
	涌泉	足少阴肾经	足心人字纹头凹陷处

(注:1寸,拇指最宽指节处为1寸的尺度)

三、总结

1. 学习健身气功·五禽戏,应掌握基本的手型与手法、步型与步法、身型与身法。

2. 学习健身气功·五禽戏学学步骤可分为调身、调息、调心三个步骤。第一步先学习肢体动作,初步掌握动作轨迹、方向,能够独立完成整套动作即可,达到"导体令柔"目的,本阶段初步掌握动作技术;第二步再学练呼吸吐纳,也就动作与呼吸配合,细化动作,密切配合呼吸,达到"导气令和"目的,本阶段要求熟练细化动作细节,并注意与呼吸的配合;第三步才学练意念的运用,本阶段要求体现五禽戏功法特点,五禽神韵,象形取义,体现仿生气功特点。

3. 学习健身气功·五禽戏不仅仅是学习动作技术,还需了解中国的传统文化,如阴阳学说、精气神学说、经络学说、脏腑学说、五行学说、天人合一、形神意气说、常用人体穴位等,有关传统气功学方面典籍,以便更好地理解动作的文化内涵、达到健身养心的作用。

四、延伸学习

学会健身气功·五禽戏者,可学习健身气功·马王堆导引术、健身气功·易筋经、健身气功·八段锦、健身气功·六字诀、健身气功·大舞、健身气功·太极养生杖、健身气功·导引养生功十二法、健身气功·十二段锦,及三线放松功、练功十八法、内养功、太极拳。

五、思考与练习题

1. 健身气功·五禽戏的习练要领?
2. 健身气功·五禽戏的功法特点?
3. 健身气功·五禽戏中的调息动作有哪些,各有什么作用?
4. 习练熊晃时提髋落步的动作要领是什么?
5. 怎样才能达到习练健身气功·五禽戏的最佳效果?

六、参考文献

[1] 国家体育总局健身气功管理中心.健身气功·五禽戏[M].北京:人民体育出版社,2003.
[2] 国家体育总局健身气功管理中心.健身气功常用词汇手册[M].北京:高等教育出版社,2012.
[3] 国家体育总局健身气功管理中心.健身气功社会体育指导员培训教材[M].北京:人民体育出版社,2007.
[4] 国家体育总局健身气功管理中心.健身气功知识荟萃[M].北京:人民体育出版社,2011.
[5] 孙广仁.中医基础理论[M].北京:中国中医药出版社,2007.

第十一章

武功整复术

一、导言

武功整复术是武术家对身体的整复术,它以武术家对身体感知、肢体控制与发劲方法为技术基底,以被动的推拿、按摩、拍打、抖震、摇扳等徒手疗法,及主动的控制肢体自我锻炼健身气功进行治疗为主要手段,从而调整身体、处理身体肌、筋、膜与骨骼、关节等运动系统失调的方法。武功整复术除可治疗武术训练过程中失当的运动伤害,也可以调整日常生活中不良习惯所形成的运动功能失调问题。

二、学习体验

(一) 动作说明

1. 基础放松手法

【推法】

(1) 推法:以指、掌、拳、肘等部位着力于被放松部位,进行单方向直线移动的手法。有指推法、掌推法、拳推法、肘推法等(图11-1-1)。

(2) 擦法:以指、掌贴附于体表被放松部位,进行直线来回摩擦运动的手法。有掌擦法、指擦法、鱼际擦法、小鱼际擦法等(图11-1-2)。

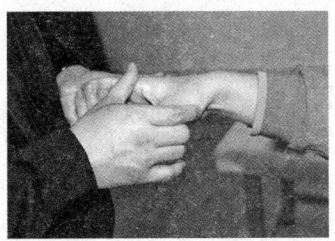
图 11-1-1　推法

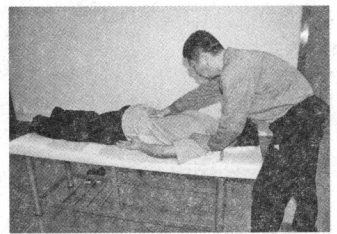
图 11-1-2　擦法

(3) 抹法:以指腹或手掌在不同部位进行往返推动的手法。有拇指抹法、掌抹法、鱼际抹法、指节抹法等(图11-1-3)。

(4) 扫散法:以拇指桡侧面,从头颞部向脑后进行较快速度单向推动的手法。如头部扫散法(图11-1-4)。

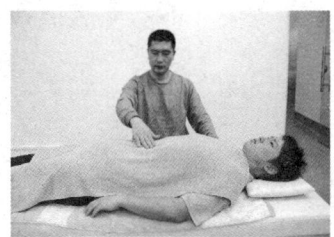
图 11-1-3 抹法

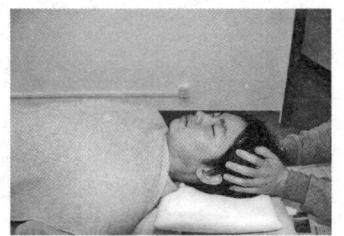
图 11-1-4 扫散法

鱼际

本指鱼际穴,为手太阴肺经穴,在手拇指第1掌指关节后凹陷处,约当第1掌骨中点桡侧,赤白肉际处。在武功整复中为整复师手掌著力的位置,整复师以手掌正面内、外侧缘由肌群构成稍隆起的部位用力,其中大拇指一侧称"大鱼际",另一侧称"小鱼际"。

【拿法】

(5)拿法:以拇指和其余四指指腹对称用力内收提起,并做捏揉的手法。有二指拿法、三指拿法、四指拿法、五指拿法等(图 11-1-5)。

(6)抓法:又称为五指抓法或五指拿法;五指分开,满把抓拿受术部位的手法。如头部五指抓法(图 11-1-6)。

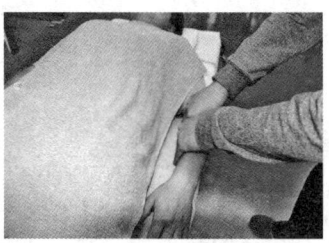
图 11-1-5 拿法

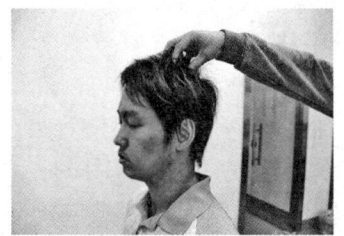
图 11-1-6 抓法

(7)捏法:以指腹相对用力,挤捏肌肤,或做捻、转、挤、拿、扯、提的对称用力动作。如捏脊法(图 11-1-7)。

(8)捻法:以拇指与食指相对捏住放松部位,稍用力进行对称的快速捻搓动作。如捻指法(图 11-1-8)。

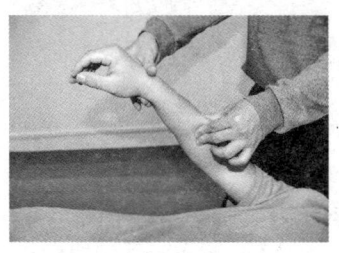
图 11-1-7 捏脊法

图 11-1-8 捻法

【按法】

(9) 按法：以手指或手掌着力于放松部位或穴位，逐渐用力向下按压的方法。有指按法（拇指按法、中指按法、三指按法）、掌按法（单掌按法、双掌按法、迭掌按法、掌根按法、鱼际按法）等（图11-1-9）。

(10) 压法：以手指、掌、肘着力于放松部位，压而抑之，持续几秒时间。有肘压法、膊压法、指压法、掌压法等（图11-1-10）。

(11) 点法：属接触面积小、压力强的按法。有拇指点法、屈拇指点法、凤眼拳点法、象鼻拳点法等（图11-1-11）。

(12) 掐法：以拇指、食指或中指的指甲重掐取穴的手法。如人中掐法、承山掐法（图11-1-12）。

(13) 弹拨法：又称为拨法、指拨法、拨络法；以指、拳、肘着力于放松部位，压按并拨动的手法。有拇指拨法、三指拨法、屈指拨法、拳拨法等（图11-1-13）。

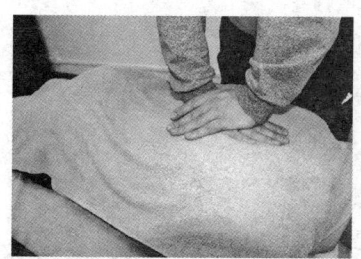
图11-1-9 按法

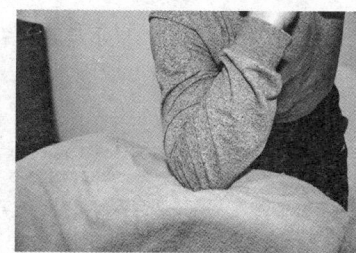
图11-1-10 压法

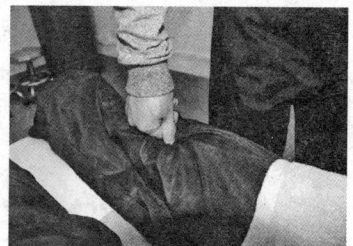
图11-1-11 点法

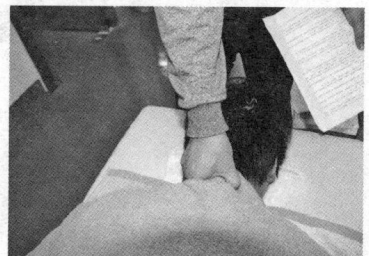
图11-1-12 掐法

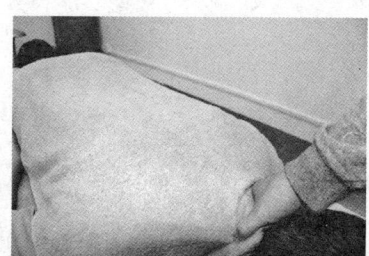
图11-1-13 弹拨法

【摩法】

(14) 摩法：以手指指腹或手掌面放于体表的放松部位，进行有节律的环形摩动的手法。有指摩法、掌摩法等（图11-1-14）。

(15) 揉法：以手指的指腹或手掌面着力于放松部位或穴位，力量渗透于该处的皮下组织，进行轻柔缓和的环旋运动的手法。有指揉法（拇指揉法、二指揉法、三指揉法、中指揉法、勾揉法、叠指揉法）、掌揉法（鱼际揉法、掌根揉法）等（图11-1-15）。

(16) 搓法：用手掌面着力于放松部位或夹住肢体作交替搓动的手法，称为搓法。有搓上肢、搓下肢、搓项部等（图11-1-16）。

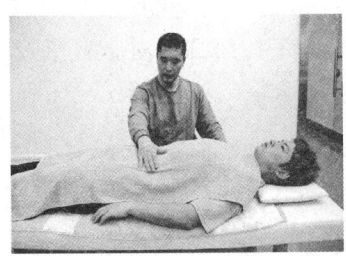 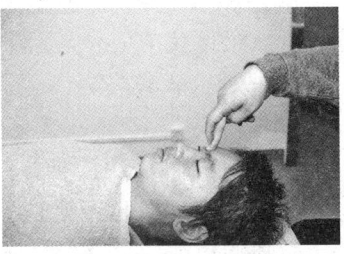 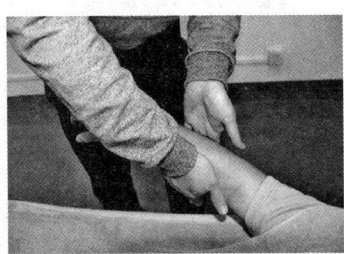

图 11-1-14　摩法　　　　图 11-1-15　揉法　　　　图 11-1-16　搓法

【拍打法】

（17）拍法：以手掌拍打体表之法（图 11-1-17）。

（18）击法：用拳、掌、指以及桑枝棒击打体表的手法。有拳击法（拳背击法、拳心击法、拳眼击法）、掌击法（掌心击法、掌根击法、掌侧击法、合掌击法）、指击法（指尖击法、二指击法）、棒击法等（图 11-1-18）。

（19）弹法：屈指，以手指弹打受术部位或穴位的手法。如眉心弹法（图 11-1-19）。

（20）啄法：又称为餐法；五指聚拢成钩手，如鸡啄米状，啄击受术部位的手法。如百会啄法（图 11-1-20）。

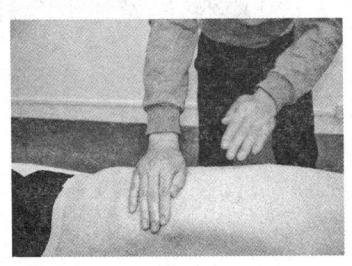 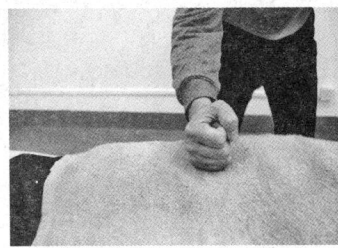 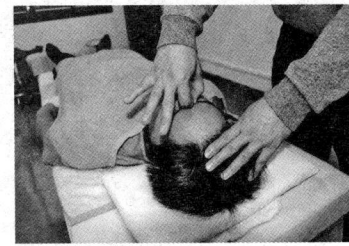

图 11-1-17　拍法　　　　图 11-1-18　击法　　　　图 11-1-19　弹法

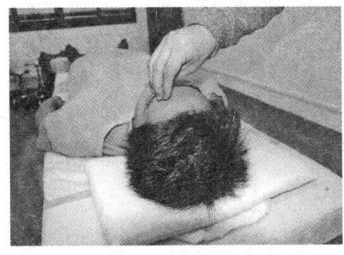 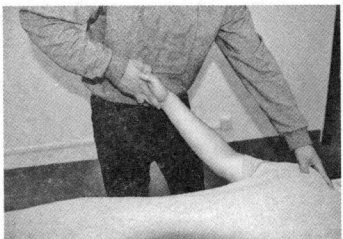 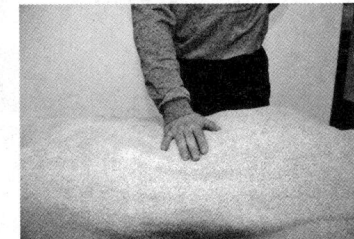

图 11-1-20　啄法　　　　图 11-1-21　抖法　　　　图 11-1-22　振法

【抖振法】

（21）抖法：以单拍法手或双手握住四肢远程，做连续的、小幅度的、频率较高的上下抖动的手法。有抖上肢法、抖下肢法、抖腕法等（图 11-1-21）。

（22）振法：又称为颤法或振颤法；以指或掌吸附于受术部位，做频率密集的快速振颤动作的手法。有指振法、掌振法等（图 11-1-22）。

【拔伸法】

（23）拔伸法：又称为牵引法或牵拉法；整复师固定受术者肢体或关节的一端，牵拉另一端；或者用对抗力量将关节或肢体进行牵拉、牵引，使其伸展的手法。有颈部拔伸法、肘关节拔伸法、腕关节拔伸法、指掌关节拔伸法、腰椎拔伸法、髋关节拔伸法、踝关节拔伸法等（图 11-1-23）。

（24）勒法：以手指夹住受术者手指或足趾，相对用力，做急速滑拉动作的手法（图 11-1-24）。

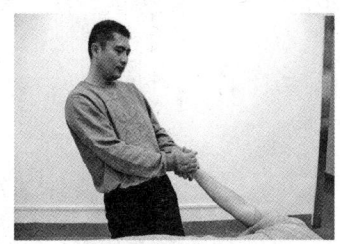
图 11-1-23　拔伸法

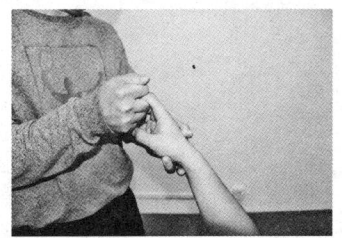
图 11-1-24　勒法

【摇扳法】

（25）摇法：以受术者关节为轴心，使肢体做被动往返旋转或环转运动的手法。有颈部摇法、肩关节摇法、肘关节摇法、腕关节摇法、指掌关节摇法、腰部摇法、髋关节摇法、膝关节摇法、踝关节摇法等（图 11-1-25）。

（26）扳法：以双手向同一方向或相反方向用力，使肌肉与关节伸展、屈曲或旋转的手法。有颈部扳法、胸椎扳法、腰椎扳法等（图 11-1-26）。

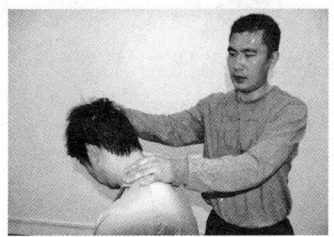
图 11-1-25　摇法

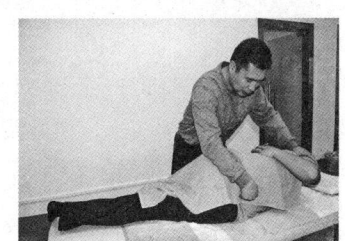
图 11-1-26　扳法

【一指禅推法】

（27）一指禅推法：又称为一指禅功；以拇指指腹前半段或指端着力，运用前臂的摆动，带动腕关节，使拇指关节做伸屈运动的手法（图 11-1-27）。

（28）一指禅偏锋推法：以拇指桡侧偏锋着力，进行一指禅推法的手法（图 11-1-28）。

（29）一指禅屈指推法：又称跪推法；以拇指第一、二指骨间关节背侧桡侧着力，进行一指禅推法的手法（图 11-1-29）。

图 11-1-27　一指禅推法

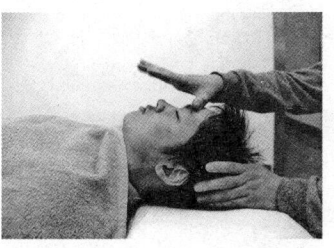
图 11-1-28　一指禅偏锋推法

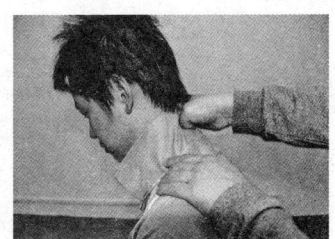
图 11-1-29　一指禅屈指推法

【滚法】

(30) 掌背滚法（丁氏滚法）：将第五掌、指关节背侧吸附于受术部位，以小鱼际及掌背尺侧在受术部位进行滚法的手法（图11-1-30）。

(31) 掌指关节滚法：以掌指关节背侧吸附于受术部位，进行滚法的手法（图11-1-31）。

(32) 指间关节滚法：以第一、二指骨间关节作为着力点，进行滚法的手法（图11-1-32）。

(33) 前臂滚法：以前臂尺侧作为着力点，进行滚法的手法（图11-1-33）。

图11-1-30　掌背滚法

图11-1-31　掌指关节滚法

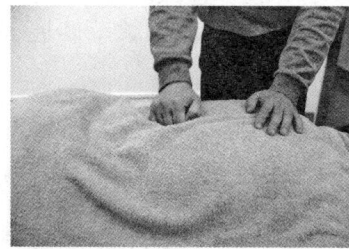
图11-1-32　指间关节滚法

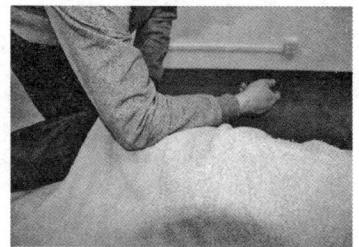
图11-1-33　前臂滚法

2. 上肢放松的操作程序

(1) 肩部放松操作

整复师立而面向坐着的受术者的背部。

分推冈上窝：以双手拇指、鱼际或掌根从胸椎向两侧分推冈上窝斜方肌及冈上肌（图11-2-1）；

指压冈上窝：以双手拇指从胸椎向两侧按压冈上窝部位之斜方肌及冈上肌。建议由内向外，分压6点（图11-2-2）；

勾揉胸肌：以双手二指、三指或四指勾揉胸肌，特别是肩夹骨喙突及锁骨下肌（图11-2-3）；

拿肩井、勾揉肩井、叩击肩井：以双手拿两侧肩井斜方肌（图11-2-4）。两手二指或三指分别勾揉两侧肩井穴（图11-2-5）。以双拳叩击肩胛上部，颈项部两侧肌肉（图11-2-6）；

指压菱形肌、天宗：以拇指按揉脊柱与肩夹骨之间的大小菱形肌（图11-2-7），以及冈下窝正中的天宗穴（图11-2-8）；

勾揉大、小圆肌：以双手二指、三指或四指勾揉肩夹骨外侧的大、小圆肌（图11-2-9）。

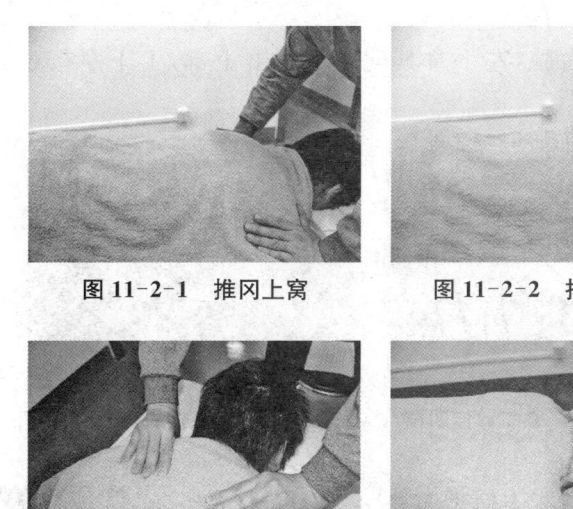

图 11-2-1　推冈上窝　　　图 11-2-2　指压冈上窝　　　图 11-2-3　勾揉胸肌

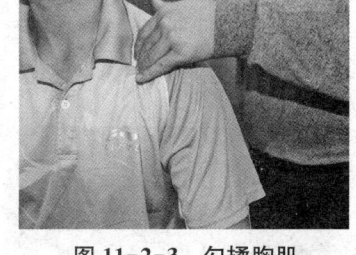

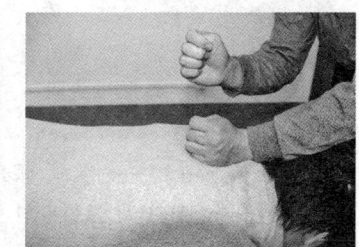

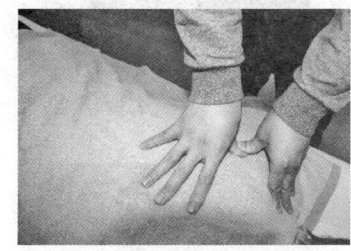　　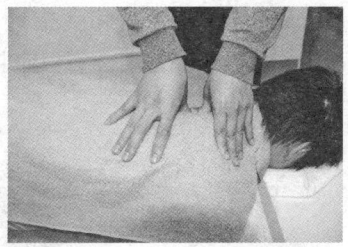　　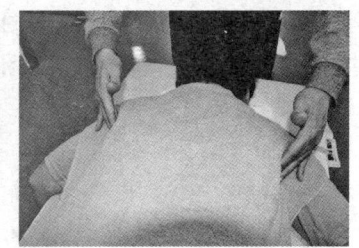

图 11-2-4　拿肩井　　　图 11-2-5　勾揉肩井　　　图 11-2-6　叩击肩井

图 11-2-7　指压菱形肌、天宗　图 11-2-8　指压冈下窝正中天宗　图 11-2-9　勾揉大、小圆肌

（2）上肢部放松操作

整复师立于受术者右侧，放松其右上肢。

拿三角肌：右手扶持受术者右手腕部，以左手掌按揉其右肩三角肌及肩胸交会处（图11-2-10）；

托揉肱三头肌：右手扶持受术者右腕部，以左手手掌托住其肱三头肌后部，进行自上而下的揉动（图11-2-11）；

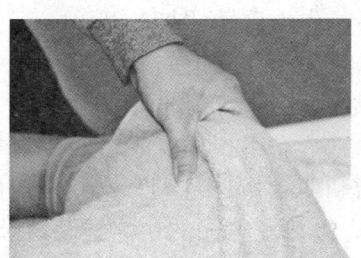　　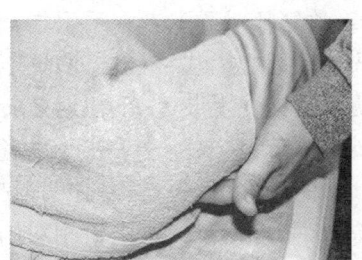

图 11-2-10　拿三角肌　　　图 11-2-11　托揉肱三头肌

拿肱二头肌：右手扶持受术者右前臂腕部，使其肘关节屈曲；以左手虎口置于受术者肘

第十一章　武功整复术

139

弯部，以五指拿肱二头肌，上下拿按(图11-2-12)；

拿前臂伸肌群：整复师右手持受术者右腕，左手拿其前臂伸肌群上部，上下拿按(图11-2-13)；

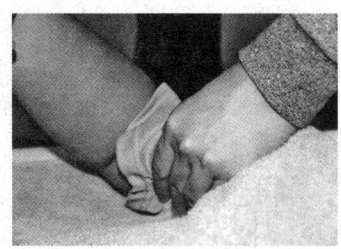
图11-2-12 拿肱二头肌

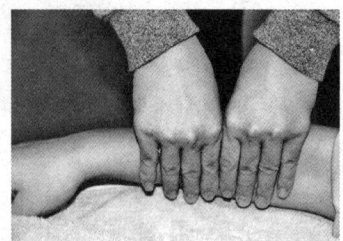
图11-2-13 拿前臂伸肌群

图11-2-14 指压前臂中线

指压前臂中线：受术者掌心向上，整复师双手拇指由上向下按压于前臂中线骨缝处(图11-2-14)；

勾揉小海，按揉曲池、内关、外关、合谷：整复师一手扶住受术者右手手腕，一手以中指勾揉小海穴(尺神经沟中)(图11-2-15)；以拇指按揉曲池穴(图11-2-16)，以拇指和食指同时捏住内关和外关，进行按揉(图11-2-17)，再按揉合谷(图11-2-18)；

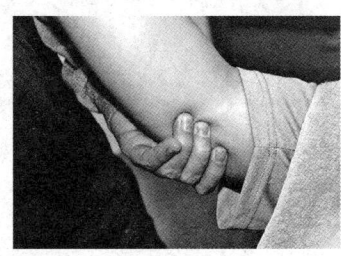
图11-2-15 勾揉小海穴

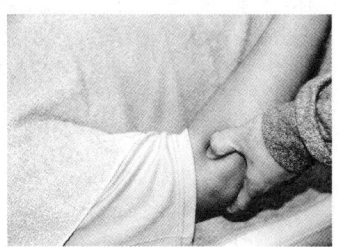
图11-2-16 按揉曲池穴

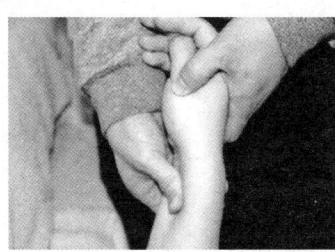
图11-2-17 捏压内关和外关

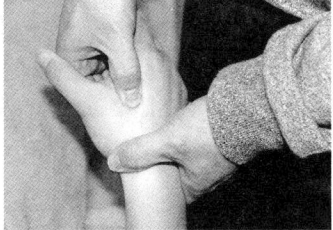
图11-2-18 按揉合谷

分推手掌、分推手背：受术者掌心向上，整复师以双手的小指和无名指扣住受术者右手的拇指和小指，以双手拇指分推其手掌的大小鱼际和掌心(图11-2-19)；受术者手背向上，整复师双手握住受术者手掌两侧，以双手鱼际分推其手背(图11-2-20)；

捻、勒手指：整复师对受术者右手手指，逐一先捻后勒(图11-2-21)；

摇上肢：选择适用之摇法，依次摇肘关节、腕关节和掌指关节(图11-2-22)；

搓上肢：两手掌夹住上肢，上下往返搓转数次(图11-2-23)；

抖上肢、抖腕关节：整复师左手扶受术者右肩，右手握住受术者右手，抖动其上肢，使动波传导肱三头肌(图11-2-24)；整复师两拇指和两食指、中指上下相对，捏住受术者右手腕关节上下横纹；双手拇指和食指、中指相对用力做相反方向的快速搓动，带动腕关节快速上下抖动(图11-2-25)；

叩击上肢作：整复师一手托住受术者上肢，一手握拳叩击受术者上肢。(图11-2-26)

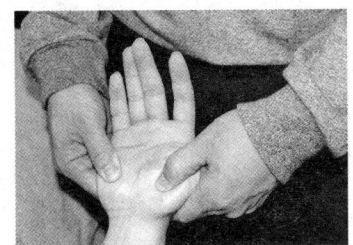
图 11-2-19　分推手掌

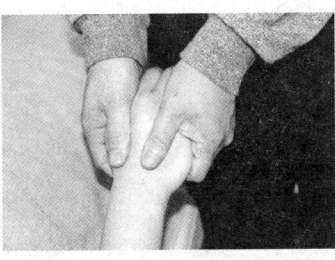
图 11-2-20　分推手背

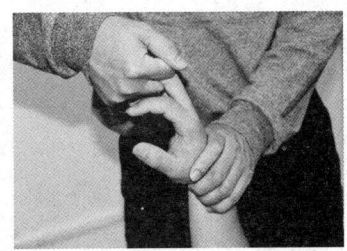
图 11-2-21　捻、勒手指

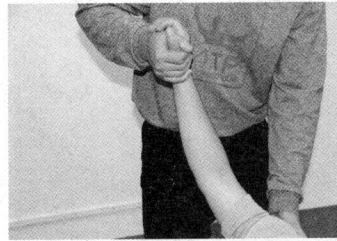
图 11-2-22　摇上肢

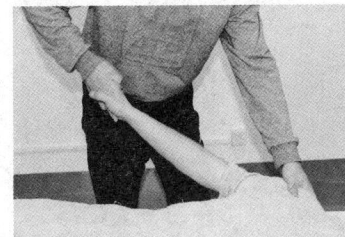
图 11-2-23　搓上肢

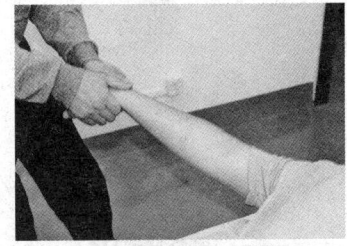
图 11-2-24　抖上肢、抖腕关节

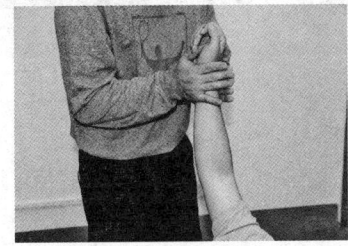
图 11-2-25　抖动腕关节

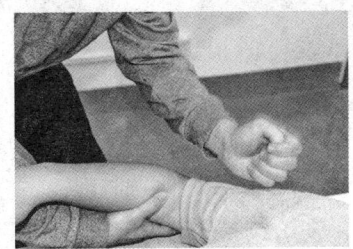
图 11-2-26　叩击上肢作

穴位与主治

肩井：大椎穴与肩峰联机中点；肩部最高处，乳头正上方与肩线交接处。主治肩背痹痛、手臂不举，颈项强痛、头酸痛、落枕。

天宗：在肩胛部，当冈下窝中央凹陷处，与第4胸椎相平。主治肩胛疼痛，肘臂外后侧痛，颈项肩背及上肢的麻痛。

小海：在肘外侧，当尺骨鹰突与肱骨内上髁之间凹陷处，尺神经沟中。主治肘臂疼痛。

曲池：屈肘成直角，肘横纹外侧端尺泽穴与肱骨外上髁联机中点。主治上肢不遂，手臂肿痛，肩肘关节疼痛、上肢瘫痪。

内关：仰掌，位于前臂正中，腕横纹上2寸，在桡侧屈腕肌腱同掌长肌腱之间。主治心痛、心悸、胸闷气急、呃逆、失眠、晕车、手臂疼痛、恶心想吐、月经痛、精神异常等。

外关：伸臂俯掌，于手背腕横纹中点直上2寸，尺桡骨之间，与内关穴相对取穴。主治肢软、手颤。

合谷：别名虎口。以一手的拇指指骨关节横纹，放在另一手拇、食指之间的指蹼缘上，当拇指尖下是穴。主治齿痛、手腕及臂部疼痛、口眼歪斜、感冒发热等症，孕妇慎用。

3. 肩关节整复手法

(1) 挺胸展臂法

整复师位于受术者后方,受术者端坐于板凳上。受术者双腕触腰,挺胸抬肩,头部后仰,轮肩胛骨向上向后放松放下(图 11-3-1);整复师调整并固定肩膀(图 11-3-2);受术者头部转正,双手松垂放下(图 11-3-3);

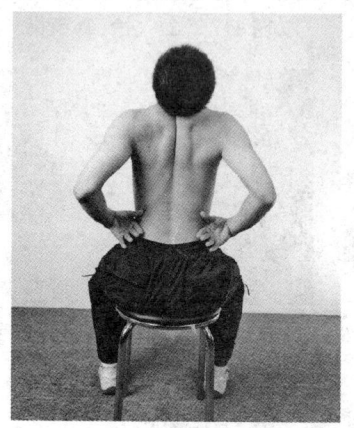

图 11-3-1 挺胸展臂法

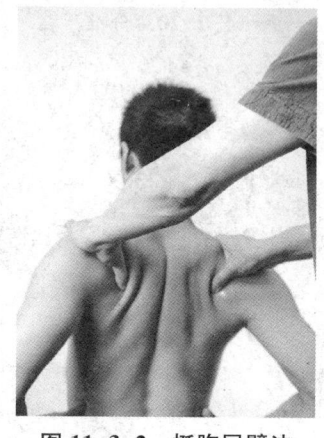

图 11-3-2 挺胸展臂法

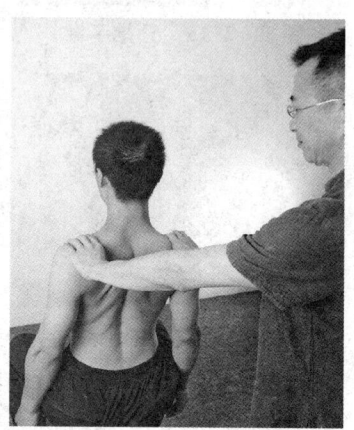

图 11-3-3 挺胸展臂法

受术者两手臂向两侧侧平举,至水平位(图 11-3-4);继续上举,同时抬头、转手心向上,直至双手朝天,开与肩齐或微开,眼看天空(图 11-3-5);

受术者放松肩膀,手臂左右下落,至水平位(图 11-3-6);头部转正,同时转手心向下(图 11-3-7);手继续下落,直至完全松垂放下(图 11-3-8)。

(2) 高低肩的调整手法

设受术者右肩不适,整复师立于受术者后方偏右侧,受术者端坐于板凳上。

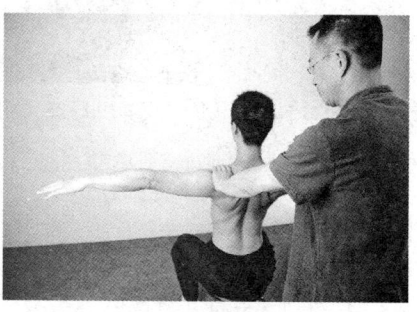

图 11-3-4 挺胸展臂法

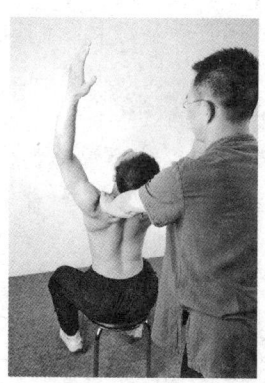

图 11-3-5 挺胸展臂法

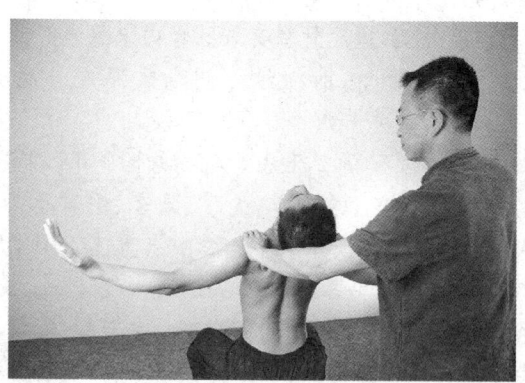

图 11-3-6 挺胸展臂法

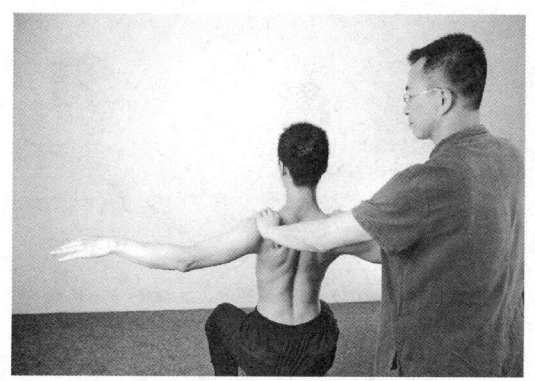
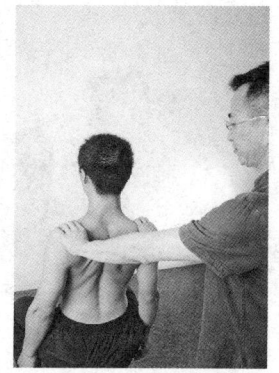

图 11-3-7　挺胸展臂　　　　　　图 11-3-8　挺胸展臂

受术者将右手臂腕部至于背后脊柱，使肩胛骨充分暴露，左手托住右手掌，防止其掉落（图 11-3-9）；

整复师右手从前方托住盂肱关节，左手从下扣住肩胛骨下角，上下、左右、前后调整肩胛骨，使其正位（图 11-3-10）；

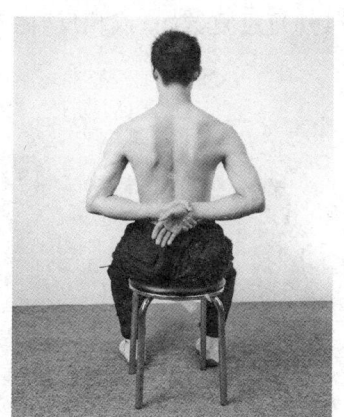
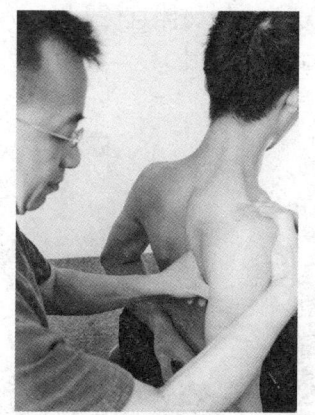

图 11-3-9　高低肩的调整手法　　　图 11-3-10　高低肩的调整手法

调控盂肱关节及肩胛下角，使成沉肩状态，并固定住肩关节（图 11-3-11）；受术者双臂从背后自然下垂；右手臂自主向前抬起，抬至最上方后松肩（图 11-3-12）；手心由外向后转，手臂顺势向后盖下来（图 11-3-13）。

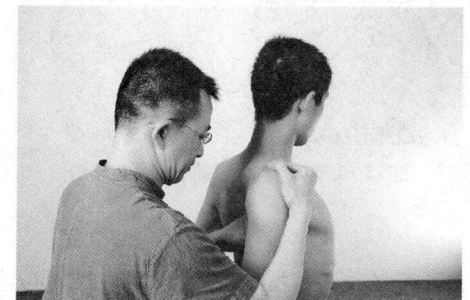
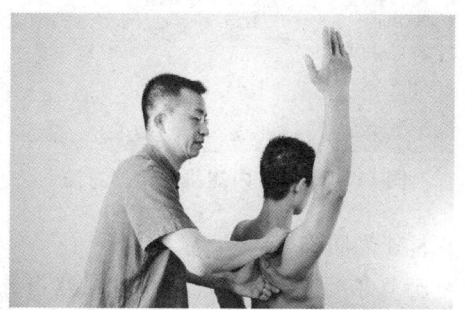

图 11-3-11　高低肩的调整手法　　　图 11-3-12　高低肩的调整手法

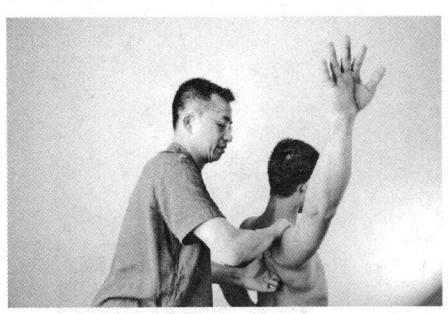 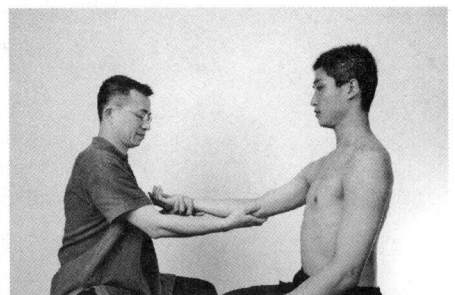

图 11-3-13　高低肩的调整手法　　　　图 11-4-1　肘内侧肌肉牵伸方法

4. 肘关节整复手法

（1）肘内侧肌肉牵伸方法

整复师立于受术者前方，右肘内侧有筋结点和压痛点的受术者坐于凳上，右手曲肘，掌心朝上，保持肩肘腕垂松状态。

整复师右手持受术者手肘，拇指扣压于少海，左手持手腕（图 11-4-1）；整复师右手固定，拇指按压固定并微内旋，左手内旋，两手相对运动，使受术者手臂内旋，掌心向下，先曲肘，后直肘，手臂微牵拉延展伸直（图 11-4-2,11-4-3）；反复数次；或相反，做外旋运动，使受术者手臂外旋，掌心向上（图 11-4-4,11-4-5）。

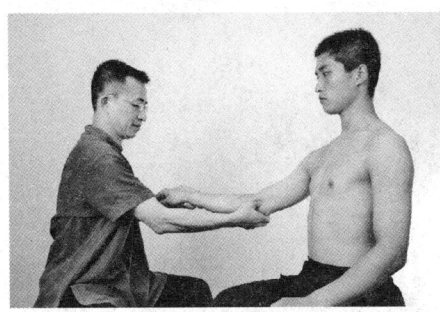 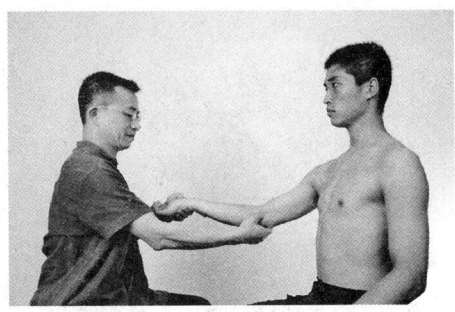

图 11-4-2　肘内侧肌肉牵伸方法　　　　图 11-4-3　肘内侧肌肉牵伸方法

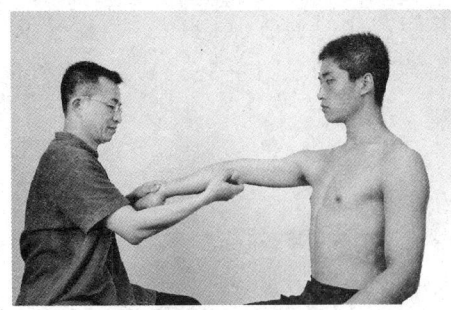 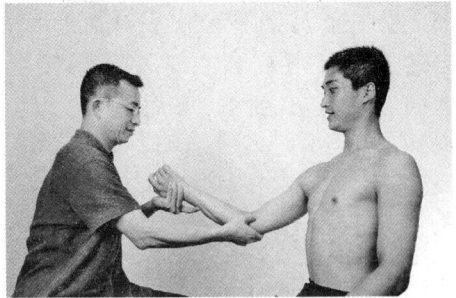

图 11-4-4　肘内侧肌肉牵伸方法　　　　图 11-4-5　肘内侧肌肉牵伸方法

（2）肘外侧肌肉牵伸方法

整复师立于受术者前方，肘外侧筋结点和压痛点的受术者坐于凳上，右手曲肘，掌心朝上，保持肩肘腕垂松状态。

整复师左手持受术者手肘,拇指扣压于曲池,右手持手腕(图11-4-6);整复师左手固定,拇指按压固定并微内旋,右手内旋,两手相对运动,使受术者手臂外旋,掌心向上,先曲肘,后直肘,手臂微牵拉延展伸直(图11-4-7,11-4-8);反复数次;或相反,做外旋运动,使受术者手臂内旋,掌心向下(图11-4-9,11-4-10)。

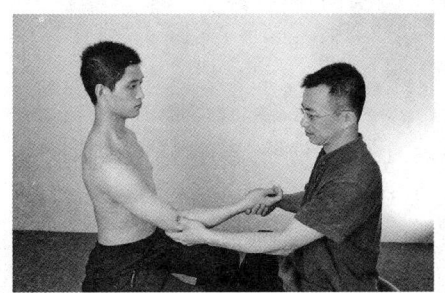
图11-4-6　肘外侧肌牵伸法

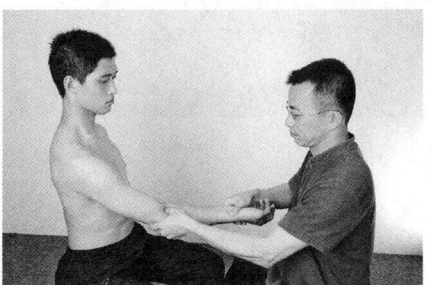
图11-4-7　肘外侧肌牵伸法

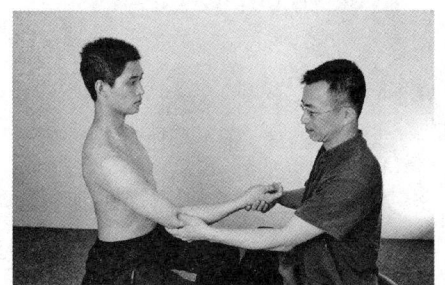
图11-4-8　肘外侧肌牵伸法

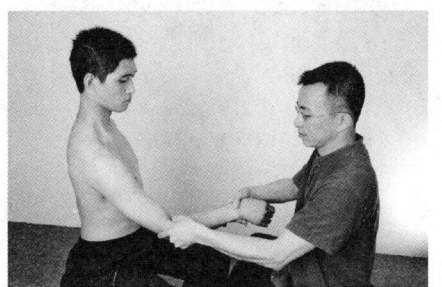
图11-4-9　肘外侧肌牵伸法

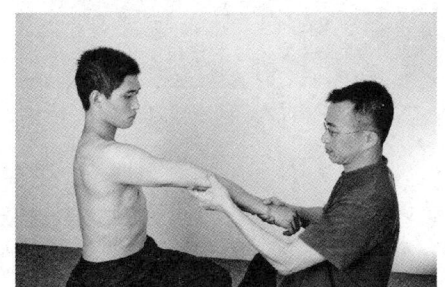
图11-4-10　肘外侧肌牵伸法

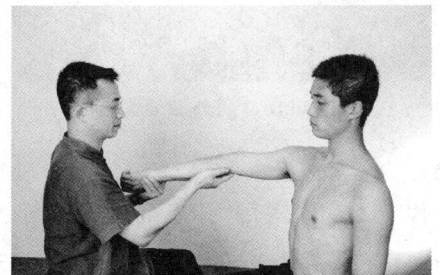
图11-4-11　肘外侧肌牵伸法

(3) 肘后侧肌肉牵伸方法

整复师立于受术者前方,右肘后侧筋结点和压痛点的受术者坐于凳上,右手曲肘,掌心朝上,保持肩肘腕垂松状态。

整复师右手持受术者手肘,食指、中指点压肘后天井或清冷渊,左手持手腕(图11-4-11);

整复师右手固定,食指、中指点压固定,左手内旋,使受术者手臂内旋,掌心向下,先曲肘,后直肘,手臂微牵拉延展伸直(图11-4-12,11-4-13),反复数次;或相反,做外旋运动,使受术者手臂外旋,掌心向上(图11-4-14,11-4-15);整复师换手,左手持肘,右手持腕;翻转肘关节,使其成擒拿反关节状态(图11-4-16,11-4-17)。

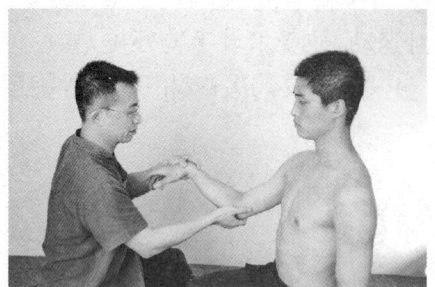
图 11-4-12　肘外侧肌牵伸法

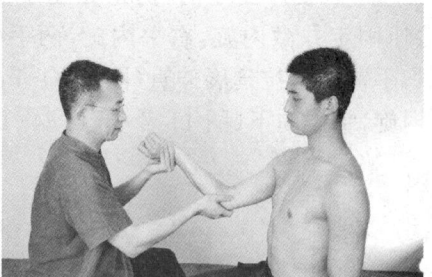
图 11-4-13　肘外侧肌牵伸法

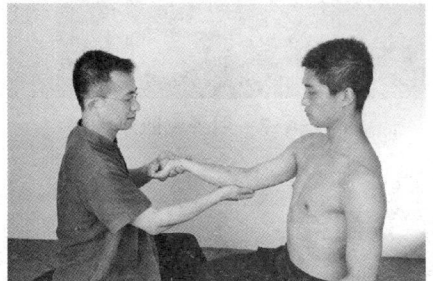
图 11-4-14　肘外侧肌牵伸法

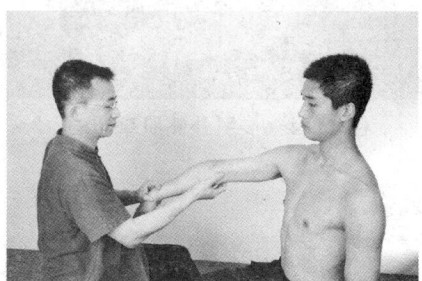
图 11-4-15　肘外侧肌牵伸法

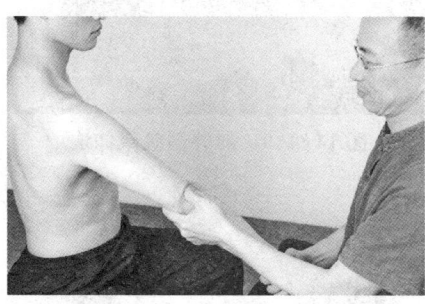
图 11-4-16　肘外侧肌牵伸法

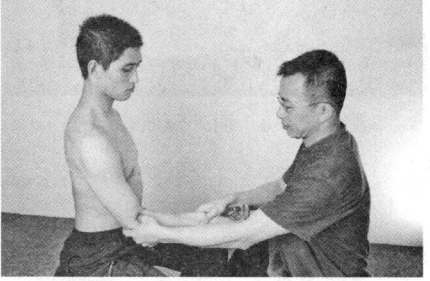
图 11-4-17　肘外侧肌牵伸法

（4）坠肘托顿手法

整复师立于受术者前方，右肘受伤的受术者坐于凳上，右手曲肘，掌心朝上，保持肩肘腕垂松状态。整复师右手托受术者手肘，左手持手掌（图 11-4-18）；略微旋动手掌使手臂内旋，掌心向下，整复师做向下托顿动作，调整肘关节（图 11-4-19）。

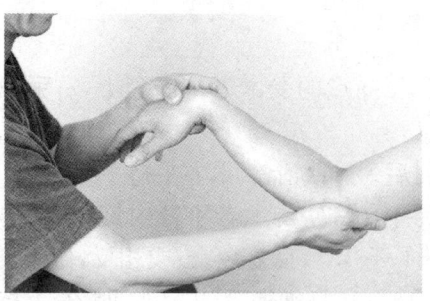
图 11-4-18　坠肘托顿手法

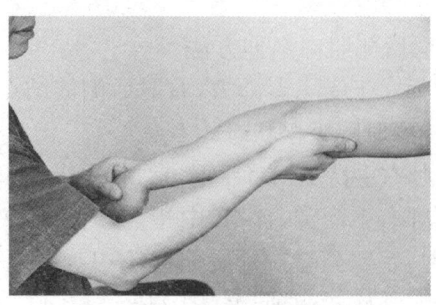
图 11-4-19　坠肘托顿手法

> **穴位与主治**
>
> 少海：屈肘，当肘横纹内侧端与肱骨内上髁联机的中点凹陷处。主治：前臂麻木及肘关节周围软组织疾患，肘臂挛痛。
>
> 天井：臂外侧，屈肘时，当肘尖直上1寸凹陷处，当肱骨鹰嘴窝部。主治，偏头痛、颈项痛、肘关节及上肢软组织损伤、落枕。
>
> 清泠渊：在臂外侧，屈肘时，当肘尖直上2寸，即天井上1寸。主治，肩臂痛不能举。

5. 腕关节整复手法

（1）牵顶旋动

整复师立于受术者前方，右腕受伤的受术者端坐于凳上，右手曲肘，掌心朝下，保持肩肘腕垂松状态。

整复师将双手的食指、无名指和小指分握在受术者的大小鱼际，食指托顶受术者腕关节下侧，双食指压按受术者腕关节上侧（图11-5-1）；

将腕关节牵拉并旋动，调整腕关节（图11-5-2）。

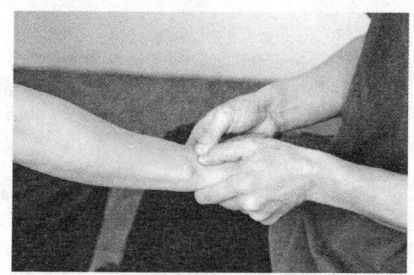 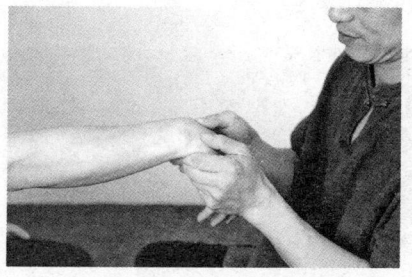

图11-5-1 牵顶旋动　　　　　　图11-5-2 牵顶旋动

（2）牵拉腕关节

整复师立于受术者前方，右腕受伤的受术者端坐于凳上，右手曲肘，掌心朝下，保持肩肘腕垂松状态。

整复师两手扣住受术者的手腕关节，水平向外、向下拉伸，使腕关节之上关节张开（图11-5-3）；

在保持腕关节之上关节张开状态下，再继续把关节以水平位拉伸开，使腕关节之下关节张开，同时按压突起之小关节使其复位（图11-5-4）；

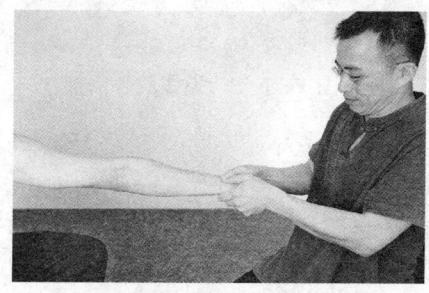 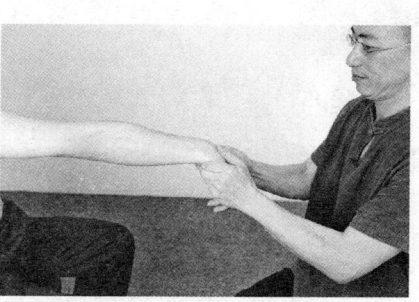

图11-5-3 牵拉腕关节　　　　　　图11-5-4 牵拉腕关节

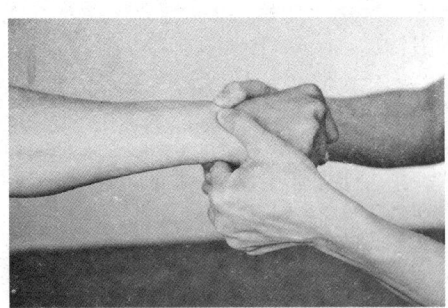

图 11-5-5 牵拉腕关节

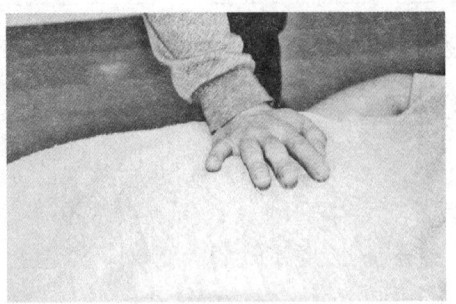

图 11-6-1 按揉近侧臀部肌群

让受术者快速握拳,放松手腕使其复位(图 11-5-5)。

6. 下肢后部放松操作程序

以放松左下肢为例,整复师立于受术者左侧,受术者俯卧床上。

(1) 整复师以左或右手掌根按揉近侧臀部肌群(图 11-6-1);以双手掌根按压大腿后部(图 11-6-2);以双手拇指并指或叠指按压大腿后部(图 11-6-3);以单掌或叠掌揉大腿后部(图 11-6-4);手虎口张开置于股后部,从股骨大转子处开始由下往上向膝部移动,以拇指弹拨股外侧部(11-6-5);

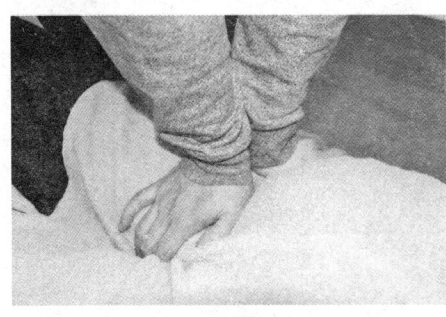

图 11-6-2 掌根按压大腿后部

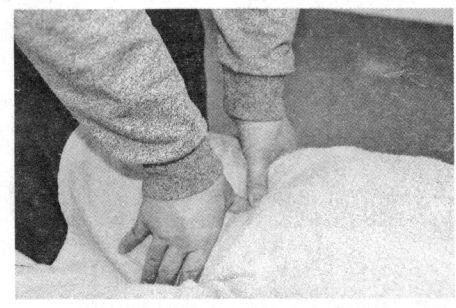

图 11-6-3 按压大腿后部

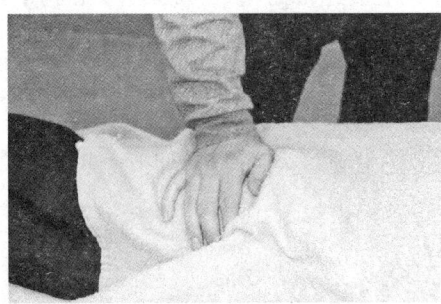

图 11-6-4 掌揉大腿后部

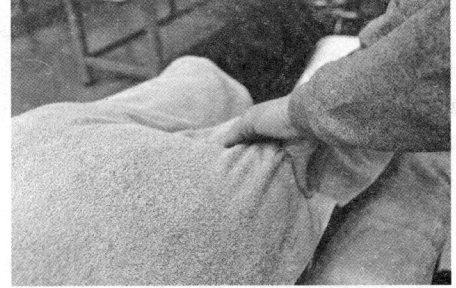

图 11-6-5 弹拨股外侧部

(2) 以单手拇指按揉小腿部委中、承山穴(图 11-6-6);双手同时拿左大腿、小腿后部肌群,直到跟腱(图 11-6-7);左掌抵住腰骶部,以右手掌从髋横纹沿下肢纵轴推进,至小腿跟腱处(图 11-6-8);左掌抵住腰骶部,以右手掌按压足跟内侧,重心落于右手,进行分离式撑压(图 11-6-9);

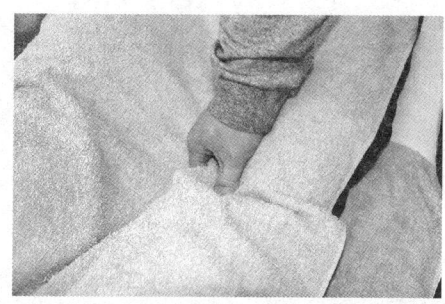
图 11-6-6 按揉委中、承山穴

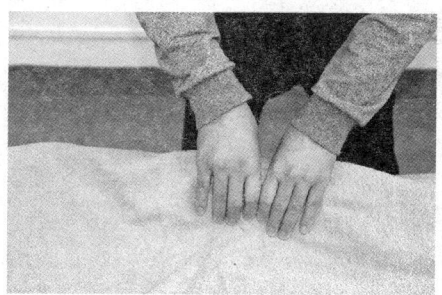
图 11-6-7 拿腿部肌群

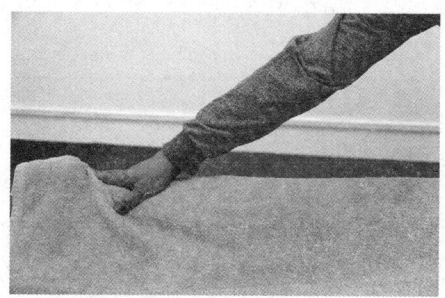
图 11-6-8 掌推

图 11-6-9 掌按

（3）以双手以击法依次施于大腿后侧、外侧，小腿后侧、外侧，往返数次（图 11-6-10）；以右手小鱼际擦足底涌泉（图 11-6-11）；左手按于髋部，右手在右膝关节屈曲后，托住膝部将髋部后伸（屈膝伸髋）扳动数次（图 11-6-12）。

（4）双掌前后夹住受术者屈膝 90°的小腿，在三阴交水平处进行快速搓动（图 11-6-13）；右手扶住屈膝 90°的左脚，左手握拳轻轻叩击其脚掌数次（图 11-6-14）。

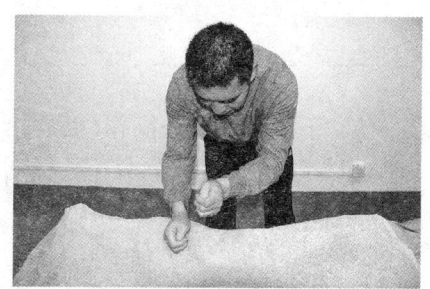
图 11-6-10 击法

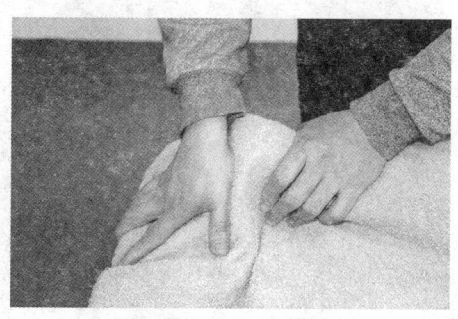
图 11-6-11 击法

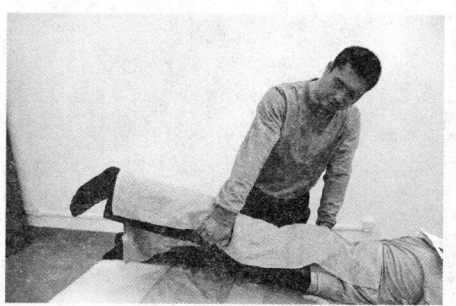
图 11-6-12 击法

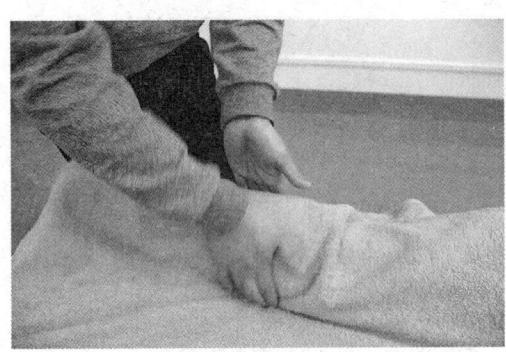
图 11-6-13　搓动

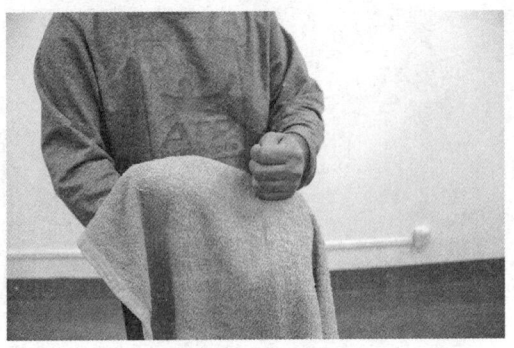
图 11-6-14　叩击

穴位与主治

委中：腘横纹中点，当股二头肌腱与半腱肌肌腱的中间。主治，腰背痛、下肢痿痹等腰及下肢病证。

承山：小腿后面正中，当伸直小腿或足跟上提时，腓肠肌肌腹下出现的尖角凹陷处即是。主治，腿部转筋，肛门疾患。

涌泉：足前部凹陷处第2、3趾趾缝纹头端与足跟连线的前三分之一处。主治，头顶痛，足心热，霍乱转筋。

7. 下肢前部放松操作（以放松左下肢为例）

（1）整复师面对受术者足底，以拇指、食指依次捏揉每一跖骨间隙（图 11-7-1），以拇指直推足背每一跖骨间隙（图 11-7-2）；以双手鱼际分推足背（图 11-7-3）；左手握住受术者五个足趾，同时向下扳动（图 11-7-4）；对受术者足趾逐一先捻后勒；左手托住受术者足跟，右手握住足掌，推伸后跟腱（图 11-7-5）；以双手拇指叠指按揉左侧足三里、阳陵泉，以食指按揉三阴交（图 11-7-6）；

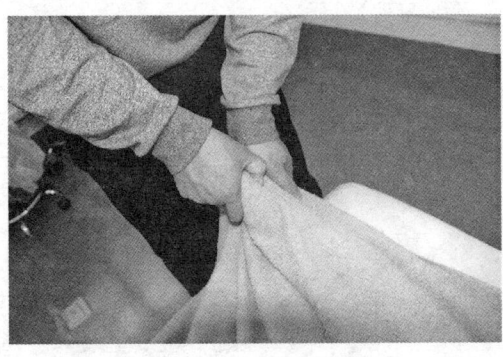
图 11-7-1　捏揉跖骨

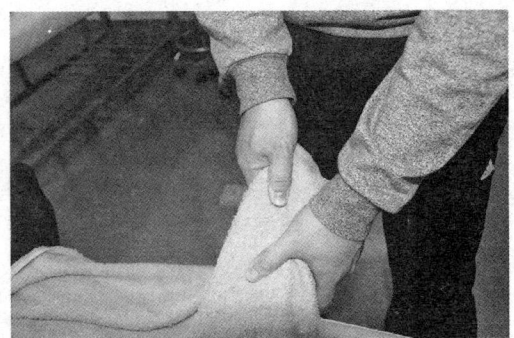
图 11-7-2　直推足背

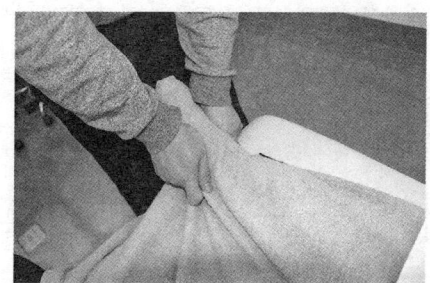

图 11-7-3　分推足背

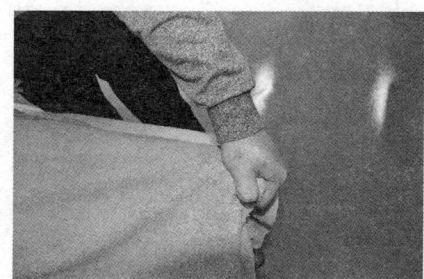

图 11-7-4　扳动足趾

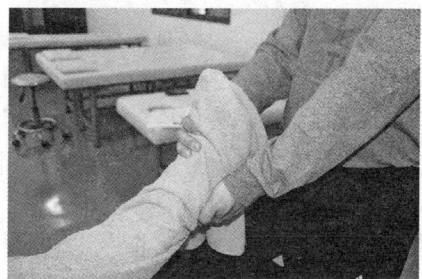

图 11-7-5　推伸后跟腱

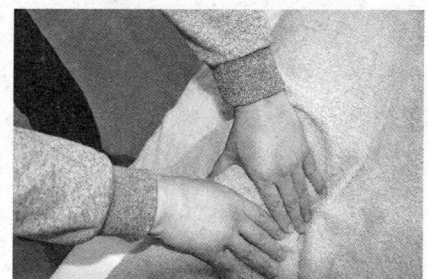

图 11-7-6　按揉足三里等

(2) 两手掌根相对,由上而下按压股前部。双手拿股四头肌(图 11-7-7);以掌跟按揉两侧膝眼。以拇指分别点按膝眼。以掌心吸附于髌骨,运用腕部活动,使髌骨进行小幅度的环形运动(图 11-7-8);以中指勾揉委中穴、承山穴(图 11-7-9);左手握受术者左踝关节,右手扶其左膝,使之屈膝屈髋,以髋关节为轴心,进行水平方向的内外摇旋数次(图 11-7-10);以其膝关节为轴心,进行垂直方向的内外摇旋数次(图 11-7-11);受术者直腿,整复师左手握住其左脚,右手握住左足跟,先拔伸足踝关节,并在此基础上以踝关节为轴心,进行小幅度的内外摇旋(图 11-7-12);

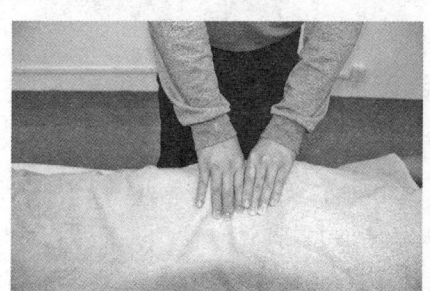

图 11-7-7　拿股四头肌

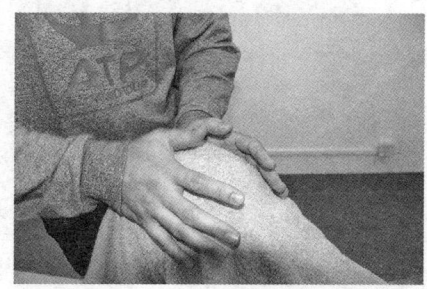

图 11-7-8　掌按揉膝眼

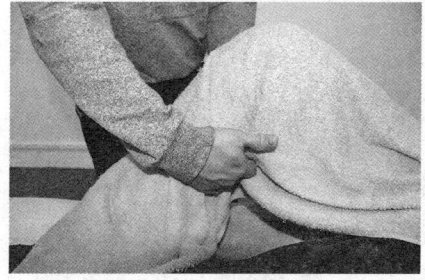

图 11-7-9　指勾揉委中穴等

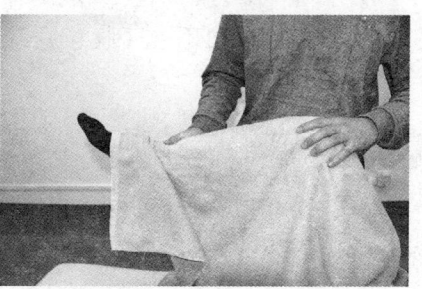

图 11-7-10　摇旋踝关节

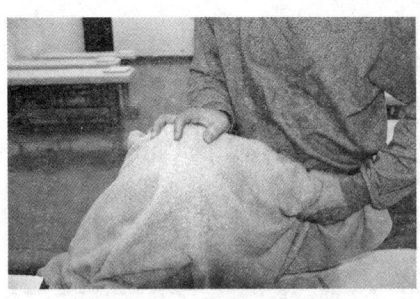
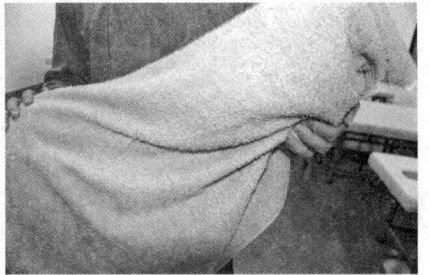

图 11-7-11　摇旋膝关节　　　　　图 11-7-12　小幅度摇旋踝关节

（3）两手掌夹住患肢，自上而下搓揉下肢，反复数次（图 11-7-13）；左手握受术者踝关节，右手置于其膝关节，将下肢轻快的反复屈伸数次（图 11-7-14）；左膝抵住受术者右腿足跟，左手握住左脚，右手握住左足跟，向后用力，逐渐牵拉，拔伸下肢踝、膝、髋关节及肌群（图 11-7-15）；左手握住左脚，右手握住左足跟，使大腿小幅度的外展，对下肢进行上下抖动（图 11-7-16）。

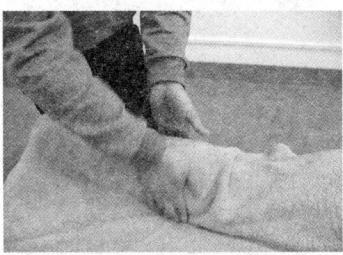

图 11-7-13　搓揉下肢　　　　　图 11-7-14　屈伸下肢

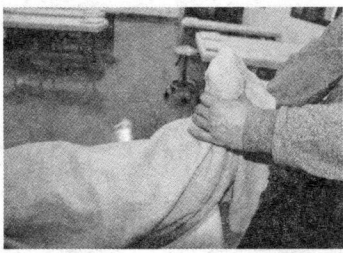
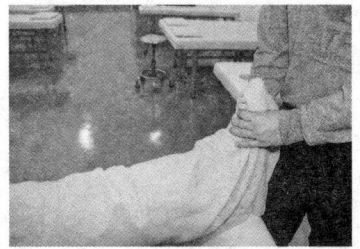

图 11-7-15　拔伸下肢　　　　　图 11-7-16　抖动下肢

穴位与主治

足三里：由外膝眼向下量 4 横指，在腓骨与胫骨之间，由胫骨旁量 1 横指。主治，下肢痹痛、肠胃病、虚劳消瘦。

阳陵泉：位于小腿外侧，当腓骨小头前下方凹陷处。主治，下肢痿痹、膝膑肿痛等下肢、膝关节疾患。

三阴交：在小腿内侧，当足内踝尖上 3 寸，胫骨内侧缘后方。主治，腹痛、腹胀、腹泻、经痛、月经不调、遗精、遗尿、失眠、神经衰弱。

8. 踝关节整复手法

(1) 抵摇踝关节

右踝关节不适的受术者仰卧于整复床上，足踝位于床外，膝下置一枕，让膝关节微屈，使小腿及足部放松，呈垂松状态（图11-8-1）。整复师立于受术者患足前方。

整复师一手掌心托受术者足跟，拇指按压于踝，一手持足掌（图11-8-2）；整复师一手掌心托足跟，拇指抵踝，一手持足掌，双手对称微微用力，沿踝关节面进行牵伸、摇转（图11-8-3）；注意：先对患侧对侧边进行抵旋摇转，再处理患侧（图11-8-4，11-8-5）。

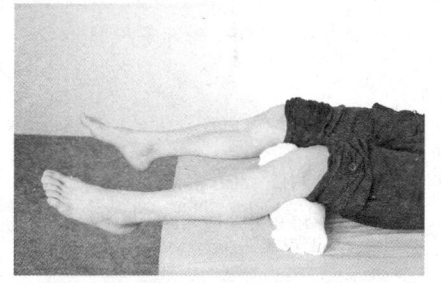

图11-8-1 抵摇踝关节

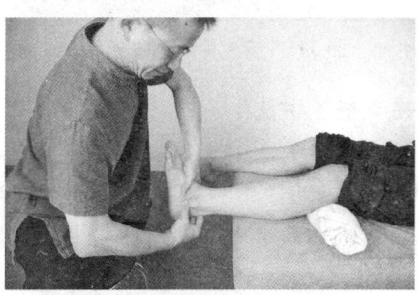

图11-8-2 抵摇踝关节

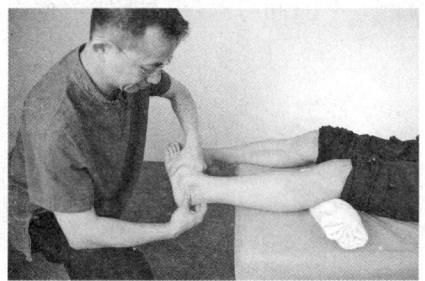

图11-8-3 抵摇踝关节

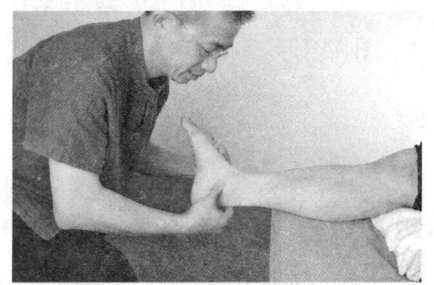

图11-8-4 抵摇踝关节

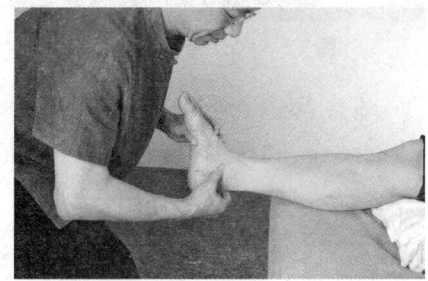

图11-8-5 抵摇踝关节

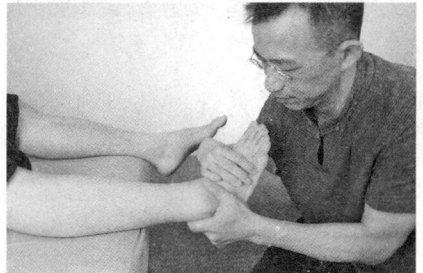

图11-8-6 牵伸踝关节

(2) 牵伸踝关节

右踝关节受不适的受术者端坐于椅子上，膝下或小腿下置支架，使腿部放松；或仰卧于整复床上，足踝悬于床外；整复师位于受术者患足前方。

整复师左手抓住患侧脚跟，右手抓握住患侧脚掌（图11-8-6）；整复师双手同时用力向后，逐渐牵拉、拔伸踝关节，使其放松；整复师摇晃受术者足踝使其放松下来以后，右手压脚掌使其背伸（图11-8-7）；在保持背伸状态下牵伸足跟，同时让脚背屈（图11-8-8）；接着放松力量使其复位。

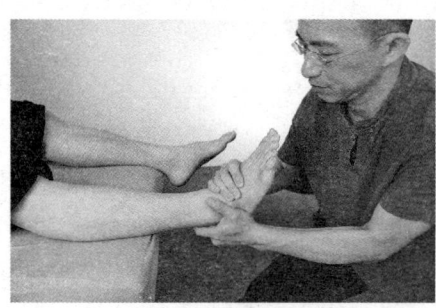
图 11-8-7 牵伸踝关节

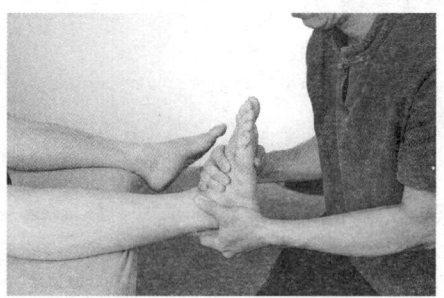
图 11-8-8 牵伸踝关节

9. 膝关节整复手法

（1）牵抵手法

右膝关节受伤的受术者体位仰卧于整复床上，整复师位于受术者患足侧。整复师左手抵患肢髌骨，右手握患肢小腿下端（图 11-9-1）；让膝关节屈伸，进行抵定与牵拉运动，调整髌骨位置。牵抵手法调整髌骨分以下几类：

上调髌骨：若患肢髌骨下移，调髌骨向上。整复师以虎口或拇指指腹抵住髌骨下缘（图 11-9-2）。整复师牵拉患肢，使患肢做膝关节屈伸的动作，同时以虎口或拇指指腹向上推髌骨，使其复位（图 11-9-3）。

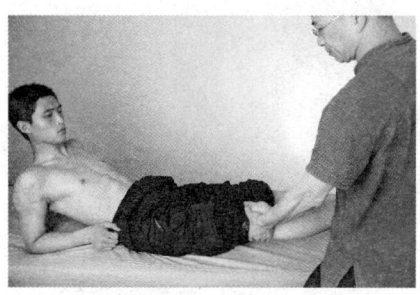
图 11-9-1 牵抵手法

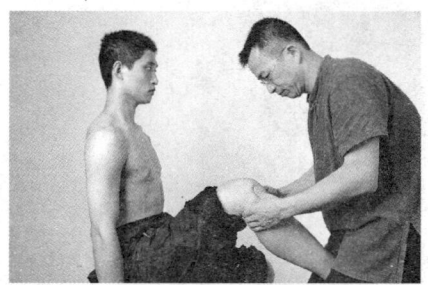
图 11-9-2 牵抵手法

下调髌骨：若患肢髌骨上移，调髌骨向下。整复师以拇指指腹抵住髌骨上缘（图 11-9-4）。整复师牵拉患肢，使患肢做膝关节屈伸的动作，同时以拇指指腹向下推髌骨，使其复位（图 11-9-5）。

其它：视需求，抵住髌骨不同角度位置进行调整。

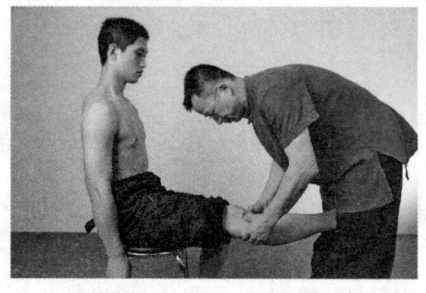
图 11-9-3 牵抵手法

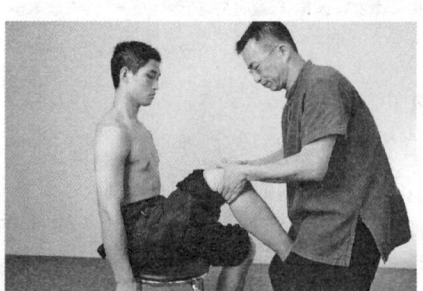
图 11-9-4 牵抵手法

(2) 腓骨上端调整法

右膝关腓骨关节不适、腓骨头上端按压时游动不固定的受术者仰卧于整复床上,整复师体位:位于受术者患足侧。

整复师左手持患足,右手虎口置于患足膝关节(图 11-9-6);整复师右手外旋受术者足踝,左手食指、中指压抵腓骨头上端,使其固定(图 11-9-7);整复师伸展受术者右足,使其直膝、屈膝,反复数次以达到固定的效果(图 11-9-8)。

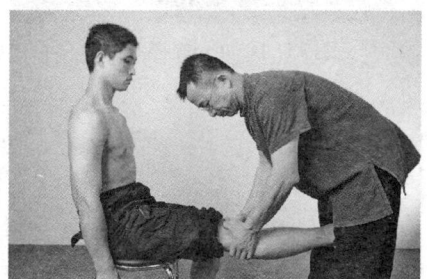

图 11-9-5　牵抵手法

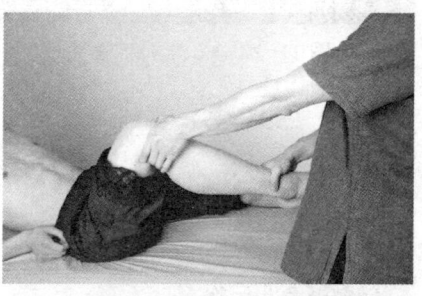

图 11-9-6　腓骨上端调整法

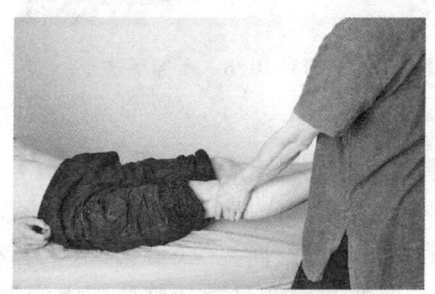

图 11-9-7　腓骨上端调整法

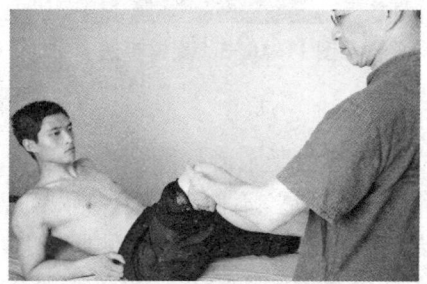

图 11-9-8　腓骨上端调整法

10. 髋关节整复手法

(1) 旋摇手法

右髋关节不适的受术者仰卧于整复床上,整复师位于受术者患足侧。

受术者右腿屈膝,整复师右手握住患肢踝部,左手放在患侧膝盖上;开始先使髋关节屈曲、内收、内旋,伸展外侧肌群,使股骨头离开髂骨(图 11-10-1 至图 11-10-3);然后将关节外旋、外展、伸直,伸展内侧肌群,使股骨头滑入髋臼(图 11-10-4,图 11-10-5);反复进行此屈膝旋摇髋关节动作数次,放松髋关节软组织及股内外侧肌群。

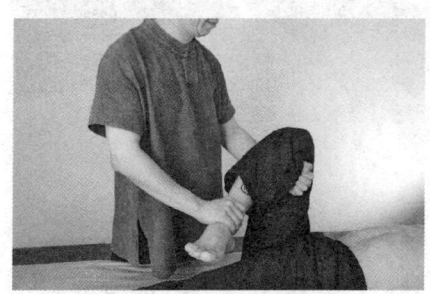

图 11-10-1　旋摇手法

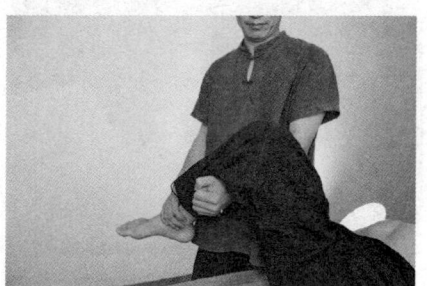

图 11-10-2　旋摇手法

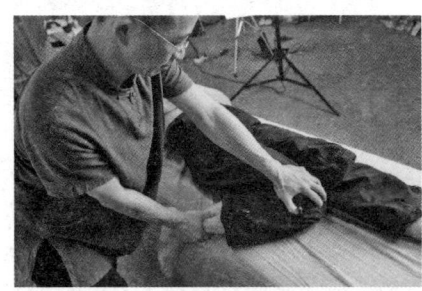

图 11-10-3 旋摇手法

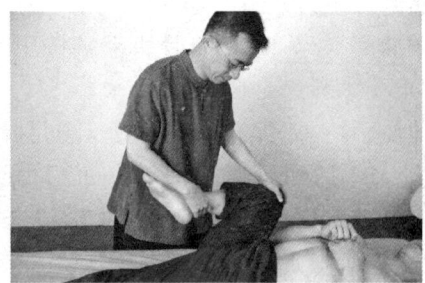

图 11-10-4 旋摇手法

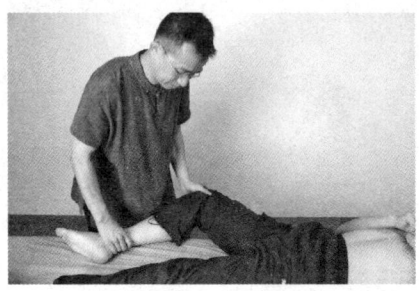

图 11-10-5 旋摇手法

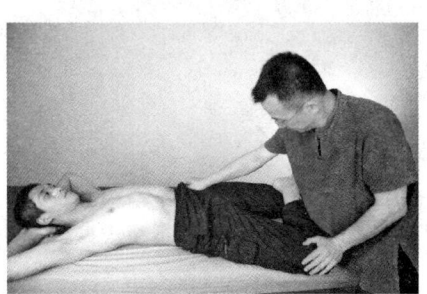

图 11-10-6 压伸手法

(2) 压伸手法

右髋关节不适的受术者仰卧于整复床上,整复师位于受术者患足侧。

将关节外旋、外展,不伸直,置患侧踝于健侧膝关节近大腿处,整复师右手固定健侧髋骨,左手按压患侧膝关节,伸展股内侧肌,使股骨头滑入髋臼而复位(图 11-10-6);亦可以轻轻摆荡的手法反复压伸膝关节与股内侧肌,同时曲髋使患侧足踝从健侧腿上慢慢滑落,渐次的伸展股内侧肌,使股骨头滑入髋臼而复位。

11. 躯干放松操作程序

(1) 项部放松操作

受术者俯卧位,整复师左侧站位。

拇指按揉项部:以两手拇指交替按揉项部两侧肌肉和项韧带,沿风池→肩井,风府→大椎两线路上下往返操作。先以右手拇指按揉右项,再以左手按揉左项(图 11-11-1)。

拿项部:以右手三指或四指捏拿项部两侧肌群(图 11-11-2)。

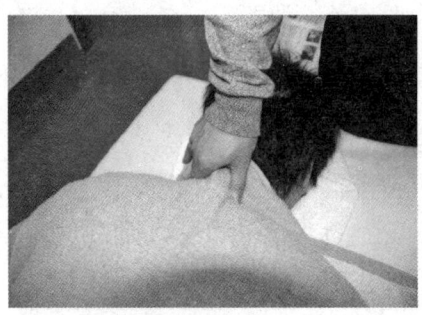

图 11-11-1 项部放松

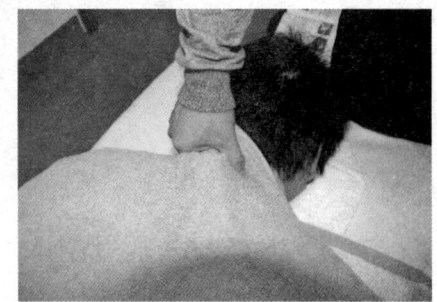

图 11-11-2 项部放松

弹拨颈项部两侧大筋：以两手拇指交替做与颈项部两侧筋肉纤维方向垂直的来回拨动，上下往返数遍（图11-11-3）。

按揉风池、后脑枕部：整复师以单手拇指和食指或双手拇指按揉风池穴，接着向两侧后脑枕部按揉（图11-11-4）。

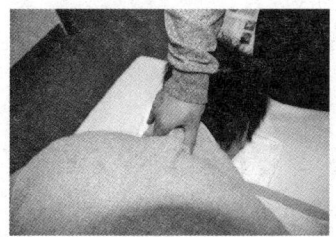
图11-11-3　项部放松

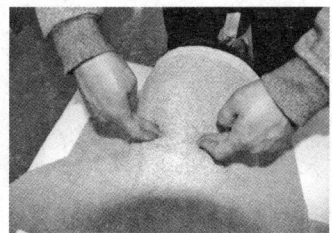
图11-11-4　项部放松

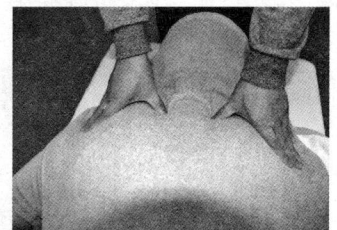
图11-11-5　项部放松

指压项肩部：以双手拇指从胸椎正中向两侧按压冈上窝斜方肌；由内向外，分压6点（图11-11-5）。

拿肩井、勾揉肩井、叩击肩井：以双手拿两侧肩井斜方肌（图11-11-6）。两手二指或三指分别勾揉两侧肩井穴（图11-11-7）。以双拳叩击肩胛上部，颈项部两侧肌肉（图11-11-8）。

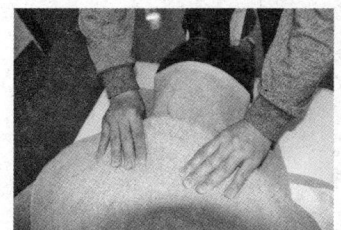
图11-11-6　项部放松

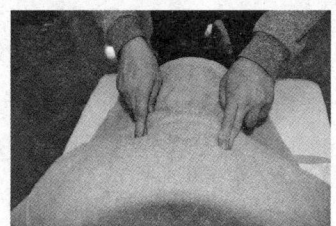
图11-11-7　项部放松

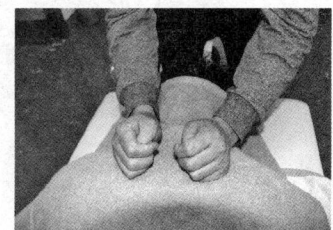
图11-11-8　项部放松

穴位与主治

风府：在项部，当后发际正中直上1寸，枕外隆凸直下，两侧斜方肌之间凹陷中。主治头痛、眩晕、项强、中风、癫狂、痴呆、咽喉肿痛、失音。

大椎：在后正中在线，第七颈椎棘突下凹陷中。主治头项强痛、热病、咳嗽、气喘、肩部肌肉痉挛、颈椎病、落枕、感冒等。

风池：在项后，与风府穴相平，当胸锁乳突肌与斜方肌上端之间的凹陷中取穴。主治落枕、肩周炎、中风后遗症、足跟痛。

（2）腰背部放松操作

受术者俯卧位，整复师左侧站位。

撑压肩髋、撑压脊柱：以两手掌分置于肩背部和对侧髂骨部，同时对称用力向外向下，两侧撑压腰背部数遍（图11-11-9）；整复师右手抵住骶骨，左手抵住上胸段脊柱，同时对称用力向外向下，两侧撑压脊柱数遍（图11-11-10）；

掌揉腰背部：双手迭掌按揉脊柱两侧竖脊肌，与脊柱平行自上而下螺旋形移动，左右各数遍（图 11-11-11）；

按揉华陀夹脊穴及膀胱经：以单手拇指或叠指按揉背部脊柱两侧华陀夹脊穴及膀胱经；先是距中线旁开 0.5 寸之华陀夹脊穴，次是距中线旁开 1.5 寸之膀胱经第 1 侧线，最后是距中线旁开 3 寸之膀胱经第 2 侧线；从上往下操作（图 11-11-12）；

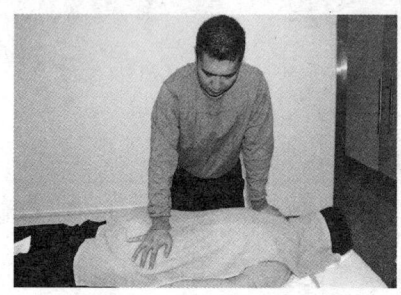

图 11-11-9　腰背部放松

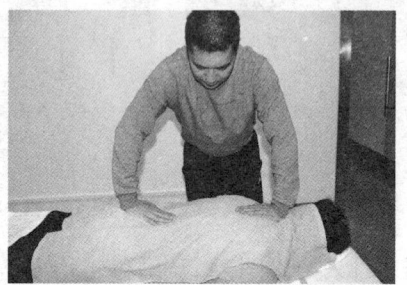

图 11-11-10　腰背部放松

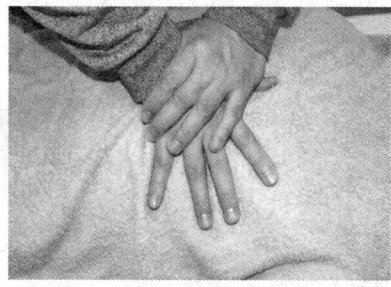

图 11-11-11　腰背部放松

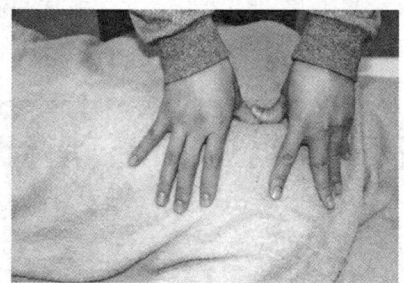

图 11-11-12　腰背部放松

掌按腰背部：两手掌根相对，由上而下按压脊柱两侧背腰部（图 11-11-13）；

指压华陀夹脊穴及膀胱经：以双手拇指同时按压背部脊柱两侧华陀夹脊穴及膀胱经；先是华陀夹脊穴，次是膀胱经第 1 侧线，最后是膀胱经第 2 侧线；从上往下操作（图 11-11-14）；

掌按脊柱：双手叠掌按压胸、腰椎和骶椎（图 11-11-15）；

弹拨背部华陀夹脊穴及膀胱经：用双手拇指叠指、肘尖或凤眼拳、象鼻拳弹拨背部脊柱两侧华陀夹脊穴及膀胱经；先是华陀夹脊穴，次是膀胱经第 1 侧线，最后是膀胱经第 2 侧线；从上往下操作（图 11-11-16）；

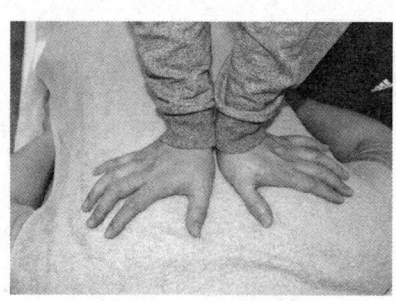

图 11-11-13　腰背部放松

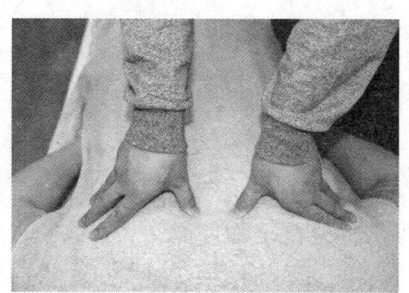

图 11-11-14　腰背部放松

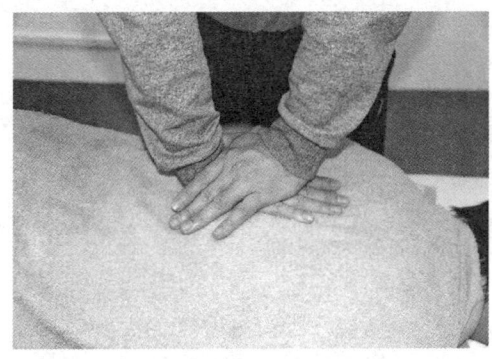
图 11-11-15　腰背部放松

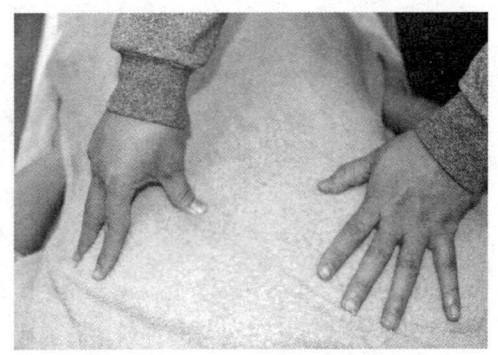
图 11-11-16　腰背部放松

掌推腰背部、肘推华佗夹脊穴：一手掌按于上胸段，另一手掌根着力，由上而下直推督脉以及两侧膀胱经，各数遍（图 11-11-17）；以肘推华佗夹脊穴，由上而下数遍（图 11-11-18）；

横擦腰骶部：全掌横擦腰骶部命门、腰阳关、八髎诸穴（图 11-11-19）；

叩击背部：双手握拳轻轻叩击背部，上下移动数遍（图 11-11-20）；

掌拍腰背部：双手虚掌拍击背部，上下移动数遍（图 11-11-21）；

搓腰部：两手夹住受术者腰部两侧，相对用力进行搓揉，并在一定范围内进行上下移动（图 11-11-22）。

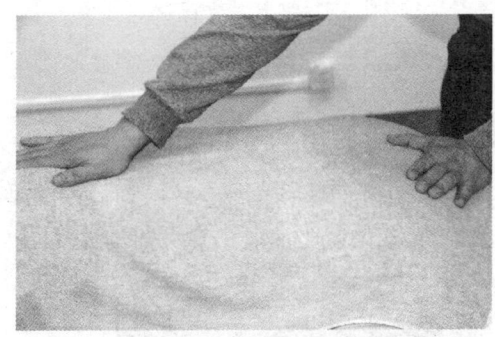
图 11-11-17　腰背部放松

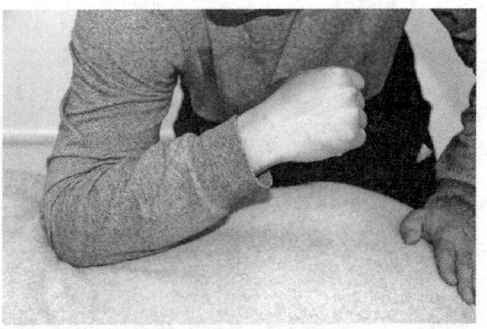
图 11-11-18　腰背部放松

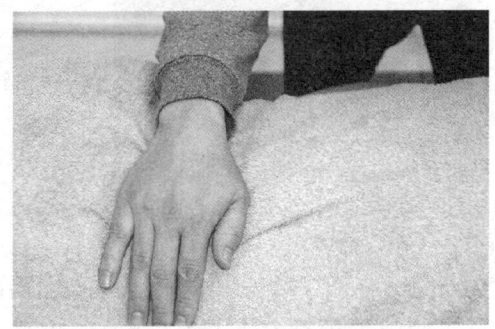
图 11-11-19　腰背部放松

图 11-11-20　腰背部放松

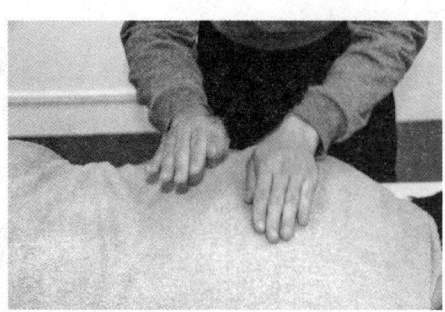
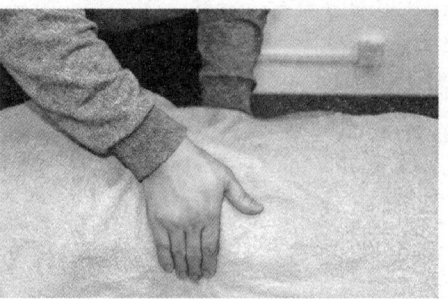

图 11-11-21　腰背部放松　　　图 11-11-22　腰背部放松

12. 颈项部整复手法

（1）摇颈部

受术者坐位，整复师位于受术者身后，一手扶住受术者头顶后部，另一手托住其下颌部。

两手臂协调运动，使受术者头颈部做顺时针和逆时针环转摇动，反复摇转数次，做被动的和缓回旋运动，使其颈项部放松；摇转次第为：若受术者前屈受限，先采后伸位摇颈（图11-12-1）；一边摇动，一边由后伸位转换到前屈位。接下来，再采前屈位摇颈（图11-12-2）。反之亦同。

摇颈时，若受术者左转受限，先右转摇颈；接下来，再左转摇颈。反之异同。共做四种方位的摇颈。

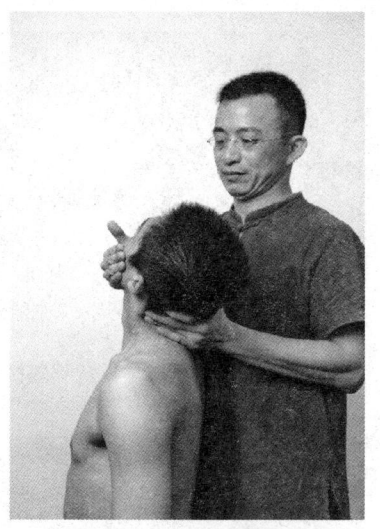
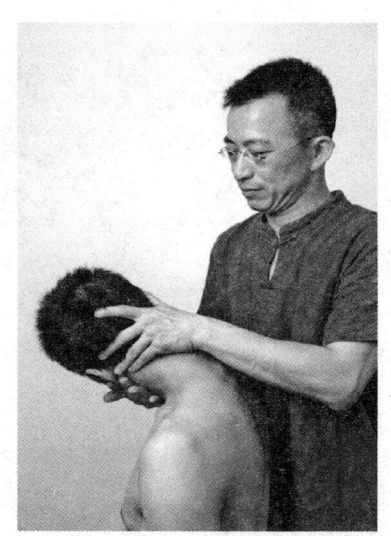

图 11-12-1　摇颈部　　　图 11-12-2　摇颈部

（2）拖抬颈椎

受术者仰躺，整复师立于受术者头部。

双手食、中二指托住受术者颈椎间关节，使之充分上抬（图11-12-3）；依次向上向后，圆弧形拖抬颈椎关节，延展颈部肌群；依次向上向后，圆弧形拖抬颈椎关节，并前后扭动以调动颈椎，达到关节复位目的。

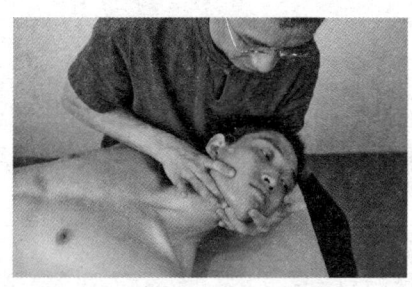
图 11-12-3　拖抬颈椎

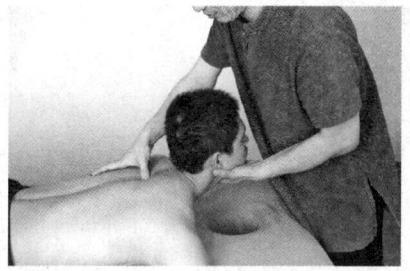
图 11-13-1　胸部整复

13. 胸部整复手法

（1）侧颈分压法：开三线

上胸段与颈部相关肌群紧张、上胸段胸椎小关节紊乱的受术者俯卧于整复床上，整复师立在床头前。

右手指按住患侧肌肉纠结点，左手拖住受术者的下巴，往上抬至极限（图 11-13-1）；待受术者呼气放松时，顺势将头部右侧摆，左颊置于整复床。注意，为脸颊部贴床面，非头侧部（图 11-13-2）；左手掌固定在被操作者右上耳处，右手按于患侧肌肉纠结点，发劲分压（图 11-13-3）；宜先延展健侧，再延展患侧。

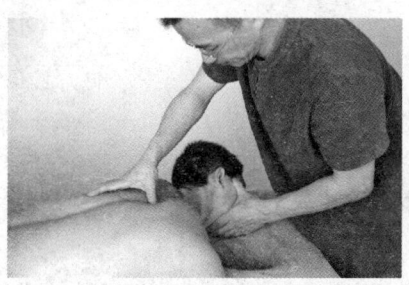
图 11-13-2　胸部整复

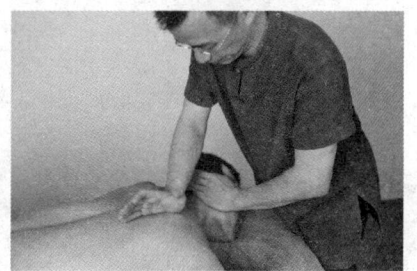
图 11-13-3　胸部整复

（2）托胸开胸法

胸肋小关节紊乱的受术者坐于整复床上，两腿伸直；整复师单足跪蹲立于受术者身后，受术者双手十指交叉抱住脖子（图 11-13-4）；整复师两手从受术者大臂和小臂之间伸过去，两手托住受术者肩胛骨部位，然后跪腿垫在患者背后胸椎上，让受术者躺在整复师大腿上（图 11-13-5）；待受术者吐气放松时，顺势托胸挑掌发劲，打开胸廓，调整胸肋关节。

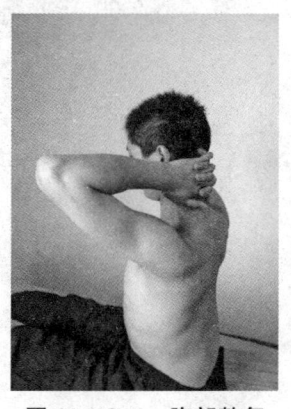
图 11-13-4　胸部整复

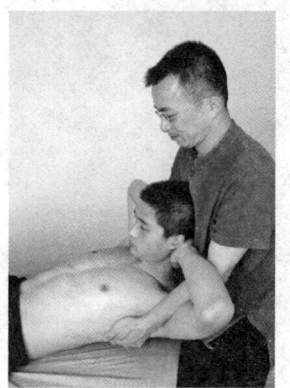
图 11-13-5　胸部整复

14. 腰部整复手法

（1）腰部牵伸斜板法

腰左侧有患的受术者仰卧、屈左腿、右腿伸直，整复师立于受术者右侧（健侧）（图11-14-1）。

受术者右侧躺，右手身于整复床外；整复师左手牵引受术者右手，右腿压顶受术者左膝腿，右手小臂内侧缘固定在受术者左臀部，右手掌指定位于患侧腰部；牵伸受术者右手、推移左膝、固定臀部，以延展患侧腰部（图11-14-2）；

左手固定在受术者左肩，右手小臂内侧缘固定在受术者左臀部，右手掌指定位于患侧胸腰交接处（图11-14-3）；左右手对称用力，摆荡受术者身体，依次放松腰椎（图11-14-4）；一边摆荡放松受术者，一边慢慢右手离开受术者腰椎；在摆荡过程中以左手推受术者肩部，小臂扳受术者臀部，使患侧腰部两端延展到极限（图11-14-5）；导引受术者吐气放松，感觉受术者身体放松以后，顺势发劲，两手同时作相反方向旋转并延展推动，使其腰部肌肉伸展，腰椎复位（图11-14-6）。建议，先处理健侧，再处理患侧。

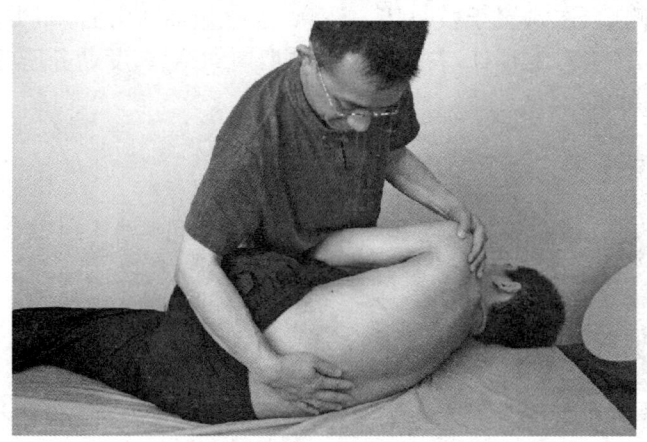
图11-14-1　腰部整复

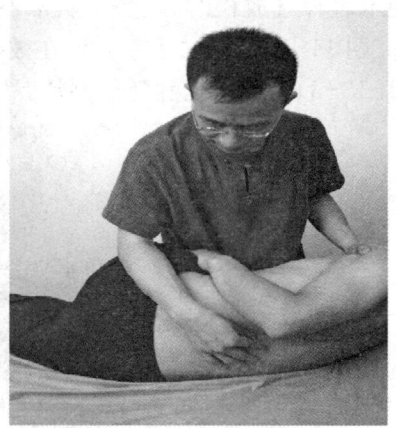
图11-14-2　腰部整复

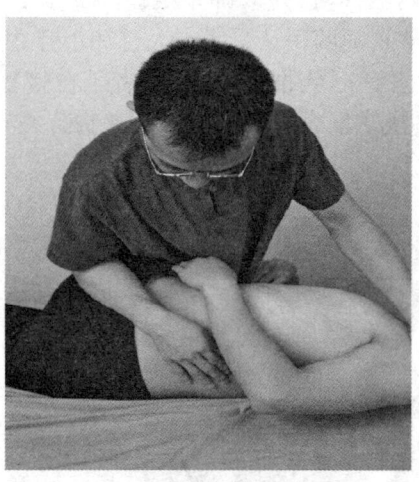
图11-14-3　腰部整复

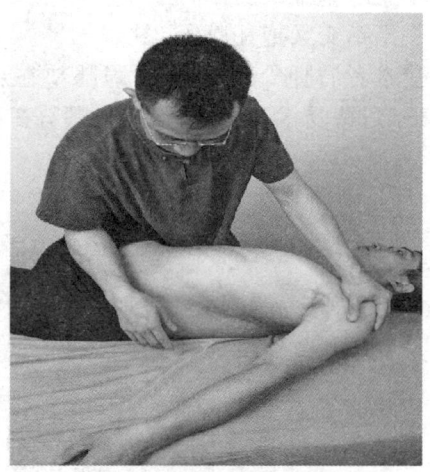
图11-14-4　胸部整复

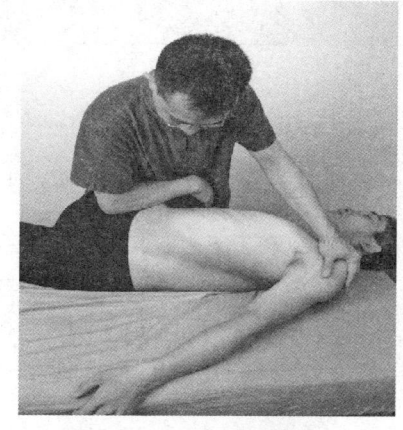
图 11-14-5　胸部整复

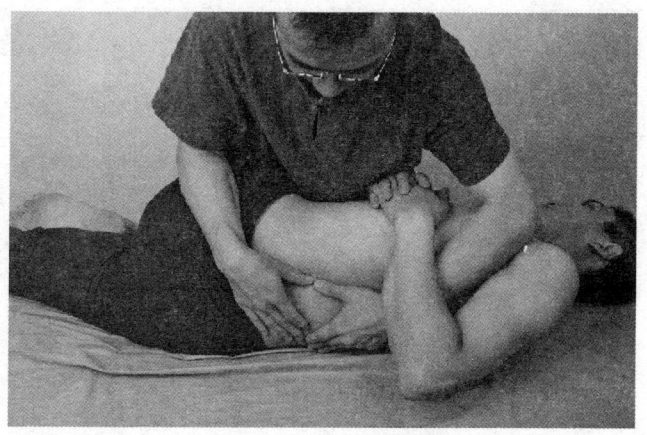
图 11-14-6　胸部整复

（2）腰椎后身扳法

腰左侧有患的受术者俯卧、腿伸直，整复师立于受术者左侧（患侧）。

左手掌指固定被操作者左侧腰椎，右手循被操作者右大腿内侧将受术者右腿抱起；左手固定，右手向左侧扳动，双边对称用力，调整腰椎（图 11-14-7，11-14-8）。

建议，宜先处理健侧，再处理患侧。

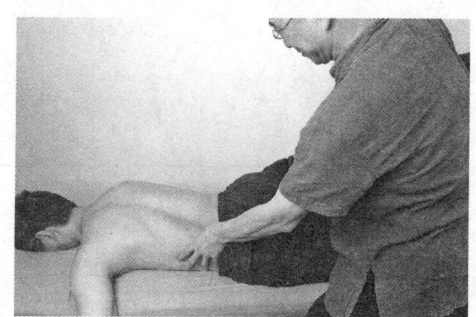
图 11-14-7　腰椎后身板法

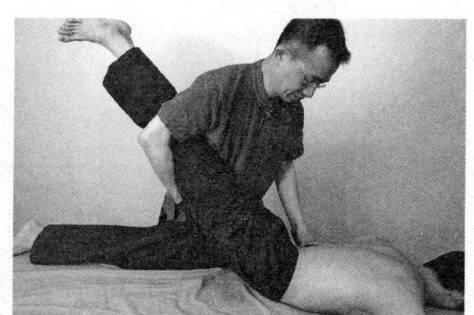
图 11-14-8　腰椎后身板法

15. 全身整复操作程序

肩部与上肢部放松（坐姿）→上肢整复：调整肩、肘、腕（坐姿）→项部放松（俯卧位）→腰背部放松（俯卧位）→下肢后部放松（俯卧位）→下肢前部放松（仰卧位）→下肢整复：调整足、膝、髋（仰卧位）→躯干整复：调整胸、腰、颈（仰卧位）。

（二）学习计划

项目	内　容
前期准备	学习武功整复术需有"武术技术的底基、健身气功、穴位知识、指力"等前期准备。 1. 武术技术的底基：发劲能力、身体感知与控制能力。 2. 健身气功：身体感知与控制能力。 3. 穴位知识：穴位定位、经络走向、肌肉位置。 4. 劲力：指力、掌力、握力

(续表)

项目	内　容
学习进度	1. 学习顺序 (1) 学习基本手法,如按摩推拿、拍打、抖震、摇扳…… (2) 知晓穴位知识、经络走向、人体结构知识,如肩井、委中、膀胱经、髂腰肌、阔筋膜…… (3) 学习不同身体部位放松的操作程序,如肩部、上肢、下肢后部、下肢前部…… (4) 学习不同身体部位整复手法,如肩部的挺胸展臂法、高低调整法,胸部的侧颈分压法、托胸开胸法……
学习进度	2. 教学安排,本课程分20次课学完,每次三节,每节45分钟。 整复功法课程介绍。 基础放松手法。 上肢放松操作程序。 肩关节整复手法。 肘关节整复手法。 腕关节整复手法。 上肢整复操作程序练习。 下肢放松操作程序。 踝关节整复手法。 膝关节整复手法
学习进度	髋关节整复手法。 下肢整复操作程序练习。 躯干放松操作程序。 颈项部整复手法。 胸部整复手法。 腰部整复手法。 躯干整复操作程序练习。 全身放松及整复操作程序。 全身放松与整复操作程序练习。 考核

(三) 技术体验

内容	要求
动作质量	1. 动作要有节奏与韵律。 2. 操作时手掌紧贴体表,用力平稳,移动缓慢均匀。着力点要吸定,用力由轻到重,移动时逐点慢移。 3. 拍打注意肩肘腕的放松与力量渗透度的关系。 4. 抖振注意过程中,身体的松紧度与幅度、频率的关系。 5. 一指禅推法注意沉肩、坠肘、悬腕、掌虚、指实。 6. 操作时搓揉要快,移动要慢。 7. 弹拨大筋时指下应有弹动感,在体表不能有摩擦;压力根据受术者情况与耐受程度而定,适可而止。 8. 无肌肉覆盖处,容易损伤,手法宜轻柔。 9. 腘窝部以及小腿后侧宜用力轻柔缓和。 10. 应避开大腿内侧中上部的敏感部位。 11. 按压膑骨动作柔和灵活,力量由轻到重,切忌暴力;使膑骨活动幅度逐渐增大。 12. 抖下肢频率略低于抖上肢,幅度稍大于抖上肢。 13. 扳法不可用暴力,重点在以摆荡方式放松肌肉关节,多做延展,少过度扭转。过程中,若受术者疼痛不能忍受,不宜继续进行操作。 14. 施术时,发劲要短、脆、有力;否则仅为伸展关节肌肉,达不到打开关节间隙的效果

(续表)

内容	要求
手感规范	1. 推法：推动过程中注意被推部位肌肉强度变化，是否有纠结点；推力要均匀，要能推压过纠紧的肌肉。 2. 拿法：注意所拿捏部位的肌理，是否有条索状纠结；拿捏时用力要对称，紧压住肌肉条索。 3. 按柔时，体验身体重心变化产生之力量变化。 4. 滚法：感受操作时来自上体前倾及沉肩坠肘时对手法的压力。 5. 拔伸法：感知被拔伸部位肌肉的伸长及关节的间隙打开。 6. 摇扳法：感知受术者关节在不同角度时肌肉松紧状态；觉察受术者肌肉与关节生理极限范围。
动作配合	1. 按法：按压过程要配合受术者呼吸，逐渐用力向下按压；注意所按压部位的肌理松紧变化，调整施力及按压位置；力量要能直接按压在紧张的肌肉或肌肉纠结点上。 2. 摩法：注意按与摩两种力量方式的结合，并配合受术者呼吸，碾压在紧张的肌肉或肌肉纠结点上。 3. 掌揉背部时应带动受术者身体同步轻轻晃动，有利于全身放松。 4. 指压或掌压背部时手臂伸直，先将重心逐步移到手指或手掌上，在重心离开手指或手掌后，再向下移动；第1遍宜轻，使受术者对按压的力量和节奏有所适应。 5. 按揉穴位，以受术者感觉酸胀为；操作时力量由轻到重，再由重到轻。 6. 整复手法需注意配合受术者呼吸，俟受术者吐气到尽，肩、背、腰皆放松时方能施术
处理程序	1. 先放松，后整复，继而再进行放松，才能达到最佳效果。 2. 放松次第为"先肩及上肢，次为颈胸腰，最后为腿"，即"先坐姿，继而俯卧姿，最后仰卧姿"。 3. 整复次第为"先上肢，后下肢及躯干"。例如，调整肩关节上连颈项，下连上肢，前连胸，后接背；需先调整肩关节后，才能调整颈、胸，或肘、腕；"腰背委中求"，先处理下肢再处理腰背部。

三、总结

1. 武功整复术是武术家对身体的整复术，需以武术为技术基底，以徒手疗法及健身气功疗法为主要手段，而调整身体、处理身体失调的方法。

2. 武功整复术需以武术劲力、动作控制、动作感知等技术作为基底，掌握肌筋膜放松与骨骼关节整复等徒手疗法，了解健身气功各动作与身体活动的相对应关系，可调整肩肘腕、髋膝足、颈胸腰等身体运动系统的失调状态。

3. 武术整复术的基本方式手法有"推、拿、按、摩、拍打、抖震、摇扳"，放松不同身体部位具有不同的操作程序，整复不同身体部位也具有不同的手法，要注意辩证施治。

4. 武功整复术应知晓穴位知识、人体结构知识。

四、延伸学习

1. 武功整复术以武术劲力为基础，需要进一步学习南拳等武术拳种的发劲技巧。例如，利用桥马发出短劲，以便在受术者关节角度不变的情况下有效地进行微距离拉伸、打开受术者关节、延展受限肌筋膜。

2. 武功整复时的身体姿态与武术要求一致，需要你在太极拳等拳种锻炼中不断调整武功整复时"沉肩坠肘、松腰坐胯、尾闾中正、虚领顶劲、周身中正"的状态。

3. 武功整复术目标是将身体调整到原先自然状态，因此需要你不仅具有良好的生理解剖知识基础，而且也需要你在武术和气功锻炼中感知自身的结构与机能、在推手等锻炼中提高对他人肢体动态的觉察能力。

4. 学会本课程后，你可进一步学习完整版武功整复学教材，也可学习保健按摩师教材（考取保健按摩师证照），还可以阅读有关肢体疗法（Body work）或身心学（Somatics）的相关资料。

五、思考与练习题

1. 武功整复术的基础放松手法有哪些？
2. 上肢放松的操作程序是什么？如何放松下肢和躯干？
3. 如何整复肩关节、腕关节、踝关节、颈项部？

六、参考文献

[1] Feldenkrais,M. 从动中觉醒[M]. 台北:世茂出版社,1998.
[2] Feldenkrais,M. 从身态改变心态[M]. 台北:世茂出版社,1998.
[3] Knaster,M. 肢体疗法百科[M]. 台北:生命潜能出版社,1999.
[4] Marian Wolfe Dixon. 肌筋膜按摩疗法[M]. 天津:天津科技翻译出版公司,2008.
[5] 金宏柱. 推拿学基础[M]. 上海:上海中医药大学,2000.
[6] 李志明. 孙禄堂拳学的身心教育观[M]. 台北:阿含文化有限公司,2003.
[7] 李志明. 武术身心整复学说研究[D]. 南京中医药大学博士后出站报告,2009.
[8] 玛丽.B.布朗,斯蒂芬.J.西蒙森. 按摩疗法导论[M]. 天津:天津科技翻译出版公司,2006.
[9] 王震,李志明. 武功整复学[M]. 上海:复旦大学出版社,2012.
[10] 萧天石. 真本易筋经、秘本洗髓经合刊——增附:述古堂钱遵王藏经写本[M]. 台北:自由出版社,1992.
[11] 詹姆斯.H.克莱,戴维.M.庞兹. 基础临床按摩疗法[M]. 天津:天津科技翻译出版公司,2006.
[12] 周信文,周哲敏. 保健按摩师(初级).[M]. 2版. 上海:中国劳动社会保障出版社,2010.
[13] 周信文,周哲敏. 保健按摩师(中级).[M]. 2版. 上海:中国劳动社会保障出版社,2009.

第十二章

南狮运动

一、南狮运动概述

南狮是起源并流行于中国南方一带的舞狮形式,是集音乐、舞蹈、编织、刺绣、绘画为一身,通过二人首尾配合模仿狮子形神动作,既表形又寓意的民间艺术和体育活动,分为佛山狮和鹤山狮两大流派。

> **舞狮的起源**
>
> 古代中国并没有狮子这种动物,最早由西亚和中亚经丝绸之路张骞出使西域打通汉朝与西域各国交往后,狮子才得以进入中原。起初舞狮只是简单地模仿狮子的动作,是配以龟兹乐的一种舞蹈,而表达人们对兽中之王的膜拜,唐代在中原地区盛行。
>
> **舞狮的发展**
>
> 舞狮源于生活,源于民间,1994 年原国家体育运动委员会正式将舞龙舞狮界定为体育竞赛项目,1995 年成立中国龙狮运动协会。1997 年 7 月,国际龙狮总会在马来西亚召开执委会和代表大会,正式决定将国际龙狮总会执委会秘书处迁至中国北京。2006 年 12 月在印度尼西亚举办的国际龙狮总会代表大会上决定,国际龙狮总会更名为国际龙狮运动联合会。截止目前,会员组织已经有 26 个国家和地区。与此同时,亚洲、欧洲和美洲也相应建立了自己的龙狮组织。

二、学习体验

(一) 动作说明

1. 握狮方法

(1) 双阳手:两手心朝上,两手虎口握于狮头两侧狮口连接处,其余四指托于狮口下端(图 12-1)。

(2) 双阴手:两手心朝下,两手虎口握于狮头两侧狮口连接处,食指握于狮口上端,其余三指托于狮口下端(图12-2)。

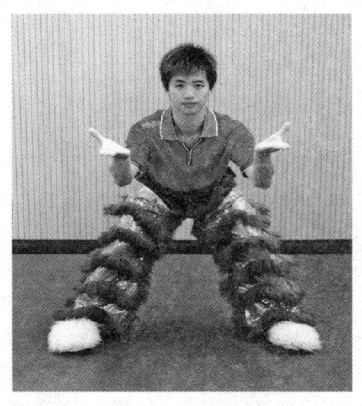
图12-1 双阳手

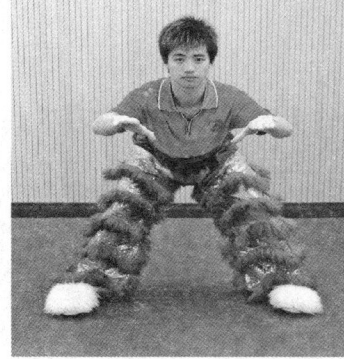
12-2 双阴手

图12-3 单握手

（3）单握手：单手手心朝上或朝下握于狮口连接处中端,拇指与其余四指分开(图12-3)。

（4）前后手：前手手心朝上托握于狮口连接处边端,后手握于狮头内横架(图12-4)。

（5）单阳握法：单手手心朝上握于狮口连接处中端,拇指与其余四指分开(图12-5)。

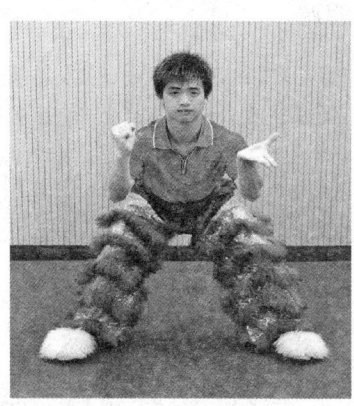
12-4 前后手

图12-5 单阳握法

2. 准备姿态
身体保持弯肘、弯腰、弯膝的"三弯姿态"(图12-1)。

3. 站立姿态
（1）上架站立(开立步、四平步、弓步、虚步)：一手握于狮头内握杆,一手手心朝上握于狮口处,狮口合闭,双手朝斜上方45°高举,狮头离开躯干,狮口与舞狮者额头平行,力达手腕左右平行短促转动(图12-6)。

（2）中架站立(开立步、四平步、弓步、虚步、左右麒麟步等)：双阳手或双阴手握于狮口连接处,背部贴于狮头内框中海绵保护垫处,手臂呈环抱形状支撑狮头,躯干前倾约40°(图12-7)。

（3）下架站立(开立步、四平步、弓步、跪马步、仆步等)：两人以仆步步型,狮头顺前腿方向平行于地面前后伸缩(图12-8)。

图 12-6　上架站　　　　　图 12-7　中架站

4. 步型、步法

（1）马步（大四平步）：两腿分立马步姿势，间距三脚半，两腿膝关节呈 135°弯屈，躯干前倾约 40°，抬头挺胸（图 12-9）。

（2）弓步：两腿前后站立，前腿膝关节呈 135 度弯屈，后腿伸直且脚掌扣于地面，躯干前倾约 40°，抬头挺胸（图 12-10）。

（3）铲步（仆步）：两腿分立，支撑腿全屈，臀部贴近支撑腿，前腿伸直且脚掌内扣于地面，躯干前倾约 40°，抬头挺胸（图 12-11）。

图 12-8　下架站

（4）探步（金鸡独立步）：单腿直立，支撑腿伸直，提膝腿呈 90°弯屈平行于腰部，立脚尖，躯干前倾约 40°，抬头挺胸（图 12-12）。

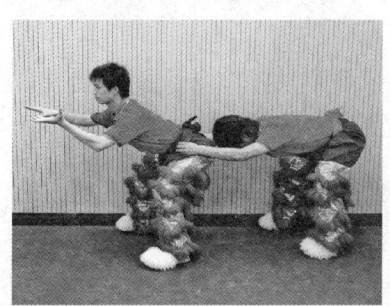
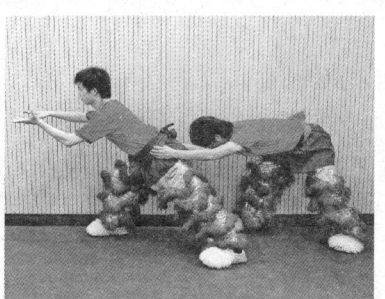

图 12-9　马步　　　　　　图 12-10　弓步

图 12-11　仆步　　　　图 12-12　金鸡独立　　　　图 12-13　跪步

（5）跪步：前腿屈膝跪于地面，后退呈 90°弯屈立于地面，躯干前倾约 40°，抬头挺胸（图

12-13)。

(6) 虚步：两腿前后分立，后支撑腿呈135°弯屈，前腿位于支撑腿前一脚处膝关节呈135°弯屈，重心在后支撑腿，躯干前倾约40°，抬头挺胸(图12-14)。

(7) 麒麟步：前腿屈膝跪于地面，后退呈90°弯屈立于地面，躯干前倾约40°，抬头挺胸(图12-15)。

(8) 插步：双腿交叉，单腿斜插于另一腿后，前腿呈约50°弯屈，后退伸直，脚尖朝前，躯干前倾约40°，抬头挺胸(图12-16)。

图 12-14　虚步

图 12-15　麒麟步

图 12-16　插步

5. 配合协助动作

(1) 配合上单腿：动作要领：狮尾握紧狮头腰带呈弓步姿势上举，狮头收腹上跳单腿落至狮尾髋关节与大腿连接处，脚掌外翻，悬空腿提膝，双手呈高架姿势，躯干正直(图12-17)。

(2) 配合上双腿：动作要领：狮头收腹上跳至狮尾髋关节与大腿连接处，两脚掌内扣或外翻，双手呈高架姿势，狮尾握紧狮头腰带呈马步姿势，躯干正直(图12-18)。

(3) 配合坐头：动作要领：狮尾握紧狮头腰带呈分腿姿势上举，狮头收腹上跳臀部落至狮尾头部，悬空腿弯屈，双手呈高架姿势，躯干正直(图12-19)。

图 12-17　配合上单腿

图 12-18　配合上双腿

图 12-19　配合坐头

（二）学习计划

项目	内 容
前期准备	1. 基本功 需具备身体柔韧、手臂力量、腰部力量、腿部力量、身体协调性、节奏感 2. 基本步 需学会"行礼步、两移步、马步（大四平步）、弓步、开合步、扑步（铲步）、麒麟步、跪步、虚步、独立步、小跑步、插步、跃步、探步、跳步"等基本动作
学习进度	1. 学习或教学的组合 组合动作一：行礼步——马步——两移步——插步——仆步 组合动作二：麒麟步——跃步——跳步——虚步 组合动作三：独立步——探步——跪步——小跑步 组合动作四：开合步——配合上单腿——配合上双腿——配合上头 2. 分教学三阶段 前期阶段：学习握狮方法的手型手法、站立姿态、步行步法 中期阶段：专项素质、配合动作、鼓乐节奏 后期阶段：步法路线、表演技巧

（三）技术体验

内容	要 求
动作规范	保持身形"三弯"，提高动作质量
动作配合	狮头狮尾的狮型配合要保持狮型完整，步型步法配合要协调一致，狮型动作配合要符合狮子形神，难度动作配合要运动连贯
狮的运动感	根据南狮运动规律要充分发挥想象模仿狮子的喜、怒、哀、乐、动、静、惊、疑，力争形态逼真、神态细腻

（四）文化体验

- **南狮"狮头"的黑、红、黄三种**

分别表示桃园三结义刘、关、张，而称之"刘备狮""关公狮""张飞狮"，的性格。其中，关公狮舞姿勇猛而雄伟，张飞狮动作粗犷好战，刘备狮则沉着刚健、威严有力。

- **南狮鼓乐**

由鼓、锣、钹构成，鼓发出"咚"音，锣发出"珰"音，钹发出"锵"音。

鼓以三星、五星、七星三种鼓法为主，钹为和音，锣为打点。

三音以鼓为主合奏发出轻、急、快、缓的韵律，而指挥舞狮节奏变化和动作转折。

- **南狮的形态动作、神态动作、难度动作**

形态动作是通过举、伸、握、摆等手法动作结合马步、弓步、虚步、麒麟步、独立步、跪步、等步法动作达到人狮合一的形态模仿过程。

神态动作是运用狮具中的口、眼、耳、尾来模仿狮子的睡、醒、醉、戏、望、惊恐、怀疑、试探等神态动作过程。

难度动作是运用抛腾、飞跃、转体、翻滚、立身、钳腰、挂桩等高难度技巧动作。

三、总结

1. 学习南狮运动初级动作和套路需掌握基本功和基本动作。
2. 南狮运动的技术由个人握狮方法、准备姿态、站立姿态、相关步型和步法,以及狮头和狮尾配合协助动作所组成。
3. 南狮运动要体现狮之形态、神态。

四、延伸学习

1. 在掌握本教学内容基础上,学习者可以根据个人构思进行"采青"套路编排。通过自己对舞狮的理解和套路所需表达的主题进行动作和套路创编,要求在创编过程中既要形似,更要神似。套路主题要富有积极健康的思想,同时要体现出狮子这种动物所包含的"威武""勇猛""矫健""多智"的形神表现,并且要符合狮子活动的逻辑。

2. 在掌握南狮基本动作和"醒狮出洞"套路后,可以开始学习南狮鼓乐配合。南狮鼓乐分为"鼓""锣""钹"三种,其中鼓为谱,锣为点,钹为合。首先学习鼓乐中的"擂、震、平、步、三、快、七"基本鼓点,然后根据舞狮动作进行合理配合练习。

五、思考与练习题

1. 中国舞狮的起源与"丝绸之路"的关系。
2. 中国南狮的分类。
3. 南狮运动的技术分类有哪些?
4. 南狮鼓乐的乐器构成有哪几种?

六、参考文献

[1] 陈耀佳. 南狮[M]. 广东:广东科技出版社,2007.
[2] 国际龙狮运动联合会. 国际舞龙舞狮竞赛规则[M]. 北京:人民体育出版社,2008.
[3] 黄益苏. 龙狮表演与竞赛[M]. 长沙:湖南文艺出版社,1999.
[4] 卫志强. 中国龙文化与龙运动[M]. 天津:天津古籍出版社,2003.
[5] 余汉桥. 中国舞龙舞狮运动现状及发展对策研究[D]. 武汉:武汉体育学院,2007.

 Chapter One

Introduction

1 Introduction

As one kind of sport and culture, wushu (known as Kungfu, or Gung fu, the same as below) has the history of thousands of years. It exists as both a way of traditional physical fitness and a carrier to express traditional culture for Chinese people. Since the 20th century, wushu being a sport has had sport competitions like World Wushu Championships, Wushu Competition in Asian Games, etc. In August, Beijing 2008 Wushu Competition was held during the period of Beijing Olympic Games. Competitive wushu had spread over 147 countries and regions according to the official website of International Wushu Association. Wushu has become one part of Chinese people's life both as a means for self-cultivation and a specific type of Chinese literature and films. Wushu spreads all over the world which not only benefits the physical and psychological health of the people in the world, but helps them know more about Chinese culture.

2 Learning experience

2.1 Directions

2.1.1 Wushu's Definition and features

(1) Definition

Wushu is defined as one kind of Chinese sports based on Chinese culture as its theoretical foundation, characterized by combat methods as basic content, combined with taolu (known as "routines", the same as below), combat, and skill (known as "Gung fu techniques", the same as below) as the major sport forms.

(2) Features

Wushu is characteristic of being "Chinese", traditional, cultural, combative, artistic and athletic.

a. Being "Chinese"

Being "Chinese" is the primary factor for wushu to exist as one part of Chinese culture and one of Chinese sports. Wushu's Chinese nature came into being with the unique culture feature during thousands of year of development, quite different from other similar sports. This makes Chinese wushu a symbol and also one window for foreigners to know about Chinese culture.

b. Being traditional

Being traditional (*Chuan Tong*), if explained from its two Chinese characters *Chuan Tong*, has two layers of meaning. The first meaning of "*Chuan*" lies in its inheritance. In the inheritance of generation after generation, wushu has experienced thousands of years of development. The second character "*Tong*" lies in wushu's unity, representing the connotation, traits and manner of the Chinese nation. In other sense of *Tong*, wushu forms various styles of boxing with orderly development, distinct theories, distinctive styles and self-contained system. In addition, wushu's traditional nature also lies in its diachronic, as it connects past, exists at present and presages the future, with a strong vitality.

c. Being cultural

By wushu's cultural nature, we mean it is the physical culture characterized by Chinese nation only. It not only means Chinese people's imagination about their physical activity patterns, forming thousands of quan styles; but it includes the nation's understanding about the relationships among heaven, earth and man. It symbolizes a mental state of peace and tolerance as well as a graceful and restrained taste. It has been one part of Chinese culture soft power.

d. Being combative

Being combative is the nature of wushu, determining wushu's function as "self-defense". In the first place, wushu's combative nature is reflected in the actual free combat between opponents, with "hitting once striking and smashing once hitting" as the principle. Secondly it is shown in the sparring training between imagined opponents, with realness as the requirement. Lastly it is also shown in the single practice of combat with an imagined opponent, with a combating setting as the requirement.

e. Being artistic

Wushu's artistic nature firstly lies in its beauty of the elements in wushu. In wushu practice, body is divided into five parts, 4 limbs and torso. It not only requires them to be "top-down balanced, left-right symmetrical and in-out proportioned", also pursues "straightness in obliqueness, rightness in oddness and oddness in rightness". It divides the practice into various kinds of state of movement, that is, dynamic and static, rise and fall, fast and slow, high and low, hard and soft, forward and backward, turn and fold, contraction and release, straightening and bending, virtual and actual, as well as light and heavy, etc. In addition, it strengthens its artistry by complementary contrast and comparison. Next, its artistry lies in the beauty of form. It creates various forms of movements, containing straightforward shomen-uchi as well as striking while going and turning; striking while standing or falling or lying as well as striking on state. There is the striking from distance, close combat as well as direct combat. Furthermore, it happens not only in a state of somber with stable physical movements but in drunkenness with erratic motions. It can be violent or smooth. Lastly, the artistic nature is also in its aesthetic implication. It not only seeks the spirit of "motion in quietness and rhythm in motion", but expresses the artistic concept of fighting state with different motions as well as the people's understanding towards athletic beauty and wushu's spiritual beauty。

f. Being athletic

Being athletic is one of the characteristics most easily understood in wushu. Its sport nature lies in the fact that wushu helps to be healthy physically, as wushu exercise has not only become the exercise prescription for the doctors to treat patients, but "the walking stick" for Chinese people taken as a way of health and also for senior citizens to reshape their physical beauty. Its athletic nature also lies in its competitiveness. So far there has been a complete competitive system, with such major events as World Wushu Championships, Wushu Sanda World Cup, World Junior Wushu Championships, World Traditional Wushu Championships, Wushu Competition of World Game, Wushu Competition of World Traditional Game, Wushu Competition of World Wushu Expo and Wushu Competition of Asian Games, etc.

2.1.2 Wushu's technical system and content

(1) **Technical system**

The technical system of wushu can be divided into taolu, combat and skill in terms of its exercise forms. (See the Fig. 1-1)

Taolu includes the movements with unarmed techniques and armed techniques. It can further be divided into soloing, paring drill and team performance, which contains paring drill armed or unarmed, and team performance armed or unarmed.

The technique of combat exercise has practical fighting technique, which is outside the category of sport, and the technique for competitions in sport, with Changbin (long range weapons), Duanbin (Chinese fencing), Sanda (empty-hand sparring) and pushing hand.

The skill exercise contains those basic skills such as waist, leg, standing on one's head and stake-standing exercise in taolu movement, and the fighting skill in combat exercise, in addition to the health exercise, body-building exercise and health-staying exercise, etc.

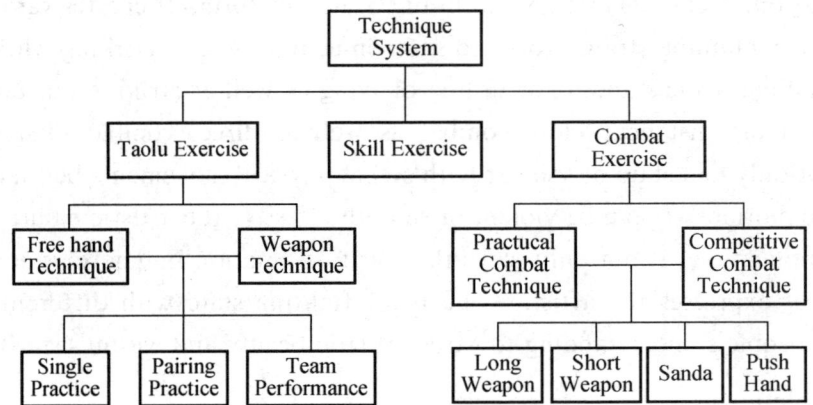

Fig. 1-1 Wushu Technique System

(2) The technique content

a. Competitivewushu

The technique in competitive wushu contains the drill techniques of Changquan, Taijiquan, Nanquan; and the combating techniques of Sanda and push hand. It requires a complete system for the competition, including required techniques, coaches, athletes, referees and certain forms. Competitive wushu comes into being on the basis of traditional wushu with the nature of sport.

Taolu of competitive Wushu in national championships contains quan styles (Changquan, Nanquan, Taijiquan), with or without short-armed weapon (broadsword, sword, Nandao and Taiji sword, or long weapons such as staff, spear and Nangun, in the form of sparring with 3 or 2 persons.

Taolu of competitive traditional wushu contains quan styles such as Xingyiquan, Baguazhang, Bajiquan, Tongbiquan, Piguaquan, Fanziquan, Ditangquan, Tanglangquan, Yingzhaoquan and other kinds of boxing such as Xiangxingquan, Zhaquan, Huaquan, Shaolinquan, Nanquan and Chen Taiji, Yang Taiji, Wǔ Taiji, Wú Taiji, Sun Taiji and 48-form Taiji. Weapons include Nandao (Southern Broadword), drunk sword, long-fringe sword, 42-form Taiji sword, men's staff, falchion, monkey staff, double broadsword, double rapier, double hook, three-section staff (two-section cudgel), single whip (including the whip with sword), rope dart (including bola), and traditional weapons for Taijiquan including broadsword, staff, sword, spear, broadsword and horsetail whisk, etc.

At present individual combating events in competitive wushu are Sanda and Pushing Hand.

b. Quan Styles

According to *Chinese Wushu History*, compiled by National Sports Commission in 1997, "there are 129 styles of quan with chronological origins, clear theories, unique features and self-evident systems all over the country, after 3-year's hard work".

The styles of quan mainly consist of Shaolinquan, Xinyi Liuhequan, Taijiquan, Xingyiquan, Baguazhang, Bajiquan, Piguaquan, Tongbiquan, Fanziquan, Chuojiao, Hongquan, Zhaquan, Huaquan, Baguaquan, Sanhuang Paochui, Liuhequan (Six-direction boxing), Taizuquan, Luohanquan, Lanshou, Mizongquan, Tanglangquan, Houquan, Zuiquan, Wuzuquan, Dishuquan, Hongjiaquan, Yongchun, Fojiaquan, Caijiaquan, Lijiaquan, Mojiaquan, Dazunquan, Longzunquan, Hequan, Cailifoquan, Sunbinquan, Yingmenquan, Famenquan, Zimenquan, Meifaquan, Gongliquan, Huaquan, Yueshilianquan, Mianquan, Changjiaquan, Wujiaquan, Baomeiquan, Sengmenquan, Yuemenquan, Dumenquan, Zhaomenquan, Hongmenquan, Huamenquan, Huimenquan, Yumenquan, Snap Kick, Qishi (Seven Postures), Jinshiquan, Huxing, Nanzhiquan, Baquan, Sunjiaquan, Sunmenquan, Yumenquan, Wangmenquan, Yanmenquan, Kongmenquan, Yuejiaquan, 36-route Songjiangquan, Yumenquan, Yangjiaquan, Liangjiaquan, Jinghequan, Cuojiaomen, Shitouquan, Hushenquan, Zhidongquan, Mingtangquan, Misiquan, Qingquan, Sitongchui, Shunshouquan, Shuipaoquan, Fohanquan, Qiangjiaquan, Dumenquan, Baohuquan, Gongliquan, Sanyiquan, Xinquan, ERlangmenquan, Fuquan, Yuanyangquan, Jiuquan, Hufuquan, and so on.

Among them, many quan styles have a system with techniques, weapons and skills. And they have various genres and have formed taolu for competitions or for physical fitness since the People's Republic of China was founded in 1949. Take Taijiquan (known as "Tai Chi" or "Shadow Boxing", the same as below) as an example. As one of the styles of Chinese wushu, Taijiquan originated from Chenjiagou of Wen County, in the Dynasty of early Qing and late Ming, with a history of over 300 years old. During the process of its development, there are Chen-style, Yang-style, Wǔ-style, Wú-style, and Sun-style, etc. in Taijiquan. Since the establishment of new China, National Sports Commission designed 24-form, 48-form and 88-form in Taiji taolu as well as the 42-form competitive taolu and other competitive taolu from other styles of Taijiquan, in order to meet the needs of physical exercises for mass people and promote Taijiquan to the international sport stage. Later, for the further spread of Taijiquan internationally, a simplified style, 8-form and 16-form Taijiquan appeared. In so doing, Taijiquan develops from the focus on the combating function of martial arts to the multiple ways of physical fitness, subsidiary medical treatment and competition performance. Especially the first two functions are playing the growing roles.

c. Weapons

Each quan style has weapons with various characteristics. In addition to the usual weapons for competition, such as broadsword, sword, staffstick and spear, there are short weapons such as whip, whip pole, hook, crutch, hammer, peg and stagger as well as long weapons including penholder fork, broadsword, dagger-axe, halberd, axe, battle-axe, fork, trident rake, spade and spiked club. There are dual weapons such as iron chopsticks, Emei thrust, iron comb, sickle knife, crescent stab, and horse halberd. Also there are soft weapons like bola, rope dart, nine-section whip, three-section staff, dragon-headed rod, fly ball, four-section staff, pole whip and others like Magistrate pen, Magistrate ring, phoenix-tail sword and bamboo spear, etc.

2.1.3 Wushu's Cultural structure and type

(1) Cultural structure

Wushu culture is in broad sense defined as "the sum of various cultures related towushu, including various forms of wushu in culture heritage, sporting field, films and televisions, literature works and school education". In narrow sense, it refers to "Chinese traditional culture, martial virtue and inheritance system which are connoted in various quan styles, with chronological origin, clear theory, unique characteristics and self-evident system".

Wushu's culture structure can be divided into 3 layers, that is, the layer of objects and techniques, system and customs, psychology and values. Among them, the first layer covers wushu techniques, instruments, tools for practice, fields and costumes, etc., showing a human-object relationship. The second layer includes wushu organizing patterns, inheritance ways, teaching methods, protocol regulations, morals and competition ways, etc., presenting the relationship between human and human. The layer of psychology and values covers national identity, national psychology and emotions, etc, presented by wushu culture. In a word, techniques and skills are superficial, rite and art are the middle layer, and reason and theory are the core.

The middle layer in wushu's culture structure is wushu's technique culture, inheritance, education system and morals, etc. The interior layer is the Chinese traditional culture spirit and connotations and they are defined in narrow sense; while the exterior layer should be considered as broad wushu, including swordsmen movies, literature and drama, mixed with other culture patterns.

(2) Cultural patterns

As a comparatively independent culture system, wushu culture belongs to local culture and mainland culture, as well as ethical culture and popular culture. The localization of wushu culture lies in its largest system, richest content with national Chinese features among the world martial arts culture. In terms of wushu's mainland culture, it means the various styles are mainly related to mainland culture of vast Chinese territory. Its popularity refers to the fact that it emerges and develops among the people, with only a small part entering into the field of sport. Its ethicality implies that not only a person's character is considered as the content of entrance examination, but the morals are included as the important part of wushu training.

Wushu culture is manifested in 4 aspects, that is, cultural wushu, educational wushu, artistic wushu and physical wushu. By cultural wushu, we mean wushu, with the integration of Chinese traditional philosophy and the introduction of traditional medicine, presents an ethical concern and military wisdom as well as a doorway to literature, drawing, calligraphy, music, dancing and theater, etc, therefore it becomes the holographic image and window of Chinese culture. By educational wushu, it means that wushu takes a dual cultivation of virtue and skill as training program, holding wushu as a means of self-cultivation. By artistic wushu, it means Chinese wushu, with the two ways of development, i.e., "attack" and "dance", for thousands of years, takes Sanda (free combat) to keep the feature of "art of attack"; in the meantime it reveals the various forms in taolu (Routine) by way of dancing, thus it enhances the artistic influence of wushu. Taolu accordingly becomes the artistic form of attack and defense. In physical wushu, it is regarded as a kind of physical exercise taken intentionally by Chinese people in a planned way. A relatively complete competition system at home and abroad has been established and it has become a relatively mature competition event since it was involved to be a sport event in modern times.

2.2 Learning program

The teaching of the chapter needs 2 periods. Students are required to know the overview of Chinese wushu, including the definition, feature, content as well as the structure, type and pattern manifestation of wushu culture.

2.3 Cultural experience

Originated from Chinese traditional culture, wushu involves many cultural elements, such as Chinese philosophy, medicine, ethics, strategic thinking, literature, drawing, calligraphy, music, dance, drama, etc., therefore wushu becomes one form of Chinese traditional culture with unique feature.

Wushu contains the theory of Chinese traditional philosophy. In ancient times, wushu masters follow skills and principles by way of absorbing traditional philosophy, thus to make the wushu theory characteristic of philosophy. For example, Taijiquan bases its theory on the principle of supreme ultimate in traditional philosophy; Baguazhang bases its theory on the Eight Diagrams while Xingyiquan takes the five elements of traditional philosophy. Chen Xin, in his *Illustrated Book of Chen's Taijiquan*, says "this book aims to teach people to digest well by opening and closing parts of body (Yin and Yang). It is named after Taijiquan because of its basic principle of Taiji." In Study of Baguazhang (Eight Diagrams Palm), Sun Lutang says, "this book is written for the purpose of self-cultivation. It follows the principles of natural development and substantiation in diagrams. So it takes the name of Eight Diagrams Palm". The above examples prove the process of combination of quan style with traditional philosophy. Various Chinese quan styles are so in shape with the principle of Book of Changes. "With Eight Diagrams and Five Elements principle established, gestures and motions are added, then Eight Diagrams Palm passes on from generation to generation".

The basic principles of Chinese traditional medicine are also introduced into wushu. Although being different disciplines, Chinese traditional medicine and wushu both aim to know the laws of people's physical activity, to understand the effect of natural environment, medical function, physical stimulation and the physical and breathing exercise on human body. While Chinese traditional medicine is to explore the ways of illness treatment through the knowledge above, wushu is to study and develop the ways of military practices. For example, the therapy of traumatic injury belongs to orthopedics of Chinese medicine, while there are also methods and principles of orthopedics in wushu, even with its unique treatment. For example, the method of patting press point with hand can be used to treat some injured acupuncture points. *Recipe for Injury by Shaolin Temple*, is a book to discuss wushu's theory of injury treatment. The typical example of the combination of wushu with traditional medicine is the famous "point pressure method". Some pressure points are exactly the acupuncture points treated in Chinese medicine. Grabbing in wushu is invented by way of the theory of grabbing nerves and pressure points. People in wushu circle use the term of "Fitness Wushu" is just for this reason. "What is the purpose to practice wushu? It is to prolong life and keep energetic forever". This line above is the reality of bodybuilding by way of wushu.

The techniques of attack and defense in wushu have the same requirement as that in Chinese military science and tactics. For example, "know yourself as well as the enemy" is the general principle of *Sun Tzu's Art of War*. So is it in wushu's art of attack and defense. Taijiquan focuses on "I must know the enemy even though he does not know me"; or "I must know the person well if I mean to approach him". When talking about the art of Xingyiquan, Guo Yunshen said, "One should be very cautious and know oneself as well as the enemy." The standpoint guided by *Sun Tzu's Art of War*, is "controlling one instead of being controlled". Yu Dayou, the wushu master in Ming Dynasty, elaborated many practical techniques about cudgel. He concluded in his *The Book of Sword*, "...to sum up from thousands of word, controlling people rather than being controlled."

Emeiquan created an art of "no hand-touching", maintaining that the strategy of no hand-touching is recommended when fighting against the enemy, in that defending tends to be passive and be easily subjugated while attacking is advised to keep active to substitute for the defensive strategy. "The way to employ the military is to give the enemy disguise" and "dispose oneself to the enemy in disguise" are the major means to achieve victory, according to Sun Tzu.

Baguazhang usually uses the tactics by "pointing at the bottom but actually targeting at the top, pointing at the left while actually meaning the right or pointing this way while hitting at that way." In Xingyiquan, the thought of giving enemy disguise or disposing oneself to the enemy in disguise" is also presented in its strategies of "attacking rightward while standing on left, attacking leftward while standing on the right, or looking straight when it is actually slanting or the vise verse." It (*Sun Tzu's Art of War*) requires "more on obtaining the victory than on lasting the long time", maintaining the quick battle and quick decision instead of protracted war. This is in accordance with the idea of winning success just by one stroke via the strategy of "grabbing the throat or crotch; pricking the eyes when confronting with the enemy" in traditional wushu. Sun Tzu holds that "it is vital to be quick in a battle". He also insists that "attacking after the enemy acts but reaching the destination ahead of the enemy even if the enemy acts first".

In contrast, it is also the key to success by quick offense. *The Script of Tongbeiquan originated* in Hongdong says that no hand is seen when hand reaches out; if the hand is seen, it is not the real hand", maintaining that the speed that hand reaches is fast enough so that the rival cannot see. *The Fighting Trick of Shaolinquan requires* a master to be "as fast as wind when rising or falling, no hand or foot can be seen when he acts." The key element in *Sun Tzu's Art of War* is to avoid the virtual strike. In Qing Dynasty, Zhang Kongzhao wrote in his *Quan Essentials*, "staying clear of the enemy's main force and choose to attack the vulnerable spot. But where are the vulnerable spots? They are chest, waist and armpit as well as the middle part of leg and ankle. They are the places where the enemy cannot use force so that we can land a blow. This is the way how to avoid the virtual strike."

The integration of wushu and ethics is embodied in the requirement of "master-practitioner succession" and "morality of wushu" (morals), such as the respect for masters, being righteous and courageous, etc. Wushu is also closely related to traditional cultures, drama, acrobatic righting, and religion, to name just a few. Therefore, wushu culture is the concentrate and carrier of Chinese culture, serving as a living witness of Chinese culture. Its cultural feature is also shown in the fact that wushu has become one part of life for Chinese people, since most of them have a "wushu complex". Some scholars hold that wushu is the way of being for Chinese. Wushu contains all "culture genes" of Chinese cultures.

3 Conclusion

- Wushu is defined as one kind of Chinese sports based on Chinese culture as its theoretical foundation, characterized by combat methods as basic content, combined with taolu (routines), combat and skill as major sport forms.
- Wushu is characteristic of being Chinese, traditional, cultural, combative, artistic and athletic.
- The technical system of wushu includes taolu, combat and skill exercise in terms of the exercise forms, competitive wushu, different quan styles and weapons.
- The structure of wushu culture can be divided into 3 layers, that is, the layer of objects and techniques, system and customs, psychology and values. Wushu culture is manifested in 4 aspects, that is, cultural wushu, educational wushu, artistic wushu and physical wushu.

4 Extensive Reading

- **Classification of quan styles**

  With abundant content inwushu, there were various classifications. For example, there are "Internal Quan" and "External Quan" in terms of the theory and method of quan; there are "Nanquan (Southern Quan)" and "Beiquan (Northern Quan)" in term of geography; there are Shaolin style, Wudang style, Emei style in terms of the division of mountains and rivers; there are "Changquan (Long Quan)" and "Duanquan (Short Quan)" in term of the features styles; and there are "Yangtze River Valley style, Yellow River Valley style or Pearl River Valley style" in term of the divisions of rivers and lakes.

- **18 kinds of weapons**

  In Ming Dynasty, wushu events contained 18 kinds, expressed in weapons, as recorded in *Wuzazu* "bow, crossbow, spear, wide sword, sword, pike, shield, axe, battle-axe, halberd, whip, mace, grabbing, bamboo knife, fork, rake head, lasso and bare-hand combat".

5 Questions and Exercises

(1) Briefly define wushu.

(2) Briefly describe the characteristics of wushu.

(3) Briefly describe the technical system of wushu.

(4) Briefly describe the classification of traditional wushu styles.

6 References

[1] Wushu Research Institute of National Physical Committee Chinese [M]. Wushu History. Eds. Beijing: People Sport Publishing House. 1996: 310-311.

[2] Textbook Committee of National Sport Universities [M]. Basics of Wushu Theory. Eds. Beijing: People Sport Publishing House. 1997: 27-28.

[3] Cai Longyun. My Viewpoint about Wushu [J]. New Sport. 1957(2):20-21.

[4] Qiu Pixiang. The Aesthetic Feature and Artistry of Wushu Taolu [J]. Journal of Shanghai University of Sport. 2004(2):39-40.

[5] Dai Guobin. Wushu: Culture of body [M]. Beijing: People Sport Publishing House, 2011:405-441.

[6] Ruan Jizheng. Wushu: The Way of Being for Chinese People [J]. Open Times. 1996(3):24-26.

[7] Guo Yucheng. Athletic Wushu and Cultural Wushu [J]. Wushu Science. 2007(5):1-3.

Chapter Two

24-Form Taijiquan

1 Introduction

Taijiquan (known as "Tai Chi" or "Shadow Boxing", the same as below) is one of the most well-known barehanded quan styles in China, which includes different styles of Taijiquan such as Chen-style, Yang-style, Wǔ-style, Wǔ-style and Sun-style. Since 1949 a series of Taijiquan taolu (known as "routines", the same as below) have been compiled by State Physical Culture and Sports Commission such as 24-form Simplified Taijiquan, 48-form and 88-form Taijiquan etc. 24-form Taijiquan includes 24 movements, back and forth for 4 times. It is composed of such technical skills as "ward-off, yielding, pressing, pushing, plucking, splitting, elbowing, bumping, stepping forward, stepping backward, turning right, turning left, and centred stability", which is the beginning taolu for Taijiquan practitioners owing to its well-balanced movements.

2 Learning experience

2.1 Movements

2.1.1 Ready position

Stand with feet together and put both arms down on either side of the thighs; keep the head straight forward, close the mouth and clench the teeth, with the abdomen relaxed and eyes looking forward (Fig. 2-1).

2.1.2 Starting posture

Step aside the left foot and keep both feet apart at shoulder-width (Fig. 2-2-1). Stretch the arms and move them upward slowly to shoulders' height, with palms facing downward (Fig. 2-2-2, Fig. 2-2-3). Bend both legs slowly into a half squat and bend the elbows and wrists with fingers facing forward, press both palms down in front of the abdomen (Fig. 2-2-4).

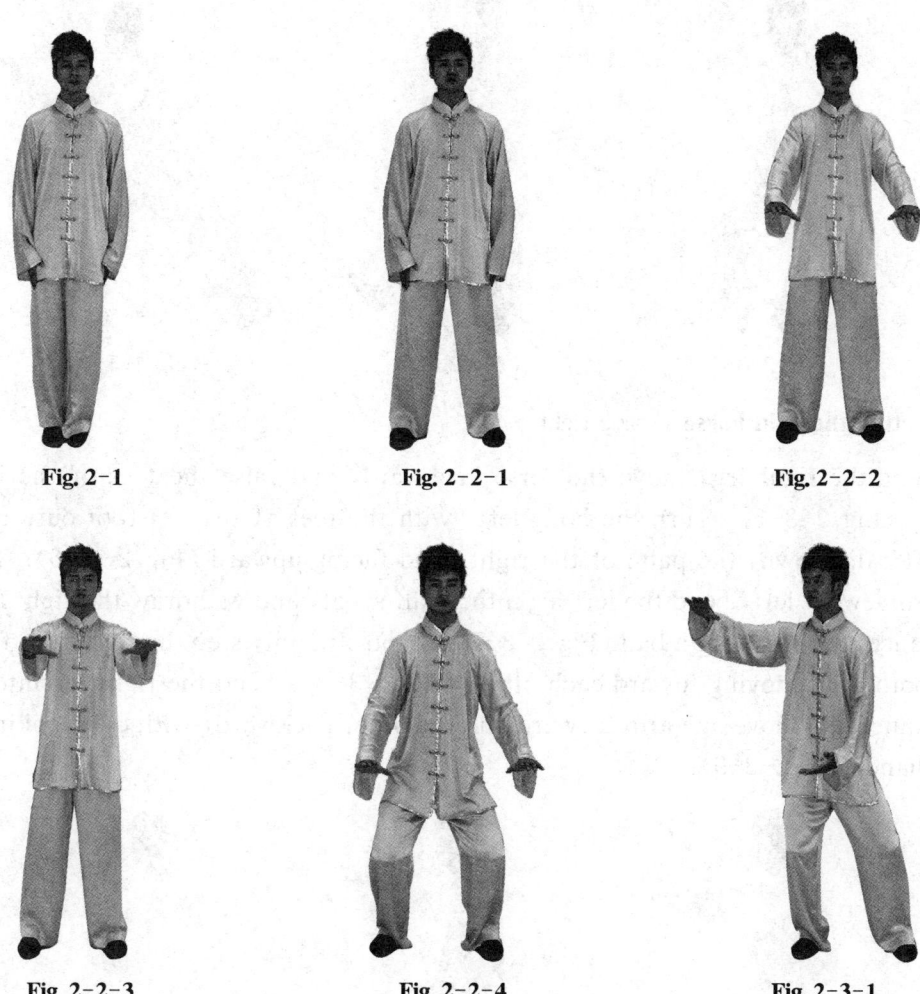

Fig. 2-1   Fig. 2-2-1   Fig. 2-2-2

Fig. 2-2-3   Fig. 2-2-4   Fig. 2-3-1

2.1.3　Parting the wild horse's mane on both sides: there are 3 movements

(1) Parting the wild horse's mane-left

　　Turn the torso somewhat right first and move the right arm up forward in a circle, the palm of left hand upward (Fig. 2-3-1). Turn the torso somewhat left, bend the right arm horizontally and move the left arm in a circle to the front of the abdomen with both palms facing each other as if holding a ball; withdraw the left foot to the inner side of the right foot, with the toes touching the floor into a T stance (Fig. 2-3-2). Stand straight, step the left foot forward, with both arms facing each other (Fig. 2-3-3); bend the left leg into a left bow stance, move one arm up forward and the other backward with the eyes looking at the left hand (Fig. 2-3-4).

Fig. 2-3-2　　　　Fig. 2-3-3　　　　Fig. 2-3-4

(2) Parting the wild horse's mane-right

　　Bend the right leg, move the torso backward, and raise the toes of the left foot slightly (Fig. 2-3-5). Turn the body left, with the toes of the left foot outward; turn the left palm down, the palm of the right hand facing upward (Fig. 2-3-6). Turn the torso somewhat left, bend the left leg into a half squat, and withdraw the right foot into a T stance, as if holding a ball (Fig. 2-3-7). Stand straight, step the right foot forward, with both arms moving toward each other (Fig. 2-3-8); bend the right leg into a right bow stance and move one arm forward and the other backward, with eyes looking at the right hand (Fig. 2-3-9).

Fig. 2-3-5　　　　Fig. 2-3-6　　　　Fig. 2-3-7

Fig. 2-3-8　　　　Fig. 2-3-9

(3) **Parting mustang**'s mane-left

The same as (1). See Fig. 2-3-2, 2-3-3, and 2-3-4.

2.1.4 White crane spreading wings

Turn the torso to the left facing forward and step the right foot half a pace forward; meanwhile fold both arms in front of the chest into a ball (Fig. 2-4-1). shift the body weight to the right leg, turn the torso right, and raise both hands up after the left hand's placing onto the right wrist (Fig. 2-4-2). Face the torso forward, lift the left foot into an empty stance; meanwhile move the right hand upward to the right front of the forehead, with the palm of the right hand facing inward. Press the left hand on the left side of the leg with eyes looking forward (Fig. 2-4-3).

Fig. 2-4-1　　　　　　Fig. 2-4-2　　　　　　Fig. 2-4-3

2.1.5 Brushing knee and twisting step on both sides: there are 3 movements.

(1) **Brushing knee and twisting step on the left**

Turn the torso somewhat right, move the right hand to the left side of the head and then down to the front of the chest (Fig. 2-5-1). Turn the torso right, move the right hand downward to the right side of the thigh and then move it up in a circle; move the left hand forward up accordingly (Fig. 2-5-2). Turn the torso further right slightly, rotate the right arm to the height of the right shoulder. Withdraw the left foot to the inner side of the right foot to form a T stance; rotate the left hand clockwise and press it to the inner side of the right elbow with the eyes looking at the right hand (Fig. 2-5-3). Step the left foot leftward; meanwhile rotate the right arm with the elbow bent counterclockwise to the height of the right ear (Fig. 2-5-4). Bend the left leg into a left bow stance, brush the left hand horizontally over the knee to the outer side of the left leg with palms of hands facing down and the fingertips forward; push the right hand out forward along the side of the right ear with the turning of body (Fig. 2-5-5).

Fig. 2-5-1　　　Fig. 2-5-2　　　Fig. 2-5-3

Fig. 2-5-4　　　Fig. 2-5-5

(2) **Brushing knee and twisting step on the right**

Bend the right leg, shift the body weight backward and raise the toes of the left foot (Fig. 2-5-6). Turn the torso left, with the left foot outward slightly; rotate the left arm on the left, and rotate the right arm upward a little with the turning of body (Fig. 2-5-7). Shift the weight to the left leg and withdraw the right foot to the inner side of the left foot to form a T stance; meanwhile turn the body further left slightly, rotate the left hand in an arc with the left palm of hand upward till the height of the left shoulder. Withdraw the right foot to the inner side of the left foot to form a T stance, rotate the right arm downward to the inner side of the left elbow with eyes looking at the left hand (Fig. 2-5-8). Step the right foot right forward; at the same time bend the left arm and withdraw the left hand to the side of the left ear (Fig. 2-5-9). Bend the right leg to form a right bow stance, at the same time brush the right hand horizontally over the right knee to the outer side of the right leg with the palm of hand facing down and the fingertips forward. Push the left hand forward along the left ear with the turning of body (Fig. 2-5-10).

Fig. 2-5-6 Fig. 2-5-7 Fig. 2-5-8

Fig. 2-5-9 Fig. 2-5-10

(3) Brushing knee and twisting step on the left

Bend the left leg, shift the body weight backward and raise the toes of the right foot (Fig. 2-5-11). Turn the torso right, with the right foot outward slightly; shift the weight to the right leg, at the same time rotate the right arm in an arc to the right and rotate the left arm upward a little with the turning of body (Fig. 2-5-12). Turn the body further right slightly and rotate the right palm upward to the right shoulder. Withdraw the left foot to the inner side of the right foot to form a T stance and rotate the left arm down in an arc to the inner side of the right elbow with the eyes looking at the right hand (Fig. 2-5-13). Step the left foot left forward, meanwhile bend the right arm and withdraw it to the side of the right ear (Fig. 2-5-14). Bend the left leg into a left bow stance, at the same time brush the left hand horizontally over the left knee to the outer side of the left leg with the palm of hand facing down and the tips of the fingers forward. Push the right palm forward along the side of the right ear with the turning of body (Fig. 2-5-15).

Fig. 2-5-11　　　　　Fig. 2-5-12　　　　　Fig. 2-5-13

Fig. 2-5-14　　　　　Fig. 2-5-15

2.1.6　Playing pipa (the Chinese lute)

Move the right foot half a pace forward behind the left foot and stretch the right arm forward slightly (Fig. 2-6-1). Shift the body weight upon the right leg, turn the torso right; meanwhile rotate the left hand slowly forward (Fig. 2-6-2). Turn the torso left slightly, and raise the left toes with the left heel on the ground to form a left empty stance. Move both arms outward with elbow bent in an arc to the front of the body, with the right hand resting upon the right side of the left elbow, the palm of the right hand facing left and eyes looking at the left hand (Fig. 2-6-3).

Fig. 2-6-1　　　　　Fig. 2-6-2　　　　　Fig. 2-6-3

2.1.7 Repulsing monkey on the left and right, including 4 movements

(1) Repulsing monkey right

Turn the torso right slightly, with the palm of the left hand facing upward; rotate the right arm outward down to the right side of the hip and then lift it up (Fig. 2-7-1). Raise the left foot, step back one pace and turn the torso left; meanwhile bend the right arm and withdraw it to the right side of the ear. Shift the body weight backward to form an empty stance on the right. Push the right hand to the front of the body; rotate the left arm from behind, down to the left side of the waist, with the palm of hand facing upward, eyes looking at the right hand (Fig. 2-7-2).

Fig. 2-7-1　　　　　Fig. 2-7-2　　　　　Fig. 2-7-3

(2) Repulsing monkey-left

Turn the torso left slightly, with the palm of the right hand facing upward; rotate the left arm outward down to the left side of the hip and then lift it up (Fig. 2-7-3). Raise the right foot and step back one pace and turn the torso right; meanwhile bend the left arm and withdraw it to the left side of the ear. Shift the body weight backward to form a left empty stance. Push the left hand to the front of the body; rotate the right arm from behind, down to the right side of the waist, with the palm of hand facing upward and eyes looking at the left hand (Fig. 2-7-4).

(3) Repulsing monkey-right

Turn the torso right slightly, with the palm of the left hand facing upward; rotate the right arm outward down to the right side of the hip and then lift it up (Fig. 2-7-5). Raise the left foot and step back one pace and turn the torso left; meanwhile bend the right arm and withdraw it to the right side of the ear. Shift the body weight backward to form an empty stance on the right. Push the right hand to the front of body; rotate the left arm from behind, down to the left side of the waist, with the palm of hand facing upward and eyes looking at the right hand (Fig. 2-7-6).

Fig. 2-7-4   Fig. 2-7-5   Fig. 2-7-6

(4) Repulsing monkey-left

Turn the torso left slightly, with the palm of the right hand facing upward; rotate the left arm outward down to the left side of the hip and then lift it up (Fig. 2-7-7). Raise the right foot and step back one pace and turn the torso right; meanwhile bend the left arm and withdraw it to the left side of the ear. Shift the body weight backward to form a left empty stance. Push the left hand to the front of the body; rotate the right arm from behind, down to the right side of the waist, with the palm of hand facing upward and eyes looking at the left hand (Fig. 2-7-8).

Fig. 2-7-7   Fig. 2-7-8   Fig. 2-8-1

2.1.8 Grasping bird's tail-left

Turn the torso slightly right, rotate the right arm backward up and move the left hand down to the front of the body (Fig. 2-8-1), as if holding a ball with both hands on the right. Step back the left foot to form a T stance (Fig. 2-8-2). Turn the torso left and step the left foot left forward. Move both arms horizontally a little to the front of the chest with the turning of body (Fig. 2-8-3). Step the left leg forward to form a bow stance; at the same time bend the left arm, stretch it straight forward with the palm of hand facing inward, move the right arm back and press it on the right side of the thigh (Fig. 2-8-4).

Fig. 2-8-2 Fig. 2-8-3 Fig. 2-8-4

Turn the torso slightly left, move the left hand upward slowly to the left; meanwhile rotate the right arm out from up, forward to the inner side of the left arm, with the palm of hand facing up (Fig. 2-8-5). Turn the torso right, shift the body weight to the back; meanwhile rotate both hands down from the front to the right, back till the front of the abdomen (Fig. 2-8-6). Turn the torso slightly right, rotate the right hand upward; rotate the left hand to the right side of the chest (Fig. 2-8-7). Turn the torso left and bend the right arm to the inner side of the left wrist (Fig. 2-8-8). Bend the left knee, shift the body weight forward to form a left bow stance; push the right forearm forward with the right hand till both arms form a circle (Fig. 2-8-9).

Turn the palm of the left hand facing downward; move the right hand to the junction of both wrists (Fig. 2-8-10). Move both hands horizontally outward at the shoulders' width (Fig. 2-8-11), shift the weight onto the right leg and bend the right knee; raise the left toes and then move back both arms with the bending of arms (Fig. 2-8-12).

Fig. 2-8-5 Fig. 2-8-6 Fig. 2-8-7

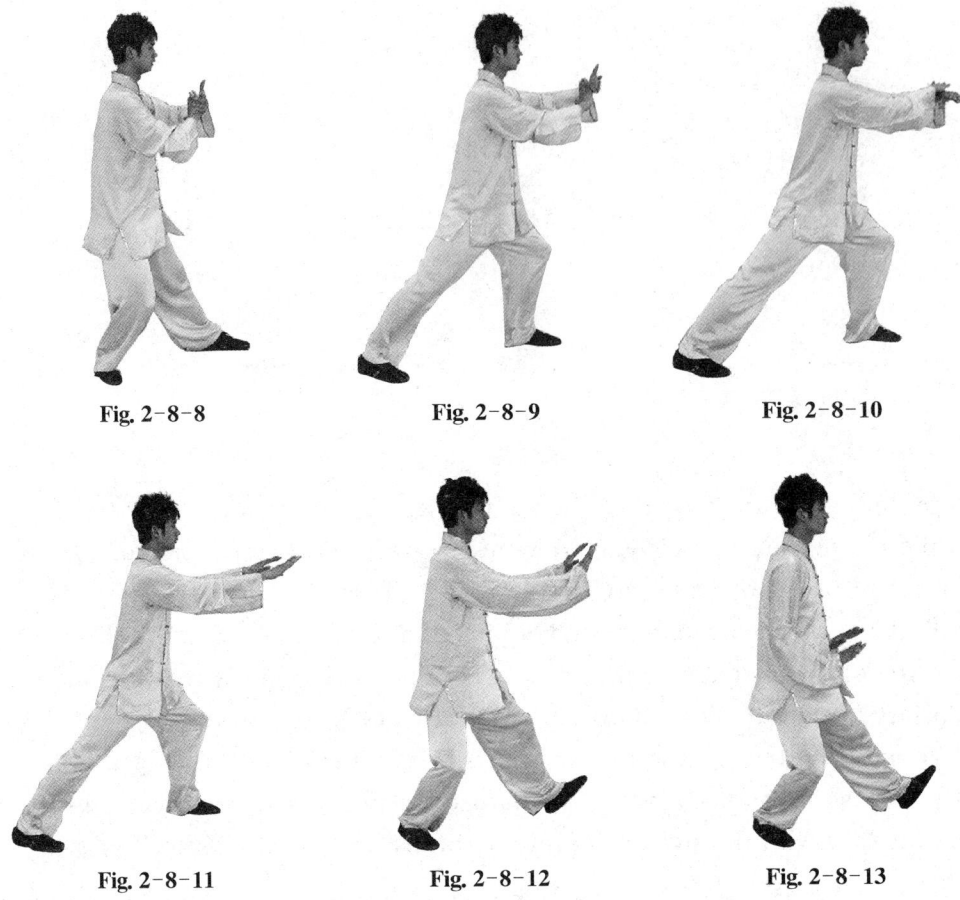

Fig. 2-8-8   Fig. 2-8-9   Fig. 2-8-10

Fig. 2-8-11   Fig. 2-8-12   Fig. 2-8-13

Move the arms to the front of the chest at a palm's width and then press them to the front of abdomen (Fig. 2-8-13), and shift the body weight to the front to form a left bow stance. Push both hands forward up at shoulder's height and then push them forward horizontally (Fig. 2-8-14).

Fig. 2-8-14   Fig. 2-9-1   Fig. 2-9-2

2.1.9 Grasping bird's tail-right

Turn the torso slightly right, shift the body weight backward and bend the right leg (Fig. 2-9-1). Turn the torso further right, rotate the right hand rightward horizontally and move the toes of the left foot inward (Fig. 2-9-2). Shift the weight to the left leg and rotate the right hand downward (Fig. 2-9-3); withdraw the right leg to form a T stance with both arms facing each other as if holding a ball (Fig. 2-9-4). Turn the torso right and step the right foot right forward; move both arms back slightly to the front of the chest (Fig. 2-9-5). Step the right leg forward and bend it into a bow stance; meanwhile bend the right elbow, stretch it forward horizontally at the shoulders' height with the palm of hand inward. Move the left arm back and press it at the right side of the thigh (Fig. 2-9-6).

Fig. 2-9-3   Fig. 2-9-4   Fig. 2-9-5

Fig. 2-9-6   Fig. 2-9-7   Fig. 2-9-8

Turn the torso slightly right, move the right hand forward slowly to the right; meanwhile rotate the left arm out from upward, forward to the inner side of the right arm, with the palm of hand facing up (Fig. 2-9-7). Turn the torso left, shift the body weight to the back; meanwhile rotate both hands down from the front to the right, back till the front of the abdomen (Fig. 2-9-8). Turn the torso slightly left and rotate the left hand upward; rotate the right hand to the left side of the chest (Fig. 2-9-9), turn the torso right and bend the left arm and place the hand to the inner side of the right wrist (Fig. 2-9-10). Bend the right knee and shift the body weight forward to form a right bow stance; push the left forearm forward with the left hand till both arms form a circle (Fig. 2-9-11).

Fig. 2-9-9   Fig. 2-9-10   Fig. 2-9-11

Turn the palm of the right hand facing downward; move the left hand to the junction of both wrists (Fig. 2-9-12). Move both hands horizontally outward at the shoulders' width (Fig. 2-9-13), shift the weight onto the right leg and bend the left knee. Raise the right toes and then move back both arms with the bending of arms (Fig. 2-9-14). Move the arms to the front of the chest at a palm's width and then press them to the front of abdomen (Fig. 2-9-15), and shift the body weight to the front to form a right bow stance. Push both hands forward up at shoulder's height and then push them forward further horizontally (Fig. 2-9-16).

Fig. 2-9-12   Fig. 2-9-13   Fig. 2-9-14

Fig. 2-9-15

Fig. 2-9-16

Fig. 2-10-1

2.1.10 Single bian (whip)

Turn the torso slightly left and shift the weight backward onto the left leg (Fig. 2-10-1). Turn the torso further left, turn the palm of the left hand outward slowly and then rotate it leftward; rotate the right hand to the front of abdomen (Fig. 2-10-2). Shift the weight to the right leg, rotate the right hand upward past the face to the right with the palm of hand inward, and move the left hand downward (Fig. 2-10-3). Bend the right leg and step back the left leg into a T stance. Rotate the right arm inward and turn the right hand into a hook when it is moved to the front of the right side at the shoulders' height; rotate the left hand up to the underneath of the left elbow with the palm of hand facing upward and the eyes looking at the direction of the hooked hand (Fig. 2-10-4). Turn the torso slightly left and step the left foot forward to the front of the left side (Fig. 2-10-5); bend the left leg and shift the weight onto it to form a left bow stance. Meanwhile turn over the palm of left hand and push it forward with the eyes looking at the front of the left hand (Fig. 2-10-6).

Fig. 2-10-2

Fig. 2-10-3

Fig. 2-10-4

Fig. 2-10-5   Fig. 2-10-6   Fig. 2-11-1

2.1.11 Cloud hands

Shift the weight backward and raise the tiptoes of the left foot (Fig. 2-11-1); turn the torso right and rotate the tiptoes of the left foot inward. At the same time turn the right hooked hand into a palm, rotate the left hand to the underneath of the right elbow (Fig. 2-11-2). Turn the torso slightly left and shift the weight to the left leg. Rotate the left hand upward with the palm of hand inward; rotate the right hand downward (Fig. 2-11-3). Step back the right foot to the left foot at a foot's width. Rotate the left hand leftward past the front of the head and then turn the palm of hand outward; rotate the right hand downward on the left (Fig. 2-11-4).

Fig. 2-11-2   Fig. 2-11-3   Fig. 2-11-4

Rotate the right hand up leftward and the left hand downward, respectively (Fig. 2-11-5). Turn the torso slightly right and shift the body weight onto the right leg; move the left leg one pace on the left with the toes facing forward. Move the right hand from the palm facing inward to outward after passing the cheek; rotate the left hand down rightward (Fig. 2-11-6). Turn the torso slightly left and shift the weight to the left leg. Rotate the left hand upward with the palm of hand inward; rotate the right hand downward (Fig. 2-11-7). Step back the right foot to the left foot at a foot's width. Rotate the left hand leftward past the front of the head and then turn the palm of hand outward; rotate the right hand downward to the left (Fig. 2-11-8).

Fig. 2-11-5　　　　　　　Fig. 2-11-6　　　　　　　Fig. 2-11-7

Rotate the right hand up leftward and the left hand downward, respectively (Fig. 2-11-9). Turn the torso slightly right and shift the body weight onto the right leg; step the left leg one pace on the left with the toes facing forward. Move the right hand from the palm of hand facing inward to facing outward after passing the cheek; rotate the left hand down rightward (Fig. 2-11-10). Turn the torso slightly left and shift the weight to the left leg. Rotate the left hand upward with the palm of hand inward; rotate the right hand downward (Fig. 2-11-11). Step back the right foot to the left foot at a foot's width. Rotate the left hand leftward past the front of the head and then turn the palm of hand outward; rotate the right hand downward to the left (Fig. 2-11-12).

Fig. 2-11-8　　　　　　　Fig. 2-11-9　　　　　　　Fig. 2-11-10

Fig. 2-11-11　　　　　Fig. 2-11-12　　　　　Fig. 2-12-1

2.1.12　Single Bian (whip)

Rotate the right hand up leftward and the left hand downward respectively (Fig. 2-12-1). Turn the torso slightly right, move the right hand from the palm of hand facing inward to facing outward after passing the cheek; rotate the left hand down rightward (Fig. 2-12-2). Bend the right leg and shift the weight onto it. Step back the left foot into a T stance; turn the right hand into a hook and rotate the left hand up to the bottom of the left elbow with the palm of hand facing forward and eyes looking at the direction of the hooked hand (Fig. 2-12-3).

Fig. 2-12-2　　　　　Fig. 2-12-3　　　　　Fig. 2-12-4

Turn the torso slightly left and move the left foot left forward (Fig. 2-12-4). Bend the left leg into a left bow stance; meanwhile turn the palm of the left hand outward and push it forward with the eyes looking at the left hand (Fig. 2-12-5).

Fig. 2-12-5   Fig. 2-13-1   Fig. 2-13-2

2.1.13 High patting on horse

Move the right foot half a pace forward and turn the right hooked hand into a palm with both palms facing upward and eyes looking at the right hand (Fig. 2-13-1). Turn the torso slightly left and raise the heel of the left foot into an empty stance; push the palm of the right hand forward past the right ear and move the left arm downward to the front of the abdomen with the palm of hand facing upward and eyes looking at the right hand (Fig. 2-13-2).

2.1.14 Kicking with the right heel

Turn the torso slightly left, step the left foot forward on the left with its heel putting onto the ground. Move the left hand slightly backward, thread the left hand forward past the back of the right hand and then cross both hands with the left palm and right palm upward and downward obliquely, respectively (Fig. 2-14-1). Rotate both arms slightly inward and turn both palms of hands outward (Fig. 2-14-2); shift the weight to the left leg and bend the knee, move the right foot back to the inner side of the left leg; move the arms further down in a circle on both sides with the hands resting upon the front of the abdomen at shoulder's width (Fig. 2-14-3). Stand straight on the left leg, bend the right leg and lift it up; meanwhile cross hands in front of the abdomen with the right hand on the outer side. Hold both arms upward to the front of chest with the palms of hands facing inward (Fig. 2-14-4). Turn the palms of hands outward and push them aside; kick forcefully with the right heel slowly forward on the right, the knee straightened, the right arm over the right leg and the eyes looking at the direction of the right hand (Fig. 2-14-5).

Fig. 2-14-1   Fig. 2-14-2   Fig. 2-14-3

Fig. 2-14-4   Fig. 2-14-5

2.1.15 Striking ears with both fists

Turn the torso right, step back the right leg with the knee bent; turn the palm of the left hand up and move it in a circle to the front of the torso at shoulders' width (Fig. 2-15-1). Bend the left leg and step the right leg forward; meanwhile put down both arms to either side of the waist (Fig. 2-15-2). Bend the right knee forward into a right bow stance, turn the palms of hands into fists and move them in a circle respectively from the side of the waist, back, out to the upper front of the head. Bend the arms like a pair of pliers with both fists facing each other at head's width and the parts between the thumb and index finger of both fists facing obliquely downward (Fig. 2-15-3).

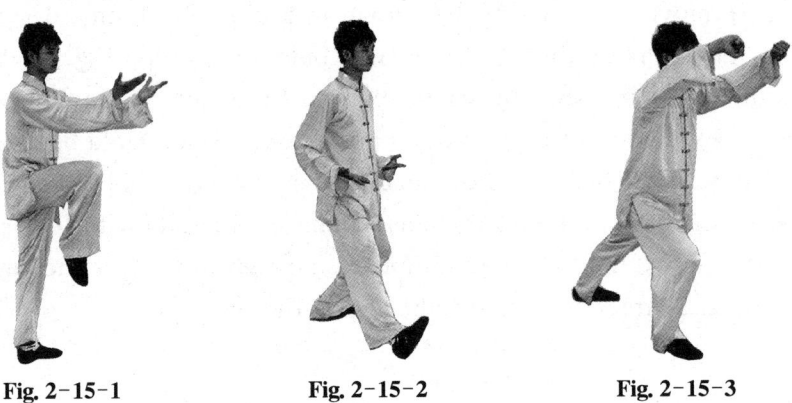

Fig. 2-15-1   Fig. 2-15-2   Fig. 2-15-3

2.1.16 Turning and kicking with the left heel

Shift body weight to the left leg and raise the tiptoes of the right foot (Fig. 2-16-1). Turn the torso left and turn the fists into palms (Fig. 2-16-2). Shift the weight to the right and move the arms in a circle downward (Fig. 2-16-3). Straighten the right leg and step back the left leg and raise it; cross both arms in front of the chest with the left hand at the outer side, both palms of hands facing inward (Fig. 2-16-4). Turn the torso slightly left and turn the palms of hands outward. kick forcefully with the left heel slowly forward on the left, the knee straightened, the left arm over the left leg and the eyes looking at the direction of the left hand (Fig. 2-16-5).

Fig. 2-16-1   Fig. 2-16-2   Fig. 2-16-3

Fig. 2-16-4   Fig. 2-16-5

2.1.17 Crouching down and standing on one leg-left style

Withdraw the left leg to the inner side of the right leg, turn the palm of the right hand into a hook and move the left hand in a circle horizontally to the right elbow with the palm of hand facing right (Fig. 2-17-1). Keep the torso still, crouch the left leg on the left (Fig. 2-17-2); turn the torso left and sink the hip into a left crouch stance. At the same time thread the palm of the left hand leftward along the inner side of the left leg with the part between the thumb and the index finger of palm facing upward (Fig. 2-17-3).

Shift body weight onto the left leg to form a left bow stance and move the left hand up forward; turn the right hooked hand inward with the hook facing upward and place it behind the body (Fig. 2-17-4). Turn the torso left and shift the weight forward. Turn down the palm of the left hand downward; turn the right hooked hand into a palm down and then lift it upward (Fig. 2-17-5). Straighten the left leg, lift the right leg up with the knee bent and stand on the left leg alone. Put down the left hand and press it to the left side of the thigh; lift the right palm further with the palm of hand leftward to the height of the eyes and bend the right arm into an arc (Fig. 2-17-6).

Fig. 2-17-1   Fig. 2-17-2   Fig. 2-17-3

Fig. 2-17-4   Fig. 2-17-5   Fig. 2-17-6

2.1.18 Crouching down and standing on one leg-right style

Land the right leg to the right front of the left foot with its anterior sole putting onto the ground (Fig. 2-18-1). Turn the torso left and move the left foot with the anterior sole as a pivot. Turn the left hand into a hook and raise it to the left side of the torso at the shoulders' height; move the right hand in a circle to the front of the left shoulder with the palm of hand facing left (Fig. 2-18-2).

Step the right leg out on the right and sink the hip into a right crouch stance. At the same time thread the palm of the right hand rightward along the inner side of the right leg with the part between the thumb and the index finger of palm facing upward (Fig. 2-18-3). Shift body weight onto the right leg to form a right bow stance and move the right hand up forward; turn the left hooked hand inward with the hook facing upward and place it behind the body (Fig. 2-18-4). Turn the torso right and shift the weight forward. Turn the palm of the right hand downward; turn the left hooked hand into a palm down and then lift it upward (Fig. 2-18-5). Straighten the right leg, lift the left leg up with the knee bent and stand on the right leg alone. Put down the right hand and press it at the right side of the hip; lift the left palm further with the palm of hand rightward to the height of the eyes and bend the left arm into an arc (Fig. 2-18-6).

Fig. 2-18-1　　　　　　Fig. 2-18-2　　　　　　Fig. 2-18-3

Fig. 2-18-4　　　　　　Fig. 2-18-5　　　　　　Fig. 2-18-6

2.1.19　Weaving shuttles on both sides

(1) Weaving shuttles right

Turn the torso left and land the left leg forward on the left with the tiptoes of the left foot outward and the palm of the left hand downward (Fig. 2-19-1). Bend the right leg and shift the body weight backward; step the right leg forward to the inner side of the left leg into a T stance. Turn the palm of the right hand upward, as if holding a ball with both hands (Fig. 2-19-2). Turn the torso right and step the right foot forward on the right. Move the right hand in a circle up forward; put down the left hand to the left side of the waist (Fig. 2-19-3). Turn the left leg with the left heel and bend the right leg into a bow stance; meanwhile raise the right arm and turn the palm of hand outward at the upper side of the right forehead. Push the left arm forward (Fig. 2-19-4).

Fig. 2-19-1　　　　Fig. 2-19-2　　　　Fig. 2-19-3

Fig. 2-19-4　　　　Fig. 2-19-5　　　　Fig. 2-19-6

(2) **Weaving shuttles left**

Shift the weight backward, turn the tiptoes of the right foot upward and then drop it down to the ground. Shift the body weight to the right leg with the palm of the left hand upward (Fig. 2-19-5). Step the left leg forward to the inner side of the left leg into a T stance. Move both arms in front of chest, as if holding a ball with both hands (Fig. 2-19-6). Turn the torso right and step the left foot forward on the left. Move the left hand in a circle up forward; put down the right hand to the right side of the waist (Fig. 2-19-7). Turn the right leg with the heel and bend the left leg into a bow stance; meanwhile raise the left arm and turn the palm of hand outward at the upper side of the left forehead. Push the right arm forward (Fig. 2-19-8).

Fig. 2-19-7 Fig. 2-19-8

2.1.20 Needling at sea bottom

Put down the left arm and draw back the right arm; move the right foot half a pace forward, shift the weight backward and bend the right leg (Fig. 2-20-1). Turn the torso right, raise the left knee and move the left hand rightward in a circle downward to the front of the left knee with the palm of hand downward and the fingertips rightward obliquely. Lift the right arm with the elbow bent to the right side of the right ear with the palm of hand facing left and the fingertips facing forward (Fig. 2-20-2). Step the left foot forward into a left empty stance and turn the torso left forward. Move the right hand forward down obliquely; move the left hand in a circle past the front of the right knee and then press it to the side of the left thigh, with the eyes looking down ahead (Fig. 2-20-3).

Fig. 2-20-1 Fig. 2-20-2 Fig. 2-20-3

2.1.21 Flashing the arms like a fan

Turn the torso right and step the left leg forward on the left. Raise the right hand up and rotate it inward with the palm of hand slanting up outward; raise the left hand with the fingertips close to the inner side of the right wrist (Fig. 2-21-1). Bend the left leg into a bow stance and turn the torso slightly right. Push the left hand out on the left, move the right hand above the head with the palm of hand upward obliquely and the eyes looking at the direction of the left hand (Fig. 2-21-2).

Fig. 2-21-1   Fig. 2-21-2

2.1.22 Turning body, pulling, blocking and punching

Shift the body weight backward and bend the right leg (Fig. 2-22-1). Turn the torso right, move the tiptoes of the left leg inward and shift the weight slowly onto the left leg; meanwhile move the right hand in a circle to the right side of the torso and the left hand to the left side of the head, respectively, with both palms of hands facing outward (Fig. 2-22-2). Bend the left leg and turn the torso further right; turn the right hand into a fist and withdraw it in front of the abdomen. Move the right leg back and bend its knee (Fig. 2-22-3); raise the right foot up slightly. Press the left hand down past the chest; move the right fist upward with the elbow bent (Fig. 2-22-4). Turn the torso slightly right and step the right foot forward; meanwhile move the right fist forward forcefully with the elbow as the pivot, the palm of fist downward. Draw back the left hand to the left hip (Fig. 2-22-5).

Fig. 2-22-1   Fig. 2-22-2   Fig. 2-22-3

Fig. 2-22-4　　　　　Fig. 2-22-5　　　　　Fig. 2-22-6

Move the tiptoes of the right foot outward and shift the body weight forward. Turn the right arm inward with the palm of fist facing downward (Fig. 2-22-6); turn the torso right and shift the weight forward. Move the right fist in a circle upward to the side of body, with the palm of fist facing downward; stretch the left arm outward and move it in a circle forward with the turning of body, the palm of hand facing downward. Move the left leg back and bend its knee (Fig. 2-22-7). Step the left foot forward and move the left arm outward a little to make the part between the thumb and index finger of the left fist facing upward to block; move the right fist back to the right waist with the palm of fist upward (Fig. 2-22-8). Turn the torso left and shift the weight forward into a left bow stance. Punch the right fist out forward with the part between the thumb and index finger of fist upward; move the left hand back with its fingers to the inner side of the right forearm, with the palm of hand facing right (Fig. 2-22-9).

Fig. 2-22-7　　　　　Fig. 2-22-8　　　　　Fig. 2-22-9

2.1.23 Apparent Sealing-up

Turn the palm of the left hand upward and thread it out from the bottom of the right forearm (Fig. 2-23-1); turn the right fist into a palm facing upward and stretch the left hand forward (Fig. 2-23-2). Part the palms of hands at shoulders' width with the palms facing upward (Fig. 2-23-3). Shift the weight backward, raise the tiptoes of the left foot and move back both arms (Fig. 2-23-4). Move back both hands in front of the chest, turn the arms inward with the palms of hands facing downward in front of the abdomen (Fig. 2-23-5). Shift the weight forward into a left bow stance, push both palms of hands slanting forward up to the horizontal level and then push them forward (Fig. 2-23-6).

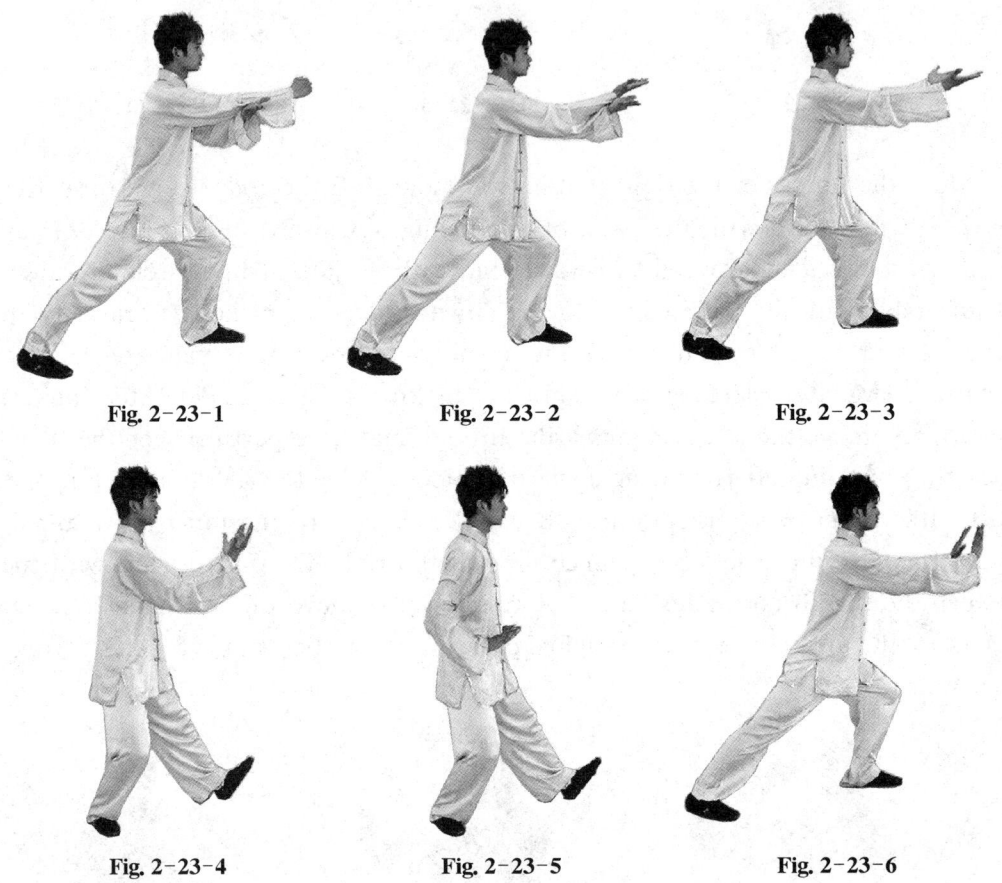

Fig. 2-23-1   Fig. 2-23-2   Fig. 2-23-3

Fig. 2-23-4   Fig. 2-23-5   Fig. 2-23-6

2.1.24 Cross hand

Shift the body weight backward and raise the tiptoes of the left foot (Fig. 2-24-1). Turn the torso right and move the tiptoes of the left foot inward; move the right hand in a circle rightward horizontally (Fig. 2-24-2). Turn the torso right and move the right foot outward; meanwhile move the right hand in a circle further (Fig. 2-24-3).

Put both arms down and cross both wrists in front of the abdomen with the right hand at the outside, palms of hands facing upward. Move the right leg back to the left leg at shoulders' width; meanwhile raise both arms upward in front of the chest with the palms of hands facing inward (Fig. 2-24-4).

Fig. 2-24-1　　　Fig. 2-24-2　　　Fig. 2-24-3

Fig. 2-24-4　　　Fig. 2-25-1　　　Fig. 2-25-2

2.1.25　Closing posture

Move both arms inward and turn both palms of hands downward (Fig. 2-25-1). Part both arms horizontally (Fig. 2-25-2). Straighten both legs; meanwhile press both arms to either side of the thighs (Fig. 2-25-3). Put down both hands with eyes looking straight ahead (Fig. 2-25-4). Step back the left foot slowly, turn back to the ready position with eyes looking forward (Fig. 2-25-5).

Fig. 2-25-3　　　Fig. 2-25-4　　　Fig. 2-25-5

2.2 Learning program

Item	Content
Preparation	1. Handwork in Taijiquan(to understand the features of physical relaxation, softness, slowness, roundness of Taijiquan movements) 2. Footwork in Taijiquan(to practice Taijiquan footwork and weight shifting) 3. Stake methods in Taijiquan(to know the physical fitness and mental health)
Syllabus	1. To learn the routes of physical movements 　　(1) Starting posture, parting wild horse's mane, white crane spreading wings 　　(2) Brushing knee and twisting step; playing pipa (the chinese lute) 　　(3) Repulsing monkey; grasping bird's tail, left and right 　　(4) Single bian (whip); cloud hands; single bian (whip) 　　(5) High patting on horse; kicking with the right heel; kicking with the left heel 　　(6) Crouching down and standing on one leg-right style; crouching down and standing on one leg-left style 　　(7) Weaving shuttles, left and right; needling at sea bottom; flashing the arms like a fan 　　(8) Turning around, blocking and punching; apparent sealing-up; cross hand; closing posture 2. To experience the movement features of Taijiquan

2.3 Technique experience

Content	Requirements
Peaceful mind & physical relaxation	"Peaceful mind" refers to a state of clearing all thoughts of the mind and concentrating on Taijiquan practice, coordinating the movements with the breathing; "Physical relaxation" does not mean you slack off, but you should take right physical positions and consciously relax joints and muscles of the whole body to the maximum.
A clear distinction between emptiness & substantiality	A clear distinction between emptiness and substantiality should be made in Taijiquan practice; the weight-carrying leg is named "substantiality" while the supporting or shifting leg is named "emptiness"; the arm leading movements is named "substantiality" while the arm supporting movements is named "emptiness." Particular attention should be paid to the shifting from emptiness to substantiality in doing Taijiquan.
Roundness, dexterity & coherence	Roundness and dexterity is featured as the most significant movement rules in Taijiquan practice. The route of the movements as well as the physical posture should follow the circular rules in Taijiquan practice. You should not be rigid and stagnant in physical movements and the whole taolu should be done smoothly and naturally. Coherence in Taijiquan can be manifested in different aspects. It not only refers to "moving one joint after another" when taking waist as its pivot, that is to say, move the waist and then downward to the hips, to the knees and to the feet in a row. Or move the waist to the back, to the shoulders, to the elbows and then to the hands in a row; but it also refers to the smooth and coherent flow among different forms.
Breathing naturally	There are three categories of breathing, including unconscious and natural breathing (taken by most people in their daily lives), diaphragmatic breathing and reversed diaphragmatic breathing. Breathing naturally in Taijiquan can only be achieved on the basis of conscious diaphragmatic breathing and gradually to a high degree of proficiency, which can be regarded as natural breathing.

2.4 Culture experience

- **Taiji**

Inspired by the book "*Books of Changes · Appended Judgments Commentary*", the famous philosopher Zhou Dunyi in the Song Dynasty explained his view on the universe in his book *The Diagram of Taiji*: Wuji produces Taiji while Taiji generates **Yang**. The extremity of mobility is motionlessness and vice versa. They are the roots of each other. Separation of Yin and Yang makes the heaven and the earth.

Taijiquan is characterized by its implicit nature, continuity, capability to overcome strength with gentleness. It has rapid while slow rhythm as well as smooth movements, elevating the practitioner to a supreme state of mind where his/her will, chi, physique and spirit are gradually integrated. The requirement of instilling the virtue of martial arts in Taijiquan calls for both building up his/her body and enhancing his/her quality, and promoting the integration and harmony between human beings and the nature as well as between human beings and the society.

- **Yin and Yang**

Yin and Yang come from the naturalistic perspective in ancient China and are the philosophical generalization of mutually related and contradicted natural phenomena such as the heaven and the earth, the sun and the moon, day and night, coldness and hotness, men and women, up and down.

The fighting method of Taijiquan accords closely with the theory of yin and yang, in which "how to guide the opponents, transform their energy, merge the energy from both sides, and strike the opponent" are the major working principles. In the process, one makes use of Tingjing (predicting the energy of the opponent) to perceive and alter the direction and strength of the opponent's strikes, "go along with the opponent's energy but change the direction of its energy", so that the energy can be transformed and returned to the opponent.

The feature of Taijiquan can be concluded as followed: overcoming the strength with the gentleness, ridding the opponent's movements with stillness, transforming straight attack into a circular direction, defeating the big with the small and conquering the strong with the weak.

- **The Thirteen Postures of Taijiquan**

The thirteen postures are to be taken seriously with the crux of the will and the energy at the waist;

Heed the shift of emptiness and subsidiarity while keeping the flow of chi without stagnation.

Stillness exists in motion while motion in stillness; the miracle lies in the process of going along and transforming the energy of the opponent. Observe and predict the fighting intention in each posture of the opponent and it is easier to be acquired.

Mind the waist all the time; relax the abdomen, purify the mind and keep smooth flow of chi. Straighten up the coccyx, hang up the vertex of the head feeling gentle and agile.

Carefully study details of each movement and reach a natural state of having an entirely free hand in opening and closing movements. Taijiquan beginner should be tutored by a master skilled in both theory and practice, then gradually learns and summarizes the gist.

Concerning how to understand the precise method of Taijiquan, it depends on the will and chi circulation rather than the strength obtained from bones and flesh.

As for the purpose of practicing Taijiquan, the answer is to promote health and prolong lives.

Every word in this lyrical poem matters a lot without losing any meaning. If one does not practice according to these principles, all the efforts will amount to nothing.

3 Conclusion

- 24-form Taijiquan is regarded as an introductory taolu to Taijiquan practitioners.
- Physical relaxation, sinuous gracefulness and slow movements are needed in Taijiquan practice after you have well memorized the movement map of its taolu.
- Having obtained the key to peaceful mind and breathing naturally, you can pursue a deeper understanding of the clear distinction between emptiness and substantiality, and the roundness, dexterity and coherence in its movements.

4 Extensive Reading

Having learnt the program of 24-form Taijiquan, you can keep on learning other Taijiquan taolu to have a deeper understanding of its movement features and expand the study, for instance, 48-form Taijiquan, 42-form Taiji Sword etc. Moreover, a profound perception of Taijiquan can be obtained with an extended study on different styles of Taijiquan, for example, Chen-style, Yang-style, Wú-style, Wǔ-style, Sun-style

Taijiquan.

5 Questions

(1) What are the four typical movements of striking, pulling, pushing, and pressing in Taijiquan?

(2) How can you breathe naturally?

(3) What is the perception of slow-acting movements in Taijiquan? What is the best way to do it?

6 References

[1] Qiu Pixiang. Chinese Wushu (Book I)[M]. Beijing: People Sport Publishing House. 2004.

[2] Textbook Committee of National Sport Universities. Wushu: A Standardized Book for General Education of Sports Majors. Eds[M]. Beijing: People Sport Publishing House. 1989.

[3] TangHao, Gu Liuxin. Study of Taijiquan [M]. Beijing: People Sport Publishing House. 1964.

[4] Wudong. An Introduction and Promotion to 24-form Taijiquan[M]. Shanxi: Shanxi Science and Technology Publishing House. 2001.

Chapter Three

Xingyiquan (Five-Element Link Fist-Play)

1 Introduction

Xingyiquan claims to originate from Shanxi Province, and is prevalent throughout Shanxi, Hebei and Henan provinces. It is based on three-in-one integral stake stance, taking Wuxingquan (punching including chopping, punching drilling, cannoning, hammering) and twelve forms of fist play (which imitate the animals of dragon, tiger, monkey, horse, rooster, sandpiper, swallow, snake, caiman, horse, hawk, bear, etc.) as its basic fist play. It includes solo taolu (known as "routine", the same as below) such as Wuxing Lianhuan (Five-element link Fist-Play), Zashichui (Fist-Play of miscellanea), 8-form Quan and sparring taolu such as Sanshoupao (Three-hand punch), Wuhuapao (Five-flower punch), Anshenpao (Body-protecting punch).

2 Learning experience

2.1 Movements

2.1.1 Ready position

With the body straight, droop both arms naturally on either side of the body; bring both feet together with eyes looking forward down (Fig. 3-1).

2.1.2 Stepping forward and chopping

Keep the body direction unchanged, step the left foot forward with heels facing each other at about two feet apart, bend both knees and shift body weight onto the right leg. Move the fists up and then change them into palms; stretch the left palm of hand forward and bend the elbow slightly, the palm of hand facing forward down and five fingers stretched apart and the palm of hand sunken at the height of the chest. Withdraw the right palm to the front of the abdomen; put the thumb close to the navel with its wrist dropped and with the eyes looking at the left index finger (Fig. 3-2).

2.1.3 Stepping forward and punching-right

Clench both palms of hands into fists and step the left leg forward with the right foot followed at the clistance of 20~30 cm, shift the body weight to the right leg; strike the right fist forward along the left arm with the part between the thumb and index finger facing upward and the palm of the fist leaning forward slightly. Withdraw the left fist to the left side of the waist with the palm of fist facing upward and the eyes looking at the right fist(Fig. 3-3).

Fig. 3-1　　　　**Fig. 3-2**　　　　**Fig. 3-3**

2.1.4 Stepping back and punching left (Blue dragon coming out of water)

Move the right leg half a step back, withdraw the left foot to the back of the right foot while punching the left fist forward with the part between the thumb and index finger facing upward; withdraw the right fist back to the right side of the waist with the palm of fist facing upward and eyes looking at the left fist (Fig. 3-4).

2.1.5 The same-side step and punching right (Black tiger coming out of cave)

Move the right foot one pace forward, the left foot half a pace followed; punch the right fist forward in the direction of the right foot with the part between the thumb and index finger facing upward at the height of the chest. Withdraw the left fist to the left side of the waist with the palm of fist facing upward and eyes looking at the right fist (Fig. 3-5).

Fig. 3-4　　　　**Fig. 3-5**

2.1.6 Stepping back and holding fists (White crane spreading its wings)

Move the left foot half a pace backward to the left, shift the body weight and form the right bow stance. At the same time bend the right arm and droop it to the front of the abdomen with the palm of fist facing upward, cross both arms in front of the abdomen and raise them upward to the front of the head, and then take them apart to either side of it (Fig. 3-6). Droop both palms down to the front of the abdomen and punch the right fist onto the palm of the left hand. Turn the torso slightly rightward, and withdraw the right foot to the front of the left foot with the eyes looking forward (Fig. 3-7).

Fig. 3-6   Fig. 3-7

2.1.7 Stepping forward and cannoning

Step the right foot forward to the front on the right with the left foot followed half a pace forward while turning over the right fist in front of the chest resting at the right side of head; turn the left palm into a fist and punch it forward with the eyes looking at the left fist (Fig. 3-8).

2.1.8 Stepping back and chopping-left

Punch the right fist to the front of the torso with the palm of fist facing up, withdraw the left fist to the left side of the waist, and step back the right foot with the eyes looking at the right fist (Fig. 3-9). Stretch the left fist forward and turn it into a palm, turn it over and press it forward, turn the right fist into a palm and press it to the front of the abdomen with the eyes looking at the left palm (Fig. 3-10).

Fig. 3-8   Fig. 3-9   Fig. 3-10

2.1.9 Twisting step and drilling-right

Turn the torso slightly to the right and turn the left palm into a fist to the front of the chest with the palm of both fists upward (Fig. 3-11). Withdraw the left foot to the inner side of the right ankle; move the right foot half a pace forward and drill the right fist forward up along the front of the left forearm at the height of the tip of the nose. Rotate the left arm inward and withdraw it to the left side of the abdomen with the palm of fist facing downward and the eyes looking at the right fist (Fig. 3-12).

Fig. 3-11   Fig. 3-12

2.1.10 Leaping and chopping with both palms (Leopard cat climbing tree)

Keep both hands motionless, move the left foot half a step forward; at the same time bend the right knee and lift the foot with the tiptoes hooked slantingly (Fig. 3-13). Land the right heel and tramp the ground forward with the left foot half a pace forward. Raise the heel from the ground with the right foot horizontal and the left foot vertical, thus to cross them into a half squat. Turn the left fist into a palm and stretch it forward from the inner side of the right arm and chop it upward, with the front hand no higher than the mouth. Withdraw the right fist to the front of the abdomen, the eyes looking at the tip of the left index finger (Fig. 3-14).

Fig. 3-13   Fig. 3-14   Fig. 3-15

2.1.11 Stepping forward and punching right

Turn both palms of hands into fists, move the right foot half a pace forward, then step the left foot forward with the right foot followed half a pace while punching the right fist forward along the left arm with the part between the thumb and index finger of fist facing upward. Withdraw the left fist to the left side of the waist with the palm of fist facing upward and the eyes looking at the right fist (Fig. 3-15).

2.1.12 Stepping back (Leopard cat climbing tree reversely)

Rotate the tip of the left foot inward, take the sole of the right foot as an axis, turn the torso 180 degree backward from the right side while bending the right fist and withdraw it to the right side of the waist with the palm of fist facing upward. Shift the weight to the left foot with the eyes looking forward horizontally. Shift the weight to the left leg, lift up the right leg with the toes of the right foot hooked upward while drilling the right fist through the chin forward up at the height of the tip of the nose (Fig. 3-16). Raise the right heels from the ground and lean the left knee joint against the right knee pit closely. Stretch the left fist upward along the inner side of the right arm and chop it down, the front hand no higher than the mouth. Turn the right fist into a palm and withdraw it to the front of the abdomen with the eyes looking at the tip of the left index finger (Fig. 3-17).

Fig. 3-16   Fig. 3-17

2.1.13 Closing position

Turn both palms into fists, move back the right foot half a pace; step back the left foot behind the right foot. Cross both legs with the left foot vertically and right foot horizontally; raise the left heel slightly above the ground and cross both legs into a half squat. Punch the left fist forward while stepping back the left foot, withdraw the right fist back to the right side of the waist with the palm of fist facing upward and the eyes looking at the left fist (Fig. 3-18). Step back the right foot to the inner side of the left foot, stand up slowly, and put both hands down on either side of the torso (Fig. 3-19).

Fig. 3-18

Fig. 3-19

2.2 Learning program

	Objectives	Content
Preliminary preparations	Basic stake-standing stance	three-in-one integral(stake-standing)
	Footwork of Xingyiquan	stepping forward, stepping backward, stepping up, withdrawing step, following-up step, shin-rubbing step, swinging step, inward-moving step, crossing-over step, back-inserting step, switching step, stepping at the same side, twisting step, jumping, giant striding, striding, leaping, bringing feet together
Schedule	To learn the taolu of Wuxingquan (Five-element link fist-paly)	chopping punching drilling cannoning hammering five-element link fist-play

2.3 Technique experience

Content	Requirements
Movement standards	1. Correct three-in-one integral stake-standing 2. Correct movement routes and movements 3. Skillful movements
External three-in-one	1. Shoulders coordinating with hips 2. Elbows coordinating with knees 3. Feet coordinating with hands
Internal three-in-one	1. Mind guiding will 2. Will guiding Qi (Chi) 3. Qi (Chi) guiding energy

Content	Requirements
Movement features	1. Unifying the internal with the external into an integrated wholeness 2. To be cohesive, coordinated, sedated and integrative 3. Three tips facing each other; three joints following each other 4. To be solid and swift

(continued)

2.4 Culture experience

- **The theory of generation-inhibition in five elements in Xingyiquan**

Wuxingquan (Five-element Fist-Paly) refers to Chopping, Punching, Drilling, Cannoning and Hammering.

Chopping is like an axe, which belongs to metal; Punching is like an arrow, which belongs to wood; Drilling is like a thunder, which belongs to water; Cannoning is like a cannon, which belongs to fire; Hammering is like a bullet, which belongs to earth. Hammering is the mother of these five fist plays, because the earth is pregnant with the world. The earth is the mother of the world, so Hammering is called the mother of fist plays.

Five-element Fist-Play is based on the natural laws of "generation-inhibition in five elements". Generation means Chopping can be turned into Drilling and Drilling into Punching, Punching into Cannoning, cannoning into Hammering. Inhibition among Five-element Fist-Play goes as "Chopping breaks through Punching; Punching breaks through Hammering; and Hammering breaks through Drilling, drilling breaks through cannoning while cannoning breaks through chopping".

- **"Internal and external cultivation" and "Dao supervises Shu and Shu represents Dao" in Xingyiquan**

"Internal" refers to organs in human body and the will of mind while "external" refers to physical movements caused by contracting and stretching of muscles; "internal" refers to human body while "external" refers to the "heaven" beyond human body. "Shu" can be defined as techniques or methods while "Dao" represents principles and rules to be followed in wushu practice.

Human body is viewed as a mini-universe in Xingyiquan while the world is regarded as a large universe. Practitioners can achievethe oneness between the large and the mini universe by doing Xingyiquan, which can be named as "oneness of human and heaven".

- **Three-in-one integral stake-standing in Xingyiquan**

The three-in-one integral stake-standing mainly refers to the stake stance, in

Xingyiquan which can be seen not only in the commencement position, in the closing position and in all kinds of taolu, but it forms a solid foundation for all kinds of other technical skills in Xingyiquan.

The three-in-one integral stake-standing in Xingyiquan grasps the ideas of Taiji, including two appearances, three sections, four tips, five elements, six-in-one unifications, seven stars, eight characters and eight musts, nine-counting in Xingyiquan, which is essential not only to preliminary practitioners but to advanced wushu masters as well, as the saying goes "all kung fu (wushu) are originated from the three-in one integral idea."

3 Conclusion

- The three-in-one integral stake standing is regarded as an introductory exercise in Xingyiquan, which tells the basic body posture of Xingyiquan.
- Five-element Link Fist-Play is the basic routine in Xingyiquan, which is the exercise of "Chopping, Punching, Drilling, Cannoning and Hammering".
- Firstly, memorize the correct map of your movements and specified movement standards of Five-element Fist-Play; secondly, attain "six-in-one unifications" mentioned above; finally, acquire the unique movement features of Xingyiquan.
- Xingyiquan emphasizes not only the stable stake-standing, but the wrapping energy, holding energy and competing energy, etc.

4 Extensive reading

Learning Xingyiquan makes you not only command a good knowledge of the technical skills of internal and external three-in-one unifications, but further the practice of "12 animal forms". "12 animal forms" imitates the unique skills of twelve animals such as dragon, tiger, monkey, horse, rooster, sandpiper, swallow, snake, Caimen, horse hawk and bear, which generates its meanings from these animals' images and adopt these images from animals' movements.

5 Questions

(1) Why are internal and external three-in-one skills key elements and should be trained intensively in doing Xingyiquan?

(2) Why should practitioners put both elbows clinging to ribs and both hands around the heart?

(3) What is your understanding of "relaxing the chest, infusing the abdomen, breathing Qi (Chi) into Dantian"?

6　References

Li Tianji, Li Deyin. Xingyiquan [M]. Beijing: People Sport Publishing House. 1981.

Chapter Four

Baguazhang (Eight-Diagram Palm-Play)

1 Introduction

Baguazhang (Eight-Diagram Palm-Play), invented by Dong Haichuan, is one of Quan styles widely spread. It is characterized by "turning in circle, changing posture while walking without any interruption, walking steadily, twisting lock clearly, and moving in crisscross patterns flexibly and coordination". The routine is called "Set Baguazhang", including 8 single palm movements, i. e. "pressing, lifting, hitting, closing, stretching, holding, standing and pushing". It is the basic taolu (known as "routines", the same as below) of Baguazhang.

2 Learning experience

2.1 Directions

2.1.1 Ready position

Stand along the circle and bring feet together, with two hands naturally hanging down the outer side of thighs, facing south. Keep the head straight, close mouth, clench teeth and relax body, eyes looking at the front straight (Fig. 4-1).

Fig. 4-1

Fig. 4-2-1

Fig. 4-2-2

2.1.2 Pressing Palms (Sinking Palms)

(1) Left form

Turn two arms outward with the palms upward and raise them from the two sides of body, the elbows bent slightly and two arms higher than the shoulder a little, looking at the front straight (Fig. 4-2-1). With the palms downward and fingers of two hands facing together, bend the two elbows and put arms down in front of the abdomen along the front of body. At the same time, bend two knees into a slight crouch, looking at the front straight (Fig. 4-2-2).

With the two palms unchanged, turn the upper body left to face the center of circle on the left. Shift the body weight onto the right leg. Meanwhile move the left foot one pace close to the inner side of the right ankle, with the toes pointing down inwardly a little and sole of the foot touching the ground emptily. Look at the center of circle on the left (Fig. 4-2-3). Shift the body weight onto the left foot and bend the knee; move the right foot one pace close to the inner side of the left ankle, with the toes pointing down inwardly a little and the sole of the foot touching the ground emptily. Keeping the two palms unchanged, look at the center of circle on the left (Fig. 4-2-4). Keep walking along the circle with two feet alternately to the place where the ready position is (Fig. 4-2-5, Fig. 4-2-6, Fig. 4-2-7).

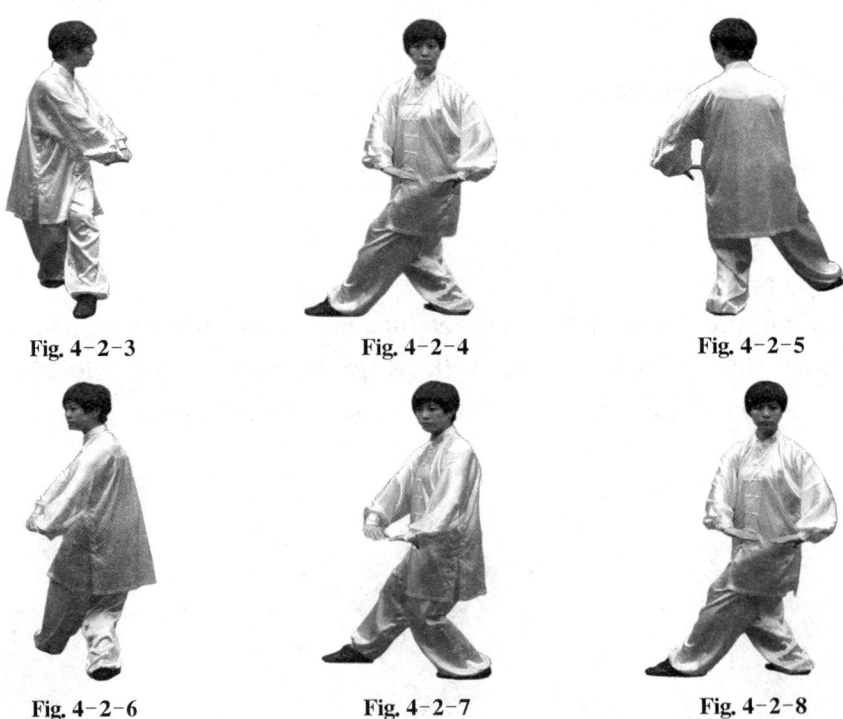

Fig. 4-2-3　　　　　Fig. 4-2-4　　　　　Fig. 4-2-5

Fig. 4-2-6　　　　　Fig. 4-2-7　　　　　Fig. 4-2-8

(2) Right form

Following the last movement till the left foot is ahead (Fig. 4-2-7), move the right foot one step to the front of the left foot, facing the center of circle with the two palms unchanged and eyes gazing at the center of circle (Fig. 4-2-8). Move the waist with the shoulder and arm moving in coordination, shift the two palms in a horizontal arc from left, front and right to the right side of the abdomen, the palms downward. Shift the body weight to the right leg and look at the palms (Fig. 4-2-9). Turn the upper body left and shift the body weight onto the left leg. Move the right leg forward along the circle with the toes straight. Turn the waist to move the upper body and arms rightward to face the center of circle, the eyes looking at the front straight (Fig. 4-2-10). Turn and walk along the circle till change it to the right form of Pressing Palm.

Fig. 4-2-9   Fig. 4-2-10   Fig. 4-2-11

2.1.3 Lifting Palms (A great hawk spreads its wings)

(1) Right form

Following the last movement, move the left leg one step to the front of the right leg; rotate two arms outward and lift them from the front of abdomen to the front of chest, with the fingers upward obliquely and arms crossed, looking at the two palms (Fig. 4-3-1). Shift the body weight onto the left leg; at the same time move it forward one pace and stretch out the two palms from forehead to the two sides of body, the elbows bent slightly and palms upward, a little higher than the shoulder, thus a Lifting Palm is formed. Turn the upper body right to face the center of circle. With the eyes looking straight, turn and walk along the circle (Fig. 4-3-2).

Fig. 4-3-1   Fig. 4-3-2

(2) Left form

Follow the last movement and move the left foot one step to the front of the right foot. Bend two knees to form a tight-horse-riding stance. Meanwhile, close two arms crossed inward and place the palms to the top front of the chest, the palms upward and eyes looking at the palms (Fig. 4-3-3). Turn the upper body right to shift the body weight onto the left leg. Turn the right leg to the back right and step it back rightward with the toes pointed. Meanwhile, turn two arms inward and turn the palms over to the two sides of knees, the palms facing outward obliquely, the fingers of two hands facing together and eyes gazing at the circle (Fig. 4-3-4). Shift the body weight rightward and move the left leg one pace to the right front, with the toes pointing outwardly a little. Meanwhile, turn two arms outward, turn the palms over and lift them up from the two sides of body, with the palms upward, higher than the shoulder slightly. Keeping the upper body unchanged, only twist waist leftward to face the circle. Turn and walk along the circle (Fig. 4-3-5).

Fig. 4-3-3　　　　　Fig. 4-3-4　　　　　Fig. 4-3-5

2.1.4　Pushing Palms (Double Pushing Palms)

(1) Left form

Following the last movement, bend elbows, turn wrists and push palms forward from the front of the shoulders, the palms outward, thumbs downward and both sets of fingers pointing towards each other. Raise the arms up in a circle to the height of the chest. Keep the upper body and legs unchanged, walk along the circle for once till the left foot is ahead and then change it to the next form, looking at the palms (Fig. 4-4-1).

(2) Right form

Follow the last movement and step the right foot forward to the front of the left foot. With the left foot unchanged, bend two knees and face the circle, the palms unchanged and eyes gazing at them (Fig. 4-4-2). Shift the body weight to the right leg and turn the upper body left slightly. Turn the left leg and step the foot left behind along with the turning of upper body. Meanwhile thread the right palm out from below the left elbow and cross the arms at the front of the chest with the left palm above the right one and eyes looking at the left palm

(Fig. 4-4-3). Move the right foot forward one step from the inner side of the left ankle and twist the upper body right slightly. Meanwhile, turn two wrists and arms to push palms forward along with the turning of the upper body, the thumbs facing downward and the palms facing the circle at the level of chest. Walk along the circle once till the right leg is ahead and then change it to the next form. Look at the palms (Fig. 4-4-4).

Fig. 4-4-1　　　　　　Fig. 4-4-2　　　　　　Fig. 4-4-3

Fig. 4-4-4　　　　　　Fig. 4-5-1　　　　　　Fig. 4-5-2

2.1.5　Bringing heels of palms together (A white monkey offers the peach)

(1) Right form

Following the last movement, bend elbows, turn wrists and push arms forward from the two sides of the waist to the below, with the heels of two palms close together, the thumbs facing upward and palms facing the circle at the level of abdomen. Walk along the circle once till the right leg is ahead and then change it to the next form (Fig. 4-5-1).

(2) Left form

Following the last movement, move the left foot one pace to the front of the right foot and bend knees to form a tight-horse-riding stance. Keep the upper body and palms unchanged, eyes looking at the palms (Fig. 4-5-2). Turn the upper body right, and move the right foot rightward half a pace with the body weight on the right leg. Meanwhile place the palms at the front of the left thigh. Look at the palms (Fig. 4-5-3). Move the left foot one pace to the right front and keep the right foot unchanged. Turn the upper body left slightly. At the same time, put the wrists close together to push the palms out toward the circle, with the heels of two palms close together, the thumbs facing upward and palms facing the circle at the level of chest. Look at the palms. Walk along the circle once till the left foot is ahead and then change it to the next form (Fig. 4-5-4).

Fig. 4-5-3

Fig. 4-5-4

2.1.6 Stretching Palms (Yinyang Zhang)

(1) Left form

Following the last movement, turn the right arm inward, bend the elbow and push the right palm to the right front horizontally, the thumb facing downward and the palm forward at the level of the head. Meanwhile turn the left arm inward and push the left palm out from the side of the left waist to the back of body, the palm facing backward as high as the hip. Eyes gazing at the circle, walk along it once till the left foot is ahead and then change it to the next form (Fig 4-6-1).

Fig. 4-6-1

Fig. 4-6-2

Fig. 4-6-3

(2) Right form

Follow the last movement and step the right foot forward to the front of the left foot. With the left foot unchanged, bend the knees to form a tight-horse-riding stance and face the circle. Keep the palms unchanged and look forward straight (Fig 4-6-2). Turn the upper body left and step the left foot to the back leftward with the toes straight; keep the right foot unchanged and bend knees to form a horse stance. At the same time, scoop the left palm out to the left front, the thumb facing downward and palm forward as high as the chest. Turn the right arm inward and place the right palm at the back right side of the body, with the five fingers facing downward and palm backward. Look at the left palm (Fig 4-6-3). Move the right foot one pace forward; meanwhile turn the right arm outward and thread it out forward from below the left arm, the palm facing upward to the level of the eyebrow. Turn the left wrist and arm to draw the left palm back and place it at the top of the inner side of the right elbow, the palm facing upward and eyes gazing at it (Fig 4-6-4). Turn the upper body right slightly, turn the left arm inward and push the palm forward to the level of head with the thumb facing downward and elbow bent. Turn the right arm accordingly inward and push the right palm out toward the back of body along the side of the right waist to the height of the hip, the palm backward. Look at the circle, walk along it once till the right foot is ahead and then change it to the next form (Fig 4-6-5).

Fig. 4-6-4   Fig. 4-6-5

2.1.7 Holding Palms (A lion opens its mouth)

(1) Right form

Following last movement and turn the right arm outward with the elbow bent and thread the right arm out toward the circle from the back of body to the level of shoulder, the palm facing upward. The left elbow bent, turn the left palm outward and place it up above the front of head, the palm facing downward obliquely. Look at the right palm and walk along the circle once till the right foot is ahead and then change it to the next form (Fig 4-7-1).

(2) Left form

Following the last movement, move the left foot one pace forward to the front of the right foot and bend knees to form a tight-horse-riding stance. Face the circle with the upper body and palms unchanged, eyes gazing at the right palm (Fig 4-7-2). Turn the upper body right and step the right foot out toward the back right along the turning of body, the toes extending outward. At the same time turn the left arm outward and thread the palm out toward the front left from below the right arm till the height of shoulder, the palm facing upward. Turn the right arm inward and twist the right palm up and place it at the right front of head, eyes gazing at the left palm (Fig. 4-7-3). Move the left foot one pace to the front of the right foot. Meanwhile lean upper body to the right backward with the palms unchanged and eyes gazing at them (Fig. 4-7-4).

Turn the upper body right with the left foot unchanged, and move the right foot one pace backward right. Turn the forearms inward and scoop them down rightward from the front of body and place them below the left side of abdomen, the palms facing downward and eyes gazing at them (Fig. 4-7-5). Turn the upper body left slightly and move the left foot one pace rightward to the front of the right foot, the toes pointed inward slightly; step the right foot forward. Meanwhile turn the left forearm outward and push the left palm out toward the left front to the height of shoulder, the palm facing upward. Turn the right arm and wrist, push the right palm out toward the front and top from below and place it at the right front above head, the palm facing the left palm downward obliquely. Look at the left palm and walk along the circle once till the left foot is ahead and then change it to the next form (Fig. 4-7-6).

Fig. 4-7-1 Fig. 4-7-2 Fig. 4-7-3

Fig. 4-7-4 Fig. 4-7-5 Fig. 4-7-6

2.1.8 Standing Palms (Pointing at sky and piercing the ground)

(1) Left form

Following the last movement, keep the left forearm turning outward and thread the left palm up out along the left side of body; with the five fingers up and palm inward, place it at the back above head. At the same time, turn the right forearm outward and pierce the right palm down and place it at the left side of hip, the fingers facing down and palm outward. Look at the circle and walk along it once till the left foot is ahead and then change to the next form (Fig. 4-8-1).

(2) Right form

Following the last movement, keep the upper body and palms unchanged. Step the right leg one pace forward to the front of the left foot to form a tight-horse-riding stance. Face the circle with eyes looking straight (Fig. 4-8-2). Turn the upper body left and step the left foot outward half a pace to the front left, the toes pointed straight. At the same time, turn two forearms outward and droop the left palm down from the top, thread the right palm out up from below and cross two palms at the front of body. With the fingers of the right hand facing upward and palm inward, thread the right palm out up along the inner side of the right arm and place it at the right back above head. With the fingers of the left hand facing down and palm outward, pierce the left palm down along the outer side and place it at the right side of hip, eyes gazing at the circle (Fig. 4-8-3). Keep the upper body and two palms unchanged, walk along the circle once till the fight foot is ahead and then change it to the next form (Fig. 4-8-4).

Fig. 4-8-1　　　　　　　　Fig. 4-8-2

Fig. 4-8-3　　　　　　　　Fig. 4-8-4

2.1.9　Pushing Palms (Black dragon displays its claws)

(1) Right form

Following the last movement, turn the right forearm inward with the elbow bent slightly and drop the right palm down to the level of eyebrow, the fingers facing upward and palm inward. Meanwhile turn the left arm inward and raise it up with the elbow bent and place the left palm below the inner side of the right elbow, the fingers facing up and the palm outward obliquely. Look at the right palm and walk along the circle once till the right foot is ahead and then change to the next form (Fig. 4-9-1).

(2) Left form

Following the last movement, move the left foot forward one pace to the front of the right foot; bend knees to form a tight-horse-riding stance. Face the circle and look at the right palm (Fig. 4-9-2). Shift the body weight leftward, turn the upper body right and move the right foot out half a pace toward the front right; bend knees to form a tight-horse-riding stance. At the same time, turn the right forearm inward and prop the right palm up in a half circle at the front right, to the level of shoulder, the fingers facing upward obliquely and the palm upward. Turn the left forearm outward and thread the left palm out to the right side of body from below the right arm and place it below the outer side of the right armpit, the eyes gazing at the left palm (Fig. 4-9-3). Move the left foot one pace forward; keep the right foot unchanged and bend knees. Continue to thread the left palm up to the level of head, turn the right wrist with the elbow bent, draw the right palm back and place it above the inner side of the left forearm, the two palms facing upward. Look at the left palm (Fig. 4-9-4). Turn the upper body left and move the left foot one pace forward. At the same time, turn the arms and wrists to push and press the palms leftward, the left palm at the front with the fingers facing up and palm outward as high as the level of eyebrow. With the right elbow bent, place the right palm below the inner side of the left elbow, the fingers facing up and palm outward. Look at the left palm (Fig. 4-9-5, Fig. 4-9-6). Walk along the circle once till the left foot is ahead and then change it to the next form.

Fig. 4-9-1   Fig. 4-9-2   Fig. 4-9-3

Fig. 4-9-4   Fig. 4-9-5   Fig. 4-9-6

2.1.10 Closing position

Following the last movement, move the right foot forward close to the front of the left foot; keep the left foot unchanged, only step the toes pointed outward, the legs straight. At the same time, turn the arms outward and lift them up at the two sides with the palms facing up as high as the level of eyebrow, the eyes gazing straight (Fig. 4-10-1). Turn the palms inward with elbows bent, press the palms downward with the set of fingers of two hands facing each other (Fig. 4-10-2). Droop the palms down and place them at the outer side of thighs along the front of body. Look forward straight (4-10-3).

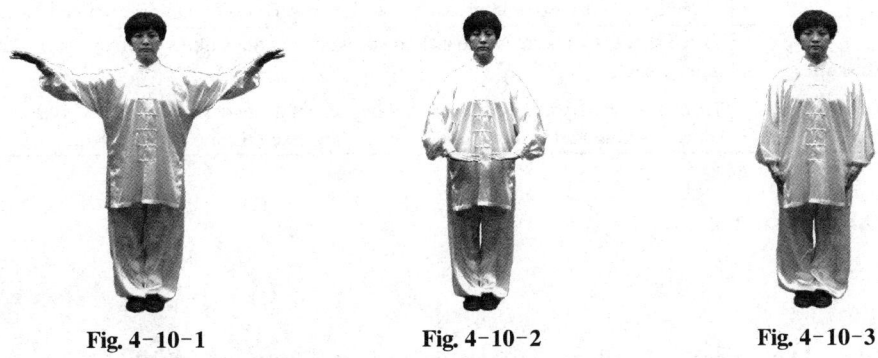

Fig. 4-10-1　　　　　**Fig. 4-10-2**　　　　　**Fig. 4-10-3**

2.2 Learning program

Item	Content
Preparations	The training of flexibility
	The basic footwork of Baguazhang
Schedule	Pressing Palms (Sinking Palms)
	Lifting Palms
	Hitting Palms (Double Hitting Palms)
	Bringing heels of palms together (A white monkey offers the peach)
	Stretching Palms (Yinyang Zhang)
	Holding Palms (A lion opens its mouth)
	Standing palm (Pointing at sky and piercing the ground)
	Pushing Palms (Black dragon displays its claws) and closing posture

2.3 Technique experience

Types	Content	Requirements
Regulations	One mind and five force exertions	One mind: stepping is like walking on mud.
		Five force exertion methods: there are five force exertion methods, i.e. heel kicking, kicking, rubbing, reaching and stamping from the ready position to closing position.
	Three hollows and three relaxations	Three hollows: palm, sole and chest should be hollow.
		Three relaxations: shoulders, palms & soles, and teeth should be relaxed.
	Three circles and three proppings-up	Three circles: back, hip and Hukou (the part between the thumb and the index finger) should be in a round shape.

(continued)

Types	Content	Requirements
Regulations	Three circles and three proppings-up	Three proppings-up: head should be propping upward, tongue should propup the jaw and palms should prop ahead.
	Four sinkings and four Quickness	Four sinkings: shoulders, waist, hip, knee should be sunken and relaxed.
		Four quicknesses: eye, hand, body and foot should be quick.
	Ten haves and three have-nots	Ten haves: mind leads action with natural breath first and abdomen breath subsequently. Waist, arm, hand and neck should be twisted to face the circle. Relax waist and wrist; lift anus and converge hip; pack elbow and twist arm; relax shoulder and elbow; stretch oneself; relax joints; be smooth all over and in coordination.
		Three have-nots: no holding one's breath; no stiffness; and no superficial movement.
Style	Three shapes	Three shapes: walking is like a flying dragon; action is like a monkey; form change is like an eagle.
	Three postures	Three postures: walking is like walking on mud; two arm's move is like twisting a rope; walking and turning along the circle is like pushing a millstone.

2.4 Cultural experience

- **Bagua**

Bagua (Eight Diagrams) is a set of symbols in ancient China, in which "—" stands for Yang, "- -"stands for Yin. With these two symbols and their combinations, which come from natural changes, 8 different forms come into being, which is called Bagua (Eight Diagrams). Each diagram (Gua) means a certain thing—Qian stands for heaven, Kun is earth, Kan is water, Li is fire, Zhen is thunder, Gen is mountain, Xun is wind and Dui represents Lake. With the combination of these eight diagrams, 64 diagrams (Gua) are obtained to represent various natural and social phenomena.

- **Walking on mud Step**

The step of walking on mud requires "one mind and five force exertion methods". "One mind" means walking is like stepping on mud, that is, one can feel the viscous force of the mud around, adhesion of the sole, viscous drag of the heel, stickiness of the feet around, viscous block from the front of feet and viscous pressure from the back of feet. "Five force exertion methods" means heel kicking, kicking, rubbing, reaching and stamping from the ready position to the closing position. It requires a driving force from sole, a forward kicking force from the angle between the foot back and the shin, a rubbing force from the two shins, as well as the reaching and stamping force at the time of foot's landing onto the ground.

3 Conclusion

- Baguazhang movement, which focuses on "walk and turn along the circle and change forms while walking", should practice the walking-on-mud Step first. One should experience a light and even walking, and clear turning.

- The set of movements is the elementary taolu for Baguazhang. The eight palm-change movements are included in this set, that is, pressing, lifting, hitting, closing, stretching, holding, standing and pushing.
- After knowing well the actions and routes, "three hollows and three relaxations", "three circles and three proppings-up", "Four sinkings and four quickness" and "ten haves and three have-nots" can be further experienced in practice.
- In practice, "three forms and three postures" should be always stressed.

4 Extensive reading

After learning "Set Baguazhang", one can go on studying such taolu as "Bagua Lianhuanzhang (The Eight Diagrams Linked Fist-Play), Youshen Baguazhang (The Flexible Diagrams Fist-Play), and Yin-Yang Baguazhang", etc. Furthermore, one can practice with weapons, Bagua Sword, Bagua Blade and Meridian Axe Pair", to name just a few. Or, one can practice the pair exercise of taolu, like Baguazhang sparring and Bagua Sixty-four Division par exercise.

5 Questions

(1) How can one practice "walking-on-mud step"?
(2) Breath movements in Baguazhang should combine the use of footwork. How can one successfully make it to realize "all dynamic and static moves represented in one's breathing"?
(3) The set of exercise can be practiced by a repeated single-form movement or continuous eight-form exercises. It is recommended that one should practice the continuous eight-form movement after knowing well the single-form movement.

6 References

[1] Taolu Textbook Committee of Chinese Wushu Series. Baguazhang [M]. Beijing: Beijing University of Sports Press. 1998.
[2] Textbook of Chinese Wushu [M]. Beijing: People Sport Publishing House. 2004.

Chapter Five

Shaolin Arhat Eighteen Hands

1 Introduction

Shaolin Arhat Eighteen Hands, the basic Shaolinquan taolu (known as "routines", the same as below), is composed of 2 sections, including 24 movements and 18 techniques which contains 6 kinds of fist techniques, 2 palm techniques, 1 elbow technique, 4 leg techniques and 5 grabbing techniques, etc, characteristic of plainness and simplicity.

2 Learning experience

2.1 Directions

2.1.1 Preparations: there are 2 movements

(1) Ready position

Bring feet together with two legs straight. Place two arms down at the two sides of body, with the set of fingers of two hands close to the outer side of legs. Straighten body and look straight forward (Fig.5-1-1).

Fig. 5-1-1   Fig. 5-1-2

(2) Bringing feet together and clenching hands into fists

Clench hands into fists, bend elbows and draw them back close to the two sides of waist, with the palm of fists upward, the little finger side of fist close to the body and eyes gazing leftward (Fig. 5-1-2).

Section 1

2.1.2 Bow stance, grabbing hand and pushing palm

Bend knees slightly and step the left foot out leftward. Change the left fist into a palm, ring it up from the left side of waist to the left top with the elbow bent, and place it at the front of the right shoulder with the fingers facing up and the thumb open. Look at the left palm (Fig. 5-2-1). Turn the left palm outward and then change it into a fist, the palm of fist facing up. Bend the elbow and draw the fist back to the left side of waist. Change the right fist into a palm and push it straight forward from the right side of waist. Meanwhile, straighten the right leg and bend the left knee into a half squat to form a left bow stance. Look at the front of the right palm (Fig. 5-2-2).

2.1.3 Empty stance and pushing palm

Shift body weight backward, bend the right knee into a half squat; draw the left foot half a pace back to point at the ground virtually with the toes, thus a left empty stance comes into being. Meanwhile, turn the right palm into a fist and draw it back to the right side of waist. Change the left fist into a palm and push it out forward. Look at the front of the left palm (Fig. 5-3).

Fig. 5-2-1　　　　　Fig. 5-2-2　　　　　Fig. 5-3

2.1.4 Bow stance, grabbing hand and raising elbow

Step the left foot onto the ground and turn the left arm inward with the thumb open downward. Stretch the right palm to the back down of body with the arm straight, the palm of fist facing forward and eyes gazing at the left palm (Fig. 5-4-1). Turn the left arm outward to make the palm of hand facing up; clench the fist to draw it back to the left side of waist with the elbow bent. At the same time, step the right foot forward and bend the knee into a half squat to form a horse stance. With the turning of body, rotate the right fist up from the back of body to the front till the level of eyebrow, the front of fist upward and the thumb side of fist rightward. Turn the head right and look at the front of the right side (Fig. 5-4-2 front; back).

Fig. 5-4-1   Fig. 5-4-2   Fig. 5-4-3

2.1.5 Horse stance, parrying & striking and punching fist

Extend the toes of the right foot outward, turn body right; step the left foot forward with the turning of body, and bend the knees into a half squat to form a horse stance. Turn the right fist inward and parry it up at the top of the right side with the elbow bent. Punch the left fist out leftward from the left side of waist, the palm of fist facing downward and eyes gazing at the front of the left fist (Fig. 5-5).

Fig. 5-5   Fig. 5-6   Fig. 5-7-1

2.1.6 Bow stance, parrying & striking and punching fist

Extend the toes of the left foot outward and turn body left to form a left bow stance. Meanwhile, change the left fist into a palm and parry it up from the front of body with the elbow bent. Punch the right fist out with the elbow bent from the right side of waist, the palm of fist facing down and eyes gazing at the front of the right fist (Fig. 5-6).

2.1.7 Bow stance and ringing elbow

Pat the back of the right fist with the left palm and hold the right wrist. Turn body right, draw the right fist and left palm in together below the right rib, close to the body, with the elbows bent and eyes gazing at the left palm (Fig. 5-7-1). Step the right foot forward to form a right bow stance. Meanwhile raise the right elbow and ring it top-down to the front. Look at the right elbow (Fig. 5-7-2).

Fig. 5-7-2　　　　　　Fig. 5-8-1　　　　　　Fig. 5-8-2

2.1.8 Turning body over, horse stance and striking

Standing straight, raise the right foot with the knee bent (Fig. 5-8-1). Thrust the left foot to the ground and jump up. Turn body right and land the right foot to the place before jumping the left foot; land the left foot on the left side followed, and bend knees into a half squat to form a horse stance. At the same time, loosen the left palm off the right fist, ring it from the top of the right arm along the elbow to the underneath and then turn it over to make the palm of hand face upward. Strike with the right fist from the inner side of the left arm to the top and forehead with the arm straight, the palm of fist facing upward and eyes gazing at the right fist (Fig. 5-8-2).

2.1.9 Horse stance, propping palm up and punching fist

Draw the right fist back from the top of the left palm and place it at the right side of waist. Stretch the left palm out straight forward from below the right arm closely to the body, with the arm turning inward, the thumb open, the part between the thumb and index finger facing upward and the palm of hand forward. Look at the left palm (Fig. 5-9-1). Punch the right fist straight out forward from the right side of waist with the palm of fist facing downward. At the same time, draw the left palm back to the front of the right shoulder with the elbow bent and keep the thumb open, the palm of hand facing rightward and the set of fingers upward. Look at the right fist (Fig. 5-9-2).

Fig. 5-9-1　　　　　　Fig. 5-9-2

2.1.10 Bow stance, blocking and punching fist

Bend the right elbow and draw the fist back to the right side of waist. Change the left palm into a fist and turn the arm outward to block leftward ina ring. Meanwhile, extend the toes of the left foot outward and turn body left to form a left bow stance. Look at the left fist (Fig. 5-10-1). Step the right foot forward to form a right bow stance, meanwhile bend the left elbow to draw it back to the left side of waist. Punch the right fist straight out forward, the palm of fist facing downward and eyes gazing at the front of the right fist (Fig.5-10-2).

Fig. 5-10-1   Fig. 5-10-2   Fig. 5-11-1

2.1.11 Bow stance, blocking and punching fist

Turn the right arm to make the thumb side of the fist downward. Ring the arm with the elbow bent to the front of abdomen to the left side of chest. Ring the forearm to the right and block with its radius side, the front of fist facing up and eyes gazing at the right fist (Fig.5-11-1). Step the left foot forward to form a left bow stance. At the same time, bend the right knee and draw the fist back to the right side of waist. Punch the left fist out forward, the palm of fist facing downward and eyes gazing at the front of left fist (Fig.5-11-2).

2.1.12 Hanging legs and kicking with toes pointed inward

Shift body weight forward and bend the left leg slightly; raise the right foot off ground at the back of body with the knee bent, the toes facing downward. Change the left fist into a standing palm; change the right fist into a palm and ring it with the arm straight from the right side of waist, underneath, back, and top of head till onto the left wrist and cross the two palms (Fig.5-12-1). Push the two palms down from the front of chest with the arms straight and then raise them to the two sides horizontally, the fingers of the left palm facing up, the palm of hand forward. Change the right palm into a hook hand with the tip of hook facing down. At the same time, with the toes of the right foot pointed inward, swing the left leg and kick with it from the back of body to the left forward obliquely. At the time of crossing the front straight, rub the ground with the heel. Look ahead straight (Fig.5-12-2).

Fig. 5-11-2   Fig. 5-12-1   Fig. 5-12-2

2.1.13 Twisting wrist, horse stance and punching fist

Bend the right knee, change the right hook hand into a fist and ring it with the arm straight from the right side to the bottom; and then with the elbow bent ring the arm from the front of abdomen, left and top till the front of chest, the palm of hand facing outward, fingers upward, and thumb open. Meanwhile, bend the left elbow, ring the palm from the left side, top, right, down till the right wrist and then hold it. Look at the right palm (Fig. 5-13-1). Turn the right arm and wrist outward and change the palm into a fist when the palm of hand is facing up. Bend the elbow and draw the fist back to the front right side of waist; hold the right wrist with the left hand. Meanwhile, turn body right, stamp with the right foot to the side of the left foot and raise the left foot at the back of the right leg with the left knee bent. Look at the right fist (Fig. 5-13-2). Land the left foot to the left side to form a horse stance. At the same time, draw the right fist back to the right side of waist. Loosen the left hand off the right wrist and change into a fist to punch it out to the left side, the palm of fist facing downward and eyes gazing at the front of the left fist (Fig. 5-13-3).

Fig. 5-13-1   Fig. 5-13-2   Fig. 5-13-3

2.1.14 Bending body and sweeping leg backward

Extend the toes of the left foot outward, bend the knee into a full squat; straighten the right leg and stoop down at the right side, the toes of the right foot pointed inward. Meanwhile, change two fists into palms, swing two arms to the right and then touch the ground with the turning right of body. Look at the right foot (Fig. 5-14-1). At the time of swinging the leg, sweep with the right straight leg half a circle close to the ground from the right to the back, eyes gazing at the movement of the right foot (Fig. 5-14-2).

Fig. 5-14-1

Fig. 5-14-2

Section 2

2.1.15 Tuning body over, bow stance and chopping

Shift body weight to the right, turn the heel of the right foot inward to make the toes forward right; turn body right, bend the knee, and straighten the left leg to form a right bow stance. Meanwhile, change two palms into fists. With the turning of body, ring the right palm from the front of the right knee to the back of body and then raise it up backward, the thumb side of fist downward; with the turning of body change the left palm into a fist and raise it up at the front of body with the arm straight, the palm of fist downward and eyes gazing at the left fist (Fig.5-15-1).

Turn the left arm inward to make the thumb side of fist downward, ring the fist with the arm straight from the top to the back and then chop with it, the thumb side of fist upward. Stretch the right fist straight down from the back of body and ring it to the front with the thumb side of fist upward. At the time of ringing two arms, turn body left and look at the left fist (Fig. 5-15-2). Keep turning body left to form a left bow stance. Meanwhile, continue to ring the two fists backward and then chop. Raise the left arm and chop with the left fist to the front of body and then draw it back to the left side of waist. Raise the right arm and chop with the right fist to the front of body, the thumb side of fist facing upward and eyes gazing at the front of the right fist (Fig.5-15-3).

Fig. 5-15-1　　　　　Fig. 5-15-2　　　　　Fig. 5-15-3

2.1.16 Punching fist and snap kick

Turn the right arm outward to make the palm of fist upward, bend the elbow and draw the fist back to the right side of waist. Following it punch the left fist out straight forward from the left side of waist, the thumb side of fist facing downward. Meanwhile, shift body weight forward, bend the left leg slightly and snap kick with the right leg. Look ahead (Fig. 5-16).

Fig. 5-16   Fig. 5-17-1   Fig. 5-17-2

2.1.17 Jumping twice and flying kick

Land the right leg forward and then jump up; swing the left foot forward. Meanwhile, change the left fist into a palm. With the palm of fist downward, raise it above the forehead. Change the right fist into a palm, stretch it down with the arm straight from the right side of waist and ring it forward. Strike the palm of the left hand with the back of the right palm, the eyes gazing in front (Fig. 5-17-1). Kick out with the right leg forward, the toes pointed forward. Extend the right arm and strike the instep of the right foot with the palm; raise the left palm to the left side horizontally. Look at the right foot (Fig. 5-17-2). Lower the body and land the left foot onto the floor (Fig. 5-17-3).

Fig. 5-17-3   Fig. 5-18   Fig. 5-18-1

2.1.18 Bow stance and pressing palm down

Step the right foot backward and turn body right to form a right bow stance.

Meanwhile, turn the right arm outward, stretch it straight down; ring it from the outer side of the right leg to the back and raise it up to the top of head. Ring the left palm up till the front above head and then press it down at the inner side of the right knee, the palm of hand downward and eyes gazing at the left front (Fig. 5-18 front, back).

2.1.19 Ringing arm and sinking elbow with the legs crossed

Shift body weight left to form a horse stance. Grab the left shoulder with the right palm from the topdown to the left. Change the left palm into a fist, turn the arm outward and ring it from the front of abdomen to the left side, the elbow bent slightly and palm of fist upward, the eyes gazing at the left fist (Fig. 5-19-1). Keep ringing the left fist up with the palm of fist rightward. Continue to shift body weight forward and step the left leg to the back of body. Look at the left fist (Fig. 5-19-2). Continue to shift body weight forward, move the left foot to the left side one pace, and bend knees to form a horse stance. Meanwhile, with the movement of body, turn the left fist to make the palm of fist face the back of body. Press it down at the outer side of the front of body till the height of eyebrow with the forearm straight. Look at the front left (Fig. 5-19-3).

Fig. 5-19-1　　　　　　**Fig. 5-19-2**　　　　　　**Fig. 5-19-3**

2.1.20 Bow stance, parrying & striking and punching fist

Turn body left and move the right foot outward accordingly; straighten the right leg, bend the left knee to form a left bow stance. Bend the left elbow and draw the fist back to the front of the right shoulder, the little finger side of fist close to the body and the palm of fistfacing forward. Change the right palm into a fist, ring it with the elbow bent from below the left forearm to the front and top and then parry it up, the thumb side of fist facing downward (Fig. 5-20-1). Shift the body weight backward, turn the body right and bend knees to form a horse stance. Meanwhile, bend the right elbow and parry the right fist above the right shoulder, the back of fist facing leftward and the palm of fist upward. Punch the left fist out immediately from the front of the right shoulder to the left side, the palm of fist downward and eyes gazing at the front of left fist (Fig. 5-20-2).

Fig. 5-20-1　　　　　　Fig. 5-20-2　　　　　　Fig. 5-21

2.1.21　Bow stance, parrying & striking and sticking elbow out

Extend the toes of the left foot and the heel of the right foot outward and turn body left to form a left bow stance. Meanwhile, change the left fist into a palm and parry it up from the front of body to the top of forehead with the elbow bent. Move the right fist with the elbow bent from the underneath, the front of right shoulder to the left armpit. Turn the arm inward to make the palm of fist downward, the tip of elbow sticking out forward. Look in front (Fig. 5-21).

2.1.22　Grabbing hand and striking with feet together

Lift the left leg straight and bring the right foot forward close together. Meanwhile, grab with the left palm and press it down from top to the front of the tip of the right elbow, the palm of hand downward. Using the right elbow as an axis, ring the right fist from the left armpit, top to the front and then strike with the straight arm, the palm of fist facing upward. At the time of striking forward with the right fist, turn the left palm up to hold the right elbow. Look at the front of the right fist (Fig. 5-22).

Fig. 5-22　　　　　　Fig. 5-23-1　　　　　　Fig. 5-23-2

2.1.23　Propping palm up, horse stance and punching fist

Turn body backward slightly and stretch the left palm out straight from below the right arm; turn the arm inward to make Hukou (the part between the thumb and index finger) upward and then prop the palm up forward. Meanwhile, draw the right fist back from the top of the left palm and place it back to the right side of waist, the palm of fist upward. Lift the right knee and look at the left palm (Fig. 5-23-1). Land the right leg forward, turn body left and bend knees into a half squat to form a horse stance. Meanwhile, parry the left palm to the top of the left shoulder, the elbow bent. Punch the right fist out to the right side, the palm of fist facing downward and eyes gazing at the front of the right fist (Fig. 5-23-2).

2.1.24 Separating palms, bow stance and pushing palms

Stand straight on the right leg and bend the left knee. Meanwhile, change the palm into a fist, raise it with the arm straight and then ring with the left palm together from down to the back, the palms of hands face to face (Fig. 5-24-1). Separate the two palms at the same time and ring them to the front and top with the elbows bent from two sides and then raise them up at the sides of ears, the fingers facing backward and body tilting backward with it (Fig. 5-24-2). Land the left foot forward to form a left bow stance. Push the two palms straight forward out at the same time, the eyes gazing at the front of palms (Fig. 5-24-3).

Fig. 5-24-1   Fig. 5-24-2   Fig. 5-24-3

2.1.25 Empty stance and body-protecting palm

Shift body weight forward, lift the left leg slightly up; bend the right knee and raise the right leg to place it behind the dent of the left knee with toes of the foot pointed inward. Meanwhile, turn two arms outward to make the palms of hands face upward and ring the arms straight from down to the back (Fig. 5-25-1). Land the right foot at the right side of body and shift body weight rightward to form a left empty stance. Meanwhile, ring the two palms from back to the top and continue to ring it when crossing the head till the front of body. And then raise it up horizontally with the elbow bent slightly. Bend the right elbow and draw the right arm back near the left elbow, the eyes gazing at the front of the left palm (Fig. 5-25-2).

Fig. 5-25-1   Fig. 5-25-2

Closing movements

2.1.26 Bringing feet together and holding fist

Turn the heel of the right foot inward. Stand upright and bring the left foot close to the right foot. Meanwhile, change two palms into fists and draw them back to the two sides of waist. Look at the left (Fig. 5-26).

Fig. 5-26   Fig. 5-27

2.1.27 Closing position

Change two fists into palms and hang two arms down straight. Turn head right at the position of attention (Fig. 5-27).

2.2 Learning program

Category	Content
Preparations	1. To possess the quality of flexibility, coordination and strength
	2. To master the basic hand forms, foot forms, handwork and footwork
Schedules	1. To learn the movements (In this set of routines, 18 movements can be learned within 8 times, including 6 for learning new and 2 for review.)
	2. To master the regulations of each movement
	3. To improve the training level of the whole set of routines
	4. To experience the techniques in each movement

2.3 Technique experience

Content	Requirements
Regulations	1. Hand form: being tight for a fist, bringing palm together and stretching, bending wrist with fingers bringing together for a hook
	2. Foot form: a stable body weight, swift movement and flexible change
	3. Body form: raising head and neck straight, throwing chest out and sinking waist, restraining abdomen and hip back, straightening body
	4. Handwork and footwork: correct method, clear route and exact force focus
Technique essentials	1. To use retreating, turning, dodging, hiding and restraining to avoid the attacking from the opponent and at the same time to attack the opponent skillfully and reasonably.
	2. To know the offence and defense in each move. For example, a sudden and forceful strength is required in "punching fist" to hit the face and chest and abdomen of the opponent correctly. "Twisting hand" asks one to use the edge of the little finger side to grab and strike the wrist joint of the opponent. In "chopping palm", one is required to use the sharp edge of the palm to chop the shin bone of the lower leg, instep of the foot or ankle joint of the opponent. "Hanging leg with toes pointed inward" requires one to use the strength from swinging of the lower leg to hook the place near the ankle joint of the opponent. "Sweeping leg" is asked to sweep the leg of the opponent by using heel. In "Yuan Yang leg (Kicking separately)", it needs to attack the crotch, abdomen and jaw of the opponent in a mixed virtual-practical way. "Separating palms" is to protect face or head from being attacked; "Parrying fist up" is to prevent the hack from the opponent and "propping palm up" is to smash the striking from the opponent.
	3. To understand the meaning and use of offence and defense in each move by constant practicing under the guidance of teachers.
Objectives	1. Smooth movement: to examine "smooth strength going, complete strength exertion and correct strength focus"; to experience the state of "eyes following the movement of hand, hands following the foot without any interruption"
	2. Proper rhythm: to experience the rhythm by "the combination of dynamic and static, fast and slow, rising and declining"
	3. The combination of form and spirit: to understand the saying in play fist, "fist has no spirit if eyes have no focus."

2.4 Learning experience

- **Fist-holding salute**

Greeting salute, originated before Zhou Dynasty, is a traditional Chinese etiquette. Fist-holding salute is commonly seen in wushu circle. It requires one to stand straight with two feet bringing together and look at the person opposite straight, holding the left palm and right fist putting together in a ring at the front of chest, with a distance of 20~30 cm in between. Behave naturally and properly.

1. The left palm implies that one has owned the quality combined with morality, intelligence, physique and aesthetic. Bending the left thumb means one is modest with humbleness; while the right fist expresses war. With the left palm covering the right fist, it means one restrains himself by reasoning instead of war.

2. With the left palm and right fist in front of the chest, the five fingers stands for the five lakes, the divisions between the five fingers are 4 seas, meaning that people all over the world coming here are friends.

3. The left palm stands for art while the right fist is war, implying the combination of art and war, a humble attitude towards the master or teacher.

4. With the two hands holding in front of chest facing outside slightly, it shows innocence, that one has no weapons in hand.

- **Twenty-four Key Elements of Changquan**

Twenty-four Key Elements of Changquan can be divided into "Four techniques (*Si Ji*), Eight Essentials (*Ba Fa*), and twelve Forms (*Shi'er Xing*).

1. Four Techniques (*Si Ji*): no wushu taolu that includes attack and defense movements is complete without the teaching of the four techniques.

2. Eight Essentials (*Ba Fa*): it refers to the general term of "hands, eyes, body, feet, spirit, energy, strength and skills." It requires that "fists should be as quick as shooting stars; eyes should be as sharp as lightening; the waist should be as supple as a snake; steps should be firmly rooted; the spirit should be vigorous; breath (*Qi*) should be kept down; strength should be exerted smoothly and skill (*Gong*) should be highly pure and proficient."

3. Twelve Forms (*Shi'er Xing*): it refers to 12 manners of movements, including motion, stillness, rising, falling, standing on both feet, keeping upright with one foot, turning, folding, and being light, heavy, swift or slow. It requires "moving like waves; still like mountains; jumping like monkeys, falling like magpies; upright like cranes, standing like pine trees, turning like wheels, bending like bows, light as leaves, quick like gales and slow like hovering eagles."

3 Conclusion

- Shaolin Arhat Eighteen Hands is the basic taolu both for Shaolinquan and wushu.
- After the movement route is known well, then the movement of regulation should be carefully examined.
- On the basis of movement regulation, one can experience the techniques of attack and defense characteristics of Shaolinquan, improve its implied morals and understand the wushu culture as well as Chinese culture.

4 Extensive reading

- Improve the regulations of movement by practicing repeatedly after learning the movement route.
- Focus on the coordination between the movement and breath, reaching the combination of breath, strength and form by producing strength via breath.
- Improve oneself from its movement rhythm as well as the unity of form and spirit.
- Sparring routine exercise can be done after learning the sole taolu practice.

5 Questions

(1) How is "the unity of form and spirit" demonstrated in taolu exercise?

(2) What is the implication of offense and defense in each move in Shaolin Arhat Eighteen Hands? And what is its factual practice?

6 References

[1] Cai Longyun. The Dhyana of Shaolin Boxing [M]. Hangzhou: Zhejiang Science and Technology Press, 1983.

[2] The Textbook Committee of National University of Sport (Eds). Textbook of Chinese Wushu (1) [M]. Beijing: People Sport Press, 2004.

Chapter Six

Fengmo Cudgel-Play

1 Introduction

Fengmo Cudgel-Play, as "one of the 72 secrets of Shaolinquan", is one of the basic cudgel play taolu (known as "routines, the same as below). This set has thirty kinds of cudgel work, emphasizing the mixed use of end and shaft of the cudgel, with the request of echo and cooperation of "up and down, left and right", esteeming generating great wind with cudgel potential, and fast but powerful splitting.

2 Learning experience

2.1 Directions

Ready Position

2.1.1 Holding the cudgel with feet together

Face east, bring feet together and stand straight; grip the cudgel with Hukou of the right hand (Hukou means the part between the thumb and index finger, the same as below), cudgel stuck to the right leg. Fingers of left hand close together against the outside of the left leg, stick the cudgel touchdown vertical, looking the shaft horizontally (Fig. 6-1).

Fig. 6-1

2.1.2 Empty stance and holding the cudgel with both hands

> **Cudgel gripping**
>
> Cudgel boasts as "the Top Weapon" as a bladeless weapon, composed of the end, body and shaft. Distant attack includes "chopping, dropping, lifting, sweeping and shoveling" while near attack has "pointing breaking, thrusting, jabbing and covering, etc." as well as the defensive techniques like "parrying, dodging and pulling, etc."

Bend the left knee, step the right foot back to make a left bow stance, rub the cudgel upward along with the right hand till the front of the right shoulder, then fully grip the cudgel. Grip the cudgel with the left hand, the Hukou of both hands facing toward the cudgel end. Raise the cudgel forward with both hands (Fig. 6-2-1). Shift body weight back and bend the right knee to form a left empty stance. Meanwhile raise the cudgel forward to the level with the left arm straight, eyes gazing at the front of the cudgel shaft (Fig. 6-2-2).

Fig. 6-2-1　　　　　　　　　　Fig. 6-2-2

Section 1

2.1.3　Bow stance and shoveling

Shift body weight forward and step the right foot forward to form a right bow stance. Fully grip the cudgel with the right hand, the arm straight; stretch the cudgel end top-down obliquely along the right side of body, the palm facing up. Fully grasp the cudgel shaft with the left hand, bend the elbow at the front of body and look at the shaft (Fig. 6-3-1). Grip the cudgel shaft and swing the cudgel with the left hand from the front to the left, and rear down; return the cudgel to the left side of the waist, the palm close to the body. Grip the cudgel end and swing the cudgel with the right hand from the rear to the right and front up obliquely. Shovel the cudgel up forward with the arm straight, the palm facing upward left, the Hukou facing forward and eyes gazing at the cudgel end (Fig. 6-3-2).

Fig. 6-3-1　　　　　　　　　　Fig. 6-3-2

2.1.4 Bow stance and piercing

Withdraw the cudgel with both hands. Keep the right hand in the same holding position and bend the right elbow to the front of chest, the palm facing up; push the cudgel shaft a little farther from the left hand and bend the left elbow to the rear of waist. Meanwhile, raise both legs with the right leg straightened and the right knee bent, eyes gazing at the cudgel end (Fig.6-4-1). Pause temporarily, step the right foot forward to make a right bow stance; meanwhile piece the cudgel end up forward with both hands obliquely. Keep the right hand at the same holding position, straighten the right arm; grip the cudgel fully and draw it back to the left side of waist, the elbow bent, the palm close to the body and eyes gazing at the end (Fig.6-4-2).

Fig. 6-4-1   **Fig. 6-4-2**

2.1.5 Close attack through armpit

Keep the right hand at the same holding position, spin the cudgel end to the left, down and right close to the ground with the arm straight. Then spin the cudgel end from front down to the right and rear. When it reaches at the rear, lift it to the right shoulder with the elbow bent. Meanwhile lift the cudgel to the left shoulder from the left side of the waist with the left hand to spin the cudgel shaft from the rear to the left and front. Straighten the left arm with that move, and loosen the hand slightly to make the cudgel stick out. Stand up with the cudgel end reaching the rear and cudgel shaft reaching the front. Step the left foot forward to the cudgel shaft (Fig.6-5-1).

Hand change

Hand change is also called hand swap. It means to change hand position from the cudgel shaft to the cudgel end, or change hand position from the cudgel end to the shaft part.

Moving one hand while the other remains still is called single change, and swap two hands to the other's earlier position is called a double change.

It is required that your swap must be swift in order to startle the enemy.

Fig. 6-5-1　　　　　　Fig. 6-5-2　　　　　　Fig. 6-5-3

Without any pause, move the cudgel to the left shoulder through the air from the right shoulder after spinning it from overhead to the left and down with the right hand, the right elbow bent. Meanwhile, lift the right foot behind off the ground and look at the cudgel end (Fig. 6-5-2). Without any pause, turn body right, step the right foot forward to from a right bow stance. Meanwhile spin the cudgel shaft from the front to the right and back with the left elbow bent and the left arm under the right armpit. Then spin the cudgel end from behind to the left and front down with the right hand, the elbow straight. Strike forward down obliquely with the cudgel end. Look at the cudgel end (Fig. 6-5-3).

2.1.6　Elevating while changing hand

The left hand releasing the shaft, grip the cudgel with the right hand, the elbow bent; and then draw it back to the right side of waist. Grip the cudgel end with the hand change, the palm facing downward and eyes gazing ahead (Fig. 6-6-1). Without any pause, continue to pull back the cudgel with the right hand and grab it with the left hand in the hand change. Spin the cudgel shaft from behind to the right and down front with the right elbow straight. Spin the cudgel end from the front to the left and right with the left hand, the elbow bent. Draw it back to the left side. Look at the cudgel shaft (Fig. 6-6-2).

Fig. 6-6-1　　　　　　Fig. 6-6-2

2.1.7　Cudgel uppercutting

Spin the cudgel end up and back from the front and pull the cudgel back near to the right ear with the right hand, the elbow bent. Poke the cudgel up with the Hukou facing down and stick it out with the left arm straight, spinning the cudgel end from behind to below and front, the Hukou facing up. Straighten the left leg, lift the right leg and look ahead (Fig. 6-7-1). Without any pause, step the right foot forward to form a right bow stance. Meanwhile spin the cudgel down and forward with the left hand. Uppercut forward down with it, eyes gazing at the end (Fig. 6-7-2).

Fig. 6-7-1　　　　　　　　　　Fig. 6-7-2

2.1.8　Bow stance and striking downward

Shift the right hand to the cudgel shaft and lift it obliquely up with the arm straight after loosening the cudgel a little by the left hand. And then shift the right hand to the cudgel end; then grip the cudgel fully with the left hand and pull it back to the left side of the waist, the palm close to the body and Hukou directing forward. Meanwhile spin the cudgel shaft with the right hand up forward to strike, the arm straight, the palm facing downward, Hukou leftward and eyes gazing at the cudgel shaft (Fig. 6-8).

Fig. 6-8　　　　　　Fig. 6-9-1　　　　　　Fig. 6-9-2

2.1.9　Changing hand and intercepting

Stretch the left arm forward; release the cudgel shaft from the right hand, pull back the right arm to the right ear with the cudgel in hand and elbow bent. Make sure both hands are tight, the Hukou of both hands are directing backward. Watch the front (Fig. 6-9-1). Without any pause, spin the cudgel end from front to the left and back with the left hand gripping the shaft, then bend the elbow to pull it back to the left side of body, the palm close to the body. Meanwhile hang the cudgel down to the right back, with the cudgel in the right hand and the arm straight. Spin the cudgel end from behind to below, right and forward to intercept. Watch the cudgel shaft (Fig. 6-9-2).

2.1.10 Bow stance and shoveling

Grip the cudgel with both hands and spin the cudgel end from near the ground front to the right and rear, the elbow of the left hand bent slightly at the front of chest and palm facing downward while the right arm stretching outward to the back of the right leg and the palm facing rightward (Fig. 6-10-1). Without any pause, grip the cudgel shaft and swing the cudgel with the left hand from the front to the left, and rear down; return the cudgel to the left side of the waist, the palm close to the body. Grip the cudgel end and swing the cudgel with the right hand from the rear to the right and front up obliquely. Shovel the cudgel up forward with the arm straight, the palm facing upward left, eyes gazing at the cudgel end (Fig. 6-10-2).

Fig. 6-10-1

Fig. 6-10-2

2.1.11 Hanging and thrusting

Stand on both feet and turn left. Meanwhile hold the cudgel with both hands to make sure the cudgel end is above the head. Watch the cudgel end (Fig. 6-11-1). Without any pause, spin the right arm to make the cudgel end circle around from above to front, down and the right. Hang the cudgel below the outer side of the right leg, and then pull it back to the right side of the waist with the elbow bent. Swing the cudgel shaft backwards with the left hand from the left side of the waist to spin the cudgel end to the left and upward front from behind. Lift the left arm horizontally in front of the chest with the elbow bent, the Hukou facing backwards. Meanwhile move the left heel outwardly and turn right; bend the right knee to lift the leg, eyes gazing forward (Fig. 6-11-2).

Without any pause, step the right foot forward and spin the cudgel end on the ground from front to the left and behind with the elbow bent. Bend the left elbow and swing the cudgel to the rear left from the front, and then send it back to the left side. Bend the right knee to form a right bow stance. Loosen the right hand, stick out the cudgel with the left arm straightened and put the right hand in front of the left hand. Tilt the body forward and watch the cudgel end (Fig. 6-11-3).

Fig. 6-11-1　　　　　　　Fig. 6-11-2　　　　　　　Fig. 6-11-3

2.1.12　Dragging and elevating

Step the right foot backward and turn body right. Change the cudgel gripping with the left hand at the front and the right hand at the rear. Meanwhile pull the cudgel back to the right side of waist. Bend knees and squat, with the body weight shifted onto the right and eyes gazing at the cudgel end (Fig. 6-12-1). Without any pause, the left leg leaping to the right side, across the right leg; push off the ground and jump with the right foot. Drag the cudgel and step back (Fig. 6-12-2). Without any pause, step the right foot to the right and squat on both knees. Make sure the body weight is still on the right. Elevate the cudgel in front of the abdomen (Fig. 6-12-3). Without any stop, move the tiptoes of the left leg and right heel outward, turn body left to form a left bow stance. Meanwhile shift the right hand-gripping inward a little and lift the cudgel above head from front with both arms straight, the left palm facing back and the right one facing up, eyes gazing forward (Fig. 6-12-4).

Fig. 6-12-1　　　　　　　　　　　　Fig. 6-12-2

Fig. 6-12-3　　　　　　　　　　　　Fig. 6-12-4

Section 2

2.1.13 Blocking while changing hand

Shift body weight forward and move the right foot forward close to the left foot; at the same time move the right hand inwardly to grab the cudgel and release the left hand off the cudgel. Spin the cudgel shaft from the right to front to make the cudgel end spin from left to right above head. Lower down the cudgel passing through the right ear, the left hand grabbing the cudgel at the front, the palm facing right and the left palm facing left (Fig.6-13-1). Without any pause, step the left foot backward and straighten the left leg to form a right bow stance. Meanwhile spin the cudgel from front to the left and back with the left hand and then draw it back to the left side with the elbow bent, the palm close to the body. Extend the right hand obliquely down right from the right shoulder, swinging the cudgel to the bottom, right and front from behind, the cudgel shaft close to the ground. Intercept the enemy with the cudgel end and twist your wrist to the other side to make the palm left upward obliquely. Look at the cudgel end (Fig.6-13-2).

Fig. 6-13-1   Fig. 6-13-2   Fig. 6-14

2.1.14 Empty stance and striking downward

Move body forward and step the left foot forward to form a left empty stance with the tiptoes slightly touching the ground. Spin the cudgel with the left hand inwardly to the left shoulder, then lift it obliquely up backward; grab at the 2nd grip spot with the right hand and spin the cudgel downward and backward before bending the elbow and send it back to the right side of the waist. Make sure the back of hand is touching the body and the Hukou is directing to the ground. At the same time, shift the left hand forward to spin the cudgel upward and forward, striking with the cudgel shaft up forward. Move the hand to grab at the 3rd grip spot naturally and grip the cudgel tight with both hands, the Hukou directing upward, the palm to the right and elbow bent. Watch the cudgel (Fig.6-14).

2.1.15 Bow stance and stirring cudgel

Extend the right arm backward with the elbow straight. Bend the left elbow to the chest and draw back the cudgel horizontally. At the same time straighten the right knee and lift the left knee. Watch downward ahead (Fig. 6-15-1). Without any pause, step the left foot forward to form a left bow stance. Meanwhile reach out the left hand and bend the right elbow to the left side of chest. Stir the cudgel down forward with both hands, the Hukou facing up, the left palm and right palm directing to the right and left respectively. Watch the cudgel end (Fig. 6-15-2).

Fig. 6-15-1   Fig. 6-15-2

2.1.16 Stepping forward and blocking

Hold the cudgel with the right hand and stretch it out with the arm straight; grab the cudgel shaft backward with the left hand. Step the right foot forward to form a right bow stance. Meanwhile, grip the cudgel fully with the left hand to spin the cudgel from front to the left and right, and then pull back the elbow to the left side. Hold the cudgel with the right hand and droop the right arm straight backward. Swing the cudgel end close to the ground from behind to below, right and front to block the enemy's weapon down forward, the palm directing upward left and eyes gazing at the cudgel (Fig. 6-16).

Fig. 6-16   Fig. 6-17   Fig. 6-18

2.1.17 Squatting, sweeping and stirring

Draw the cudgel back a little with both hands. Grip the cudgel and spin its end in a round shape with 2/3 meter-radius from below to the right, up and left then down. When the cudgel end comes to the left, turn left and bend the left knee; when the cudgel tip comes below, turn right a little. Draw back to the left side with the cudgel in the left hand, eyes gazing at the cudgel end (Fig. 6-17).

2.1.18 Withdrawing and controlling

Following the last move, draw back the cudgel slightly with both hands. Stir the cudgel end from below to the right and up in a half-circle. When stirring the cudgel end to the left, turn the right arm inwardly and grab the cudgel while twisting the wrist to swing the cudgel to the left and down, turning the palm down to the ground. Grip the cudgel with the left hand to stir it at the rear naturally with the swinging of the cudgel. While stirring, turn left and straighten the right leg, the body weight shifting onto the left and eyes gazing left (Fig. 6-18).

2.1.19 Lifting and fending off

Move the body weight to the right and bend the right knee. Turn right a little and swing the right arm outwardly with the cudgel in hand. Stick up the cudgel to spin it from below to slightly left, up, then slightly right, the palm obliquely facing up. Swing the left arm inwardly with that move and move it down to the left side of hip, the palm close to the body and eyes gazing at the cudgel end (Fig. 6-19-1). Pause for a while, draw the cudgel back with the left hand and shift the right hand forward to the cudgel end. Turn right and step the right foot back to form a left bow stance. While retreating, send back the right elbow to the left side of chest. Loosen the left grip to stick out the cudgel end from behind. And then move the hand to the middle part of the cudgel; spin the cudgel from behind to the left and front. Fend off the enemy's weapon down forward with the cudgel end, the left and right palm facing the right and left respectively, the Hukou of both hands facing up. Watch the cudgel (Fig. 6-19-2).

Fig. 6-19-1　　　　　　　　　　Fig. 6-19-2

2.1.20 Stirring with feet together

With the cudgel holding in hands, stretch the right hand obliquely down backward passing through the right shoulder; bend the left elbow to pull it back to the left shoulder. At the same time stick the cudgel end obliquely down backward. Stand up and turn left 180° on the right sole. Bring the left foot off ground to the right foot and watch the cudgel end (Fig. 6-20-1). Without and pause, stir the cudgel end in an arc shape from below to the right forward with the right hand and bend the right elbow naturally. Stir the cudgel end in a circle from above to the south and down with the left hand, and naturally bend the left elbow. Meanwhile, squat a little and turn right to face the east with eyesight straight (Fig. 6-20-2).

Fig. 6-20-1   Fig. 6-20-2   Fig. 6-21

2.1.21 Hopping step

Following the last move, stir the cudgel end in an arc from above to the left. Push off the ground and leap in the air at the same time (Fig. 6-21).

2.1.22 Empty stance and striking downward

Turn right to make sure the right foot touches the ground first, the tiptoes outwards; and then step the left foot down and touch the ground with the tiptoes pointing emptily. Bend both knees to make a left empty stance. Meanwhile, swing the right arm outwardly, bend the right elbow, then send it back to the right side of the waist, the back of the hand close to the body and Hukou directing to the ground. Grip the cudgel with the left hand and spin the cudgel end upward front to strike with it. Watch the cudgel. (Fig. 6-14)

2.1.23 Bow stance and stirring

Same as the 3rd move in Section 2 (Fig. 6-15-1, Fig. 6-15-2).

2.1.24 Stepping forward and blocking

Same as the 4th move in Section 2 (Fig. 6-22).

2.1.25 Bow stance and shoveling

Same as the 8th move in Section 1 (Fig. 6-10-1, Fig. 6-10-2).

2.1.26 Hanging and thrusting

Same as the 9th move in Section 1 (Fig. 6-11-1, 6-11-2, 6-11-3).

2.1.27 Dragging and elevating

Same as the 10th move in Section 1 (Fig. 6-12-1, 6-12-2, 6-12-3, 6-12-4).

Closing position

Bring the right foot forward close to the left foot together. Stand straight. Meanwhile, hold the cudgel with both hands and pull it back at the outer side of the right leg with the elbow straight; bend the left elbow and lift the left hand upward to the forehead from behind, and send the cudgel back to the right side of body, the cudgel end facing upward. Make sure the cudgel is vertical (Fig. 6-22-1). Release the left hand off the cudgel and draw the hand back to the outer side of the left leg from front with the arm straight, the fingers together and the finger tips directing to the ground. Grip the right hand around the cudgel with the thumb close to the body, both elbows bent and eyes gazing ahead. Stand upright with the cudgel in the right hand (Fig. 6-22-2).

Fig. 6-22-1   Fig. 6-22-2

2.2 Learning program

Category	Content
Preparations	1. Basic skills: to acquire the cudgel gripping, hand changing, spinning, and other skills such as chopping, flipping, thrusting, etc. 2. Basic moves: to learn the basic stances: bow stance, horse stance, crouching step, empty step, as well as the basic cudgel moves combined with those stances.

Learning arrangement	Lesson 1:
	1. Holding the cudgel with feet together 2. Empty stance and holding the cudgel with both hands
	Section 1: 1. Bow stance and shoveling 2. Bow stance and piercing
	Lesson 2:
	Section 1: 3. Close attack through armpit 4. Elevating while changing hand 5. Cudgel uppercut
	         6. Bow stance and striking downward
	Lesson 3:
	Section 1: 7. Changing hand and intercepting 8. Bow stance and shoveling 9. Hanging and
	         thrusting 10. Dragging and elevating
	Lesson 4:
	Section 2: 1. Blocking while changing hand 2. Empty stance and striking downward 3. Bow stance
	         and stirring cudgel 4. Stepping forward and blocking
	Lesson 5:
	Section 2: 5. Squatting, sweeping and stirring 6. Withdrawing and controlling 7. Lifting and
	         fending off 8. Stirring with feet together
	Lesson 6:
	Section 2: 9. Hopping step 10. Empty stance and striking downward 11. Bow stance and stirring
	         12. Step forward and block
	Lesson 7:
	Section 2: 13. Bow stance and shoveling 14. Hanging and thrusting 15. Dragging and elevating
	         Closing position
	Lesson 8:
	Review and improvement

2.3 Technique experience

Category	Requirements
Move Accuracy	Move accuracy is crucial for cudgel play. Make sure to observe the moves closely and conduct the route attentively.
Cudgel play Skill	Mastering the routines is the key of cudgel play. Make sure to change the cudgel-holding techniques flexibly. And the striking point should be correct.
Cudgel play training	While training, we focus on the vigour that "a cudgel can sweep down a group of enemies" and the horizontal or vertical posture when holding the cudgel. Fengmo Cudgel-Play is a traditional type of cudgel paly. It has simple and brisk moves. Move accuracy and routine operation can judge the training effect.

2.4 Cultural experience

- A cudgel can sweep down a group of enemies

With a bigger attacking range than sword or spear, the function and strength of the cudgel is never undervalued. It is featured with swift and fierce moves. The control of a cudgel is fierce and flexible with single hand or both hands. Its attacking area is so huge that the saying goes like this: "a cudgel can sweep down a group of enemies at one stroke".

- Thirteen Monk Cudgel-Masters in Shaolin

In the early Tang Dynasty, the end of the Sui Dynasty, Wang Shichong, a General of Sui, proclaimed himself Emperor with his military force. In the 3rd year of Wude, Tang Dynasty (620 AD), Li Shimin conducted a military expedition against Wang. After Li lost the first battle, thirteen Shaolin monks who guarded the Bogu Village started an uprising, including Zhicao, huixi and Tanzong, due to Wang Renze's plundering Shaolin's fiefs. They attacked the camp and captured Wang Renze, then handed him over to Li Shimin. The event benefited Li Shimin (known as Highness Qin) greatly before he reunited China.

3 Conclusion

1. Fengmo Cudgel-Play is the basic taolu of Shanlinquan, as well as the basic taolu of wushu cudgel play.
2. The practice should begin with the cudgel-gripping methods.
3. The practitioner should get to know the style of cudgel play and its strength features by means of the body movements.

4 Extensive Reading

1. After the mastery of the movement routes, one can get to learn the method of cudgel-gripping change to experience the unity of body and cudgel.

2. After the mastery of the basic taolu, one can learn competition routines or other cudgel plays like Changquan

5 Questions

(1) Are the cudgel-gripping in Fengmo Cudgel-play fixed or flexible?

(2) To deliver the force when striking, what is the key point?

(3) Explain the "cudgel can sweep down a group of people at one stroke".

6 References

[1] Cai Longyun. The Zen of Boxing and Cudgel-play in Shaolin Temple [M]. Hangzhou: Zhejiang Science & Technology Press. 1983.02.

[2] Textbook Committee of National Sport Universities. Textbooks for Chinese Wushu (1). People's Sports Press. 2004

Chapter Seven

Qixing Sword

1 Introduction

Qixing Sword is the basic taolu (known as "routines", the same as below) of sword play. The set of structured movement is put in order, graceful and generous, which belongs to Gongjia sword taolu.

2 Learning experience

2.1 Directions

2.1.1 Preparations, with two movements

(1) Ready position

Stand facing south, grip the hilt in the left hand backward, turn the right hand into the swordfinger (*jianzhi*, which is a handwork, with the index finger and middle finger straight brought together, the ring finger and little finger bent, the thumb pressing onto them, the same as below), and close to the right leg, with eyes looking horizontally (Fig. 7-1-1).

Fig. 7-1-1

Fig. 7-1-2

(2) Lifting the knee and holding the sword

Step the right foot forward to form a right bow stance. Stretch the right swordfinger from the right side of the waist out forward; watch the swordfinger (Fig. 7-1-2). Stand straight on the right leg, raise the left knee, bend hands in front of the chests, and look at the sword tip (Fig. 7-1-3).

Fig. 7-1-3   Fig. 7-2   Fig. 7-3-1

Section 1

2.1.2 Lifting knee and stabbing forward

Hold the sword with the right hand and stab forward, draw the left swordfinger back in front of the right shoulder, and watch the tip of sword (Fig. 7-2).

2.1.3 Holding up sword from left to right, lifting leg and propping up sword

Turn the right arm inward to hold the sword to swing its tip up from toward to upward, backward, downward, and then forward on the right side of the body, with palms facing up (Fig. 7-3-1). Hold the sword with the right hand on the left side of the body, swinging the sword tip from the front to the upwards and left behind; cut with the blade out backward, the palms facing right and eyes gazing left (Fig. 7-3-2). Hold the sword with the right hand and make its tip ring from below to the front; lift the right arm and put the sword above the head. Meanwhile, turn the right heel inward and body right; kick the left leg with heel to the left, the left swordfinger pointing eastward and eyes gazing at it (Fig. 7-3-3).

Fig. 7-3-2   Fig. 7-3-2(A)   Fig. 7-3-3

2.1.4 Bow stance and splitting with sword backward

Hold the sword with the right hand and put the right arm down, ring the left arm upward and rightward and then put it before the right shoulder. Meanwhile, lift the left knee and watch the sword tip (Fig. 7-4-1). Put down the left foot on the left into a left bow stance. Hold the sword with the right hand and ring it from down to left, up into a circle, and then split backward on the right side. Ring the left swordfinger in front of the right shoulder from down to the left, and then horizontally lift it up. Watch the sword (Fig. 7-4-2).

Fig. 7-4-1   Fig. 7-4-2   Fig. 7-5

2.1.5 Lifting the right knee and holding sword

Hold the sword with the right hand and thrust it rightward down. Straighten the left leg and shift the body weight from left to the rear. Place the left swordfinger above the head, lift the right knee, bend the right arm and withdraw the sword back in front of the chest, eyes gazing at the right side (east) (Fig. 7-5).

2.1.6 Horse stance and holding sword; bow stance and stabbing down

Put down the right foot on the right into a horse stance; meanwhile, hold the sword with the right hand and put the hilt before the abdomen, so that the tip faces the right top obliquely as high as the head. Put the left swordfinger down to the inner side of the right wrist and watch the tip of sword (Fig. 7-6-1). After a little pause, extend the right toe a little into a right bow stance; meanwhile, hold the sword with the right hand and stab it straight down forward, raise the left swordfinger backward up obliquely and watch the tip of sword (Fig. 7-6-2).

Fig. 7-6-1   Fig. 7-6-2   Fig. 7-6-3

2.1.7 Stepping forward, turning the body and splitting with sword

Step the left foot forward, hold the sword with the right hand and ring it outward from front, top, to left and down. Meanwhile, put the left swordfinger straight down backward, then bend the elbow and ring the arm forward till below the right armpit. Keep eyes on the blade (Fig. 7-7-1). Continue to spin the sword with the right hand from down, forward, upward in a circle, turn the body right, move the right foot to the rear of the left leg and keep the left swordfinger unchanged (Fig. 7-7-2). Turn right, hold the sword with the right hand and split with it down forward from the head. Raise the left swordfinger from down to backward in an arc, eyes gazing at the front down (Fig. 7-7-3).

Fig. 7-7-1   Fig. 7-7-2   Fig. 7-7-3

2.1.8 *Wanhua*, horse stance and holding sword

Turn left, spin the right arm inward to make the sword tip facing down, whirl the sword from the outside of the left leg to backward, place the left swordfinger onto the right wrist, and watch the sword tip (Fig. 7-8-1). Hold the sword with the right hand and move it upwards; sink the hilt before the chest with the body turning right and keep the left swordfinger on the right wrist. Meanwhile, step the left foot back, bend the left leg and keep eyes on the sword tip (Fig. 7-8-2). Hold the sword with the right hand and ring its tip from front down, along the outer side of the right leg to the backward and upward in an arc, that is *wanhua* (Fig. 7-8-3). Hold the sword with the right hand and raise it from the outer side of the right leg to backward in an arc, the sword tip facing down and arms lifting horizontally. Bend the left elbow and place the left swordfinger in front of the right shoulder, eyes gazing at the sword hilt (Fig. 7-8-4). Stretch the left swordfinger out leftward and watch the swordfinger (Fig. 7-8-5).

2.1.9 Hanging sword to the left and right and cross-legged resting stance

Hold the sword with the right hand and ring its tip along the front, left, up, right in a circle, then hang it in front of the head; bend the left elbow and place the swordfinger onto the right wrist. Meanwhile, turn right, straighten the left leg and watch the sword tip (Fig. 7-9-1). Hold the sword with the right hand and ring its tip from the outer side of the right leg to the backward, up, front in a circle, then hang it

Fig. 7-8-1   Fig. 7-8-2   Fig. 7-8-3

Fig. 7-8-4   Fig. 7-8-5   Fig. 7-9-1

above the head. Bend the left elbow and place the swordfinger under the right shoulder when the sword tip arrives at the below. When the sword tip moves up forward, step the left foot forward to form a left bow stance, and keep eyes on the sword tip (Fig. 7-9-2).

Hold the sword with the right hand and ring its tip from the outer side of the left leg to the backward, up, front in a circle, then hang it in front of the head. Bend the left elbow and place the swordfinger onto the right wrist when the sword tip arrives backward. Step the right foot forward when the sword tip moves up forward (Fig. 7-9-3). Hold the sword with the right hand and ring its tip from the outer side of the right leg to the backward, up, front in a circle, then hang it above the head; meanwhile, turn the body right to face south and bend legs into a left cross-legged resting stance. Bend the left elbow and place the swordfinger before the right shoulder when the sword tip moves to the below; stretch it down forward obliquely with the arm straight when the sword tip moves to the front and a cross-legged resting stance is formed, eyes gazing at the swordfinger (Fig. 7-9-4).

Fig. 7-9-2   Fig. 7-9-3   Fig. 7-9-4

Section 2

2.1.10 Jumping, turning around and stabbing

With legs rising straight, put the right sole onto the ground and turn around (facing the west); with the body turning ring the sword with the right hand over the head for one and half a circle horizontally and then droop it down outward. Move the left swordfinger with the body turning and then lift it up leftward at the rear with the arm straight (Fig. 7-10-1). Shift the body weight forward, move the left foot forward and then push off ground (Fig. 7-10-2). At the same time, hold the sword with the right hand and ring it back, up and forward. Following that movement rotate the body from right to the rear. Ring the left swordfinger from up to the front when the sword tip moves backward, and move it down backward when the tip rings up forward (Fig. 7-10-3). Hold the sword with the right hand and ring the tip down backward, the left swordfinger ringing upward. Meanwhile, rotate the body right backward facing north, with the right foot landing first and the left foot later to form a horse stance. At this time, stab the sword rightward horizontally and watch the tip of sword (Fig. 7-10-4).

Fig. 7-10-1   Fig. 7-10-2

Fig. 7-10-3   Fig. 7-10-4

2.1.11 Rolling over, empty step and pointing with sword

With legs straighten up, move the right foot to the left from behind. Hold the sword with the right hand and ring it leftward till the front of the shoulder. Ring the left swordfinger down till below the right armpit with the elbow bent. Watch the sword (Fig. 7-11-1). Roll over the body backwards from the right. Hold the sword with the right hand and lift it rightward, the left swordfinger ringing with the turning of body (Fig. 7-11-2). Turn the body half straight toward the right slightly forward to form a right empty stance. Hold the sword with the right hand and ring it down westward pointing and hitting; lift the left swordfinger up obliquely, eyes gazing at the tip of the sword (Fig. 7-11-3).

Fig. 7-11-1

Fig. 7-11-2

Fig. 7-11-3

2.1.12 Horse stance and cutting with sword

Hold the sword with the right hand and ring it in the air (that is, *wanhua*) backward down with the tip of sword along the outer side of the left leg. Place the left swordfinger forward onto the right wrist (Fig. 7-12-1). Hold the sword with the right hand and *wanhua* with the tip of sword ringing up, forward and downward from behind. Place the left swordfinger onto the right wrist (Fig. 7-12-2). Hold the sword with the right hand and *wanhua* with the tip of sword ringing from the outer side of the right leg to the rear up; place the left swordfinger onto the right wrist. At the same time, shift the body weight forward, lift the left foot forward and push off the ground with the right foot and jump in the air (Fig. 7-12-3). With the left foot landing forward, turn the body left (facing south) and land the right foot on the right side of the body to form a horse stance. At the same time, hold the sword with the right hand and use the middle section of the blade to cut down toward the outer side of the right leg, the sword flat and the tip of sword facing toward the body. Lift the left swordfinger up with the elbow bent and watch the sword (Fig. 7-12-4).

Fig. 7-12-1   Fig. 7-12-2   Fig. 7-12-3

2.1.13 *Wanhua*, bow stance and chopping with sword

Hold the sword with the right hand and *wanhua* with the tip of sword ringing left, up and rightward; place the left swordfinger onto the right wrist. At the same time, turn the body right (facing west), shift the body weight onto the left leg to form a right empty stance and watch the tip of the sword (Fig. 7-13-1). Hold the sword with the right hand to ring the tip down (Fig. 7-13-2). Shift the body weight forward, place the right foot onto the ground and move the left foot forward to form a left bow stance. At the same time, hold the sword with the right hand and *wanhua* with the tip of sword backward up along the outer side of the right leg and then chop with it forward straight. Withdraw the left swordfinger in front of the right shoulder and watch the sword (Fig. 7-13-3).

Fig. 7-12-4   Fig. 7-13-1   Fig. 7-13-2

2.1.14 Exploring Sea and stabbing

Bring the right foot close to the left foot together, shift the body weight rightward and point to the ground emptily with the toes of the left foot. At the same time, hold the sword with the right hand to make the tip of sword stand as high as the head, the left stretching to the right wrist and eyes looking at the tip of the sword (Fig. 7-14-1).

Pause for a while, straighten the right leg and lift the left leg straight backward, the instep of the left foot stretching straight forward and the toes backwards. Hold the sword with the right hand and stab straight to the front down with it. Ring the left swordfinger down, back, upward to above the head along the outer side of the left leg and watch the tip of sword (Fig. 7-14-2).

Fig. 7-13-3   Fig. 7-14-1   Fig. 7-14-2

2.1.15 Turning around, bow stance and horizontal striking

Lean the body down, move the left foot next to the right foot and place the left sword finger onto the right wrist (Fig. 7-15-1). Step the right foot backward and turn back (facing east) to form a right bow stance. At the same time, hold the sword with the right hand and strike with it horizontally to the east front down obliquely with the body turning. Lift the left swordfinger up back on the left and watch the tip of sword (Fig. 7-15-2).

Fig. 7-15-1   Fig. 7-15-2

2.1.16 Lifting knee and holding sword

Straighten up the right leg and move the left foot forward. Hold the sword with the right hand and *wanhua* with the tip of sword ringing from up forward to the back, down and forward once along the outer side of the right shoulder with the straight arm. At the same time, ring the left swordfinger from down to the rear along the outer side of the left leg with the elbow bent and then place it in front of the right shoulder. Watch the tip of sword (Fig. 7-16-1). Turn the right heel outward and turn the body back from the left side (facing west). Lift the left leg with the knee bent; hold the sword with the right hand and lift it up. Stretch the left swordfinger forward straight at the time of lifting the left leg, eyes gazing at the tip of sword (Fig. 7-16-2).

Fig. 7-16-1   Fig. 7-16-2

2.1.17 Cross-legged stance and pushing sword

Place the left foot steps forward and lift the right foot behind the body with the knee bent. Hold the sword with the right hand and droop the sword tip behind the body; withdraw the left swordfinger before the right shoulder (Fig. 7-17-1). Hold the sword with the right hand and ring the sword hilt from upper to the left, from the left shoulder to the below till the right waist and then stop, the sword tip pointing forward in front of the body. Ring the left swordfinger down, left, and up till above the head. At the same time, swing the right foot to the west, push off the ground with the left foot and then stretch it at the rear of the right leg, eyes gazing at the below of the right side of the body (Fig. 7-17-2). With the right foot first touching the ground first, bend the right knee into a half-crouch; cross the left foot to the rear of the right leg to form a cross-legged stance. At the same time, hold the sword with the right hand and push it to the below of the left side obliquely and watch the sword (Fig. 7-17-3).

Fig. 7-17-1   Fig. 7-17-2   Fig. 7-17-3

Section 3

2.1.18 Empty stance and holding sword

Straighten up the right leg, step the left foot eastward and step the right foot eastward from the front of the left foot. At the same time, hold the sword with the right hand and swing the sword tip to the right side of the body. Ring the sword horizontally from the right to the front and place the left swordfinger onto the right wrist, eyes following the sword (Fig. 7-18-1). Move the left foot one more pace to the east and turn the body left; at the same time, hold the sword with the right hand and ring it horizontally to the east with the body moving. Bend the elbow and pull the sword next to the waist, the sword tip pointing up forward obliquely, slightly higher than the head; place the left swordfinger onto the right wrist. Shift the body weight backward, bend the right knee, and point forward with the toes of the left foot to form a left empty stance. Watch the sword tip (Fig. 7-18-2).

Fig. 7-18-1

Fig. 7-18-2

2.1.19 Bow stance and stabbing forward

Step the left foot forward to form a left bow stance with the knee bent. Hold the sword with the right hand, together with the left swordfinger, and stab up forward straight with the tip of sword, the tip as high as the head. Watch the sword tip (Fig. 7-19).

Fig. 7-19

Fig. 7-20

2.1.20 Crouch stance and sweeping with sword

Turn the body right to form a right crouch stance; at the same time, hold the sword with the right hand, swing and sweep with the blade towards the right and rear down obliquely. Lift the left swordfinger up on the left obliquely and watch the sword (Fig. 7-20).

2.1.21 *Wanhua*, cross-legged resting stance, and backward pulling

Stand straight, turn the left heel outward, turn the body right and move the right foot back half a pace, the two legs bent slightly. At the same time, hold the sword with the right hand and lift the hilt upward to the front of chest, with the left swordfinger attached to the right wrist; watch the sword hilt (Fig. 7-21-1). Hold the sword with the right hand and *wanhua* with the sword tip ringing from the outer side of the right leg to the rear and top (Fig. 7-21-2). Step the right foot backward, turn the body right (facing north), cross the left foot at the rear of the body and bend knees to form a left cross-legged resting stance. At the same time, hold the sword with the right hand and take a backward pull to west, down, east and then up; withdraw the left swordfinger before the right shoulder. Watch the sword tip (Fig. 7-21-3).

Fig. 7-21-1　　　　　Fig. 7-21-2　　　　　Fig. 7-21-3

2.1.22 Stepping back and stabbing straight

Straighten the body and turn left (facing the west); step the right foot back to form a left bow stance. Hold the sword with the right hand and stab out with the sword tip top-down via the waist, with the left swordfinger attached to the right shoulder. Watch the sword tip (Fig. 7-22).

Fig. 7-22　　　　　Fig. 7-23-1　　　　　Fig. 7-23-2

2.1.23 Lifting knee and chopping with sword

Step the left foot back, hold the sword with the right hand and ring it downward;

move the left swordfinger to the right wrist and watch the sword tip (Fig. 7-23-1). Hold the sword with the right hand and ring the sword tip from down to the rear left; turn the right arm inward and lift the hilt via the left shoulder. Chop with the blade forward; draw the left swordfinger back to the front of the right shoulder. At the same time, straighten the left leg straight, lift the right leg with the knee bent and watch the sword (Fig. 7-23-2).

2.1.24 Empty stance and holding sword

Bend the left knee, step the right leg to the rear and straighten it. Hold the sword with the right hand to lift it upward and place the left swordfinger onto the right wrist (Fig. 7-24-1). Turn the toes of the left foot inward and the body backward to form a right empty stance. Hold the sword with the right hand and move it, together with the left swordfinger, the hilt slightly sunk at the height of waist and eyes following the blade (Fig. 7-24-2).

Fig. 7-24-1   Fig. 7-24-2

2.1.25 Horse stance and lifting sword

Step the left foot forward, turn the body right and bend knees to form a horse stance. At the same time, hold the sword with the right hand and ring the hilt down, right and then up, with the sword tip pointed to the ground, the left swordfinger pulled back to the front of the right shoulder. Watch the sword hilt (Fig. 7-25-1). Stretch the left swordfinger out to the left, eyes gazing at it (Fig. 7-25-2).

Fig. 7-25-1   Fig. 7-25-2

2.1.26 Turning back, pointing forward, empty stance and lifting sword

Hold the sword with the right hand and hang it to the left in front of the body; at the same time, cross the right foot to the left rear of the body, lift the left swordfinger upward and turn the body backward, eyes following the sword tip (Fig. 7-26-1). Turn the body right backward, hold the sword with the right hand and hang the sword to the right side with the body turning(Fig. 7-26-2). Hold the sword with the right hand and point forward, the left swordfinger attached to the right wrist from up to the front and eyes gazing at the sword tip(Fig. 7-26-3). Hold the sword with the right hand, with the sword hilt down, pull the sword back from the outer side of the right leg to the back, then put it behind the body, with the sword tip facing down forward obliquely. At the same time, shift the body weight backward to form a left empty stance; stretch the left swordfinger out forward horizontally, eyes gazing at it(Fig. 7-26-4). At the same time, Shift the body weight backward and form a right empty stance. Stretch the left swordfinger out foward and eyes looking at the sword tip. (Fig. 7-26-5)

Fig. 7-26-1 Fig. 7-26-2 Fig. 7-26-3

Fig. 7-26-4 Fig. 7-26-5

Section 4

2.1.27 Pointing onto the ground and stabbing forward

Step the right foot forward and then step the left foot forward, the left toes pointing onto the ground. At the same time, hold the sword with the right hand and move the sword hilt across the right side of the waist and then stab upward straight before the body with the sword tip, the left swordfinger drawn back to the front of the right shoulder, eyes looking at the sword tip (Fig. 7-27).

Fig. 7-27　　　　　　Fig. 7-28-1　　　　　　Fig. 7-28-2

2.1.28 Cross-legged resting stance and chopping down

Hold the sword with the right hand and ring the sword tip leftward and then pull the sword hilt back in front of the abdomen; ring the left swordfinger down, left, and then up obliquely. Watch the front below (Fig. 7-28-1). With two legs bent, fully squat to form a cross-legged resting stance. Hold the sword with the right hand and chop down forward horizontally with the sword blade; lift the left swordfinger up backward on the left. Watch the sword (Fig. 7-28-2).

2.1.29 Lifting knee and holding sword

Stand straight and lift the right knee. At the same time, hold the sword with the right hand and lift the hilt up to the left side of the left ear, with the sword tip pointing down obliquely. Place the left swordfinger onto the right wrist. Watch the front below (Fig. 7-29).

Fig. 7-29　　　　　　Fig. 7-30-1　　　　　　Fig. 7-30-2

2.1.30 Jumping forward, cross-legged resting stance and cutting down

Step the right foot forward; hold the sword with the right hand and ring the tip from the outer side of the right leg toward back, up, and left. Following that movement withdraw the swordfinger of the left hand back to the front of the right shoulder. Move the left foot forward at the time of ringing the tip upward; push off the ground and jump with the right foot from behind to the left, body in the air (Fig. 7-30-1). Land the left foot first and land the right foot on the left side to form a cross-legged resting stance. At the same time, hold the sword with the right hand and cut down with it on the left in front of the body; stretch the left swordfinger out to below the right armpit accordingly. Stoop forward, turn head left and watch the sword tip (Fig. 7-30-2).

2.1.31 Rolling over body, bow stance and chopping with sword

Hold the sword with the right hand and pull the sword hilt rightward, with the left swordfinger stretching to the left. At the same time, straighten two legs to form a right cross-legged stance (Fig. 7-31-1). Turn the body right toward the back (facing west) and move the right foot half a pace to form a right bow stance. Hold the sword with the right hand and swing it with the body turning over and then chop forward; lift the left swordfinger above the head from the left behind. Watch the sword (Fig. 7-31-2).

Fig. 7-31-1   Fig. 7-31-2

2.1.32 Raising knee and stabbing straight

Hold the sword with the right and ring the sword to *wanhua* with the tip of sword ringing back, up and forward for one circle from the outer side of the right leg. Bend the elbow and withdraw the hilt behind the right waist, with the left swordfinger attached to the right wrist. At the same time, stretch the toes of the right foot outward and step the left foot half a pace forward to form a left cross-legged resting stance. Watch the back of the right side (Fig. 7-32-1). Turn the body left, step the left foot forward (facing west), straighten the left leg and lift the right knee. At the same time, hold the sword with the right hand and stab forward with the sword tip; ring the left swordfinger horizontally from the front of the body to the rear left. Watch the sword tip

(Fig. 7-32-2).

Fig. 7-32-1   Fig. 7-32-2

Concluding movements

2.1.33 Bringing feet together and holding sword

Turn the left heel inward, turn the body left and land the right foot west to form a right bow stance. At the same time, hold the sword with the right hand and lift the hilt up to overhead, the left swordfinger carrying the hilt and eyes looking at the hilt (Fig. 7-33-1). Turn the body right to form a right crouching stance, grip the hilt and lift it up with the left hand backhand; change the right hand into a swordfinger to cross the right side, eyes following the right swordfinger (Fig. 7-33-2). Straighten two legs, bring the left foot close to the right foot and step together. Lift the right swordfinger above head; hold the sword with the left hand down next to the left side of body. Watch the left side (Fig. 7-33-3).

Fig. 7-33-1   Fig. 7-33-2   Fig. 7-33-3

2.1.34 Closing position

Ring the swordfinger of the right hand from up to right downward. Change them into a palm and place it close to the right leg. With two elbows slightly bent naturally, turn the head forward and watch the front (see Fig. 7-1-1).

2.2　Learning program

Category	Content
Preparations	To require the flexibility, coordination and strength; To master the basic wushu footwork; To understand the structure of a sword; To know the basic skills of sword play (splitting, stabbing, pointing, hanging, lifting, *wanhua*, etc.).
Learning Schedule	To learn the movement routes (a set of 34 movements, with four movements in each lesson. It needs about 10 times, 20 class hours to complete the learning task); To improve the movements.

2.3　Technique experience

Content	Requirements
Healthy body and strong bone	Qixing Sword belongs to GongJia (which focuses on the movements and postures of an actor on stage) Sword which needs neat movements and postures. Therefore, mastering basic stances, gait and balanced actions, are the basic requirements of studying Qixing Sword.
Correct ways	Swordsmanship of Qixing Sword includes the movements of "Stab, point, lift, split, cut, hit, raise over head, chop, hang, spin" and so on. So you need to find out the skills in each movement. For example, stabbing and pointing focus on the sword tip; in lifting and splitting, the strength should be on the front blade; cutting needs the arm and sword in a straight line; hitting with sword means that you should place down the wrist to make the tip straight up abruptly; raise your sword higher than your head to make the strength up to the sword; chopping is to push the sword left or right horizontally between the head and the shoulder, with the strength onto the sword; hanging must be in a circle and close to the body; spin is to ring the sword horizontally overhead or in the front of the front head.
Coordination with the body and sword	In action, the body movements need to work closely with the action of sword, make strength of the body's movement up to the sword blade. For example, coordination betweenthe swordfinger and sword, sword and gait (stance following the sword and sword following the stance), the sword moves and body moves (the body moving with sword and sword moving with the body), etc.

2.4　Cultural experience

- **Arms sword and Chinese wushu sword**

　　As a "gentleman in hundreds of weapons", arms sword fights in two ways: one is going into battle straight, together with shield; the second is as a back-up weapon.

　　Chinese wushu combines the arms sword's "stabbing" and "cutting" (hitting) with blade, and deepen the people's understanding toward the sword into "three tips and four blades", which not only constructs the technology system with different methods, but also forms a unique practice pattern.

- **Light and neat in a sword play**

　　Sword has two blades, so you can't touch the sword when holding it. Therefore, the movements of pointing, hitting, cutting and twisting need to be agile, light and accurate, with strength on the sword tip or the front of the sword. In the course of light footwork, natural and unrestrained jumps and adroit dodging of the sword play drills, the maneuver of sword needs the strength to arrive at one part of the sword in the adroit attacking and chopping or stabbing, showing the features of softness with stiffness, the lightness with neatness in the movement of a sword.

- **Gongjia Sword focus on the movement structure**

"Gongjia Sword" focuses on the standard movement or posture, like the regular script in Chinese calligraphy, Therefore, it asks for a balanced structure in the sword movement, including the symmetry of the postures and overall layout.

- **How to hand a sword and hold a sword**

The manner of handing sword

1. Handing the sword with hands: stand upright naturally, with two feet bringing together, the palms facing upward. Hold the hand guards and place it in the front of the body horizontally, with sword standing straight and the blade toward the left and right sides; watch the person who will get the sword.

2. The manner of handing the sword with one hand: stand upright naturally, with two feet bringing together, the left hand close to the hand guard. Hold the hilt with the Hukou facing upward and watch the person who gives you the sword.

The manner of holding the sword

Stand upright naturally, with two feet bringing together. Hold the sword with the left hand, bend the arm and lift it up to make the sword close to the outer side of the forearm and then place it in front of chest obliquely. Change the right hand into a palm and attach it to the index finger bottom of the left hand with the outer edge of the palm, the same height as chest. The distance between hands and chest is 20 to 30 cm.

3 Conclusion

- Qixing Sword is the basis taolu of the sword play in wushu weapons, so it includes the basic sword skills, such as stabbing with sword, hanging with sword, chopping with sword, lifting with sword, spinning with sword, pointing with sword and splitting with sword and so on.

- Qixing Sword belongs to Gongjia Sword, so it needs to regard "standard movements" and "neat sword maneuver" as the basis; and every movement should reflect its dignified appeal.

- Practicing Qixing Sword needs coordination between the swordfinger and sword, sword and gait, the sword moves and body moves, etc., so that the imposing manner in sword play can be shown in sword play.

- To learn the "lightness and neatness in sword movement" in Qixing Sword practice, and to understand the cultural spirits of "loving the sword and despising the death, being dead rather than giving up".

4 Extensive Reading

- After learning the route of Qixing Sword, you need to correct mistakes repeatedly and improve the standard movements.

- After learning the taolu of Qixing Sword, you can improve the appeal of the exercise from "the coordination of sword and body", "coherent momentum" and other aspects.

- After learning the route of Qixing Sword, you can continue another set of Gongjia Sword (Pan-long sword play), you can also choose Sanhe Sword as further study.

5 Questions

(1) How do you understand the unique pattern in sword maneuver;

(2) What are the movement features in Qixing Sword.

(3) What is the relationship between sword drill style and Chinese traditional culture.

6 References

[1] Cai Longyun. Swordsmanship [M]. Nanchang: Jiangxi People's Publishing House, 1982.

[2] The National Sports Colleges and Universities Teaching Material Committee. Chinese Martial Arts Tutorial (I) [M]. Beijing: People's Sport Publishing House, 2004.

[3] Dai Guobin. Cultural Biography of Sword [J]. Journal of Physical Education and Science, 2009 (5): 11-13.

Chapter Eight

Nunchakus

1 Introduction

It is said that nunchakus was invented by the first emperor of Song Dynasty, Zhao Kuangyin. It was used to sweep the horse hoofs of the enemies, break their Armour and weaponry or hard weapons at that time. Later nunchakus was spread southward to Philippines, eastward to Japan, and then brought to screen by Bruce lee, thus being widely circulated and even becoming the defence of American police. Nowadays, nunchakus not only combines the wushu moves of broadsword, spear, sword, staff and nine-section whip and so on together, but also absorbs the elements of modern music and dance, becoming a fashion sport with the combination of fighting and performance. It is also a popular martial arts fitness activity with the combination of self-defense and bodybuilding, which features "flexible fierce, moderate hardness and softness, dynamic and static state, and free unlimited state".

The Structure of Nunchakus

It consists of staff A, staff B, the length of which both is 30cm, and the in-between chain with a length of 12cm. Each staff is divided into two parts, the far-side section which is the farther part away from the chain and the near-side section which is near the chain.

---

2 Learning experience

2.1 Directions

2.1.1 Ready position

Set two feet open with a distance of 10-15cm between the front and back foot, the whole sole of each foot touching the ground. The hand holding the near-side section of the staff A should keep a consistent direction with the front supporting leg. And meanwhile the practitioner should hold the head up, keep chest out and two eyes leveled (Fig. 8-1).

Fig. 8-1　　　　　　　　　　　　Fig. 8-2-1

Fig. 8-2-2　　　　　　　　　　　Fig. 8-2-3

2.1.2　Meteors catching up with the moon

Pivot the right hand on the right elbow, swing the staff downward from inside, then forward and upward, and then outward and backward, and finally downward and forward, thus to make the staff B spin into a flower like a big "8" (Fig. 8-2-1, 8-2-2, 8-2-3).

2.1.3　Both ways

Extend the right arm forward (straight or slightly bent) and pivot the right hand on the wrist joint downward from inside, upward, outward, backward, and downward and then forward and upward, thus to spin the staff B into a flower like a small "8" (Fig. 8-3-1—Fig. 8-3-6).

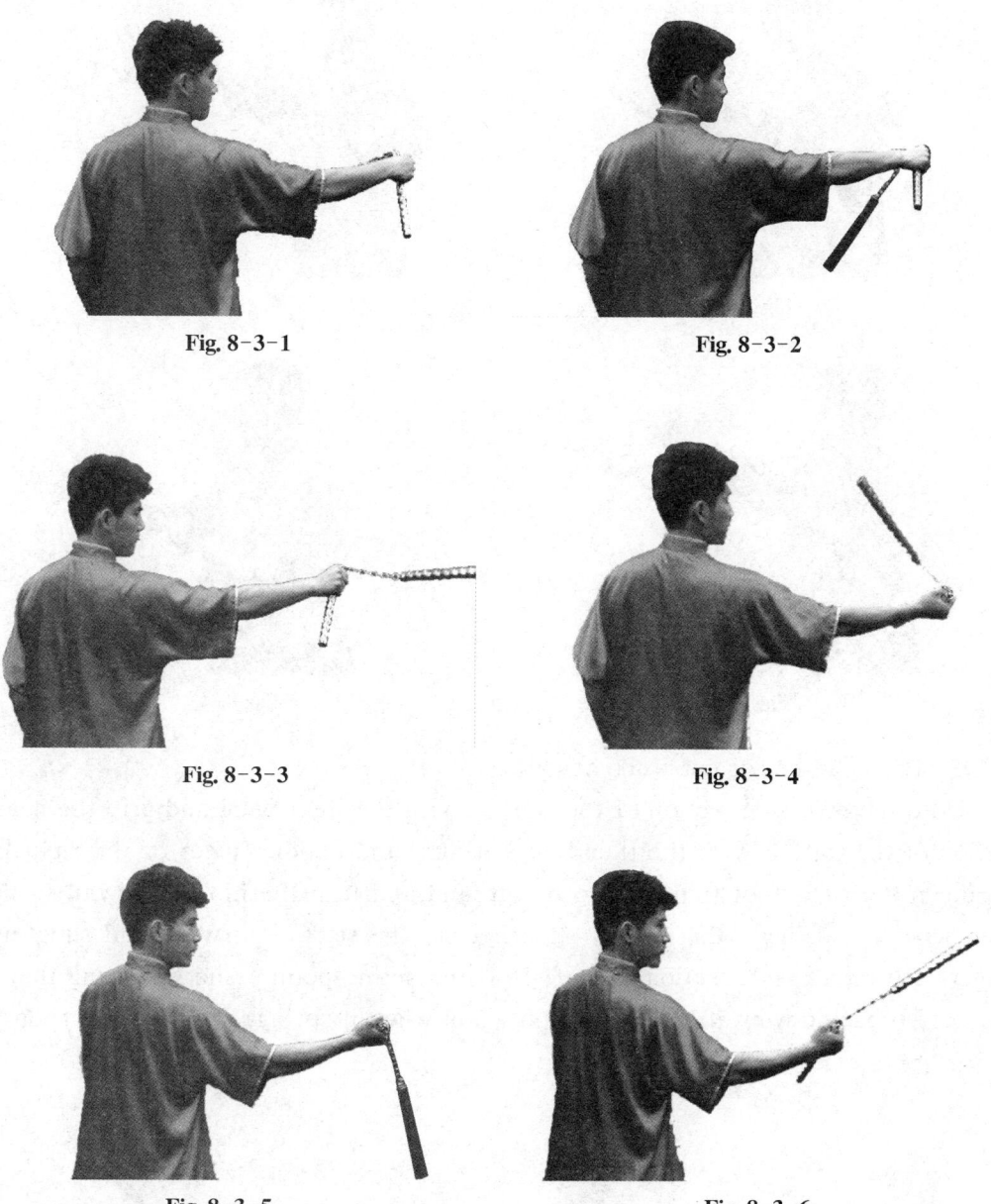

Fig. 8-3-1　　　　　　　　　　Fig. 8-3-2

Fig. 8-3-3　　　　　　　　　　Fig. 8-3-4

Fig. 8-3-5　　　　　　　　　　Fig. 8-3-6

2.1.4　The viper spits out its tongue

Hold the near-side section of staff A and clamp the staff B under the armpit. Set down the right foot tightly onto the ground and turn the hip; meanwhile send the shoulder out and jiggle the elbow, shooting off the staff B forwardly, just like a snake spitting its tongue out. Following that move, draw the staff B back downward to the armpit again conveniently, ready for a second attack (Fig. 8-4-1, 8-4-2, 8-4-3, 8-4-4).

Fig. 8-4-1   Fig. 8-4-2
Fig. 8-4-3   Fig. 8-4-4

2.1.5 The Viper comes out of the cavern

Hold the near-side section of the staff A with the right palm and grip the near-side section of the staff B with the thumb, forefinger and middle finger of the right hand. Set down the right foot tightly onto the ground and turn the hip, meanwhile send the shoulder out and jiggle the elbow, shooting off the staff B forward and shooting the target with the far-side section of staff B as the acting point. And following that draw the staff B back downward to the armpit again when it springs back from outside (Fig. 8-5-1, 8-5-2, 8-5-3).

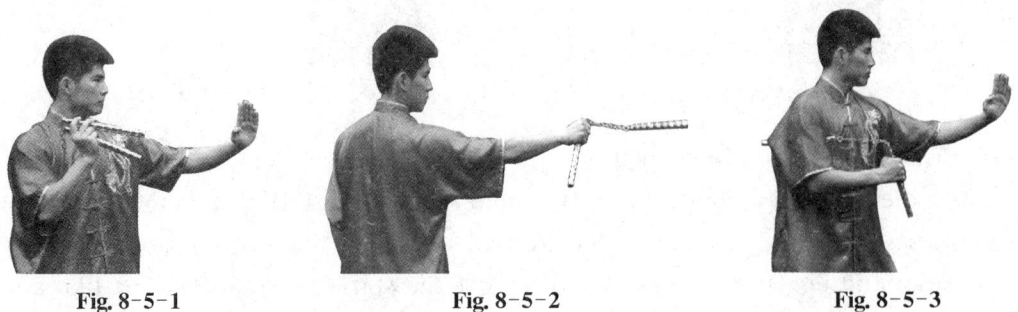

Fig. 8-5-1   Fig. 8-5-2   Fig. 8-5-3

2.1.6 Waist turning

Hold the staff A on the right shoulder with the right hand, and then hack toward the front on the left obliquely where the strength should focus on. Then draw the staff back naturally to the left rear and block it with trunk. Draw the staff B back downward to the right armpit when it springs back (Fig. 8-6-1, 8-6-2, 8-6-3, 8-6-4).

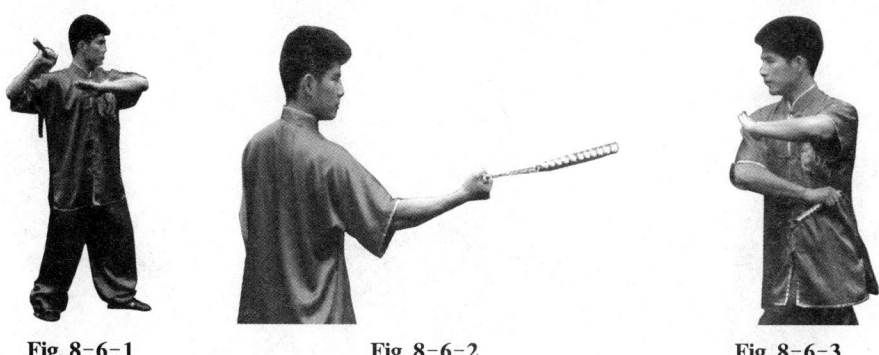

Fig. 8-6-1　　　　　　　Fig. 8-6-2　　　　　　　Fig. 8-6-3

2.1.7　Arm turning

Hold the staff on the shoulder with the right hand and hack forward and downward, which should take the elbow joint as the axis. And then hold the staff when it bounces back to the shoulder from the upper arm. And then repeat all the above-mentioned movements to practice. The movement of the left hand is the same as that of the right hand (Fig. 8-7-1, 8-7-2, 8-7-3, 8-7-4).

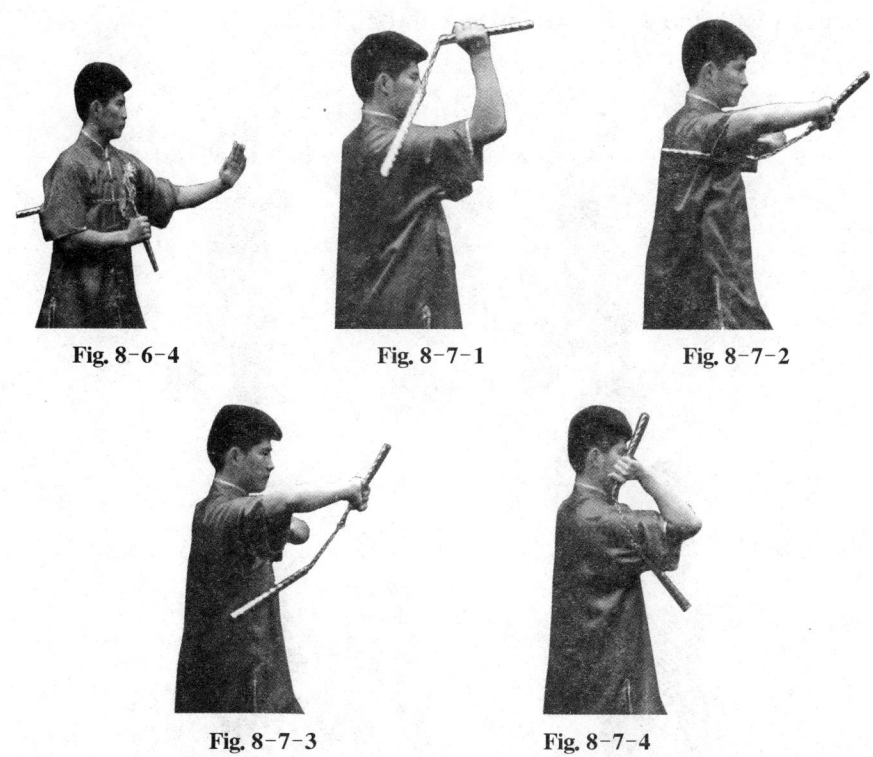

Fig. 8-6-4　　　　　　　Fig. 8-7-1　　　　　　　Fig. 8-7-2

Fig. 8-7-3　　　　　　　Fig. 8-7-4

2.1.8 Leg turning

Hold the staff A on the shoulder with the right hand. Then hack with it left forward while lifting the left knee to block the chain part of the nunchakus by the shank, making the staff B rebound to the thigh accordingly (Fig. 8-8-1, 8-8-2, 8-8-3).

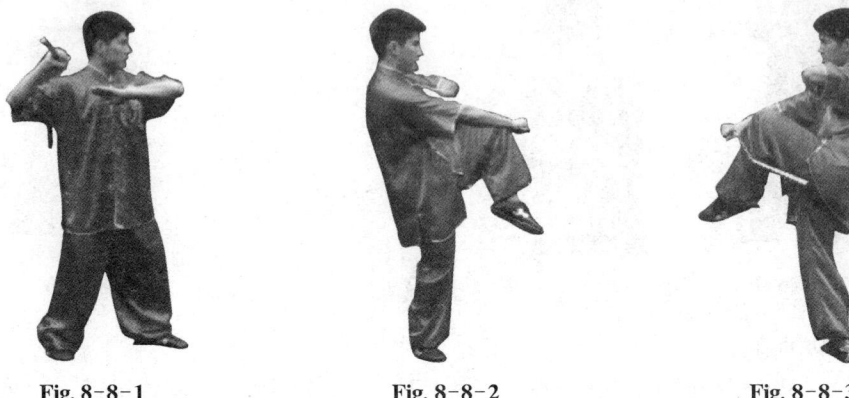

Fig. 8-8-1   Fig. 8-8-2   Fig. 8-8-3

2.1.9 Body turning

Hold the staff A with the right hand and rotate it backward around the body with the left foot in the front and right foot in the rear. And then turn the body backward to the right when the staff B is moving upward in the front, which makes the rotation become forward with the right foot in the front and the left foot in the rear (Fig. 8-9-1, 8-9-2, 8-9-3, 8-9-4).

Fig. 8-9-1   Fig. 8-9-2

Fig. 8-9-3   Fig. 8-9-4

2.1.10 Back pass

Hold the near-side section of the staff A and sweep it horizontally from the left bottom to the right rear. And then catch the near-side section of the staff B with the left hand at the back of the body (Fig. 8-10-1, 8-10-2, 8-10-3).

Fig. 8-10-1　　　　　Fig. 8-10-2　　　　　Fig. 8-10-3

2.1.11 Front pass

Hold the near-side section of the staff A and hack it up and down. And then hold the same section with the other hand when the staff is vertical to the ground while hacking (Fig. 8-11-1, 8-11-2).

Fig. 8-11-1　　　　　Fig. 8-11-2

2.1.12 Shoulder pass

Hold the near-side section of the staff A. Swing the staff B bottom-up and then to the back. And when the staff B gets to the right upper arm, catch the near-side section of the staff B from the right armpit quickly with the left hand. It is the same with backhand (Fig. 8-12-1, 8-12-2, 8-12-3).

Fig. 8-12-1

Fig. 8-12-2

Fig. 8-12-3

2.1.13 Forehand clockwise spinning

Hold the near-side section of the staff A with the right hand and swing it downward to the left side. And then throw the staff A off when the staff B is moving to the upper right, making the in-between chain slide around the back of the right hand. Meanwhile catch the near-side of the staff B with the right hand backhand (Fig. 8-13-1, 8-13-2, 8-13-3, 8-13-4).

Fig. 8-13-1

Fig. 8-13-2

Fig. 8-13-3

Fig. 8-13-4

2.1.14 Backhand clockwise spinning

Hold the staff A with the right hand backhand and swing it to the right rear. And when the staff B gets to the upper right rear, throw the staff A off, making the in-between chain slide around the back of the right hand and then catch the near-side section of the staff B with the right hand forehand (Fig. 8-14-1, 8-14-2, 8-14-3).

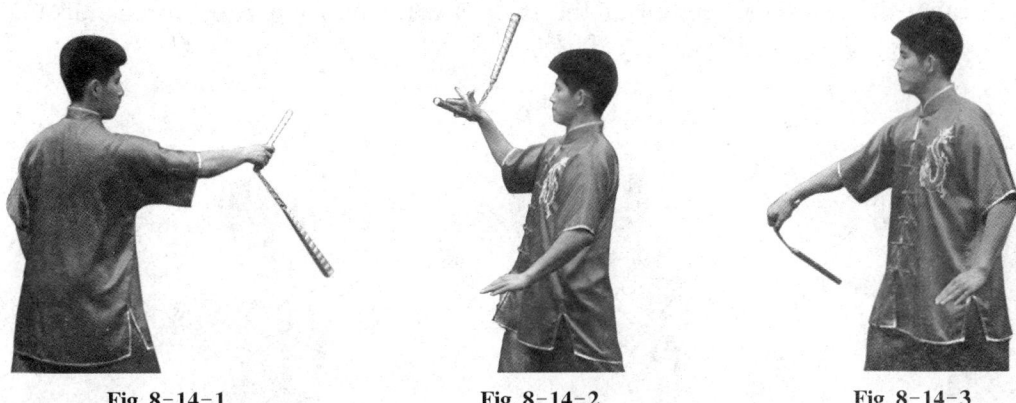

Fig. 8-14-1   Fig. 8-14-2   Fig. 8-14-3

2.1.15 Forehand counterclockwise spinning

Hold the near-side section of the staff A with the right hand and swing it upward in the front. And when the staff B arrives at the lower right, throw the staff A off, making the in-between chain slide around the back of the right hand. And then catch the near-side section of the staff B with the right hand backhand (Fig. 8-15-1, 8-15-2, 8-15-3, 8-15-4).

Fig. 8-15-1   Fig. 8-15-2

Fig. 8-15-3   Fig. 8-15-4

2.1.16 Backhand counterclockwise spinning

Hold the staff A backhand with the right hand and swing it bottom-up to the front. And when the staff goes to the lower back, push it to the left lower back with the right arm. And then throw the staff A off, making it slide around the back of the right hand, and then catch the near-side section of the staff B with the right hand forehand (Fig. 8-16-1, 8-16-2, 8-16-3, 8-16-4, 8-16-5).

Fig. 8-16-1   Fig. 8-16-2   Fig. 8-16-3

Fig. 8-16-4   Fig. 8-16-5

2.1.17 Clockwise and horizontal spinning in front of chest

Hold the near-side section of the staff A with the right hand backhand and swing the staff horizontally for a circle from the right side to the left side of the body. Then throw the staff A off, making the in-between chain slide around the back of the right hand, and then catch the near-side of the staff B with the right hand forehand (Fig. 8-17-1, 8-17-2, 8-17-3, 8-17-4).

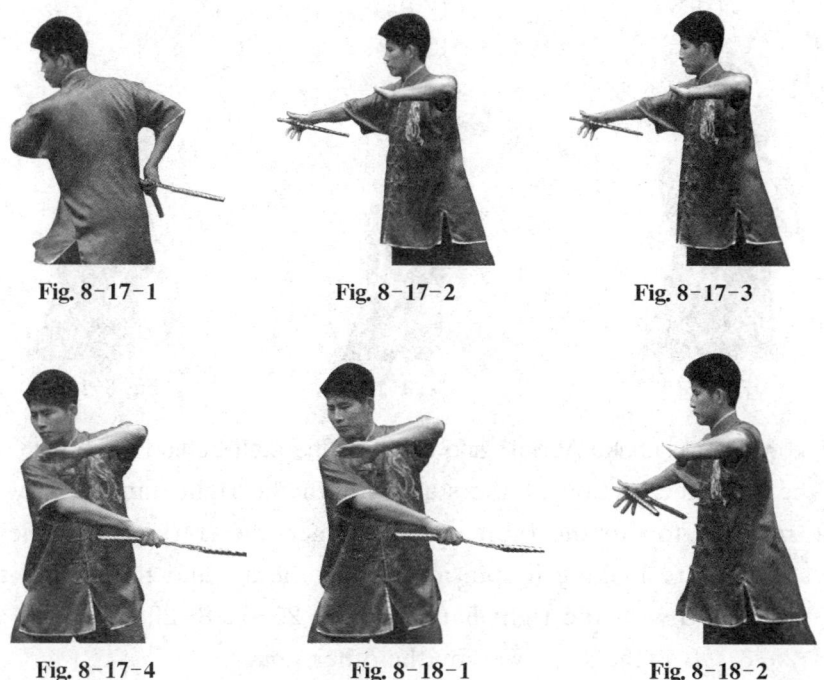

Fig. 8-17-1   Fig. 8-17-2   Fig. 8-17-3

Fig. 8-17-4   Fig. 8-18-1   Fig. 8-18-2

2.1.18 Counterclockwise and horizontal spinning in front of chest

Hold the near-side of the staff A with the right hand forehand and swing the staff horizontally for a circle from the left side to the right side of the body. Then throw the staff A off, making the in-between chain slide around the back of right hand, and then catch the near-side of staff B with the right hand backhand (Fig. 8-18-1, 8-18-2, 8-18-3, 8-18-4).

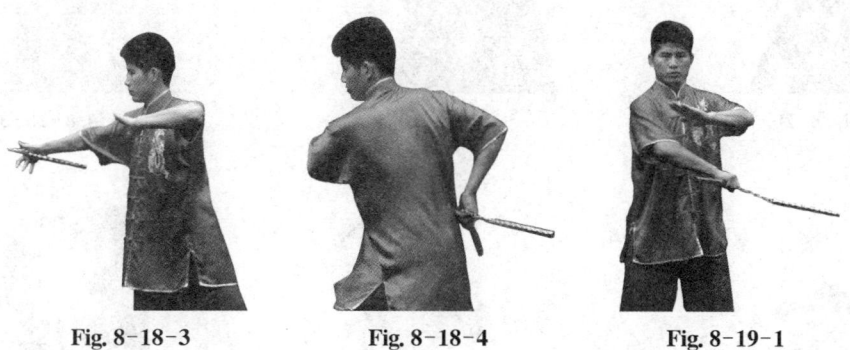

Fig. 8-18-3   Fig. 8-18-4   Fig. 8-19-1

2.1.19 Throwing (Nunchaku Aerial) and catching staff by the sides of the body

Hold the near-side section of the staff A with the right hand and swing the staff towards the left armpit. And when the staff reaches the upper rear, throw the staff A off, making it spin a circle in the air and then catch the near-side section of the staff B with the left hand (Fig. 8-19-1, 8-19-2, 8-19-3, 8-19-4). It is the same way by the other side.

Fig. 8-19-2

Fig. 8-19-3

Fig. 8-19-4

2.1.20 Throwing (Nunchaku Aerial) and catching the staff behind the body

Hold the near-side section of the staff A with the right hand and swing the staff downward from the top to the right armpit. When the staff gets to the upper rear, throw the staff A off, making it spin a circle in the air and then catch the near-side section of the staff B with the right hand (Fig. 8-20-1, 8-20-2, 8-20-3, 8-20-4, 8-20-5, 8-20-6). It is the same way by the other side.

Fig. 8-20-1 Fig. 8-20-2 Fig. 8-20-3

Fig. 8-20-4 Fig. 8-20-5 Fig. 8-20-6

2.1.21 Drawing the staff back

When the staff gets to the farthest point, take it back, making it waggle; and then catch the near side of the staff with the forefinger and middle finger of the right hand when it swings back (Fig. 8-21-1, 8-21-2, 8-21-3).

Fig. 8-21-1   Fig. 8-21-2   Fig. 8-21-3

2.2 Learning program

Category	Content
Preparations	1. Good coordination 2. Mastery of the basic skills, simple wushu taolu with weapon
Learning Progress	1. Phase One: to master the four basic skills (2 class hours); 2. Phase Two: to learn to exchange the two hands, aiming to exercise with both hands on the basis of Phase one (2 class hour); 3. Phase Three: to learn to shift the direction, aiming to exercise on the move (2 class hours); 4. Phase Four: to master the spinning movements and reach the state that the staff spins like flowers and that nothing but the staff can be seen (8 class hours). 5. Phase Five: to master the throwing (Nunchaku Aerial) and catching movements. Combine the spinning and throwing and catching organically and experience the high-level state of staff moving with body and the spinning around, coordinating with foot work and body techniques (2 class hours).

2.3 Technique experience

Content	Requirements
Movement Standards	1. To master the movement route; 2. To know the methods and parts of body when exerting force; 3. The movements should be stretched, the body and the weapon should be coordinated and the body should move fast and stand stable.
Key techniques	1. Hit the opponent's eyes or face with the endpoint of the staff, just like the action of viper spitting out its tongue or viper coming out of the cavern. 2. Hit the opponent's critical parts with the far-side section of the staff, like the hacking forward with the staff in the action of the waist turning. 3. Strangle the opponent's neck or other joint parts with the in-between chain.

(continued)

Content	Requirements
Exercise levels	1. On the basis of mastering the basic actions, speed up the actions constantly. 2. After improving the action speed, stress the training tempo, making the speed coordinate and the body move fast and stand stable. 3. After improving the action speed, experience the dynamics of the actions. (Taking the waist as the position to exert force, the wrist should be relaxed.) 4. After improving the action dynamics, experience the body-weapon coordination, which is "the staff moving with the hand and the eyes rolling with the staff", as well as the requirement of full spirit and energy.

3　Conclusion

- The actions mentioned above are the basic actions of nunchakus, which is also the basis of all the other group actions the practitioners need to exercise further.

- The practitioners should master the movement route and learn to protect themselves first, trying to avoid hurting themselves or dropping the staff.

- When practicing the actions, practitioners should relax the wrists. After lowering the speed and acquainting the route, experience the positions of exerting force and the tempo of the actions. Meanwhile try to understand the key techniques and experience the requirements of Chinese wushu, which is "body combining with weapon, eyes rolling with hands and footsteps moving with body", finally trying to coordinate the body and the weapon into one.

4　Extensive reading

- After mastering the single actions, the practitioners can change hands to exercise, trying to use the nunchakus flexibly with both hands.

- After mastering the single actions, the practitioners can deepen their understanding of the techniques by the simulation training (e.g. hitting the sandbag or the tree trunk, etc.).

- After mastering the single actions, the practitioners can learn the group actions (like grading system) to improve the coherence between single actions.

5　Questions

(1) What is the purpose and meaning of practicing nunchakus?

(2) How can we overcome the psychological fear of practicing nunchakus?

(3) How can we improve thetraining level of nunchakus?

6 References

[1] Yu Hongying, MaYe. Development of Domestic Nunchaku Sports [J]. Bulletin of Sport Science & Technology. 2011(2):89-104.

[2] http://www.lz1980.com/

[3] General Administration of Sport of China. Chinese Wushu Duan Wei System Coursebooks—Nunchakus [M]. Beijing: Higher Education Press, 2009(9).

Chapter Nine

Mawangdui Daoyin Exercise

1 Introduction

"Health Qigong · Mawangdui Daoyin Exercise" is a kind of health Qigong officially introduced abroad by Chinese Health Qigong Association, which is compiled by experts from Shanghai University of Sport on the basis of "Daoyin Illustration" excavated in Changsha, Hunan Province. It is a popular health Qigong, combining the basic theory of health Qigong with modern health promotion theories.

2 Learning experience

2.1 Directions

2.1.1 Ready position

Stand straight with feet together. Straighten your neck with your chins slightly in, sink your chest in and straighten your back. Put both arms down; lock your lips and teeth with the tongue leaning against the palate, the eyes looking forward(Fig. 9-1-1). Hold the palms up to the height of your navel, suspend Baihui (GV20) upward, and keep your body straight in a natural, relaxed and comfortable manner(Fig. 9-1-2). When lifting up the palms, resting your mind at Laogong (PC8) with eyes looking afar forward down(Fig. 9-1-3). Press your palms down resting your mind at Shenque (RN8) with your toes grasping the ground slightly and eyes looking forward (Fig. 9-1-4).

Fig. 9-1-1

Fig. 9-1-2

Fig. 9-1-3   Fig. 9-1-4

Functions and effects: to guide the fresh upward and the stale downward; to promote the blood circulation to the nerve end of your hands and your feet so that it causes warming effects on your limbs

2.1.2 Form One: Drawing a bow

Bring the palms apart and close them rhythmically as you breathe in and out with the diastole and compression of the thorax, with your eyes looking forward down (Fig. 9-2-1 and 9-2-2). When stretching the arm, put your mind on the flow of Qi (also called Chi, an exercise of breath, the same as below) along the Lung Meridian of Hand Taiyin from middle thorax (Zhongfu LU1, at 6 cun lateral to the anterior midline and parallel to the 1st intercostal space), via chelidon (Chize, in the middle of the cubital crease and in the dent of the radial side of the biceps muscle) and to the tip of your thumb (Shaoshang LU11, on the radial side of the thumb, 0.1cun posterolateral to the corner of your fingernail) as illustrated below (Fig. 9-2-3). Stretch the palms forward roughly at the height of your eyes or eyebrows. Look at the palm forward while drawing back the other arm with the palm of hand facing upwards to the height of Zhongfu (LU1).

Fig. 9-2-1   Fig. 9-2-2   Fig. 9-2-3

Functions: These movements which involve expanding the chest, stretching shoulders and raising the hip can bring effective stimulus to your internal organs and flex your shoulder muscles so as to prevent and alleviate discomfort resulting from excessive neck and shoulder exercises. If the movements mentioned above are conducted together with breathing exercise, they are conducive to purging the physical discomfort such as chest tightness and asthma.

Lung Meridian of Hand Taiyin

Meridian line: It starts from Zhongfu (LU1) (in the superior lateral part of the anterior thoracic wall, 1cun below the Yunmen (LU2), parallel to the 1st intercostal space, 6cun lateral to the anterior midline.), ends at Shaoshang (LU11) (on the radial side of the thumb, 0.1cun posterolateral to the corner of the fingernail).

Running route: The Lung Channel of Hand-Taiyin originates from the middle energizer, and descends to connect with the large intestine. It then returns and travels along the upper orifice of the stomach, passing through the diaphragm and entering the lung. It exits transversely from the arm pit from the lung system, where the lung communicates with the throat. It descends along the anteriomedial side of the upper arm, going in front of the Heart Channel of Hand-Shaoyin and the Pericardium Channel of Hand-Jueyin, where it reaches the elbow. It then goes from the elbow downward along the anterior border of the radial side on the medial aspect of the forearm and enters Cunkou, or the anterior margin of the styloid process of the wrist (where the radial artery is palpated at the wrist). It then passes through the major thenar eminence, traveling along its radial border and going out to terminate at the medial side of the tip of the thumb. A branch of this channel splits from the styloid process of the wrist and runs to the radial side of the tip of the index finger, where it connects to the Large Intestine Channel of Hand-Yangming.

Pressure points: there are 11 pressure points involved at each side of the body: Zhongfu (LU1), Yunmen (LU2), Tianfu, Xiabai, Chize, Kongzui, Lieque, Jingqu, Taiyuan, Yuji, and Shaoshang (LU11).

2.1.3 Form Two: Stretching the back

When raising heels and bending the back, rotate the arms inwards pivoting on the index fingers to make sure the distance between the index fingers equals the width of your ala nasi, your eyes looking at your index fingers. As you bend your back, guide your mind from the tip of index finger (Shangyang, on the radial side of the index finger, about 0.1 cun posterior to the corner of the fingernail) via lateral side of your elbow (Quchi RC3, at the place of bending your elbow into a right angle, at the midline between the lateral end of the cubital crease and the lateral side of humeral epicondyle) to the both sides of ala nasi (Yingxiang HN8, beside the midpoint of the lateral side of ala nasi, in the middle of the nasolabial groove) as illustrated in Fig. 9-3-1. As you stretch your arms forward, hook your hands and bend your back into a bow, the distance between your wrists should equal the width of your ala nasi, your eyes looking at your wrists. When bending your back, guide your mind from Shangyang on your index fingertips (the same pressure points mentioned above), via Quchi (RC3) on the lateral side of your elbow, to Yingxiang (HN8) on either side of your ala nasi (Fig. 9-3-2). Push the palms down gently with your index fingers slightly tilted, looking into the distance (Fig. 9-3-3).

Fig. 9-3-1

Fig. 9-3-2

Fig. 9-3-3

Functions: Stretching arms and bending the back can fully stretch the muscles of your wrists, shoulders and the back and alleviate discomfort caused by incorrect exercises of fingers, wrists, shoulders and the back. Stretching your ribs on both sides with eyes looking near and far helps prevent and mitigate discomfort of eyes.

Large Intestine Meridian of Hand Yangming

Meridian line: It starts from Shangyang (on the radial side of the end of your index finger, about 0.1cun posterior to the corner of the fingernail) and ends at Yingxiang (at the upper part of your nasolabial groove, horizontal to the midpoint of your ala nasi, 1 cun above the lateral side of Kouheliaoxue).

Running route: The Large Intestine Channel of Hand-Yangming starts from the tip of the index finger, proceeding upward along the radial side of the index finger, through the interspace of the first and second metacarpal bones and entering the depression between the two tendons (extensor pollicis longus and brevis). It then goes upwards along the lateral anterior aspect of the forearm and enters the lateral side of the elbow. From the elbow it proceeds upwards along the lateral anterior aspect of the upper arm and reaches the highest point of the shoulder joint. From there, it crosses the anterior border of the acromion upwards and reaches the Governor Vessel. It then enters the supraclavicular fossa and descends to connect with the lung channel. It continues to travel through the diaphragm further, where it enters the large intestine, its pertaining organ. Its branch splits from the supraclavicular fossa and runs upwards along the neck, passes through the cheek and enters the gums of the lower teeth. It then curves around the corner of the mouth and intersects at the philtrum with the opposite side of the same channel, with this intersection the channel on the right hand proceeds to the left while the left to the right. It finally terminates on the lateral side of the nose.

Pressure points: there are 20 Pressure points involved at either side of the body: Shangyang (Jing), Erjian (Xing), Sanjian (Shu), Hegu (Yuan), Yangxi (Jing), Pianli (Luo), Wenliu, Xialian, Shanglian, Shousanli, Quchi (He), Zhouliao, Shouwuli, Binao, Jianyu, Jugu, Tianding, Futu, Heliao and Yingxiang.

Mnemonic Formula: The Meridian of Hand Yangming starts from Shangyang; runs through Erjian,

Sanjian, Hegu, Yangxi, Pianli, Wenliu, Xialian, Shanglian, Shousanli, Quchi (He), Zhouliao, Shouwuli, Binao, Jianyu, Jugu, Tianding, Futu, Heliao and ends at Yingxiang beside the midpoint of the nasal ala.

2.1.4 Form Three: Wild duck swimming

Swing your arms to the rear of your body with your upper hand at head-high and twist your hips to the other side. Look forward sideways (Fig.9-4-1). Then shake your waist around and look behind. In that process, the bent knees should not exceed the tips of your toes (Fig.9-4-2). When you put down your arms slowly, guide your mind from your face (Chengqi ST1, in the face, directly below the pupil, between the eyeball and the infra-orbital ridge), via the lateral side of your abdomen (Tianshu ST25, 2cun lateral to your navel) and the outer side of tibia (Zusanli ST36, on the fore and lateral side of the foot, 3cun below the lateral side of your knee dent (generally referred to as knee eye), one finger-breadth lateral to the lateral side of the tibia) to tiptoes (Lidui ST45, on the lateral side of the 2nd toe, about 0.1cun posterior to the corner of the toenail) (Fig.9-4-3).

Fig. 9-4-1   Fig. 9-4-2   Fig. 9-4-3

Functions: Waving arms from side to side and rotating the body are very effective in reducing fat around the waist. Twisting hips, waving arms and turning waist around can help prevent and soothe the discomfort caused by incorrect exercises of shoulders and waist.

Stomach Meridian of Foot Yangming

Meridian line: it starts from Touwei (at 0.5cun above the hairline of the forehead, 4.5cun lateral to the midline of the head) and Chengqi (in the face, directly below the pupil, between the eyeball and the infraorbital ridge) and ends at Lidui (on the lateral side of the 2nd toe, about 0.1cun posterior to the corner of the toenail).

Running route: The Stomach Channel of Foot-Yangming starts from the lateral side of the nose. It travels upward to the root of the nose where it meets the Channel of Foot-Taiyang. Turning downward along the lateral side of the nose, it enters the upper gum. Coming around the lips, it meets Chengjiang(CV24) in the mentolabial groove. It then traverses the posterior aspect of the mandible passing through the facial artery, ascending in front of the ear and following the anterior hairline, it reaches the forehead. Its cheek branch splits from the front of the Daying(ST 5) point and passes through the carotid artery. Passing along the throat, it enters the supraclavicular fossa. It further descends and passes through the diaphragm, and then enters its pertaining organ, the stomach, and connects to the spleen, the related organ. The straight branch of the channel in the chest and abdomen arises from the supraclavicular fossa, which descends and passes through the nipple (at 4 cun lateral to the midline of the chest). It then reaches the lateral side of the umbilcus (at 2 cun lateral to the anterior midline of the abdomen) and enters the inguinal groove. The branch of the abdomen starts from the lower orifice of the stomach, and descends inside the abdomen, reaching the inguinal groove, where it merges with the previous branch of the channel. From there, it further descends to the front of the coxa joint, reaches the quadriceps muscle and enters the knee. From the knee, it continues further down along the anterior border of the lateral aspect of the tibia to the dorsum of the foot and reaches the lateral side of the tip of the second toe. The tibial branch of the chanel splits from the place 3 cun below the knee and runs downward and ends at the lateral side of the middle toe. Another branch on the foot emerges from the dorsum of the foot to enter the medial side of the tip of the big toe, where it links with the spleen channel.

Pressure points: There are 45 pressure points involved at either side of the body: Chengqi, Sibai, Juliao, Dicang, Daying, Jiache, Xiaguan, Touwei, Renying, Shuitu, Qishe, Quepen, Qihu, Kufang, Wuyi, Yingchuang, Ruzhong, Rugen, Burong, Chengman, Liangmen, Guanmen, Taiyi, Huroumen, Tianshu, Wailing, Daju, Shuidao, Guilai, Qichong, Biguan, Futu, Yinshi, Liangqiu, Dubi, Zusanli, Shangjuxu, Tiaokou, Xiajuxu, Fenglong, Jiexi, Chongyang, Xiangu, Neiting, and Lidui.

Mnemonic Formula: The Stomach Meridian of Foot Yangming runs through 45 acupoints listed in sequence as follows: Touwei, Xiaguan, Jiache, Chengqi, Sibai, Juliao, Dicang, Renying, Daying, Shuitu, Qishe, Quepen, Qihu, Kufang, Wuyi, Yingchuang, Ruzhong, Rugen, Burong, Chengman, Liangmen, Guanmen, Taiyi, Huroumen, Tianshu, Wailing, Daju, Shuidao, Guilai, Qichong, Biguan, Futu, Yinshi, Liangqiu, Dubi, Zusanli, Shangjuxu, Tiaokou, Xiajuxu, Fenglong, Jiexi, Chongyang, Xiangu, Neiting, and Lidui at the terminal point.

2.1.5 Form Four: Dragon flying

Squat down with your heels staying on the ground. You can choose a full squat or half squat considering your age and physical flexibility (Fig. 9-5-1). As you raise your hands with the palms of hands facing upwards, guide your mind to go ascending from the hallux toe (Yinbai, on the medial side of the big toe, about 0.1cun posterior to the corner of the toenail), via the inner side of your knee-joint (Yinlingquan, on the medial side of the leg, in the dent posterior and inferior to the medial condyle of the tibia) to oxter (Dabao, on the lateral side of the chest, on the mid-axillary line of your armpit, to the 6th intercostal space) (Fig. 9-5-2). Maintain the balance of your body when stretching the palms outwards, raise heels and look downwards and make sure to fully stretch your entire body. (Fig. 9-5-3)

Fig. 9-5-1　　　　　Fig. 9-5-2　　　　　Fig. 9-5-3

Functions: Stretching arms can help to get rid of discomforts like chest compression, stagnation of Chi, and asthma. Standing with raised heels could lengthen muscles and ligaments of planta pedis and enhance the balancing capability of your body. Stretching and squatting can also mitigate the discomfort caused by incorrect exercises of neck, shoulders, waist and legs.

Spleen Meridian of Foot Taiyin

Meridian line: It starts from Yingbai (on the medial side of the great toe, about 0.1cun posterior to the corner of the toenail) and ends in Dabao (on the lateral side of the abdomen, on the mid-axillary line, 6cun lateral to the anterior midline).

Running route: The Spleen Channel of Foot Taiyin originates from the tip of the big toe, and travels along the border between the red and white skin of the medial aspect of the foot, ascending anteriorly to the medial malleolus toward the medial aspect of the leg. It crosses over and goes in front of the Liver Channel of Foot-Jueyin 8 cun above the medial malleolus, passing through the anterior medial aspect of the knee and thigh, it then enters the abdomen and spleen, its pertaining organ, and connects with the stomach (the external pathway of the channel distributes in the abdomen 4 cun lateral to the anterior midline). From there it traverses the diaphragm (the external pathway of the channel distributes in the chest 6 cun lateral to the anterior midline), and runs alongside the esophagus. It arrives at the root of the tongue and spreads over the lower surface of the tongue. The abdominal branch of the channel goes from the stomach through the diaphragm and finally enters the heart to link with the Heart Channel of Hand-Shaoyin.

Pressure points: There are 21 pressure points involved at either side of the body: Yingbai, Dadu, Taibai, Gongsun, Shangqiu, Sanyinjiao, Lougu, Diji, Yinlingquan, Xuehai, Jimen, Chongmen, Fushe, Fujie, Daheng, Fuai, Shidou, Tianxi, Xiongxiang, Zhourong, and Dabao.

Mnemonic Formula: The Spleen Meridian of Foot Taiyin involves 21 pressure points with the spleen at the central position. It starts from Yinbai on the great toe, run through Dadu, Taibai, Gongsun, Shangqiu, Sanyinjiao, Lougu, Diji, Yinlingquan, Xuehai, Jimen, Chongmen, Fushe, Fujie, Daheng, Fuai, Shidou, Tianxi, Xiongxiang, Zhourong, and Dabao.

2.1.6　Form Five: Bird spreading its wings

Swing your arms on both sides of your body and guide your mind from the oxter

(Jiquan, in the center of the axilla, where the axillary artery is palpable), via elbow (Shaohai, at the midpoint of the line connecting the medial end of the cubital crease and the medial epicondyle when bend the elbow) to the tip of the little finger (Shaochong, on the radial side of the little finger, about 0.1cun posterior to the corner of the fingernail) (Fig. 9-6-1). Swing your arms again, squat down, then raise hips, stretch abdomen and chest out, crane your neck and bend your body forward to make the back parallel to the ground (Fig. 9-6-2). Withdraw your chin slightly; stretch your lumbar, thoracic and cervical vertebra section by section slowly, which is immediately followed by swinging your hands forward and pressing down the palms of hands. Then raise your head right away to look straight ahead. The move of head and neck should be consistent with that of spine(Fig. 9-6-3).

Fig. 9-6-1   Fig. 9-6-2   Fig. 9-6-3

Functions: Stretching your arms forward are beneficial to prevent and alleviate the discomfort resulting from incorrect exercises of neck and shoulders. Stretching the spine slowly has the same effect on mitigating the discomfort of your waist and the back.

Heart Channel of Hand Shaoyin

Meridian line: It starts from Jiquan (in the center of the axilla, where the axillary artery is palpable) and ends at Shaochong (on the radial side of the small finger, about 0.1 cun posterior to the corner of the fingernail).

Running route: The Heart Channel of Hand Shaoyin originates from the heart and pertains to the Heart System (the tissues where the heart connects with other organs). It then descends through the diaphragm to connect with the small intestine. A branch of the channel separates from the heart system and ascends along the esophagus to connect with the Eye System (the tissues where the eyes link with the brain). The straight part of the channel derived from the Heart System runs upward toward the lungs, running downwards and emerging from the axilla. It follows along the posterior border of the medial aspect of the upper arm and enters the elbow. From there it travels along the posterior border of the medial aspect of the forearm to the pisiform bone of the wrist, and then it enters the palm and travels along the radial side of the little finger to terminate at its tip, where it links with the Small Intestine Channel of Hand-Taiyang.

Pressure points: There are nine pressure points involved at either side of the body: Jiquan, Qingling, Shaohai, Lingdao, Tongli, Yinqie, Shenmen, Shaofu, and Shaochong.

Mnemonic formula: Chi and blood reaches their zenith at the Heart Meridian of Hand Shaoyin during the period between 11am and 13pm. It runs through Jiquan, Qingling, Shaohai, Lingdao, Tongli, Yinqie, Shenmen, Shaofu, and Shaochong.

2.1.7 Form Six: Stretching the abdomen

Rotate your arms inwards and outwards slowly, relax your abdomen, and raise your hips accordingly (Fig. 9-7-1). Stretch both arms upwards with the little finger of the hand facing upwards pointing at the rear of your shoulders (Naoshu, on the shoulder, directly above the rear of the axillary crease, in the depression of the lower border of the scapular spine), the thumb of the hand facing downward pointing at the hips (Huantiao, on the lateral side of the thigh, at the junction of the 1/3 middle and 1/3 lateral of the line connecting the prominence of the great trochanter and the sacral hiatus) (Fig. 9-7-2). When holding up the palm or pressing it down, guide your mind from the tip of your little finger (Shaoze, on the ulnar side of the little finger, about 0.1 cun posterior to the corner of the fingernail), via medial side of your elbow (Xiaohai, on the medial side of the elbow, in the depression between the olecranon of the ulna and the medial epicondyle of the humerus) to the anterior of your ear (Tinggong, on the face, anterior to the ear, posterior to the ridge of the madibular bone, in the dent when opening the mouth).

Fig. 9-7-1 **Fig. 9-7-2**

Functions: Rotating your arms inwards and outwards is very useful in preventing and soothing the discomfort caused by incorrect exercises of shoulders, elbows and hands. The movements of arms associated with twisting hips can bring proper stimulus to internal organs, prevent and alleviate discomfort like dyspepsia and abdominal distension.

Small Intestine Channel of Hand Taiyang

Meridian line: It starts from Shaoze (on the ulnar side of the small finger, about 0.1cun posterior to the corner of the fingernail) and ends at Tinggong (on the face, anterior to the ear, posterior to the process of the mandibular bone, in the depression when opening the mouth).

Running route: The Small Intestine Channel of Hand Taiyang originates from the ulnar side of the tip of the little finger. It goes along the ulnar side of the dorsum of the hand, to the wrist, and emerges at the styloid process of the ulna. It then runs upwards along the posterior border of the lateral aspect of the forearm, and passes between the olecranon of the ulna and the medial epicondyle of the humerus. Ascending along the posterior border of the lateral aspect of the upper arm, it then reaches and emerges at the shoulder joint and proceeds in a zigzag course along the scapular region arriving at the top of the shoulder. From there, it descends through the supraclavicular fossa and connects with the heart, going downwards along the esophagus, passing through the diaphragm to the stomach, and finally ending at the small intestine. A branch from the supraclavicular fossa ascends to cross the deck and cheek to the outer canthus of the eye, and finally turns and enters the ear. Another branch separates from the previous branch on the cheek and ascends to the zygomatic bone, reaching the side of the nose. It finally terminates at the inner canthus to link with the Bladder Channel of Foot-Taiyang.

Pressure points: There are 19 pressure points involved at either side of your body: Shaoze, Qiangu, Houxi, Wangu, Guyang, Yanglao, Zhizheng, Xiaohai, Jianzheng, Tianzong, Bingfeng, Quyuan, Jianwaishu, Jianzhongshu, Tianchuang, Quanliao, and Tinggong.

Mnemonic formula: The Meridian of Hand Taiyang involves 19 acupoints; it runs through Shaoze, Qiangu, Houxi, Wangu, Guyang, Yanglao, Zhizheng and Xiaohai on the elbow; links up to Jianzheng, Tianzong, Bingfeng, Quyuan, Jianwaishu, Jianzhongshu, Tianchuang and Quanliao at the tip of the capitulum ulnae and Tinggong.

2.1.8 Form Seven: Hawk glaring

Swing your arms forward, bend the elbows and gently rub the ribs (Fig. 9-8-1). Stretch out your arms slightly forward with the palm of hand facing outwards when kicking out (Fig. 9-8-2). Stretch your head slightly forward with the eyes looking forward up when hooking your tip toes. The flow of your mind starts from the head, the back and the popliteal (Weizhong, at the midpoint of popliteal crease, between the biceps muscle of the thigh and the semitendinous muscle), then to the tiptoes (Zhiying, on the lateral side of the little toe, 0.1cun posterior to the toenail) (Fig. 9-8-3).

Fig. 9-8-1　　　　　Fig. 9-8-2　　　　　Fig. 9-8-3

Functions: Stretching out arms, pulling the shoulders and craning the head and the neck mind prevent and mitigate the discomfort caused by incorrect exercises of the neck and the shoulders. Stepping up, lifting the leg and kicking help enhance the balancing capability of your body, prevent and mitigate the discomfort from lower limbs. Holding up the arms and hooking the foot can reinforce the circulation of Bladder Meridian of Foot.

Bladder Channel of Foot Taiyang

Meridian line: It starts from Jingming (in the face, in the dent above the canthus) and ends at Zhiyin (on the lateral side of the little toe, 0.1 cun posterior to the toenail).

Running route: The Bladder Channel of Foot Taiyang originates from the inner canthus of the eye. It then goes upwards toward the forehead, and connects at the vertex. Its branch from the vertex descends to the upper corner of the ear. The straight branch from the vertex enters the brain, and then emerges to descend at the nape of the neck, where the channel splits into two branches. The first branch runs downwards along the medial border of the scapular region parallel to the vertebral column, reaching the lumbar region, and then entering the body cavity via the paravertebral muscle to connect with the kidney and end at the bladder. Another branch separates into the lumbar region, descends via the hip, and enters the popliteal fossa of the knee. The branch separates at the nape of the neck and descends along the medial aspect of the scapular region, crosses the hip joint, and then descends along the posterior-lateral aspect of the thigh to meet with the previous branch of the channel in the popliteal fossa. From there, it descends through the gastrocnemius muscle, emerges posterior to the lateral malleolus, and follows along the fifth metatarsal bone to the lateral side of the tip of the little toe, where it communicates with the Kidney Channel of Foot-Shaoyin.

Acupoints: There are 67 acupoints involved at either side of the body: Jingming, Cuanzhu, Meichong, Qucha, Wuchu, Chengguang, Tongtian, Luoque, Yuzhen, Tianzhu, Dashu, Fengmen, Feishu, Jueyinshu, Pangguangshu, Zhonglushu, Baihuanshu, Shangliao, Ciliao, Zhongliao, Xialiao, Huiyang, Chengfu, Yinmen, Fuque, Weiyang, Weizhong, Fufen, Pohu, Gaohuangshu, Shentang, Yixi, Geguan, Hunmen, Yanggang, Yishe, Weicang, Huangmen, Zhishi, Baohuang, Zhibian, Heyang, Chengjin, Chengshan, Feiyang, Fuyang, Kunlun, Pucan, Shenmai, Jinmen, Jinggu, Shugu, Zutonggu and Zhiyin.

Mnemonic formula: The Meridian of Foot Taiyang involves 67 acupoints. It runs through Jingming, Cuanzhu, Meichong, Qucha, Wuchu, Chengguang, Tongtian, Luoque, Yuzhen, Tianzhu, Dashu, Fengmen, Feishu, Jueyinshu, Pangguangshu, Zhonglushu, Baihuanshu, Shangliao, Ciliao, Zhongliao, Xialiao, Huiyang, Chengfu, Yinmen, Fuque, Weiyang, Weizhong, Fufen, Pohu, Gaohuangshu, Shentang, Yixi, Geguan, Hunmen, Yanggang, Yishe, Weicang, Huangmen, Zhishi, Baohuang, Zhibian, Heyang, Chengjin, Chengshan, Feiyang, Fuyang, Kunlun, Pucan, Shenmai, Jinmen, Jinggu, Shugu, Zutonggu and Zhiyin. .

2.1.9 Form Eight: Stretching the Waist

Put your hands on the anterior of your abdomen with thumbs and index fingers linked respectively to form a circle before gently rubbing the belt channel (Fig. 9-9-1). As you push against the waist forward with four fingers of each hand, render them with certain degree of strength; withdraw your chin slightly while looking straight ahead (Fig. 9-9-2). Make sure to lift your left or right shoulder in the same direction as the head turns. While bending forward, do not lower your head (Fig. 9-9-3). As you lift your hands, your mind flows upstream from the soles of the feet (Yongquan, on the sole, in the dent when the foot is arched, the point is at the junction of the 1/3 and 2/3 on the line connecting the 2nd and 3rd metatarsal bones and the sole), via the inner side of knee joint (Yingu, on the medial side of the popliteal fossa, between the tendons of the semitendinous and semimembranous muscles when bend the knee) up to the lower part of clavicle (Shufu, on the chest; on the lower border of the clavicle, 2cun lateral to anterior median line).

Fig. 9-9-1   Fig. 9-9-2   Fig. 9-9-3

Functions: Bending forwards and backwards as well as bending sideways and twisting the body can build on muscles on the back and waist, prevent and soothe discomfort caused by incorrect waist exercise. Twisting the neck slightly in the process of bending the body forward could reinforce the effect of stretching muscles on the back and waist and do good to the prevention and alleviation of discomfort in these parts.

Kidney Meridian of Foot Shaoyin

Meridian line: It starts from Yongquan (on the sole, in the dent when the foot is arched, the point is at the junction of the 1/3 and 2/3 on the line connecting the 2nd and 3rd metatarsal bones and the sole) and ends at Shufu (on the chest, on the lower border of the clavicle, 2cun lateral to anterior median line).

Running route: The Kidney Channel of Foot Shaoyin originates from the inferior aspect of the little toe, and proceeds diagonally to the center of the sole of the foot emerging from the lower border of the navicular tuberosity. It runs posterior to the inner malleolus and enters the heel. It then ascends along the medial aspect of the lower leg and emerges from the medial aspect of the popliteal fossa. From the popliteal fossa, it proceeds upwards along the medial and posterior aspect of the thigh and goes towards the vertebral column. It then pertains to the kidney and connects with the bladder. The branch with points emerges from the lower abdomen and travels along the upper abdomen, chest and terminates at the lower border of the calvicle. A straight branch from the kidney ascends through the liver and diaphragm, enters the lung, and then travels upward along the throat to reach the root of the tongue. Another branch emerges from the lung to connect with the heart, and disperses into the chest to link with the Pericardium Channel of Hand-Jueyin.

Pressure points: There are 27 pressure points involved at either side of the body: Yongquan, Rangu, Taixi, Dazhong, Shuiquan, Zhaohai, Fuliu, Jiaoxin, Zhubin, Yingu, Henggu, Dahe, Qixue, Siman, Zhongzhu, Huangshu, Shangqu, Shiguan, Yinyu, Tonggu, Youmen, Bulang, Fengshen, Lingxu, Shencang, Yuzhong and Shufu.

Mnemonic formula: The Meridian of Foot Shaoyin involves twenty-seven acupoints; it runs through Yongquan, Rangu, Taixi, Dazhong, Shuiquan, Zhaohai, Fuliu, Jiaoxin, Zhubin, Yingu, Henggu, Dahe, Qixue, Siman, Zhongzhu, Huangshu, Shangqu, Shiguan, Yinyu, Tonggu, Youmen, Bulang, Fengshen, Lingxu, Shencang, Yuzhong and ends at Shufu.

2.1.10 Form Nine: Wild Goose Flying

Raise your arms with elbows straight on either side of your body to the height of shoulders (Fig. 9-10-1). Raise one hand and lower the other until they form an angle of 45 degrees to the ground (Fig. 9-10-2). Bend the knees but ensure the knee joints do not exceed the range of your tiptoes (Fig. 9-10-3). When turning your head and looking in the direction of the lower hand, guide your mind from the ribcage (Tianchi PC1, on the chest, in the 4th intercostal space, 1cun lateral to the nipple, 5cun lateral to the anterior midline), via cubital crease (Quze, on the transverse cubital crease, on the ulnar side of the tendon of the biceps muscle of the arm) to the tip of middle finger (Zhongchong PC9, in the central part of the tip of your middle finger) (Fig. 9-10-4).

Fig. 9-10-1   Fig. 9-10-2

Fig. 9-10-3   Fig. 9-10-4

Functions:

Tilting the body from side to side could better regulate the circulation of Qi and blood, stabilize them and ease the mind.

Pericardium Meridian of Hand Jueyin

Meridian line: It starts from Tianchi (on the chest, in the 4th intercostal space, 1cun lateral to the nipple, 5cun lateral to the anterior midline) and ends at Zhongchong (in the center of the tip of the middle finger).

Running route: The Pericardium Channel of Hand Jueyin originates in the center of the chest, and pertains to the pericardium. It descends through the diaphragm into the abdomen passing through the upper, middle and lower energizers. One branch runs from inside the chest to emerge in the costal region, 3 cun inferior to the anterior axillary fold and ascends into the axilla. It then proceeds along the medial aspect of the upper arm, goes downward between the Lung Channel of Hand-Taiyin and the Heart Channel of Hand-Shaoyin to enter the cubital fossa. From there, it travels along the forearm between the two tendons (the tendons of the m. palmaris longus and m. flexor carpi radialis) to enter the palm, passing along the middle finger to end at its tip. Another branch splits from the Laogong (PC 8) and goes along the ring finger to its tip, where it connects with the Tripple Energizer Channel of Hand-Shaoyang.

Pressure points: There are 9 pressure points involved: Tianchi, Tianquan, Quze, Qiemen, Jianshi, Neiguan, Daling, Laogong and Zhongchong.

Mnemonic formula: The Pericardium Meridian of Hand Jueyin involves nine acupoints. It runs through Tianchi, Tianquan, Quze, Qiemen, Jianshi, Neiguan, Daling, Laogong and Zhongchong.

2.1.11 Form Ten: Crane Dancing

Swing your arms to the height of shoulders with one arm forward and the other backward (Fig. 9-11-1). Turn the torso and press the palms down to the navel level like pressing the ball floating onto the water (Fig. 9-11-2). Withdraw your shoulders, elbows and hands in turns (Fig. 9-11-3). Stretch the palms in the direction of shoulders with your eyes looking at the rear hand. As you detect a sense of distension at the tip of your ring finger, infuse your mind on the tip of your ring finger (Guanchong, on the ulnar side of the ring finger, 0.1cun posterior to the corner of the fingernail), via the lateral side of your elbow (Tianjing, on the lateral side of your forearm, in the dent 1cun above the tip of your elbow when the elbow is bent) to the face (Sizhukong, on the face, in the depression at the lateral end of the eyebrow) (Fig. 9-11-4).

Fig. 9-11-1   Fig. 9-11-2

Fig. 9-11-3   Fig. 9-11-4

Functions:

Waving the arms forward and backward and twisting the trunk in a moderate manner can not only stimulate the circulation of Chi and blood, but also work effectively in preventing and mitigating the discomfort caused by incorrect exercises of the neck, the shoulders, the back and the waist.

Triple Energizer Meridian of Hand Shaoyang

Meridian line: It starts from Guanchong (on the ulnar side of the ring finger, 0.1cun posterior to the corner of the fingernail) and ends at Ermen (anterior to the supratragic notch, in the dent posterior the condyloid process of the mandible)

Running route: The Triple Energizer Channel of Hand Shaoyang originates from the tip of the ring finger and runs upward between the 4th and 5th metacarpal bones along the dorsum of the hand. It then emerges between the radius and ulna on the lateral aspect of the forearm, passing through the tip of the elbow, it ascends along the lateral aspect of the upper arm to the shoulder. In the shoulder region, it crosses and passes behind the Gallbladder Channel of Foot-Shaoyang and goes forward into the supraclavicular fossa, spreading into the chest and connecting with the pericardium. It then descends through the diaphragm into the abdomen, connecting along its pathway with the upper, middle and lower energizers. One branch separates in the chest region, ascending to emerge from the supraclavicular fossa and rising along the neck to the posterior border of the ear. It crosses from the superior aspect of the ear to the corner of the forehead, turning downward toward the cheek and reaching the inferior aspect of the eye. Another branch separates behind the ear and enters the ear, and reemerges in front of the ear, crossing the previous branch on the cheek. It then goes to the outer canthus, where it connects with the Gallbladder Channel of Foot-Shaoyang.

Pressure points: There are 23 pressure points involved at each side of the body: Guanchong, Yemen, Zhongzhu, Yangchi, Waiguan, Zhigou, Huizong, Sanyangluo, Sidu, Tianjing, Qinglengyuan, Xiaoluo, Naohui, Jianliao, Tianliao, Tianyou, Yifeng, Chimai, Luxi, Sunjiao, Ermen, Erheliao, and Sizhukong.

Mnemonic formula: The Meridian of Hand Shaoyang involves 23 acupoints; it runs through Guanchong, Yemen, Zhongzhu, Yangchi, Waiguan, Zhigou, Huizong, Sanyangluo, Sidu, Tianjing, Qinglengyuan, Xiaoluo, Naohui, Jianliao, Tianliao, Tianyou, Yifeng, Chimai, Luxi, Sunjiao, Sizhukong, Erheliao and Ermen.

2.1.12　Form Eleven: Exhaling with the Head Rose

Raise your arms above the head with the palms of hands facing each other, just like holding up a ball of energyor Chi of harmony (Fig. 9-12-1). Then rest your arms on either side of your body at the shoulder level and relax muscles on the neck as if the neck were pillowing the head; meanwhile raise your hips (Fig. 9-12-2). When turning over the palms, descend and rub either side of your body downwards, infuse Chi from the face (Tongziliao, on the face, 0.5cun lateral to the outer canthus, in the dent on the lateral side of the orbit) to tiptoes (Zuqiaoyin, on the lateral side of the 4th toe, 0.1 cun posterior to the corner of the toenail) via the lateral side of your body (Huantiao, on the lateral side of the thigh, at the junction of the 1/3 middle and 1/3 lateral of the line connecting the prominence of the great trochanter of femur and the sacral hiatus) (Fig. 9-12-3).

Fig. 9-12-1　　　　　Fig. 9-12-2　　　　　Fig. 9-12-3

Functions: The series of movements of raising arms and stretching out, expanding the chest and breathing out can purge discomfort like asthma, chest compression from the body, prevent and mitigate neck and shoulder discomfort. Lifting heels can help strengthen the muscle groups of the calf, lengthen the muscles and ligaments of the sole and enhance the balancing capability.

Gallbladder Channel of Foot Shaoyang

Meridian line: It starts from Tongziliao (on the face, 0.5cun lateral to the outer canthus, in the dent on lateral side of the orbit) and ends at Zuqiaoyin (on the lateral side of the 4th toe, 0.1cun posterior to the corner of the toenail).

Running route: The Gallbladder Channel of Foot Shaoyang originates from the outer canthus, ascends to the corner of the forehead, and then descends to the posterior of the ear. Descending further along the neck to the shoulder, it enters the supraclavicular fossa. One branch emerges from behind the ear and enters the ear, re-emerging in front of the ear, and then reaching the posterior aspect of the outer canthus. Another branch starts from the outer canthus, descends to the Daying (ST 5) and ascends to the infraorbital region passing near Jiache (ST 6) and descending along the neck where it joints the previous branch at the supraclavicular fossa. From there, it further descends into the chest, crosses the diaphragm to connect with the liver and pertain to the gallbladder. It then travels along the inside of the hypochondriac region to reach the femoral artery in the inguinal region, curving along the margin of the public hair and running transversely into the hip region. The straight branch of the channel descends from the supraclavicular fossa to the hip joint to meet the previous branch passing through the axillary region, the lateral side of the chest and the free ends of the floating ribs. It continues down the lateral aspect of the thigh and knee, descending along the anterior aspect of the fibula to reach the anterior aspect of the lateral malleolus. It then follows the dorsum of the foot to end on the lateral side of the tip of the 4th toe. One branch on the dorsum of the foot splits up and proceeds between the 1st and 2nd metatarsal bones toward the tip of the big toe, then through the nail of the big toe, ending at the hairy region of big toe, where it connects with the Liver Channel of the Foot-Jueyin.

Pressure points: There are 44 pressure points involved at either side of the body: Tongziliao, Tinghui, Shangguan, Heyan, Xuanlu, Xuanli, Qubin, Shuaigu, Tianchong, Fubai, Touqiaoyin, Wangu, Benshen, Yinbai, Toulinqi, Muchuang, Zhengying, Chengling, Naokong, Fengchi, Jianjing, Yuanye, Zhejin, Riyue, Jingmen, Daimai, Wushu, Weidao, Juliao, Huantiao, Fengshi, Zhongdu, Xiyangguan, Yanglingquan, Yangjiao, Waiqiu, Guangming, Yangfu, Xuanzhong, Qiuxu, Zulinqi, Diwuhui, Xiaxi, and Zuqiaoyin.

Mnemonic Formula 1: The Gallbladder Meridian of Foot Shaoyang starts from Tongzijiao and moves all the way along the forty-four acupoints which are involved as the following sequence: Tinghui, Shangguan, Heyan, Xuanlu, Xuanli, Qubin, Shuaigu, Tianchong, Fubai, Touqiaoyin, Wangu, Benshen, Yinbai, Toulinqi, Muchuang, Zhengying, Chengling, Naokong, Fengchi,

Jianjing, Yuanye, Zhejin, Riyue, Jingmen, Daimai, Wushu, Weidao, Juliao, Huantiao, Fengshi, Zhongdu, Xiyangguan, Yanglingquan, Yangjiao, Waiqiu, Guangming, Yangfu, Xuanzhong, Qiuxu, Zulinqi, Diwuhui, Xiaxi. And it ends at Zuqiaoyin on the 4th toe.

Mnemonic Formula 2: The Meridian of Foot Shaoyang runs through Tongzijiao, Tinghui, Shangguan, Heyan, Xuanlu, Xuanli, Qubin, Shuaigu, Tianchong, Fubai, Touqiaoyin, Wangu, Benshen, Yinbai, Toulinqi, Muchuang, Zhengying, Chengling, Naokong, Fengchi, Jianjing, Yuanye, Zhejin, Riyue, Jingmen, Daimai, Wushu, Weidao, Juliao, Huantiao, Fengshi, Zhongdu, Xiyangguan, Yanglingquan, Yangjiao, Waiqiu, Guangming, Yangfu, Xuanzhong, Qiuxu, Zulinqi, Diwuhui and Xiaxi just 1cun below the Diwuhui. But where is Zuqiaoyin? It is on the lateral side of the 4th toe.

2.1.13 Form Twelve: Body Bending

Take a step forward on the left, lift your right arm upwards and stretch your torso fully. Stretch the upper palm and the lower palm of hand to the opposite direction with the lower palm resting at the same level of your rear hips (Fig. 9-13-1). Rotate your upper arm inwards and put it down to the body side (Fig. 9-13-2). Raise your arms from either side of your torso to shoulders' level (Fig. 9-13-3), move them in an arc horizontally to the front as if holding an air ball (Fig. 9-13-4), bend the body as if embracing Chi (Fig. 9-13-5), and hold up Chi to the abdomen (Fig. 9-13-6). Lift both arms along the inner side of your lower limbs, infuse Chi from tiptoes (Dadun LR1, on the lateral side of the distal segment of the big toe, 0.1cun posterior to the corner of the toenail), via the knee joint (Ququan, at the medial side of the knee, when bend the knee, at the medial end of the knee joint, posterior to the medial epicondyle of the tibia, in the depression anterior to the insertion of the semitendinous and semimembranous muscles) to the lateral abdomen (Qimen, on the chest, directly below the nipple, in the 6th intercostal space, 4 cun lateral to the anterior midline).

Functions: The stretching, raising and lowering of arms can help prevent and mitigate the discomfort caused by the incorrect shoulders exercises. Bending the body by bending forward can effectively stimulate the internal organs and achieve favorable effect with spinal discomfort.

Fig. 9-13-1

Fig. 9-13-2

Fig. 9-13-3

Fig. 9-13-4

Fig. 9-13-5

Fig. 9-13-6

Liver Channel of Foot Jueyin

Meridian line: It starts from Dadun (on the lateral side of the distal segment of the great toe, 0.1cun posterior to the corner of the toenail) and ends at Qimen (on the chest, directly below the nipple, in the 6th intercostal space, 4 cun lateral to the anterior midline).

Running route: The Liver Channel of Foot Jueyin originates from the dorsal hairy region of the big toe that proceeds upwards along the dorsum of the foot anterior to the medial malleolus. It then travels to the place 8cun above the medial malleolus where it crosses and runs behind the Spleen Channel of Foot-Taiyin and ascends along the medial aspect of the knee. It can further along the medial aspect of the thigh and enters the lower abdomen, going around the stomach, where it pertains to the liver and connects with the gallbladder. It then ascends through the diaphragm, spreading over the hypochondriac region. From here it runs upwards along the posterior aspect of the throat, entering the nasopharynx, and connecting with the "Eye System". It then proceeds upward and emerges on the forehead and connects with the Governor Vessel at the vertex. One branch in the eye descends along the inner cheek, and curves around the inner surface of the lips. Another branch splits from the liver, crosses the diaphragm and proceeds upwards to converge in the lung, where it connects with the Lung

Channele of Hand-Taiyin.

Pressure points: There are fourteen pressure points involved at either side of the body: Dadun, Xingjian, Taichong, Zhongfeng, Ligou, Zhongdu, Xiguan, Ququan, Yinbao, Zuwuli, Yinlian, Jimai, Zhangmen, and Qimen

Mnemonic formula 1: The meridian runs through Dadun at the tip of the great toe. Xingjian and Taichong are on the dorsum of the foot, Zhongfeng 1cun anterior to the medial malleolus, Ligou the 5cun above the tip of the medial malleolus, Zhongdu 7cun above the tip of the medial malleolus, Xiguan 1cun posterior to Yinlingquan, Ququan at the medial end of the transverse popliteal crease. Yinbao is 4cun above the medial epicondyle of the femur, Zuwuli 3cun directly below the Qichong, Yinlian 2cun directly below Qichong, Jimai 2.5cun lateral to the anterior midline Zhangmen on the lateral side of the abdomen and Qimen on the chest, directly below the nipple.

Mnemonic Formula 2: The Meridian of Foot Jueyin involves fourteen acupoints; it runs through Dadun, Xingjian, Taichong, Zhongfeng, Ligou, Zhongdu, Xiguan, Ququan, Yinbao, Zuwuli, Yinlian, Jimai, Zhangmen, and Qimen.

2.1.14 Form Thirteen: Closing Position

When bringing the palms together in front of the body, adjust your position to maintain balance (Fig. 9-14-1). Move the palms of hands in turns from the chest (Shanzhong RN17, on the chest, along the anterior midline, at the level of the 4th intercostal space, i.e. at the midpoint of the line connecting two nipples) (Fig. 9-14-2), to the upper abdomen (Zhongwan RN12, at the upper abdomen, 4 cun above the navel, on the anterior midline) (Fig. 9-14-3) and the lower abdomen (Shenque RN8, in the center of the navel, in the middle of abdomen) (Fig. 9-14-4). As you gradually lower your hands with the palms of hands facing downwards, infuse your mind into Yongquan (Fig. 9-14-5).

Functions: It is to guide Chi to where ultimate energy originates, ease the mind; to infuse your mind to Yongquan and tranquilize the breath.

Fig. 9-14-1

Fig. 9-14-2

Fig. 9-14-3

Fig. 9-14-4

Fig. 9-14-5

2.2 Learning program

Category	Content
Preparations	1. To know the brief history of Health Qigong 2. To know the origin of Mawangdui Daoyin Exercise 3. To learn health-promoting and breath-regulating exercises 4. To memorize the main meridians and their running routes.
Schedule	1. Learning sequence 　(1) To learn and grasp the directions of each movement; 　(2) To master the coordination between breath and movements; 　(3) To gradually integrate the flow of the mind with physical movements and convey the romantic charm in your performance. 2. Teaching syllabus 　This course can be divided into 5 sections, each of which has three periods with each period in 45 minutes. 　(1) To learn basic movements; 　(2) To practice the entire taolu of the movements; 　(3) To become familiar with the techniques of Daoyin Exercise; 　(4) To familiarize yourself with the integration of movements and the mind; 　(5) To examine the technical movements

2.3 Technique experience

Content	Requirements
Stretching tendons and bones with the alternation of tightness and relaxation	Stretching tendons and bones can extensively pull and connect tissues including tendons and ligaments, which can also attain the goal of stretching your body to make it more flexible with the alternation of tightness and relaxation. For example, in the fourth form "Dragon Flying", the movement of stretching the palm outwards and raising heels while lifting up arms can stretch tendons and bones.

(continued)

Content	Requirements
Twisting and bending in a gentle, slow, flexible and graceful manner	Many movements in the Health Qigong • Mawangdui Daoyin Exercise involves twisting and folding their limbs and the trunk, which can not only stretch and stimulate their internal organs but flex the joints all over the body. The whole routine features with gentleness, slowness, gracefulness and variety. Also the frequent twisting, rotating, stretching and bending movements can help create an artistic reality for the practitioners.
Guiding the breath to achieve harmony and stretching the body to enhance flexibility	"Guiding the breath to achieve harmony" means coordinating the breath with physical movements to regulate the circulation of Chi and blood. Regulating breath to be fine, even, deep and long can render our body to a natural state, beef up the diaphragm effectively, stimulate and massage the vital organs extensively and make the flow of Chi and blood smoother. "Guiding the breath to achieve harmony" is one of the core essences of Health Qigong • Mawangdui Daoyin Exercise in which regulating breath to be fine, even, deep and long is a must. "Stretching the body to enhance flexibility" means to attain flexibility by doing exercises that can stretch limbs and flex joints. Guiding the body can improve the bending and stretching ability of all parts of the body, enhance flexibility and agility, thus to improve physical stability and endurance. It also contributes to lubricating joints, alleviating adhesion, unblocking meridians and reinforcing the circulation of Chi and blood. In compiling the Health Qigong • Mawangdui Daoyin Exercise, much importance has been attached to the health concept mentioned above since many designed movements involve twisting, bending and stretching of tendons and bones.
Inhale the stale and exhale the fresh; Integrate the body and the mind	The distinguishing feature between Health Qigong and other traditional sports is that the former emphasizes the significance of breath and integration of the body and the mind. Breathing naturally and smoothly, keeping the serenity of the mind and coordinating the flow of mind with physical movements are the basic requirements of Health Qigong • Mawangdui Daoyin Exercise to attain the goal of integrating the body and the mind.
The whole body movements; Combining the inner being with the external world	The taolu of Health Qigong • Mawangdui Daoyin Exercise is compiled from an integrative perspective, which starts with regulating your body as a whole. The spine is the binding joint that brings into full play of the overall movements such as bending forward and backward, lateral bending, twisting, folding, stretching and contracting, lifting and lowering of limbs and the trunk. In the process, it attaches continuous emphasis to keeping the serenity of the inner world, connecting the mind to the movements, and integrating the inner being with the external world so that the purpose of promoting health can be attained.
Guiding the body along the route of meridians; connecting the flow of mind to physical movements	Guiding the body along the route of meridians refers to conduct regular physical movements with breathing exercise along the route of meridians in human body. The compilation of Health Qigong • MaWangDui Daoyin Exercises has absorbed the essence of the meridians theory. Practitioners should know the major routes of meridians in order to understand the essence of the physical movements. For example, in the first form "bending bow", stretch and contract the chest and breathe in the fresh and breathe out the stale in the lung, infuse and guide the mind along the direction of Lung Meridian of Hand Taiyin when turning the torso and stretching the arms. The oneness of physical movements and the flow of the mind means that physical movements should be coordinated with the flow of the mind along the route of the meridians, which is the key point of this taolu.
Guiding the mind along the route of meridians to unblock meridians	Guiding the mind along the route of meridians which attach much emphasis to the coordination of the flow of the mind and physical movements so as to promote the circulation of Chi and blood. The coordination of physical movements with the flow of the mind in conducting Health Qigong • Mawangdui Daoyin Exercises reinforces the idea that unblocking the meridians is the key to health promotion theory.

2.4 Cultural experience

Table 1 Mawangdui Daoyin Exercises and the starting & ending point of Hand Taiyin and Foot Taiyin

Name of movements	Drawing a bow	Stretching the back	Wild duck swimming	Dragon flying
Hand Taiyin-Foot Taiyang	Lung Meridian of Hand Taiyin	Large Intestine Meridian of Hand Yangming	Stomach Meridian of Foot Yangming	Spleen Meridian of Foot Taiyin
Starting point	Zhongfu	Shangyang	Chengqi	Yinbai
Location	Parallel to the 1st inter-costal space, 6cun lateral to the anterior midline.	On the medial side of the index finger	Directly below the pupil	On the medial side of the big toe
Direction	thorax→hand	hand→head	head→foot	foot→abdomen
Ending point	Shaoshang	Yingxiang	Lidui	Dabao
Location	On the medial side of the thumb	Beside the midpoint of the nasal ala	On the lateral side of the 2nd toe	On the 6th rib, on the midline below the armpit

Table 2 Mawangdui Daoyin Exercises and the starting & ending point of Hand Shaoyin and Foot Shaoyin

Name of movements	Bird spreading its wings	Stretching Abdomen	Hawk glaring	Stretching the waist
Hand Shaoyin—Foot Shaoyin	Heart Meridian of Hand Shaoyin	Small Intestine Meridian of Hand Taiyang	Bladder Meridian of Foot Taiyang	Kidney Meridian of Foot Shaoyin
Starting point	Jiquan	Shaoze	Jingming	Yongquan
Location	In the center of the axilla	On the lateral side of the pinkie finger	In the medial side of the eye	On the sole
Direction	thorax→hand	hand→head	head→foot	foot→abdomen
Ending point	Shaochong	Tinggong	Zhiyin	Shufu
Location	On the medial side of the pinkie finger	Anterior to the ear	On the lateral side of the little toe	below the clavicle, 2 cun lateral to anterior median line

Table 3 Mawangdui Daoyin Exercises and the starting & ending point of Hand Jueyin and Foot Jueyin

Name of the movements	Wild goose flying	Crane dancing	Exhaling with Head Raised	Body bending
Hand Jueyin—Foot Jueyin	Pericardium Meridian of Hand Jueyin	Triple Energizer Meridian of Hand Shaoyang	Gallbladder Meridian of Foot Shaoyang	Liver Meridian of Foot Jueyin
Starting point	Tianchi	Guanchong	Tongziliao	Dadun
Location	On the chest, in the 4th intercostal space, 1cun lateral to the nipple	On the lateral side of the ring finger	In the depression on lateral side of the orbit	On the lateral side of the distal segment of the great toe

(continued)

Name of the movements	Wild goose flying	Crane dancing	Exhaling with Head Raised	Body bending
Direction	thorax→hand	hand→head	head→foot	foot→abdomen
Ending point	Zhongchong	Sizhukong	Zuqiaoyin	Qimen
Location	on the tip of the middle finger	In the dent at the lateral end of the eyebrow	On the lateral side of the 4th toe	On the chest, directly below the nipple, in the 6th intercostal space

3 Conclusion

1. The Health Qigong • Mawangdui Daoyin Exercises is a kind of Daoyin exercise that can "guide the body to make it flexible."

2. The Health Qigong • Mawangdui Daoyin Exercises should be done along the route of the twelve meridians to achieve the harmony of body, mind and breath.

3. The circulating route of the meridians in Health Qigong • Mawangdui Daoyin Exercises is the cycle from thorax to hand, from hand to head, from head to foot and from foot to thorax and abdomen. The twelve meridians are divided into three circulating systems: Taiyin-Yangming, Shaoyin-Taiyang, Jueyin-Shaoyang. The teaching program can be planned according to these 3 circulation system above.

4 Extensive reading

The Health Qigong is a kind of health-promoting sports program put forward by Chinese government. It is characterized by graceful movements, diversified connotation and simple to learn and practice and is an excellent health promotion program for the public. Those who has learnt the Health Qigong . Mawangdui Daoyin Exercises can keep on learning the other 8 health Qigong in the future.

5 Questions

(1) What is the relationship between the physical movements in Qigong •Mawangdui Daoyin Exercises and the circulation of Chi in meridians?

(2) What are the technical features of the Health Qigong •Mawangdui Daoyin Exercises?

(3) How can one have a good mastery of the Health Qigong •Mawangdui Daiyin Exercises?

6 References

[1] Yu Dinghai, Wu Jingmei. Traditional Chinese Health Preservation Movement [M]. Shanghai: Shanghai Science and Technology Press. 1990.

[2] Shi Qi Eds. Collected Works of Chinese Health Preservation [M]. Shanghai: Academic Press. 1990.

[3] Shen Shou. Illustration Album of Daoyin Health Preservation [M]. Beijing: People Sport Publishing House. 1992.

[4] Xiao Bing, Ye Shuxian. A Cultural Interpretation on the Book of Lao Tzu [M]. Hubei: Hubei People's Press. 1993.

[5] Liu Tianjun. An Introduction to the Meditation in Qigong [M]. Beijing: People Sport Publishing House. 1995.

[6] The Seven Tablets in a Cloudy Satchel [M]. Complied by Zhang Junfang. Collated and annotated by Jiang Lisheng et al. Beijing: Huaxia Publishing House. 1996.

[7] Wu Zhichao. The analects of Daoyin Health Preservation History [M]. Beijing: Beijing Sport University Press. 1996.

[8] Tang Yijie Eds. Essentials for Taoism [M]. Beijing: Beijing Publishing House. 1996.

[9] Yang Li. Books of Changes and Traditional Chinese Medicine [M]. Beijing: Beijing Science and Technology Press. 1997.

[10] Zhou Yimou. Mawangdui Medical Texts with Critical Annotations [M]. Tianjin: Tianjin Science and Technology Press. 1998.

[11] The Expert Group of Silk Books from Mawangdui a Han Tomb. Daoyin Diagram: Silk Books Unearthed from Mawangdui a Han Tomb [M]. Beijing: Cultural Relics Publishing House. 1979.

[12] Chen Yingning. Taoism and Health Preservation [M]. Beijing: Chinese Publishing House. 2000.

[13] Hou Liang. The Sealed Civilization [M]. Hunan: Hunan People's Press. 2002.

[14] Wu Changxin. 44 Tips for Emperors to Preserve Health [M]. Beijing: Solidarity Press. 2000.

[15] Pan Yuting. I-Ching Studies and Health Preservation [M]. Shanghai: Fudan University Press. 2001.

[16] Health Qigong Management Center of General Administration of Sport. Training Materials for Social Health Qigong Instructors [M]. Beijing: People Sport Publishing House. 2007.

[17] Health Qigong Management Center of General Administration of Sport. Mawangdui Daoyin Exercises • Health Qigong [M]. Beijing: People's Sport Publishing House. 2010.

[18] Mawangdui Monograph of Medical Research [M]. Changsha: Journal of Traditional Chinese Medicine University of Hunan. 1980, 1981.

[19] Zhanghe. Theory of Qigong in China [M]. Beijing: China Intercontinental Press. 1984.

[20] Jiao Guorui. Qigong Essentials for Health Preservation [M]. Beijing: People Sport Publishing House. 1984.

[21] Zhou Renfeng, Li Ziran. Qigong Essentials for Rehabilitation & Health Promotion [M]. Tianjin: Tianjin Science and Technology Press. 1987.

[22] Ma Jiren. Qigong in China [M]. Shanxi: Shanxi Science & Technology Press. 1987.

[23] Li Zhiyong. The history of Chinese Qigong [M]. Henan: Henan Science and Technology Press. 1988.

[24] Li Yuanguo. Taoist Health-promoting Qigong[M]. Sichuan: Sichuan Academy of Social Science Press. 1988.

[25] Wang Boxiong, Zhou Shirong. The Historical Development of the Chinese Art of Qigong [M]. Changsha: Hunan Science & Technology Press. 1989.

Chapter Ten

Health Qigong · Wu Qin Xi

1 Introduction

Wu Qin Xi or Five-Animal Exercises is an animal-imitating Qigong originally compiled by Hua Tuo, a leading physician of the Eastern Han, who combines the typical movements of five animals like tiger, deer, bear, ape and bird with health promotion practice in ancient China such as Daoyin, a precursor of Qigong and controlled inhalation and exhalation and some theories in TCM like Zang-fu organs in human body, channels and collaterals, Chi (known as "Qi" or "qi", the same as below) and blood conception. "Health Qigong · Wu Qin Xi" is compiled by Shanghai University of Sport based on the recorded historical five-animal movement findings written by Hua Tuo and incorporated according to the feature of the era and the scientific health-building methods.

2 Learning experience

2.1 Directions

2.1.1 Ready position

Movement One: bring your feet together, straighten both legs with both arms drooping down on either side of your body, relax your chest and abdomen, straighten the vertex of your head, withdraw your chin slightly with tongue against the palate, eyes looking forward (Fig. 10-1-1).

Movement Two: move your left foot a step leftward, a bit wider than your shoulder width, bend your knees slightly, stand still in a natural posture; inhale and exhale for several times, concentrate your mind on Dantian (about 2 cun below the navel) or elixir field (Fig. 10-1-2).

Movement Three: bend your elbows slightly, move your forearms forward up till it is in front of your chest horizontally at the height of Danzhong or RN 17 (Fig. 10-1-3).

Movement Four: droop your elbows down and outstretch them, rotate your forearms inward; meanwhile turn both palms over and slightly press them to the front of your abdomen with eyes looking forward (Fig. 10-1-4).

Repeat Movement Three and Movement Four twice and droop your arms down on either side of your body (Fig. 10-1-5).

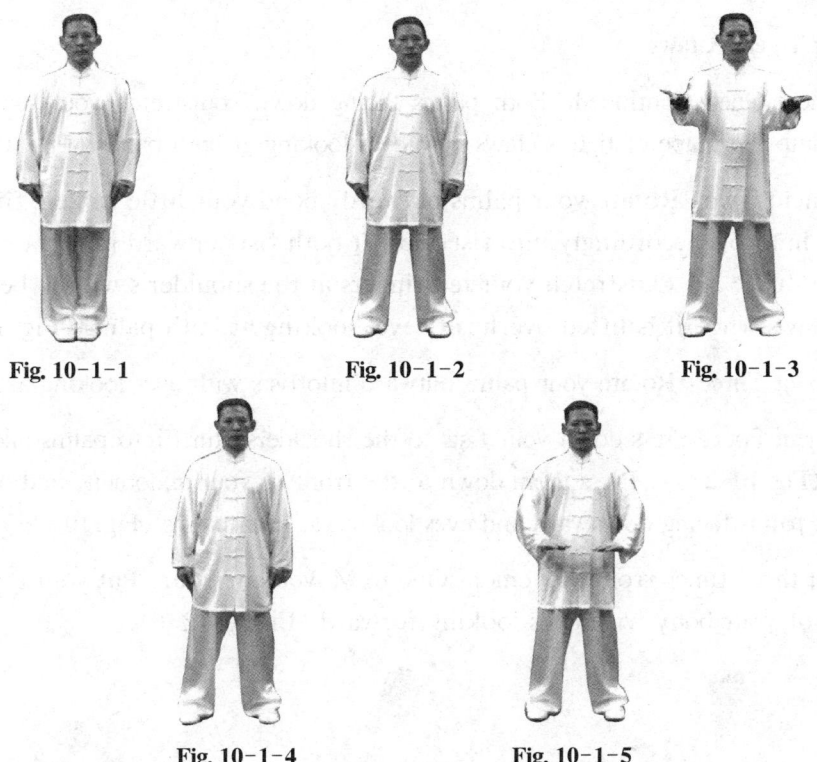

Fig. 10-1-1　　　　　Fig. 10-1-2　　　　　Fig. 10-1-3

Fig. 10-1-4　　　　　Fig. 10-1-5

Key Points: Concentrate your mind on Laogong (PC 8) pressure point in your palms; meanwhile raise your arms and pressing your palms and do it in a gentle, even and coherent manner. Your movements should go with your respiration, that is to say, inhale when raising your arms and exhale when pressing your palms.

Application of Mind: Feel the warmth on Laogong (PC 8) of your palms. You feel like lifting heavy weights with your arms. Promote Chi through central Diantian (Danzhong or RN17) down to lower Diantian (Qihai).

Functions and Effects: it is to eliminate all distracting thoughts, calm down your mind with controlled inhalation and exhalation and soothe your heart and mind; it is to exhale the stale and inhale the fresh, ascend the fresh and descend the stale and promote Qi and regulate your physical mechanism.

2.1.2　Tiger Form

It includes raising tiger's claws and seizing the prey. You should perform it in a tough-outside-with-gentle-inside manner, for the inner gentle manner produces its outer tough power, so that you can be tough outside and gentle inside as coupling the tough with the gentle will render you greater forces; your spirit is demonstrated by your eyes so you should stare like a tiger. The masculinity of a tiger is seen in its paw that is described as forceful, formidable and regal. The regal of a tiger is delivered in its thunderous motion that can't be blocked and the unshakable, like deeply rooted Mount Tai.

(1) Raising Tiger's Claws

Movement One: Continued. Both palms facing down, outstretch your ten fingers and bend them into the shape of tiger's claws with eyes looking at both palms (Fig. 10-2-1).

Movement Two: Rotate your palms outward, bend your little fingers first and then ring finger in a row accordingly into fist and lift both fists upward in front of your body slowly (Fig. 10-2-2). Outstretch your ten fingers at the shoulder's width, bend them into tiger's claws when it is lifted overhead, eyes looking at both palms (Fig. 10-2-3).

Movement Three: Rotate your palms outward into fists with eyes looking at both fists.

Movement Four: Press down your fists to the shoulders, turn into palms and press them downward (Fig. 10-2-4); Press them down to the front of your abdomen, and outstretch ten fingers, the palms facing downward and eyes looking at both palms (Fig. 10-2-5).

Repeat three times from Movement One to Movement Four. Put your arms down on either side of your body with eyes looking forward (Fig. 10-2-6).

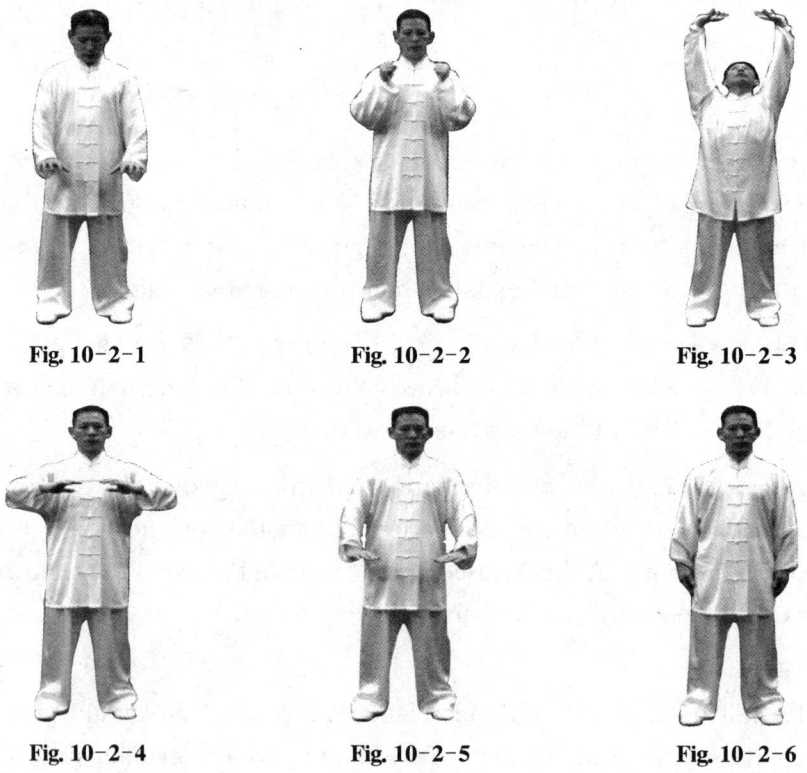

Fig. 10-2-1   Fig. 10-2-2   Fig. 10-2-3

Fig. 10-2-4   Fig. 10-2-5   Fig. 10-2-6

Key Points: Outstretch your ten fingers, bend them into tiger's claws and rotate them outward into fists; concentrate your mind on strength when doing the three movements illustrated above; lift your palms upward as if carrying heavy weights, tuck your abdomen in. Meanwhile lift your chest and stretch your body upward; press down both palms like pulling double loops, draw your chest in and relax your abdomen and hibernate Chi in Dantian (at about 2cun below the navel); inhale while lifting both palms and exhale while pulling down your palms.

Application of Mind: Outstretch your palms and claw your fingers; concentrate your mind on tiger's claws; strength is transferred to the tips of your tiger's claws; empty out Laogong or PC8; lift your palms as if carrying heavy weights; turn over your palms as if seeing the sun after dispelling the clouds or like upholding the sky and standing firmly rooted into the ground which symbolizes the oneness of human and nature.

Functions and Effects: When upholding both palms, inhale the fresh; when pressing down both palms, exhale the stale. One ascends and the other descends to regulate and promote the function of Sanjiao or the three visceral cavities housing the internal organs. When you turn palms into tiger's claws and then into fists, it can enhance the power of your handgrip and stimulate the far end of the blood circulation of your upper body.

(2) Tiger's Claw

Movement One: Clench both hands into empty fists and uplift them along either side of your body to the front of your upper shoulders (Fig. 10-2-7).

Movement Two: Draw an arc with both hands upward and forward to your fingers into "Tiger's Claw" with both palms' facing downward. Meanwhile lean your torso forward, the chest out; sink your waist with eyes looking forward (Fig. 10-2-8, Fig. 10-2-8 side).

Fig. 10-2-7

Fig. 10-2-8

Fig. 10-2-8 side

Movement Three: Bend both legs into a half squat and suck in your abdomen with chest in; meanwhile draw an arc with both hands downward to either side of your knee with the palms facing downward and eyes looking forward down (Fig. 10-2-9). Straighten both legs, lean the coxa forward, stick out your abdomen and lean your torso backward while clenching both palms into empty fists and uplifting them to either side of your chest with eyes looking forward up (Fig. 10-2-10, Fig. 10-2-10 side).

Fig. 10-2-9   Fig. 10-2-10   Fig. 10-2-10 side

Movement Four: Lift your left leg and raise both hands upward (Fig. 10-2-11). Step forward your left leg with its heel touching the ground and rotate your right leg 45 degrees outward; shift your weight onto the right leg and bend your knees into a left empty stance. Meanwhile lean your torso forward, turn your fists into tiger's claws and swoop forward down to either side of your knees, the chest in; suck in your abdomen with the palm facing downward and eyes looking forward down (Fig. 10-2-12). Straighten your torso and step back your left leg with both steps at shoulder's width, putting both arms downward at either side of your torso with eyes looking forward (Fig. 10-2-13).

Fig. 10-2-11   Fig. 10-2-12   Fig. 10-2-13

Movement Six to Movement Eight is the same as Movement One to Movement Four, but on the opposite side (Fig. 10-2-14, 10-2-15, 10-2-16, 10-2-17, 10-2-18, 10-2-19, 10-2-20).

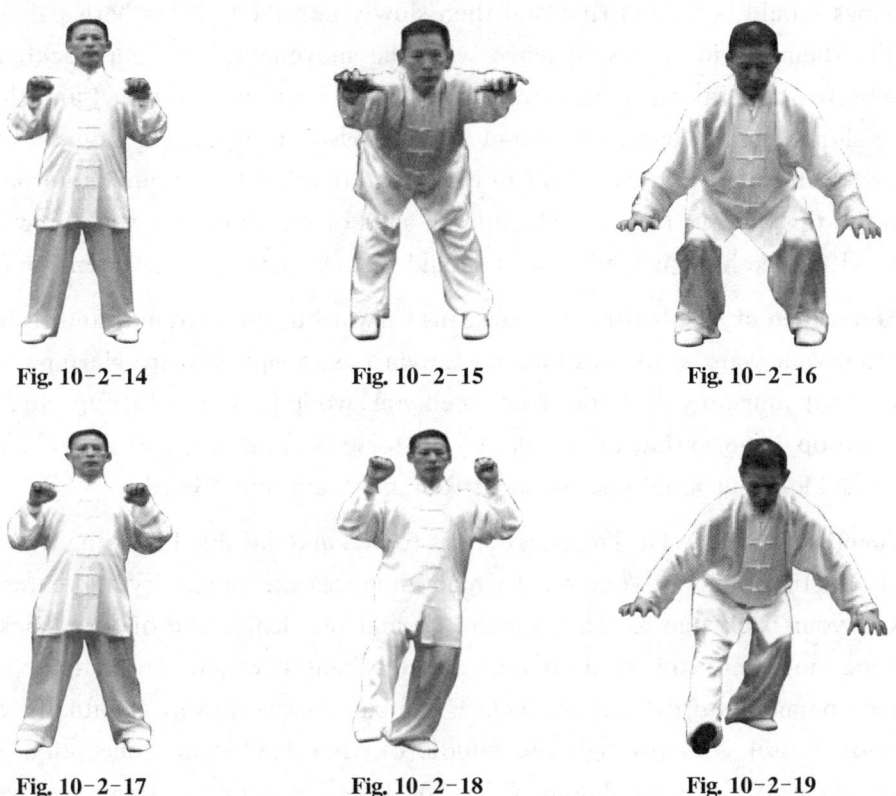

Fig. 10-2-14   Fig. 10-2-15   Fig. 10-2-16

Fig. 10-2-17   Fig. 10-2-18   Fig. 10-2-19

After repeating from Movement One to Movement Eight, raise both palms upward on either side of your torso to the height of your chest with both palms facing upward and eyes looking forward (Fig. 10-2-21). Bend both elbows, press palms downward and put them naturally on either side of your torso with eyes looking forward (Fig. 10-2-22).

Fig. 10-2-20   Fig. 10-2-21   Fig. 10-2-22

Key points: Lean your torso forward with both hands stretching forward to its utmost and arms stretching backward so that the backbone will be stretched to its extreme. Bend your knees, keep your buttocks in and squat, suck in your abdomen with the chest in, lean the coxa forward, stick out your abdomen and lean your torso in a row. The backbones should be folded first and then slowly unfolded. Press both palms down and then lift them up in correspondence with the movements of your backbones. When swooping forward in empty stance, you should do it at an even speed and the swooping gesture should be as tough as steel and as ferocious as a tiger, which implies hardness in softness. Remember to breathe in Chi into Dantian and Chi can guide internal Jin (energy) to the tips of your fingers. The middle-aged or senior or the weak practitioners and people with knee hurt or lumbar hurt should reduce their exercise intensity.

Application of Mind: Stretch your arms forward to the extreme, and sit backward to outstretch your waist with eyes looking forward as though you are glaring at your prey; imagine that your prey is at your foot when you swoop forward. Lift up, stretch out forward, swoop down so that the trunk of your torso is in motion as if a man is rotating the ground-tackle, your mind goes through Ren and Governor Vessel.

Functions and Effects: The backbone is folded and unfolded in doing tiger's claw, especially in stretching out your waist which enhances the flexibility and extension of the joints of your backbone to maintain the normal physical curve of your backbone. The backbone movement can build up your muscle strength which can be a good prevention to some common waist disorders such as lumbar muscle strain, habitually waist twist. Governor Vessel goes through the middle of your back and Conception Vessel goes through the center of your abdomen. The backbone is folded and unfolded when moving forward and backward which stimulates Conception Vessel (conception vessel) and Governor Vessel, stretch your waist, dredge the channels and collaterals to warm and nourish Blood and Chi.

2.1.3 Deer Form

It includes butting with its antlers and running like a deer.

When doing deer exercises, bear in mind the features of deer. For example, deer prefers to stand up and look out, to butt with its antlers and run swiftly, so they move its coccyx to bridge Conception Vessel (conception vessel) with Governor Vessel.

(1) Butting with its antlers

Movement One: Continued. Bend both legs slightly and shift your weight onto your right leg; meanwhile move your left leg from the inner side of your right leg forward 45 degrees on your left side with its heel stretching the ground; meanwhile turn your torso right, clench both palms into empty fists and draw an arc on the right side with the palm of your fist downward at the shoulders' height. Your eyes follow your hands and look at your right fist (Fig. 10-3-1).

Movement Two: Shift your weight forward and bend your left knee. Rotate the tips of your toes outward 90 degrees to the left side, straighten and outstretch your right leg; meanwhile rotate your body to the left side, turn your palms into antler and draw an arc with your left arm to the left side with your palm facing outward, the tips of your fingers pointing to the left. Bend your left arm and stretch it vertically and withdraw your left elbow to the left side of your waist. Lift your right arm overhead and stretch out to the back on the left with your palm facing outward, the tips of your fingers facing backward, eyes looking at the heel of your right foot (Fig. 10-3-2). Then rotate your torso to the right, step back your left foot with both feet apart at shoulders' width; meanwhile draw your hands in an arc upward, then to the right and then downward, turn both "antlers" into empty fists at the front of your shoulders and put them to the front of your torso with eyes looking forward (Fig. 10-3-3).

Movement Three and Movement Four is the same as Movement One and Movement Two but in the opposite direction. Movement Five to Movement Eight is the same as Movement one to Movement four (Fig. 10-3-4, 10-3-5, 10-3-6). Repeat them from Movement One to Movement Eight.

Fig. 10-3-1 Fig. 10-3-2 Fig. 10-3-3

Fig. 10-3-4 Fig. 10-3-5 Fig. 10-3-6

Key Points: Lift your leg and step forward and then back in a swift and fluid way; bend and twist your waist to full extreme to its side. It should be strained on one side of your waist, and lift your arms upward and stretch back on the other side of your waist so that your waist will be stretched to its full extreme. The heel of your back foot should be straightened as the anchor of your lower body; twist and move your waist and abdomen to your coccyx. Inhale when drawing an arc upward with both palms while exhaling when butting with your antlers backward; inhale when swinging to the front of your shoulders; exhale when turning back and put down your arms.

Application of Mind: Look at the heel of your foot with your mind resting at the coccyx. Imagine that two deer are butting with its antlers for fun.

Functions and Effects: When twisting your waist to stretch the entire backbone to its full extreme, it can build up the muscle strength of the waist and prevent the disposition of your excessive fat. Look at the heel of your back foot and twist your waist as possible as you can, which can prevent small joints disorders of your lumbar spine, thoracic vertebrae and cervical spine. In terms of Chinese Traditional Medicine, "waist is the house of kidney". The movement of your coccyx can build up the muscle of your waist, tonify your kidney and strengthen your muscles and bones.

(2) Running like a deer

Movement One: Continued. Lift your left foot and step forward and bend your knee; straighten your right leg into a left bow stance. Meanwhile clench your palms into empty fists, draw an arc forward up to the front of your torso and bend your wrist at shoulders' height and at shoulders' width as well with the palms of your fists facing downward and eyes looking forward (Fig. 10-3-7).

Movement Two: Shift your weight backward and straighten your left knee with the entire sole on the ground. Bend your right leg, sit backward, lower your head with the chest in, bend your back like a bow, suck in your abdomen and keep your buttocks in while rotating both arms inward and stretching them forward, the back of fists facing each other. Turn your fists into "antlers" (Fig. 10-3-8, Fig. 10-3-8 side).

Fig. 10-3-7   Fig. 10-3-8   Fig. 10-3-8 side

Movement Three: Shift your weight forward and straighten your torso. Straighten your right leg and bend your left leg into a left bow stance. Relax your shoulders and sink your elbows, rotate both arms outward and clench your "antlers" into empty fists at shoulders' height, the palms of your fists facing downward and eyes looking forward(Fig. 10-3-9).

Movement Four: Step back your left leg and stand straightforward at shoulders' width. Turn both fists into palms and put them naturally at either side of your torso with eyes looking forward (Fig. 10-3-10).

Movement Five: Movement Five to Movement Eight are the same as what is illustrated from Movement One to Movement Four, but in the opposite direction (Fig. 10-3-11, 10-3-12, 10-3-13, 10-3-14). After repeating from Movement One to Movement Eight again, raise both palms forward up at the height of your chest, your palms facing upward and eyes looking forward (Fig. 10-3-15). Bend your elbows inwardly and press both palms downward and put them naturally at either side of your torso, your eyes looking forward (Fig. 10-3-16).

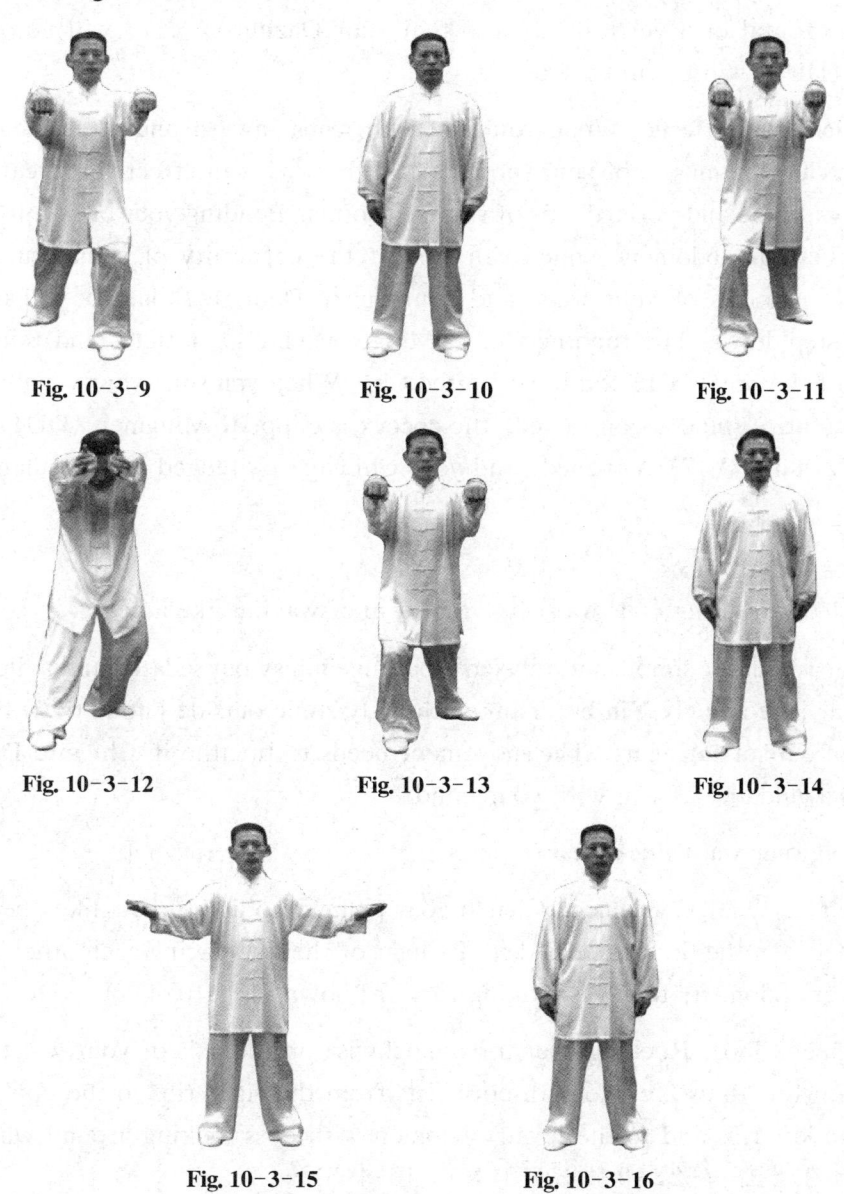

Fig. 10-3-9 Fig. 10-3-10 Fig. 10-3-11

Fig. 10-3-12 Fig. 10-3-13 Fig. 10-3-14

Fig. 10-3-15 Fig. 10-3-16

Key Points: Lift your leg and stride forward with an arc; put it on the ground with delicacy in a graceful and elegant manner of deer. Sit backward, stretch both arms forward with chest in and contract your back into a bow. Lean your head forward, contract your back and abdomen and keep your buttocks in, so that your torso is shaped into a vertical bow, which stretches your waist backward to the full extent. Do this exercise consciously with breath. Inhale when lifting your leg and exhale when dropping your leg into a bow stance. Sit back consciously with breath. Inhale when sitting back; exhale when shifting your weight forward.

Application of Mind: Running or lifting legs in giant strides or small steps should be like a deer in a graceful and flexible manner. Stretch forward and bend your back to shape a horizontal or a vertical bow, so that your Dazhui (CV17) will be opened and Mingmen (DU4) will be protruded.

Functions and Effects: When rotating both arms inward and stretching forward, which stretches the muscle of your shoulders and back, it can effectively treat your neck shoulder syndrome and periarthritis of shoulder joints. Bending your back into a bow can help suck in your abdomen, which can correct the deformity of spinal curvature and build up the muscles of your waist and your back. Dantian should be filled with Chi when you step down. The running Chi at Mingmen (DU4) initiates and reinforces the exchange of the innate Chi and the acquired Chi. When you shift your weight backward so that the entire spine is contracted, the coccyx is clipped, Mingmen (DU4) is protruded and Dazhui (CV17) is opened, and your Chi can be dredged and circulates with vitality.

2.1.4 Bear Form

It includes rotating your waist like a bear and swaying like a bear.

A bear is sedate, simple and relaxed, looking clumsy but sedated and agile. The motion of bear is seemingly Yin but Yang within, dynamic outside but static within, seemingly tough but soft at heart. The movement needs to breathe in Chi into Dantian and conduct the guidance of Chi with your mind.

(1) Rotating your waist like a bear

Movement One: Continued. Clench your palms into empty fists like "bear palms", the part between the thumb and index of finger of the fists facing each other and resting at the lower abdomen; the eyes looking forward down (Fig. 10-4-1).

Movement Two: Rocking your torso clockwise on the axis of your waist and abdomen; meanwhile draw a circle with both fists from the right ribs to the upper abdomen then to the left ribs and to the lower abdomen with eyes looking around when rocking your torso (Fig. 10-4-2, 10-4-3, 10-4-4, 10-4-5).

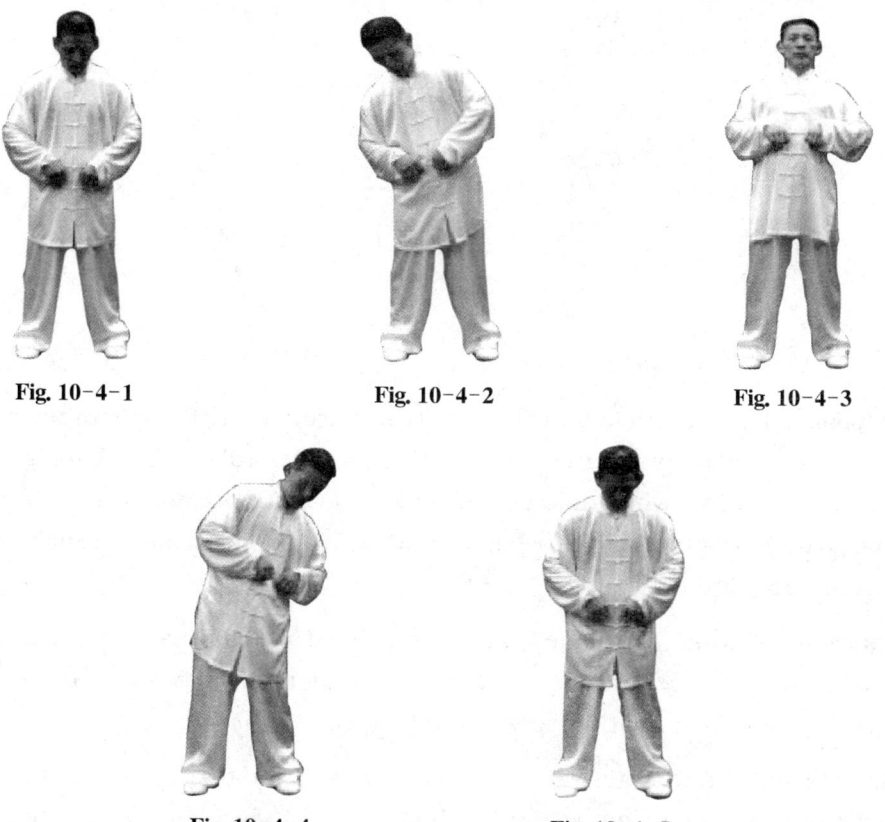

Fig. 10-4-1 Fig. 10-4-2 Fig. 10-4-3

Fig. 10-4-4 Fig. 10-4-5

Movement Three and Four is the same as Movement One and Movement Two. The Figures from Movement Five to Movement Eight is the same as that from Movement One to Movement Four, but in the opposite direction, that is, to rock your torso counter-clockwise with both fists drawing a circle (Fig. 10-4-6, 10-4-7, 10-4-8, 10-4-9). After finishing the last movement, turn both fists into palms and put them down naturally on either side of your body with eyes looking forward (Fig. 10-4-10).

Fig. 10-4-6 Fig. 10-4-7 Fig. 10-4-8

Fig. 10-4-9   Fig. 10-4-10

Key points: Draw a circle with both fists in harmony with the movements of your waist and abdomen. Draw a circle with both fists outwardly while shaking your waist and abdomen inwardly, which initiates the inner Chi in Dantian of your abdomen under the guidance of your mind. Inhale when leaning your torso backward, exhale when leaning your torso forward.

Application of Mind: Imagine you are the hand of clock and revolve your torso clockwise and counterclockwise. The outward movement is triggered by inward guidance to strengthen the transformation between kidney and stomach.

Functions and Effects: Activating the muscles and joints of your waist can prevent the lumbar muscle strain and soft tissue injury. Revolving your waist and abdomen, drawing a circle with both palms and moving your torso under the guidance of innate Chi can strengthen the transformation between kidney and stomach. Massage digestive organs in your body when revolving your waist and abdomen, which can prevent disordered digestion, abdominal distention, constipation and diarrhea, etc.

(2) Swaying like a bear

Movement One: Continued. Shift your weight to the right, lift up your left hip and your left foot is away from the ground. Bend your left knee and clench both palms into empty fists like "bear's palms" with eyes looking forward on your left (Fig. 10-4-11).

Movement Two: Shift your weight forward and put your left leg forward about 45 degrees on the left. With the entire sole on the ground and the tips of your left foot facing forward, straighten your right leg. Sway your torso to the right, rotate your left arm inward; swing your left arm forward with the palm of your fist facing to the left. Swing your right fist to the back of your torso with the palm of fist facing backward and eyes gazing left forward (Fig. 10-4-12).

Movement Three: Sway your torso to the left, shift your weight backward and sit backward. Bend your right knee and straighten your left leg. Twist your waist and shake your shoulder so that your arms are swayed forward or backward with an arc. Sway your right fist to the front of your left knee with the palm of your fist facing the right; sway your left fist to the back of your torso with the palm of your fist facing back and eyes gazing left forward (Fig. 10-4-13).

Fig. 10-4-11　　　　　　Fig. 10-4-12　　　　　　Fig. 10-4-13

Movement Four: Shift your weight forward and sway your torso to the right; bend the knee of your left leg and straighten your right leg. Meanwhile rotate your left arm inward and swing your left arm forward; sway your left fist forward to the front of your left knee with the palm of your fist facing the left; sway your right fist to the back of your torso with the palm of your fist facing back and eyes gazing left forward (Fig. 10-4-14).

Movement Five to Movement Eight is the same as Movement One to Movement Four, but in the opposite direction (Fig. 10-4-15, 10-4-16, 10-4-17, 10-4-18).

Fig. 10-4-14　　　　　　Fig. 10-4-15　　　　　　Fig. 10-4-16

Fig. 10-4-17　　　　　　Fig. 10-4-18

After repeating from Movement One to Movement Eight again, step your left leg forward with both feet a step apart at shoulders' width; meanwhile put both hands down at either side of your torso (Fig. 10-4-19). Raise both palms up to the front of torso at the height of your chest with the palm of your palms facing upward and eyes looking forward (Fig. 10-4-20). Bend your elbows inwardly and press both palms downward and put them down naturally at either side of your torso with your eyes looking forward (Fig. 10-4-21).

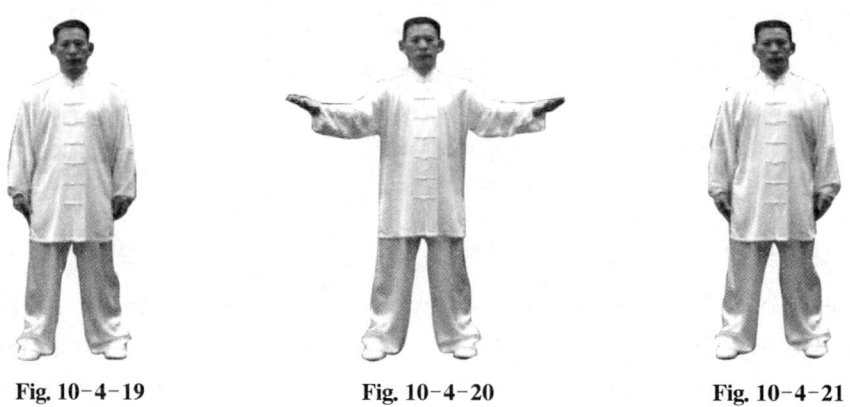

Fig. 10-4-19   Fig. 10-4-20   Fig. 10-4-21

Key Points: Contract the muscle groups on your waist and lift up your left thigh. The sequence of lifting your leg should be to lift your hip, then your leg and then to bend your knees. Move both feet forward with the lateral spacing slightly wider than your shoulders and shift your weight forward with the entire sole on the ground so that the stamping effect of your leg is sensitive enough to the joints of your hips, indicating that the bear steps in a sedate and bulky manner.

Application of Mind: Lift your hips and sink your shoulders, guide your mind through the middle of your ribs. Imitate bear to sway your torso to the left and to the right, exchange Jin between your waist and your crotch.

Functions and Effects: Swaying your torso to the left and right is to guide your mind through the middle of your ribs to regulate your liver and kidney. Lifting your hips and walk, plus the slight stamping on the ground, can build up the muscles around your hips, improve your balance ability and is effective to prevent syndromes such as the weakness of lower limbs, the strain of hip joints and knee injuries.

2.1.5 Monkey Form

It includes lifting monkey's paws and picking fruits.

Monkey is tactful, agile and good at climbing, so you improve the agility of your limbs and discipline a peaceful mind within by imitating the movement of a monkey.

(1) Lifting monkey's paws

Movement One: Continued. Put your palms in front of your torso with its fingers stretching apart (Fig. 10-5-1) and bend your wrists with your fingertips together into "monkey's hook" (Fig. 10-5-1).

Movement Two: Lift palms up to your chest and shrug your shoulders; suck in your abdomen and lift anus. Meanwhile raise your heels up and rotate your head to the left with your eyes following your head, looking at the left of your torso (Fig. 10-5-3, Fig. 10-5-3 side).

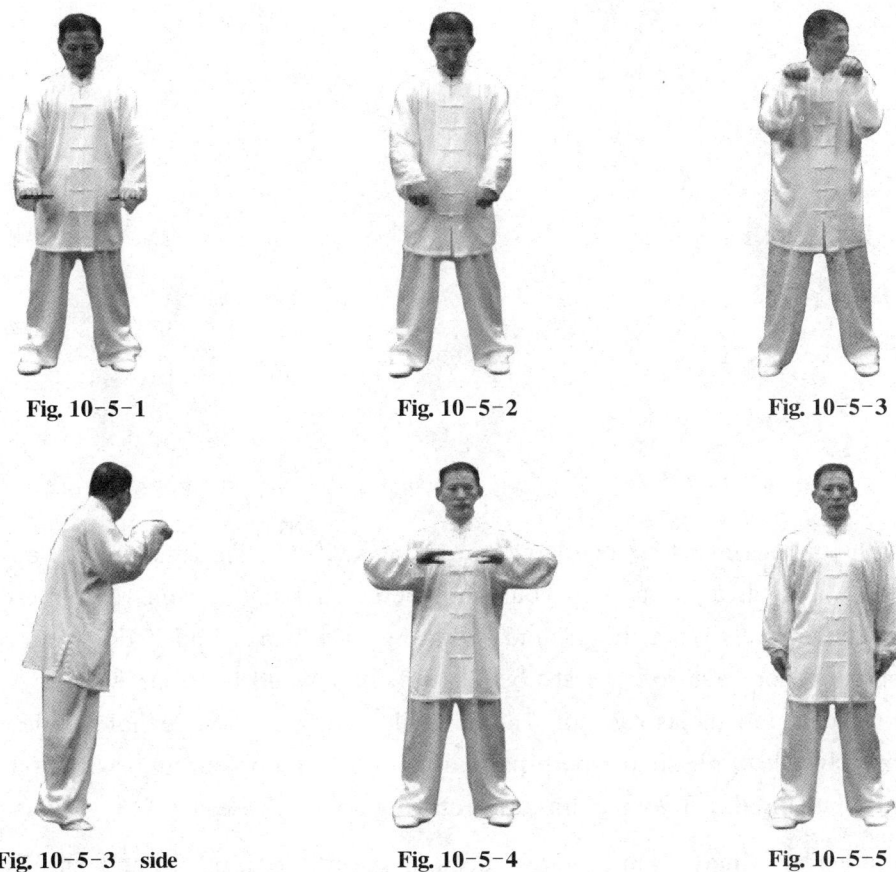

Fig. 10-5-1   Fig. 10-5-2   Fig. 10-5-3

Fig. 10-5-3 side   Fig. 10-5-4   Fig. 10-5-5

Movement Three: Move your head to the front, sink your shoulders, relax your abdomen and anus at ease and put your heels down to the ground. Turn your "monkey's hook" into palms with the palms facing downward and eyes looking forward (Fig. 10-5-4).

Movement Four: Put both palms down to either side of your torso with eyes looking forward(Fig. 10-5-5).

Movement Five to Movement Eight is the same as Movement One to Movement Four, but you should rotate your head to the right. Repeat them from Movement One to Movement Eight (Fig. 10-5-6, 10-5-7, 10-5-8, 10-5-9, 10-5-10).

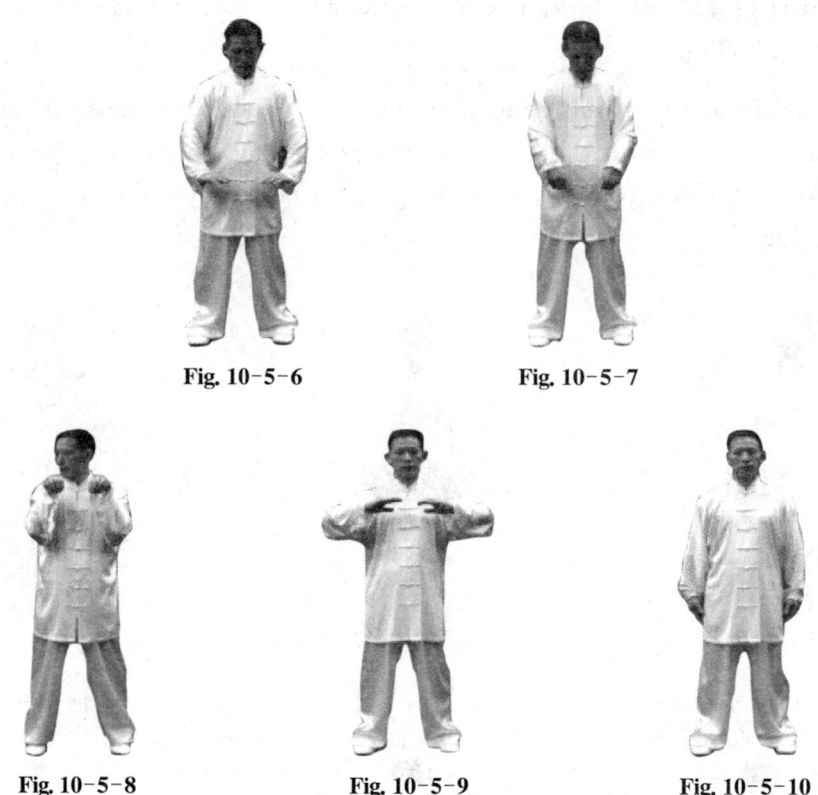

Fig. 10-5-6 Fig. 10-5-7

Fig. 10-5-8 Fig. 10-5-9 Fig. 10-5-10

Key Points: Put fingertips together into a hook swiftly. The sequence of your movements should be such as shrugging your shoulders, sucking in your abdomen, lifting anus, raising your heels from the ground, rotating your head, and lifting your weight. Shrug shoulders, contract your chest, bend your elbows and lift your wrists. And they should be done as possible as you can. Inhale while lifting anus and exhale while relaxing anus at ease. Inhale while lifting both paws up and lifting up your anus with your mind; exhale while putting down your palms and relaxing anus at ease.

Application of Mind: Stand there like a monkey, looking around shrewdly and sharply. Shrugging shoulders and tucking in your elbows with the chest in mean to massage your heart with your mind.

Functions and Effects: The swift change of "monkey's hook" is to enhance the agility of your nerves and muscular response. Lift up both palms, contract your neck, shrug your shoulders, breathe in air and circle your chest, so that they can squeeze your chest and the veins of your neck. Press your palms down, straighten your neck, sink your shoulders, relax your abdomen, and they can increase the volume of your chest, which can enhance your breathing, massage your heart and better the blood flow of your brain and prevent shoulder-neck syndromes. Raise your heels and stand straight, and they can build up your leg strength and improves your balance ability.

(2) Picking fruits

Movement One: Continued. Step your left leg back to the left with the tip of your foot touching the ground; meanwhile bend your left elbow, turn your left palm into "monkey's hook" to the left side of your waist; swing your right palm forward to the right with the palm facing downward (Fig. 10-5-11).

Movement Two: Shift your weight backward to your left foot, bend your knees and squat and withdraw your right foot to the inner side of your left leg with the tips of its toes on the ground into a right T stance. Meanwhile draw an arc with your right palm through the front of your abdomen to the front of your left with the palm facing your Taiyang (temple), eyes following your right palm. Then turn your head to the right upward (Fig. 10-5-11).

Movement Three: Rotate your right palm inward with the palm facing downward and press it down to the left side of your hip with eyes looking at your right palm (Fig. 10-5-13). Stride your right foot forward to the right, straighten your left leg and shift your weight forward; straighten your right leg with the tips of your left foot touching the ground. Meanwhile draw an arc with your right palm through the front of your torso to the front on the right, lift it up to the right overhead and turn it into "monkey's hook", slightly higher than your shoulders' height. Stretch your left palm forward up and bend your wrist into a hook as if you are picking fruits, eyes gazing at your left palm (Fig. 10-5-14).

Fig. 10-5-11

Fig. 10-5-12

Fig. 10-5-13

Movement Four: Shift your weight backward; turn your left palm into "monkey's hook" and clench it firmly. Turn your right hand into a palm and put it to the side of your torso with the Hukou facing forward (Fig. 10-5-15). Bend your left knee and squat and withdraw your right foot to the inner side of your left foot with the tips of your toes touching the ground into a T stance. Meanwhile bend your left arm to the left of your ear with fingers stretching apart and the palm facing upward as if you are holding a peach. Draw an arc with your right palm across the front of your torso under the left elbow as if you are lifting something up with your eyes looking at your left palm (Fig. 10-5-16).

Movement Five to Movement Eight is the same as Movement One to Movement Four, but in the opposite direction. (Fig. 10-5-17, 10-5-18, 10-5-19, 10-5-20, 10-5-21, 10-5-22).

Fig. 10-5-14   Fig. 10-5-15   Fig. 10-5-16

Fig. 10-5-17   Fig. 10-5-18   Fig. 10-5-19

Fig. 10-5-20   Fig. 10-5-21   Fig. 10-5-22

After repeating from Movement One to Movement Eight again, step your left foot apart to the left and straighten both legs; meanwhile put both hands down to either side of your torso (Fig. 10-5-23). Lift both palms up to the front of your torso at the height of your chest with the palm facing upward and eyes looking forward (Fig. 10-5-24). Bend your elbows inwardly and press both palms down to either side of your torso with eyes looking forward (Fig. 10-5-25).

Fig. 10-5-23　　　　Fig. 10-5-24　　　　Fig. 10-5-25

Key Points: Look around with the changing movements of your upper limbs to indicate the agility of monkey. Bend your knees and squat, contract your whole body. Kick with your heel and stride forward to pick fruits; stretch your limbs to the full extent. Turn into "monkey's hook" when picking fruits. Put fingertips together swiftly and agilely. After clenching your fist, turn it into a palm as if holding a peach with fingers stretching apart. Do the exercise as if you were a monkey and imagine the artistic reality but do not exaggerate it too much.

Application of Mind: Swing forward to gather Chi and fill it into Taiyang (temple). A monkey finds peaches in the tree, so it climbs the tree to pick up the peach and feels satisfied. Imagine in an artistic reality to differentiate the detailed changes in the whole process.

Functions and Effects: Looking left and right is good to your neck to stimulate the blood circulation of your brain, which can prevent cervical spondylosis and stiff shoulders. The diversified movement coordinates the nerve system and the corresponding physical movement. You should be in light mood when imitating monkey to pick fruits, which can release the pressure of your nerve system to prevent syndromes such as intensified nervousness and mental depression.

2.1.6　Bird Form

Take the image of a crane, including its stretching upward and flying. The crane is standing up haughtily and leisurely. The imitation of a flying crane upward and downward, open and close movements can circulate the channels and collaterals and enhance the agility of your limbs.

(1) Stretching upward

Movement One: Continued. Bend your legs slightly and squat; fold your palms in front of your abdomen (Fig. 10-6-1).

Movement Two: Raise your palms upward overhead with the palms facing downward and the tips of your fingers facing forward. Lean your torso forward, raise your shoulders, contract your neck, protrude your chest out and sink your waist, eyes looking forward down (Fig. 10-6-2, Fig. 10-6-2 side).

Movement Three: Bend your legs slightly and squat. Meanwhile fold both palms in front of your abdomen and press them down with eyes looking at the palms (Fig. 10-6-3).

Fig. 10-6-1

Fig. 10-6-2

Fig. 10-6-2 side

Movement Four: Shift your weight to the right, straighten your right leg, stretch and swing your left leg backward. Meanwhile take apart both palms like bird's wings and sway backward to either side of your torso with the palms facing upward. Raise your head, stretch your neck, protrude your chest out and sink your waist, your eyes looking forward (Fig. 10-6-4, Fig. 10-6-4 side).

Movement Five to Movement Eight is the same as Movement One to Movement Four, but you should exchange the left direction to the right (Fig. 10-6-5, 10-6-6, 10-6-7, 10-6-8).

Fig. 10-6-3

Fig. 10-6-4

Fig. 10-6-4

Fig. 10-6-5 　　　　　　　　 Fig. 10-6-6

After repeating from Movement One to Movement Eight, put down your left leg with both feet a step apart. Put your hands down on either side of your torso with eyes looking forward (Fig. 10-6-9).

Fig. 10-6-7 　　　　　 Fig. 10-6-8 　　　　　 Fig. 10-6-9

Key Points: Fold your palms in front of your torso and put one palm upon another as you like. Bear in mind the contraction and relaxation of your movements. Contract your neck, shoulders and hips while lifting your palms up; relax your neck, shoulders, hips at ease while bending your legs slightly. Swing both arms backward, stretch your torso upward and shape it into a reversed bow stance.

Application of Mind: Fold your palms and lift them up. Imagine that Baihui is connected with coccyx. Sway both arms backward, straighten your neck and your head forward and imagine you are a crane ready to fly.

Functions and Effects: Inhaling is to enlarge the chest when lifting both palms up; pressing both palms down and breathing in Chi into Dantian are to exhale the stale, which can enhance your lung capacity by inhalation and exhalation to release the syndromes such as chronic bronchitis, pulmonary emphysema and other neck-shoulder related diseases. Lifting both palms up will massage Dazhui (CV17) and coccyx of Governor

Vessel. Swaying both palms backward and shaping your body into a reversed bow stance can stretch the Conception Vessel (conception vessel). The contraction and relaxation exercises can dredge the circulation of Chi in Conception Vessel (conception vessel) and Governor Vessel.

(2) Flying like a bird

Continued. Turn your palms into bird's wings and hold them in front of your abdomen with both palms facing each other and eyes looking forward down (Fig. 10-6-10).

Movement One: Straighten your right leg, stand single-legged, bend your left knee and lift it up with your lower leg hanging down and the tips of your foot facing downward. Meanwhile turn both palms into bird's wings and lift them up slightly higher than the height of your shoulders with the palms facing downward, eyes looking forward (Fig. 10-6-11).

Fig. 10-6-10

Movement Two: Put your left leg down to the side of your right leg with the tips of your toes touching the ground while closing both palms in front of your abdomen with both palms facing each other and eyes looking forward down (Fig. 10-6-12).

Movement Three: Straighten your right leg and stand single-legged, bend your left foot and lift it up with your lower leg hanging and the tips of your foot facing downward while lifting both palms upward overhead along your body, with the back of your palms facing each other and eyes looking forward (Fig. 10-6-13).

Fig. 10-6-11　　　　　　　Fig. 10-6-12　　　　　　　Fig. 10-6-13

Movement Four: Put your left leg down to the side of your right foot with the entire sole on the ground and bend both legs slightly while closing both palms in front of your abdomen with both palms facing each other and eyes looking forward down (Fig. 10-6-14).

Movement Five to Movement Eight is the same as Movement One to Movement Four, but you should exchange the left direction to the right (Fig. 10-6-15, 10-6-16, 10-6-17, 10-6-18). After repeating from Movement One to Movement Eight, raise both palms up along the side of your body to the height of your chest with palms facing upward and eyes looking forward (Fig. 10-6-19). Bend your elbows inwardly and press both palms down and put them down at the side of your body with eyes looking forward (Fig. 10-6-20).

Fig. 10-6-14

Fig. 10-6-15   Fig. 10-6-16   Fig. 10-6-17

Fig. 10-6-18   Fig. 10-6-19   Fig. 10-6-20

Key Points: Lift your arms up laterally and stretch out as possible as you can to either side of your chest freely. Put down and close your arms and press them at either side of your chest. Coordinate your arms with your legs, lift them up and put them down at the same time. Inhale when lifting up your palms and exhale when putting them down.

Application of Mind: Lifting your knee above your waist and lifting both arms up mean to lifting anus with your mind and sucking in your abdomen. Looking afar is to keep your balance. Exertion force onto your thumb, index finger and little finger, combined with your breath, and it looks as if you were light enough about to fly. And the gentle landing the ground seems as if dragonfly skimmed water surface.

Functions and Effects: The movements of both arms can change the capacity of your chest, which can massage your heart and lung if you do it with the movement of breath. It can strengthen the exchange capacity of oxygenation of the blood and prevent syndromes such as joint problems in shoulders, elbows, wrists and fingers. Straining and tilting up your thumb and index fingers can stimulate Lung Channel of Hand-Taiyin and to enhance the circulation of Chi in Lung Channel and to improve the functions of your heart and lungs. Lifting your knee and standing single-legged can improve your balance ability and prevent slips and falls.

2.1.7 Closing form [Restoring Chi (Qi) to its origin]

Movement One: Lift your palms up overhead along the side of your body with the palm facing downward (Fig. 10-7-1).

Movement Two: Press your palms down to the front of your abdomen with fingertips of both palms facing each other and eyes looking forward (Fig. 10-7-2). Repeat them twice from Movement One to Movement Two.

Movement Three: Draw a flat arc with both palms in front of your torso slightly with the palms facing each other at the height of your navel and eyes looking forward (Fig. 10-7-3).

Movement Four: Cross both hand in front of your abdomen at the Hukou, overlap your palms, close your eyes and stand still. Breathe evenly with your will resting at Dantian (Fig. 10-7-4).

Fig. 10-7-1

Fig. 10-7-2

Fig. 10-7-3

Fig. 10-7-4

Movement Five: Open your eyes slowly after a few minutes, close both hands and rub them till they are warmed(Fig. 10-7-5).

Movement Six: Put your palms on the face and rub them up and down as if you were washing your face, do it three to five times(Fig. 10-7-6).

Movement Seven: Rub your palms from the top of your head to behind your ears and the front of your chest and put them down on either side of your torso with eyes looking forward (Fig. 10-7-7).

Movement Eight: Lift your left foot and put both feet together with the fore sole touching the ground first and then the whole sole stand firm to restore to the ready position with eyes looking forward (Fig. 10-7-8).

Fig. 10-7-5   Fig. 10-7-6

Fig. 10-7-7   Fig. 10-7-8

Key Points: Press both palms down and relax every part of your body to Yingquan (K11). Draw a flat arc with both palms in front of your abdomen naturally and dexterously as if you were gathering and restoring Chi into Dantian with your mind.

Application of Mind: Holding both arms up seems that you were holding Chi upward. Closing your arms and pressing them down mean to guide your Chi going through Baihui (GV20), down to central Diantian (Danzhong or RN17), down to lower Diantian(Qihai) and down to Yongquan(K11). Chi(Qi) is eventually restored to lower Dantian (Qihai).

Functions and Effects: Restoring Chi into Dantian with a peaceful mind is to guide the innate and external Chi around you into Dantian, which will nourish your breath and blood, dredge Channel, regulate visceral and bowels. By rubbing your hands and washing your face, it is restored to its origin and the exercises are done.

2.2 Learning program

Table 10-1 Teaching Syllabus

Category	Content
Preliminary Preparations	1. Learn handwork, foot stance and footwork of Wu Qin Xi and other subsidiary fundamentals; 2. Learn to do health-oriented breathing exercises
Learning Process	1. Imitate the movements of tiger, deer, bear, monkey and bird. Learn and memorize the movement first and then master the technical skills of each movement and understand the precise essence of each movement to be applied to promote health. 2. Coordinate your breath with your movements for the purpose of regulating your breath. 3. Integrate the body, spirit, mind and Chi into one; unify the internal with the external to regulate your mental health.

2.3 Technique experience

Table 10-2 Technical Skills of Wu Qin Xi

Content	Requirements
Movement standards	Do standardized movement; especially have a clear distinction of the upper and lower, heavy and light, slow and swift, empty and solid. Do exercises gently and dexterously without stiffness.
The Combination of breath and movement	When doing Wu Qin Xi, a kind of Health Qigong, breathing should be combined with movement in accordance with the following rules: inhale when up; exhale when down. Inhale when open; exhale when close. Inhale first and then exhale. Inhale and accumulate energy while exhale and strike. There are several types of breathing manners such as natural breathing, abdominal breathing and lift anus breathing, which can be applied according to the energy requirements and your movements. Inhale when lifting up your palms and exhale when putting down your palms in doing commencement form. Abdominal breathing can be applied in rotating your waist like a bear, that is, inhale when rotating to the right and then upward; exhale when rotating to the left and then downward. Anus-lifting abdominal breathing is applied in lifting monkey's paws. Inhale when lifting both arms up and raising your heels and turning your head; exhale when putting them down.
Physical and mental harmony	The four layers of practice should be kept in mind when doing Wu Qin Xi, a Health Qigong, that is, "physical movement, spirit, mind and Chi circulation". It is better to combine four in one, to combine your physical movements when practice, mental charm with the application of mind and breathing. "Physical movement" is the movements you do in your practice. When doing it correctly, Chi is circulated smoothly. A peaceful mind arrives and you are mentally concentrated. Do different animal movements in accordance to the connotation of its animal names, which should meet the requirements of standardized movements. Do tiger exercise like a tiger while doing bear exercise like a bear as possible as you can. Shen is its look and its manner. When doing given exercises, the look and the manner of the given animal should be acquired. Only when you know well the look of the five animals and how they play games can you imitate them vividly and acquire their manners and looks. "Mind" refers to imaginary reality. When doing the given exercises, imitate animal movements with corresponding mental image. Imitate tiger swooping on its prey, deer running, bear walking, monkey climbing and bird flying.

Content	Requirements
Physical and mental harmony	Your mind goes with your movement and Chi circulation goes with your mind, so that the oneness of mind, Chi and physical movements can be acquired. Chi (refers to the breathing exercises in doing Health Qigong exercises, which is also named "breath-regulating skills". Learn physical movements first, understand its connotation, regulate your breath, combine your movement with your breath, your mind and the mental image, and perceive the connotation of physical skill and mental image so that the internal and external oneness of physical skill and mental image can be acquired.
The mental image of the animal's move	Tiger is ferocious, casting a greedy eye on its prey, so tiger symbolizes a terrifying warrior. Deer is swift and graceful, running in a free and unrestrained manner, so deer symbolizes comfortable and at ease. Bear is simple and frank, sedate in its steps, so bear symbolizes sedated composure. Monkey is nimble and agile, swift and lively, so monkey symbolizes nimble and dexterity. The image of bird is borrowed from crane as crane stands haughty, elegant and distinguished, so bird symbolizes delicacy.

2.4 Cultural experience

- Basic handwork

Tiger's claws: Stretch five fingers apart with the Hukou shaped in a circle. Bend the first and the second knots inward.

Deer's antlers: Straighten the thumb, index finger and little finger, and bend the middle finger and ring finger inward.

Bear's paws: Press the thumb onto the tip of the index finger and bend and put the other four fingers together with the Hukou shaped into a circle.

Monkey's hook: Put five fingertips together and bend the wrist.

Bird's wings: Straighten five fingers, tilt up the thumb, index finger and little finger, and lower the middle finger and ring finger.

Clench fist: Press the tip of the thumb onto the tail of the ring finger; fold the other four fingers to the center of the palm.

- Three regulations in one:

Three regulations are to regulate your body, your breath and your mind. Three regulations are combined into one when doing exercises, combining the physical movements with breath and mind. Three regulations in one is the door to perfection of Qigong.

Five Impairments:

It refers to the impairments of five viscerae of liver, heart, spleen, lung and kidney, which is caused by overstraining.

The five kinds of impairment by overstraining are: protracted watching will overstrain the heart and impair the blood; protracted lying will overstrain the lung and impair the energy; protracted sitting will overstrain the spleen and impair the muscle; protracted standing will overstrain the kidney and impair the bone; protracted walking will overstrain the liver and impair the tendon. *Yellow Emperor's Canon of Internal Medicine • Expounding on the Energies of Five Viscera* has the records as such.

- Breathing Methods:

Abdominal breathing: when inhaling, your abdominal muscles are relaxed; your musculus diaphragm decreases and the abdominal wall are gradually protruded. When exhaling, your abdominal muscles are contracted; your abdominal walls is contracted as well or slightly sunken and your musculus diaphragm is restored to its origin, which is seen in breath regulating in commencement form of Wu Qin Xi.

Reversed Abdominal Breathing: when inhaling, your abdominal muscles are contracted; your abdominal wall is contracted as well or slightly sunken and your musculus diaphragm is decreased and the capacity of abdominal cavity shrinks. When exhaling, your abdominal muscles are relaxed and your abdominal walls are gradually protruded. Your musculus diaphragm is increased and restored to make the capacity of abdominal cavity swell, which is seen in rotating your waist like a bear in Wu Qin Xi.

Anus-lifting abdominal breathing: It is to combine anus-lifting movement with breathing exercise. Contract anus and perineal muscles consciously when inhaling; relax anus and perineal muscles when exhaling, which is seen in lifting monkey's paws.

Table 10-3 Common Acupuncture Points of Health Qigong

Body Part	Name of acupoint	Channels and Vessels	location
Head	Bei Hui	Governor Vessel	the central part on the top of the head, in the middle of both ear tips
	Yin Tang	Non-Channel Extra Acupoint	in the middle of both eyebrows, facing the tip of the nose
	Tai Yang	Non-Channel Extra Acupoint	a pit about 1cun at the back from between your eyebrow and the outer corner of the eyes
	Ren Zhong	Governor Vessel	at the 1/3 point of the upper lip's Renzhong Line
	Cheng Jiang	Conception Vessel	a pit just in the middle of the lower lip
Neck	Yu Zhen	Bladder Channel of Foot-Taiyang	at the outer side of upper external occipital protuberance
	Feng Chi	Gallbaldder Channel of Foot-Shaoyang, GB	a pit between the hairlines of the rear neck
	Tian Zhu	Bladder Channel of Foot-Taiyang	at 1.3cun apart from Yamen, a pit at the outer side of trapezius muscle

(continued)

Body Part	Name of acupoint	Channels and Vessels	location
Back waist chest	Da Zhui	Governor Vessel	a pit under the seventh cervical spine
	Ming Men	Governor Vessel	a pit under the second lumbar vertebra
	Shen Yu	Bladder Channel of Foot-Taiyang	at 1.5cun beside Mingmen (DU4)
	Shan Zhong	Conception Vessel	in the middle point of both nipples
Abdomen	Zhong Wan	Conception Vessel	at 4cun above the navel
	Shen Que	Conception Vessel	in the middle of the navel
	Qi Hai	Conception Vessel	at 1.5cun below the navel
	Guan Yuan	Conception Vessel	at 3cun below the navel
Hips and crotch	Hui Yin	Conception Vessel	at the midpoint of two Yin
shoulder	Jian Jing	Large Intestine Channel of Hand-Yangming	a pit on the shoulder when lifting shoulders forward up
Arm	Qu Chi	Large Intestine Channel of Hand-Yangming	a pit at the side of the radial bone on the stripe wrinkle when bending the elbow
	Nei Guan	Pericardium Channel of Hand-Jueyin	at 2cun above the strip wrinkle of the wrist
Hand leg	Lao Gong	Pericardium Channel of Hand-Jueyin	at the middle finger when clenching the fist
	Zu San Li	Stomach Channel of Foot-Yangming	at 3cun below the knee, at the outer side of the front ridge of shin bone
	Cheng Shan	Bladder Channel of Foot-Taiyang	a pit below the tip of the belly of the Gastrocnemius muscle
	Wei Zhong	Bladder Channel of Foot-Taiyang	in the center of the stripe wrinkle of the rear knee
	San Yin Jiao	Three Yin Channel up	at 3cun above the tip of medial malleolus, behind the inner side of tibia
Foot	Tai Xi	Kidney Channel of Foot-shaoyin, KI	a pit behind the inner malleolus and above heel bone
	Tai Chun	Liver Channel of Foot-Jueyin, LR	in front of the joint between the first and the second metatarsus of the foot
	Yong Quan	Kidney Channel of Foot-shaoyin, KI	a pit at the tip of the character "Ren" on the sole

Notes: 1) 1 cun equals to the width of the widest joint of one's thumb

2) Acupuncture point is also called acupoint, or pressure point.

3 Conclusion

1. The basic hand shape and handwork, foot shape and footwork, body shape and body work should be acquired when learning Health Qigong · Wu Qin Xi.

2. Three steps can be taken to learn Health Qigong, that is, to regulate your body, your

breath and your mind as well. First of all, learn the physical movements and memorize their movement routes and directions. You should achieve them alone, which is the initial purpose of making your body gentle and soft; technical skills should be mastered in this phase. Secondly, learn to breathe in and out, combine physical movements with breathing and perceive the details of physical movements combined with your breath, which attains the purpose of guiding Chi into harmony, familiarize yourself with the details of each movement combined with your breath. Thirdly, learn to apply your mind. The features of five animals are characterized in this phase; and you should acquire the looks and the manners of five animals.

3. To learn Health Qigong • Wu Qin Xi is not only to learn technical skills but to perceive Chinese traditional culture, such as the theory of Yinyang, physique-Chi-spirit, channels and collaterals, viscerae and bowels, five elements, unification of heaven and human, physique-spirit-mind-Chi, the commonly used acupuncture points, etc. as well as the classics on traditional Qigong, so that its cultural connotation of physical movements can be better perceived to promote health and cultivate mind.

4 Extensive reading

Besides Health Qigong • Wu Qin Xi, you can also learn Health Qigong • Mawangdui Daoyin Exercises, Health Qigong • Yi Jin Jing, Health Qigong • Ba Duan Jin, Health Qigong • Liu Zi Jue, Health Qigong • Da Wu, Health Qigong • TaiChi Health Cudgel, Health Qigong • 12-Step Daoyin Health Qigong, Health Qigong • 12-Routine Exercises Shi Er Duan Jin, Relaxation Training Along Three Lines, 18-Routine exercises, Health Cultivation Exercise, Tai Chi Chuan.

5 Questions

(1) What are the key points in practicing Health Qigong • Wu Qin Xi?

(2) What are the skills featured in Health Qigong • Wu Qin Xi?

(3) What are the breathing methods and their effects applied in Health Qigong • Wu Qin Xi?

(4) What are the key technical skills of lifting hip and dropping down foot when swaying like a bear?

(5) How can you attain the perfect effects when practicing Health Qigong • Wu Qin Xi?

6 References

[1] Health Qigong Management Center, State General Administration of Sports. Health Qigong · Wu Qin Xi [M]. Beijing People's Sports Press. 2003.

[2] Health Qigong Management Center, State General Administration of Sports. Training Textbooks for Health Qigong [M]. Beijing: People's Sports Press. 2007.

[3] Health Qigong Management Center, State General Administration of Sports [M]. Vocabulary List for Health Qigong. Beijing: Higher Education Press. 2012.

[4] Health Qigong Management Center, State General Administration of Sports [M]. Assembled Knowledge for Health Qigong. Beijing: People's Sports Press. 2011.

[5] Sun Guangren. The Basic Theories of Traditional Chinese Medicine [M]. Beijing: China Traditional Chinese Medicine Press. 2007.

Chapter Eleven

Wushu Chiropractic

1 Introduction

Wushu chiropractic is one method of physical chiropractic by wushu experts. It follows the way that wushu experts, based on their perception to physical condition, body control and force exertion, use massage, rub, pat, rock, shake or bend, etc., as well as the active body control by practicing Qigong to serve as the treatment means to adjust body, and treat the disorder of kinetic system such as muscle, tendon, membrane, bone or joint, etc. Wushu chiropractic can be used at the period of wushu practice when hurt happens owing to the improper practice; or in daily life when the disorder of sport function occurs owing to the bad habit of physical exercise.

2 Learning experience

2.1 Directions

2.1.1 Basic Relaxation methods

Push

(1) Push (*Tui*): Exert force onto the affected part of body with finger, palm, fist or elbow. Move it in a straight line or in one direction, such as finger-push method, palm-push method, fist-push method and elbow-push methods, etc. (Fig. 11-1-1).

(2) Rub (*Ca*): Attach finger or palm to the affected part of body. Rub it in a straight line back and forth. There are palm-rub method, finger-rub method, thenar (*Yuji*) rub method and hypothenar (*Xiaoyuji*) rub method, etc. (Fig. 11-1-2).

(3) Wipe (*Mo*): To push the affected part (generally the small ones such as eye, finger knuckle, or ear) with finger tip or palm back and forth. There are wipe-with-thumb method, wipe-with-palm method, wipe-with-thenar method and wipe-with-knuckle method, etc. (Fig. 11-1-3).

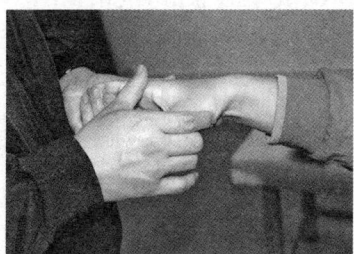

Fig. 11-1-1

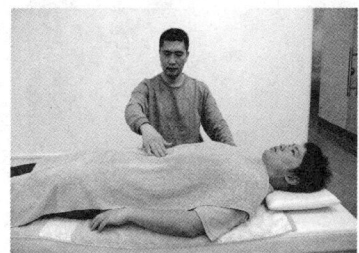

Fig. 11-1-2

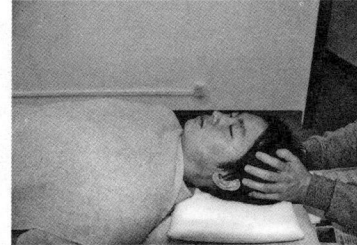

Fig. 11-1-3

Fig. 11-1-4

(4) Sweep (*Saosan*): Push quickly from tempora towards the back of head in a single way with radial of thumb, such as head-sweeping method (Fig. 11-1-4).

Thenar (Yuji) [LU10]

It originally means thenar (Yuji) pressure point. It is the pressure point of lung meridian of hand, at the dent behind the first knuckle of thumb. It is the place where the chiropractor exerts force, when he does so with the slight bulge caused by the interior muscle group and exterior muscle group. Among them, the side of thumb is called thenar (Da Yuji) and the other side is hypothenar (Xiao Yuji).

Grab

(5) Grab (*Na*): Use the thumb and four fingers to lift the affected part of body with abduction force and knead it, 2 fingers, 3 fingers, four fingers or 5 fingers can be used (Fig. 11-1-5).

(6) Grasp (*Zhua*): Or Five-Finger Grasp, with five fingers apart, grasp the affected part of body, such as grasp the patient's head with 5 fingers (Fig. 11-1-6).

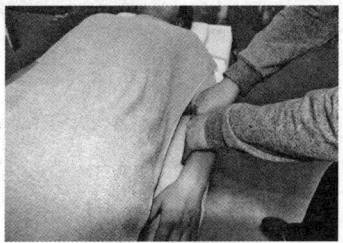

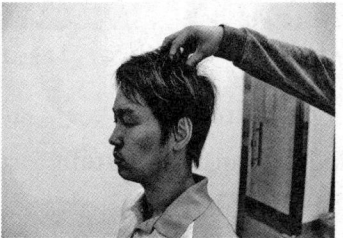

Fig. 11-1-5

Fig. 11-1-6

(7) Nip (*Nie*): Use the finger tips with force to nip skin (generally the small area), or do twisting, turning, pressing, grasping, pulling or lifting symmetrically, such as spine nipping (Fig. 11-1-7).

(8) Finger Rub (*Nian*): Grasp the affected part of body (generally the finger) with the thumb and finger and then with slight force twist and rub it quickly (Fig. 11-1-8).

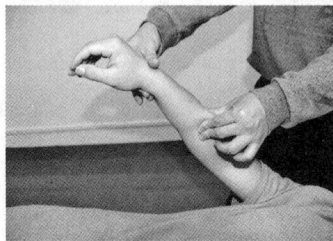 

Fig. 11-1-7   Fig. 11-1-8

Press

(9) Push-down (*An*): Exert force onto the affected part of body or pressure point with fingers or palm and push down gradually. There are push-down with finger (push-down with thumb, push-down with the middle finger, push-down with three fingers), and push-down with palm (single palm, double palms, two palms overlap, bottom of palm and Yuji) (Fig. 11-1-8).

(10) Press (*Ya*): It is to use finger, palm or elbow to exert force onto the affected part of body, and stop for several seconds. It can be done with elbow, with arm, with finger or palm (Fig. 11-1-10).

(11) Point press (*Dian*): It is a method of pressing at a small contact area and pressure. It can be done with thumb or with the bent thumb (Fig. 11-1-11).

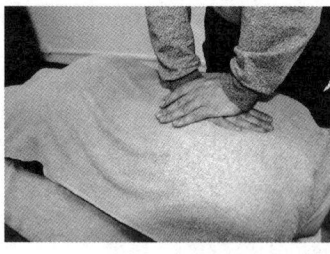 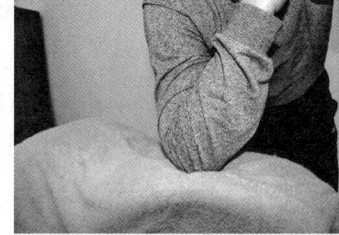 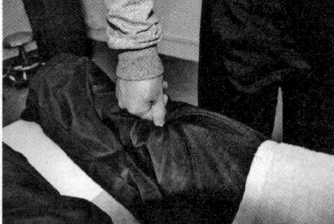

Fig. 11-1-9   Fig. 11-1-10   Fig. 11-1-11

(12) Pinch (*Qia*): It is to press the affected part or pressure point with thumb, index finger or middle finger forcefully, such as pinch with philtrum (Renzhong) or Chengshan (B57) (Fig. 11-1-12).

(13) String-pluck method (*Tanbo*): Exert force onto the affected part of body with

finger, fist or elbow, press and pluck it as if pluck the strings. This can be done with thumb, with three fingers, with fingers bent or with fist (Fig. 11-1-13).

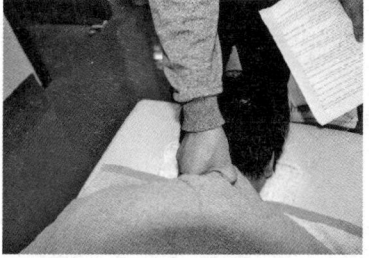
Fig. 11-1-12

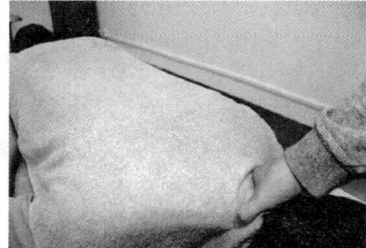
Fig. 11-1-13

Massage

(14) Stroke (*Mo*): Place the tip of finger or palm onto the affected part of body and stroke it in regular rings, such as stroke with finger or with palm (Fig. 11-1-14).

(15) Knead (*Rou*): Place tip of finger or palm onto the affected part of body or pressure point and exert force powerfully in a circular shape till the subcutaneous tissue of the part. This can be done with finger (such as thumb, two fingers, three fingers, middle finger, hook kneading or fingers overlapping), or with palm (such as thenar or heel of palm), etc. (Fig. 11-1-15).

(16) Rub (*Cuo*): Exert force onto the affected part of body or pinch the limb to rub alternatively, such as rubbing upper limb, rubbing lower limb or rubbing rear neck, etc. (Fig. 11-1-16).

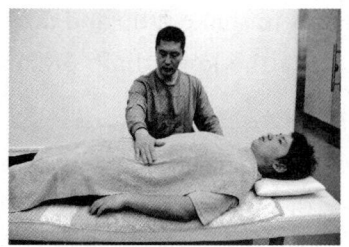
Fig. 11-1-14

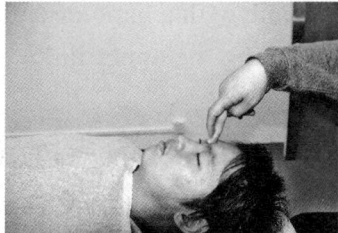
Fig. 11-1-15

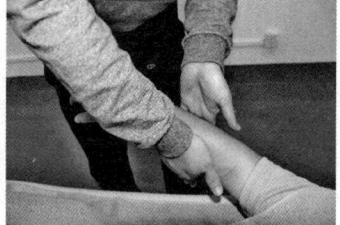
Fig. 11-1-16

Pat and strike

(17) Pat (*Pai*): Pat the relaxed part of body with palm (Fig. 11-1-17).

(18) Strike (*Ji*): Strike the affected part of body with fist, palm, finger or ramulus mori stick. It can be done with fist (fist back, palm of fist, thumb side of fist, etc.), with palm (palm of hand, bottom of palm, side of palm or two palms together), with fingers (finger tip or two fingers) and with a stick and so on (Fig. 11-1-18).

(19) Flip (*Tan*): Bend finger to flick and strike the affected part of body or pressure point, such as flipping between the eyebrows (Fig. 11-1-19).

(20) Peck (*Zhuo*): Bring five fingers together into a hook hand like a chick pecking at rice, and peck at the affected part of body, such as pecking at Baihui pressure point(Fig. 11-1-20).

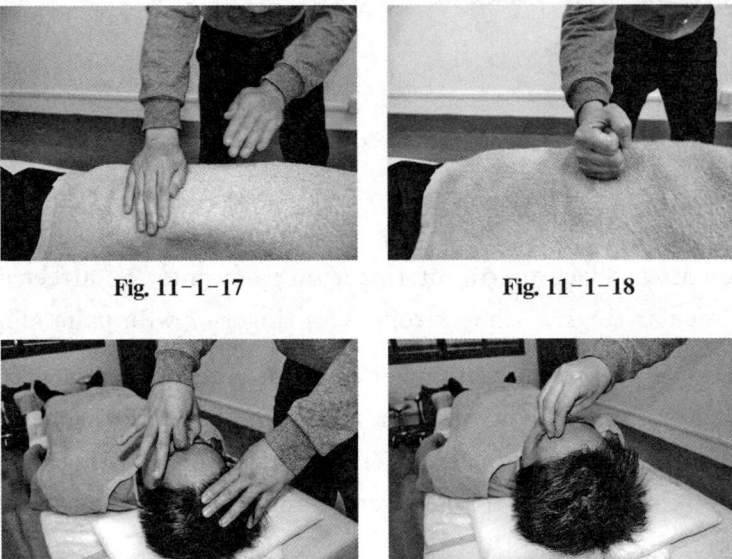

Fig. 11-1-17　　　　　　　　　　Fig. 11-1-18

Fig. 11-1-19　　　　　　　　　　Fig. 11-1-20

Shake and vibrate

(21) Shake (*Dou*): Hold the limb with a hand or two hands to shake it up and down slightly and intensively, such as shaking the upper limb, shaking the lower limb or shaking wrist, etc.(Fig. 11-11-21).

(22) Vibrate (*Zhen*): place the finger of palm closely onto the affected part of body to vibrate it quickly and intensively, such as vibrating with finger or vibrating with palm (Fig. 11-1-22).

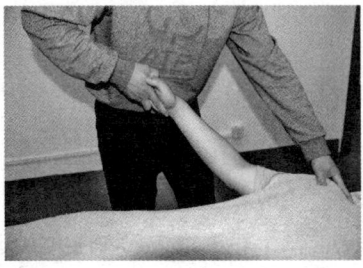 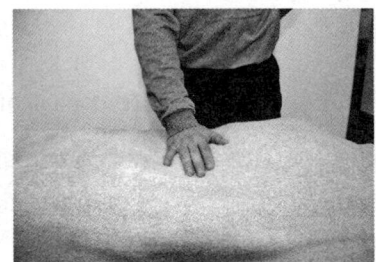

Fig. 11-1-21　　　　　　　　　　Fig. 11-1-22

Stretch

(23) Stretch (*Bashen*): Fix one end of the limb or joint and drag the other end. Or, stretch the joint or limb in the opposite direction, such as stretching neck, stretching elbow joint, stretching wrist joint, stretching finger knuckle, stretching lumbar vertebra, stretching hip joint or stretching ankle etc. (Fig. 11-1-23).

(24) Rub with force (*Lei*): Pinch the finger or toe of the patient and pull it quickly with force (Fig. 11-1-24).

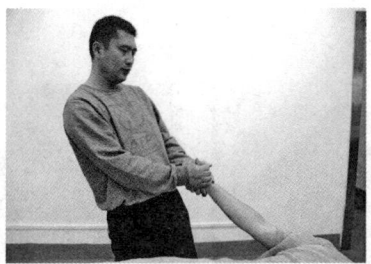
Fig. 11-1-23

Fig. 11-1-24

Rock and bend

(25) Rock (*Yao*): Use the joint of patient as the axis to rock body in circular movement, such as rocking neck, rocking shoulder joint, rocking elbow, rocking wrist, rocking finger knuckle, rocking waist, rocking hip joint, rocking knee or rocking ankle joint, etc. (Fig. 11-1-25).

(26) Bend (*Ban*): Exert force in the same direction or the opposite direction with two hands, to stretch, bend or turn muscle and joint, such as turning neck, turning thoracic vertebra, or turning Lumbar vertebrae (Fig. 11-1-26).

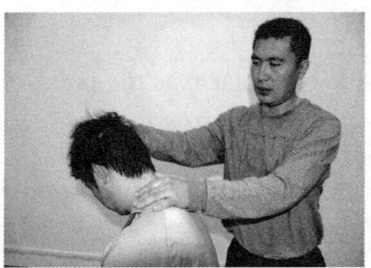
Fig. 11-1-25

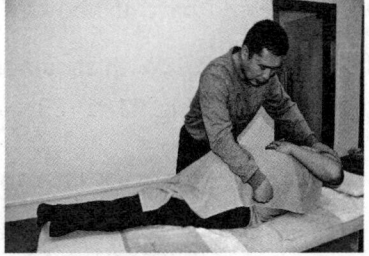
Fig. 11-1-26

Pushing Manipulation with One-finger Meditation (*Yizhi Chan*)

(27) Push Manipulation with One-finger Meditation (*Yizhi Chan*): also called One Finger Zen. It is to exert force with the first half of thumb tip or the front of thumb, by

way of the swinging of forearm to bring along the wrist joint to extend and bend the thumb joint (Fig. 11-1-27).

(28) Push Manipulation with The-Lateral-Side-of-One-finger Meditation: It is to exert force with the radial side of the thumb and then use the method of pushing Manipulation with One-finger Mediation (Fig. 11-1-28).

(29) Push Manipulation with One-Bent-finger Meditation: It is to exert force with the lateral side of the first and second finger knuckle joints (interphalangeal joints of hand) and then use the method of pushing Manipulation with One-finger Meditation (Fig. 11-1-29).

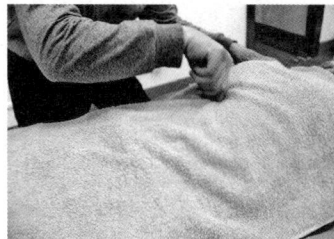
Fig. 11-1-27

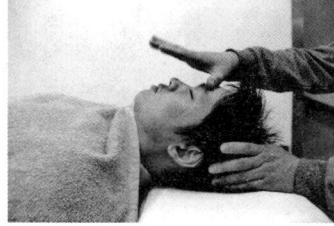
Fig. 11-1-28

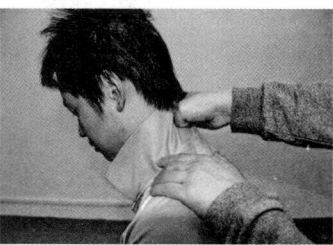
Fig. 11-1-29

Roll

(30) Roll with the back of hand (opisthenar) (Ding's Rolling): It is to place the side of the fifth finger closely to the affected part of body and roll on it with hypothenar (*Xiao Yuji*) or the ulnar side of the back of hand (opisthenar ulnar side) (Fig. 11-1-30)

(31) Roll with finger knuckle joints: It is to place the finger knuckle joints (metacarpophalangeal joints) onto the affected part of body and roll it (Fig. 11-1-31).

(32) Roll withinterphalangeal joint: It is to use interphalangeal joint as the point of strength, roll the affected part of body (Fig. 11-1-32).

(33) Roll with forearm: With theulnar side of forearm as the point of strength, roll the affected part of body (Fig. 11-1-33).

Fig. 11-1-30

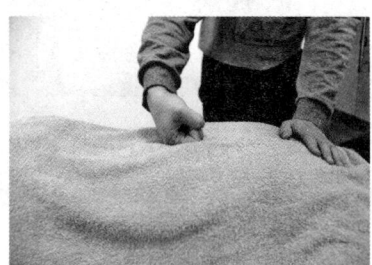
Fig. 11-1-31

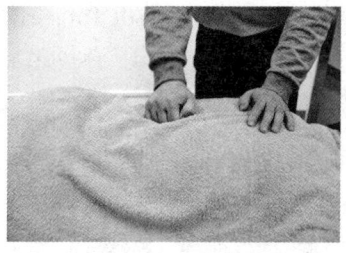
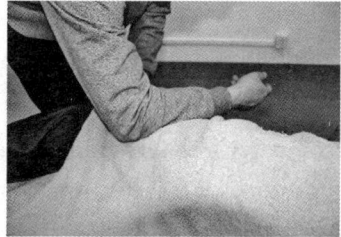

Fig. 11-1-32   Fig. 11-1-33

2.1.2 Upper limb Relaxation

(1) Shoulder relaxation

The chiropractor stands to face the back of the patient.

Pushing supraspinous fossa respectively: Use the thumbs of two hands, thenar (Yuji) or bottom of palm to push trapezius of supraspinous fossa and supraspinatus towards both sides (Fig. 11-2-1).

Pressing supraspinous fossa: With two thumbs, press supraspinous fossa and push trapezius of supraspinous fossa and supraspinatus towards both sides from thoracic vertebra. Do it from inside to outside and press 6 places respectively (Fig. 11-2-2).

Kneading pectorals: Use the index finger, middle finger or ring finger of two hands to knead pectorals, especially shoulder blade coracoids and subclavius (Fig. 11-2-3).

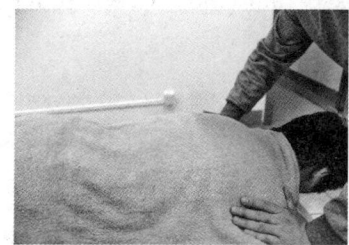
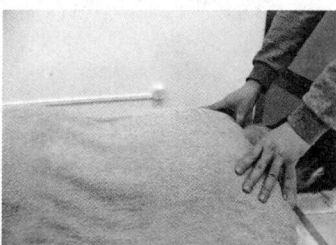
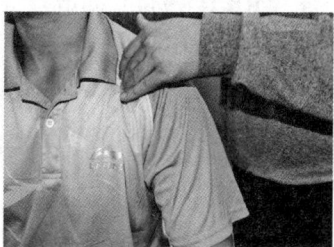

Fig. 11-2-1   Fig. 11-2-2   Fig. 11-2-3

Grabbing, kneading and tapping Jianjing: Grab trapezius of two sides of shoulder with hands (Fig. 11-2-4). Knead Jianjing pressure point with the index finger or middle finger respectively (Fig. 11-2-5). Tap the top of scapular and both sides of the neck muscle with fists (Fig. 11-2-6).

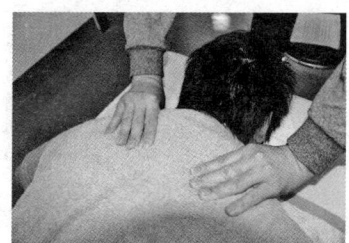
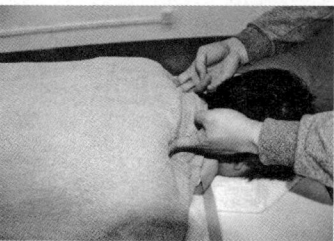
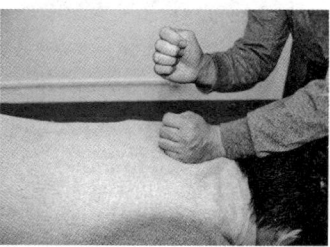

Fig. 11-2-4   Fig. 11-2-5   Fig. 11-2-6

Pressing rhomboid muscle and Tian zong pressure point with fingers: Press the major and minor rhomboid muscles between spine and shoulder blade as well as Tianzong pressure point on infraspinous fossa with the thumb (Fig. 11-2-8).

Kneading teres major and teres minor: use the index finger, middle finger or ring finger to knead teres major and teres minor outer side of shoulder blade (Fig. 11-2-9).

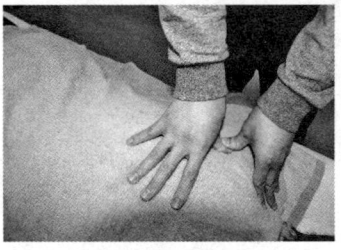
Fig. 11-2-7

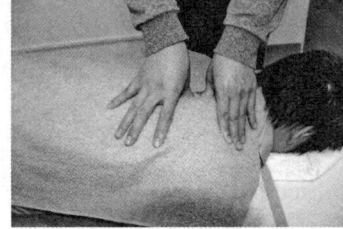
Fig. 11-2-8

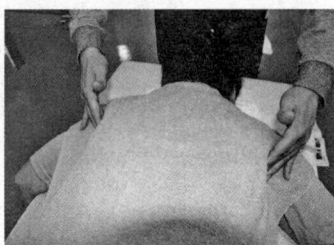
Fig. 11-2-9

(2) Upper limb relaxation

The chiropractor stands on the right side of the patient to help him the right upper limb.

Grabbing deltoid: hold the right wrist of the patient with the right hand, press and knead the junction betweem deltoid and the right shoulder (Fig. 11-2-10).

Holding and kneading musculus triceps brachii: It is to hold the right wrist of the patient with the right hand, use the left palm to hold the back of musculus triceps brachii to knead it up and down (Fig. 11-2-11).

It is to hold the right wrist of the patient with the right hand to bend his elbow joint. With Hukou (the part between the thumb and index finger, the same as below) of the left hand onto the crook of the patient's elbow, press it up and down (Fig. 11-2-12).

Grabbing forearm extensor muscle: It is to hold the right wrist of the patient with the right hand; knead the forearm extensor muscle with the left hand up and down (Fig. 11-2-13).

Pressing forearm center line with finger: It is for the chiropractor to use his thumbs to press the sutura of forearm center line up and down, with the patient's palm facing up (Fig. 11-2-14).

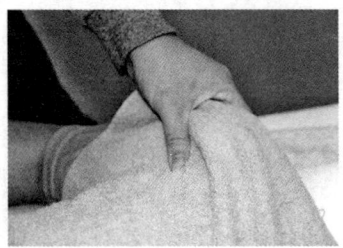
Fig. 11-2-10

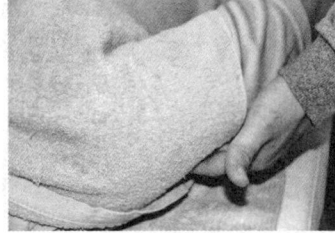
Fig. 11-2-11

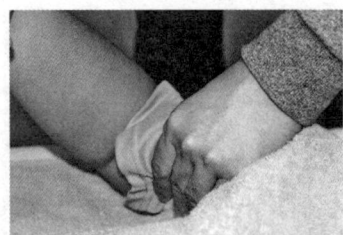
Fig. 11-2-12

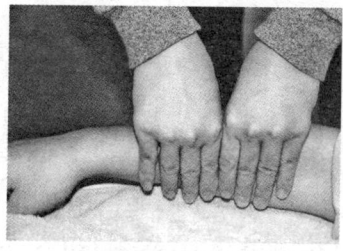
Fig. 11-2-13

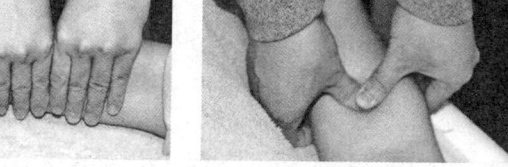
Fig. 11-2-14

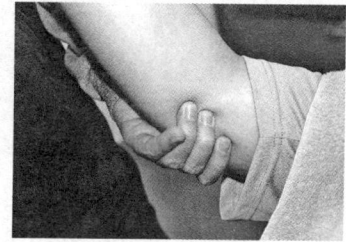
Fig. 11-2-15

Kneading Xiaohai pressure point, Quchi pressure point, Neiguan pressure point, Waiguan pressure point and Hegu pressure point: It is for the chiropractor to hold the right wrist of the patient with one hand, and knead Xiaohai pressure point(in ulnar nerve groove)with the middle finger of the other hand (Fig. 11-2-15); use the thumb to knead Quchi pressure point(Fig. 11-2-16); use the thumb and index finger together to pinch Neiguan and Waiguan and then knead them (Fig. 11-2-17); and then knead Hegu (Fig. 11-2-18).

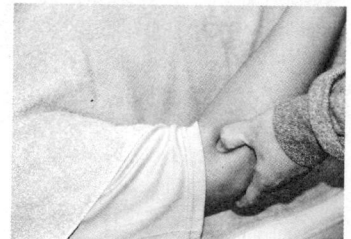
Fig. 11-2-16

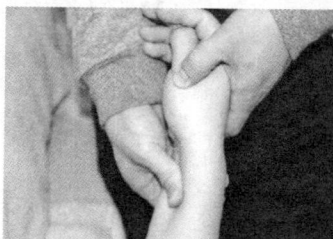
Fig. 11-2-17

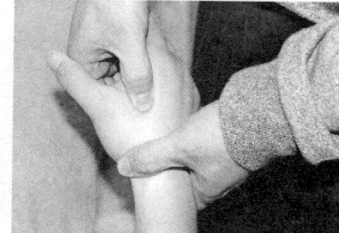
Fig. 11-2-18

Pushing palm of hand and back of hand (opisthenar) respectively: with the palm of the patient facing up, the chiropractor uses his little finger and ring finger to buckle the thumb and little finger of the patient's right hand. Then he pushes thenar and hypothenr respectively as well as palm of hand with the thumbs of two hands (Fig. 11-2-19). With the patient's back of hand facing up, the chiropractor holds the two sides of the palm of the patient with two hands, and pushes it respectively with the thenar of two hands (Fig. 11-2-20).

Twisting and rubbing fingers with force: The chiropractor twists the fingers of right hand of the patient and then rubs them with force one by one (Fig. 11-2-21).

Shaking upper limbs: Choose the proper method to shake the elbow joint, wrist joint, and metacarpophalangeal joints one by one (Fig. 11-2-22).

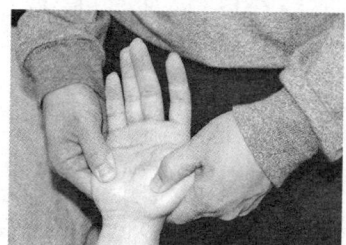
Fig. 11-2-19

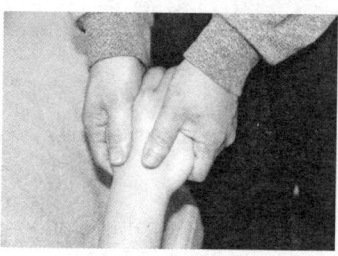
Fig. 11-2-20

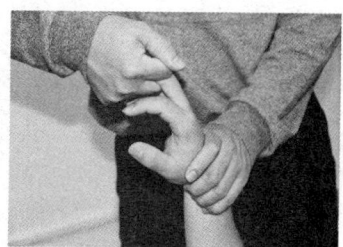
Fig. 11-2-21

Rubbing upper arm: With two palms holding the upper arm, rub it up and down for several times (Fig. 11-2-23).

Shaking upper arm and wrist joints: holding the right shoulder of the patient with the left hand, the chiropractor holds the right hand of the patient with the right hand, shake the upper arm to conduct the force to the musculus triceps brachii (Fig. 11-2-24). The chiropractor pinches the two strips of the right wrist joints with the two thumbs, index fingers and middle fingers facing opposite. And then rub them in opposite direction thus to bring the wrist joint to vibrate up and down quickly (Fig. 11-2-25).

Tapping upper arm: holding the upper arm of the patient with one hand, the chiropractor taps it with clenched fist (Fig. 11-2-26).

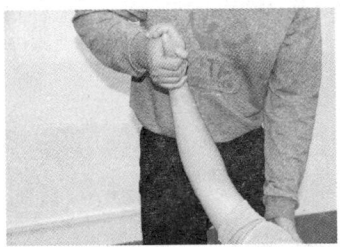
Fig. 11-2-22

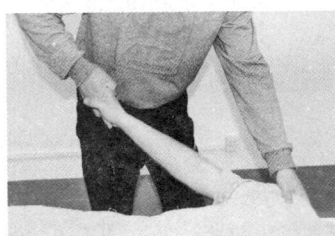
Fig. 11-2-23

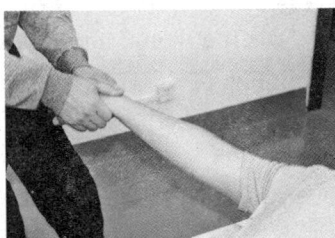
Fig. 11-2-24

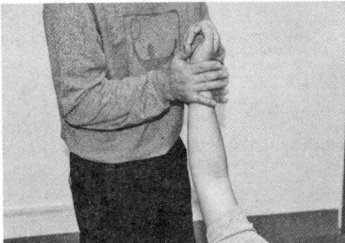
Fig. 11-2-25

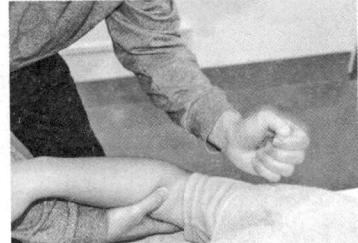
Fig. 11-2-26

Pressure point and indications

Jianjing: located at the midpoint of Dazhui pressure point and acromion, the top of shoulder, the connection place over the papilla and shoulder line

Indications: shoulder and back impediments, arm stretch difficulty, neck pain, headache and stiff neck

Tianzong (SI11): located at scapular, the central sunken place of infraspinous fossa, at the same plane of the fourth thoracic vertebra

Indications: shoulder blade aches, the pain of outer side of the back of elbow, and the pain & numbness of neck, shoulder and upper limb

Xiaohai (SI8): located at the lateral elbow, the sunken place between olecranon and Medial epicondyle of Humerus, in the sulcus for ulnar nerve

Indications: the pain of elbow and arm

Quchi: located at the place where elbows bend to be a right angle, the connection midpoint of Chize pressure point, the end of outer side of Cubital crease and Lateral epicondyle of Humerus

Indications: paralysis of upper arm, swelling of arm, pain of shoulder or elbow joint or upper limbs paralysis

Neiguan (PC6): located at the middle point of forearm when the palm is facing up, 2cun above the wrist strip between Scratching lateral flexion wrist tendons and Tendon palmaris longus

Indications: heart ache, palpitation, chest tightness and shortness of breath, hiccup, insomnia, car sickness, arm pain, nausea, dysmenorrhea and mental disorder

Waiguan: 2cun above the middle point of the wrist strip when the palm is facing down, between ulna and radius, the opposite of Neiguan pressure point

Indications: limb asthenia, hand tremor.

Hegu (LI4): or Hukou, on the edge of fingerweb between the thumb and index finger when the thumb joint strip of one hand is placed between the thumb and index finger of the other hand

Indications: toothache, pain of wrist and arm, facial distortion, cold and fever Note that pregnant women should be used with caution.

2.1.3 Shoulder chiropractic

(1) Throwing chest and extending arms

The chiropractor stands behind the patient and the patient sits straight on the bench.

(The patient) Touch the waist with two wrists, throw his chest and raise his shoulder, the head leaning backward. Move the shoulder blade up, back and down in relaxation(Fig. 11-3-1).

The chiropractor adjusts and fixes the shoulder of the patient (Fig. 11-3-2).

(The patient) Turn the head straight, with arms down in relaxation (Fig. 11-3-3).

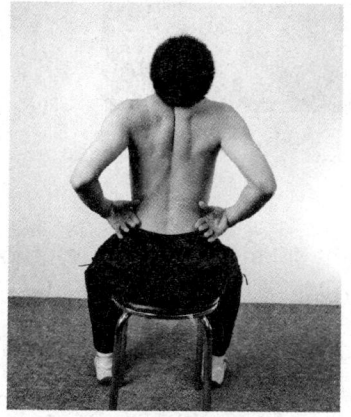
Fig. 11-3-1

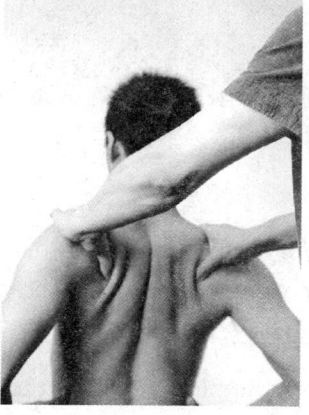
Fig. 11-3-2

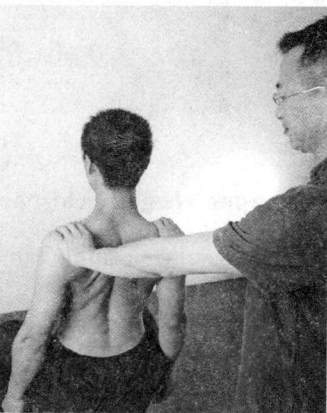
Fig. 11-3-3

(The patient) Raise two arms on two sides at shoulder level (Fig. 11-3-4.). Go on raising the head and then turn the palm up till the two hands are facing up. Open the arms at the shoulder level, eyes looking at the sky (Fig. 11-3-5).

(The patient) Relax the shoulder; put the two arms down at the level (Fig. 11-3-6). Turn the head straight, at the same time turn the palm of hand down (Fig. 11-3-7). Go on putting down hands till they are completely down in relaxation (Fig. 11-3-8).

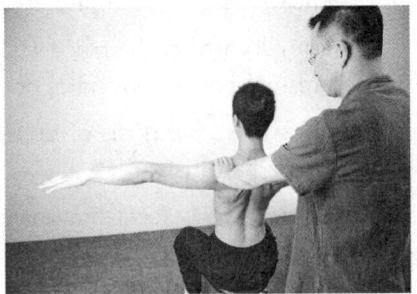

Fig. 11-3-4

Fig. 11-3-5

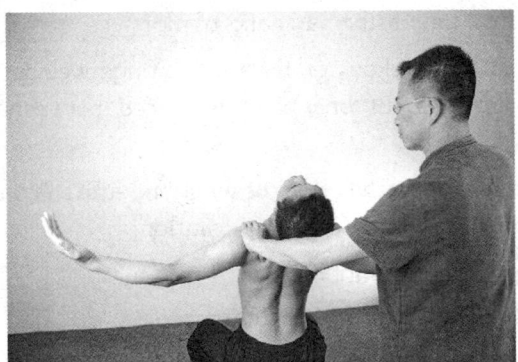

Fig. 11-3-6

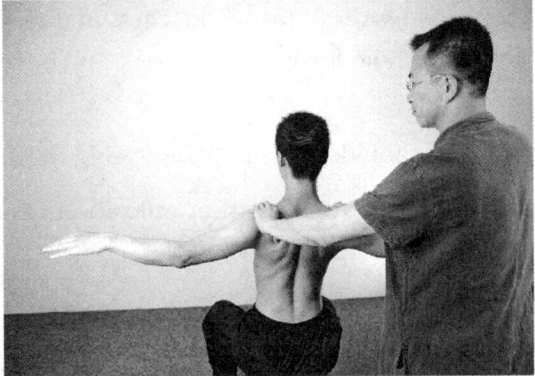

Fig. 11-3-7

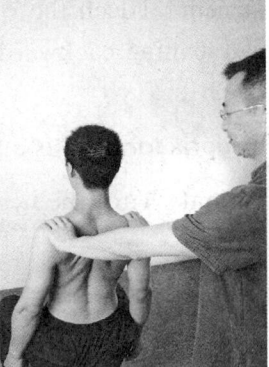

Fig. 11-3-8

(2) High-low shoulder chiropractic

Suppose the patient has something wrong with his right shoulder. The chiropractor stands behind the patient on the right slightly, and the patient sits straight on the bench.

(The patient) Put the right wrist on the back spine of the back so that the shoulder blade can complete appear. At the same time, hold the right hand with the left hand, in case it falls down (Fig. 11-3-9).

(The chiropractor) Hold the glenohumeral joint from the front with the right hand; clasp the lower part of the shoulder blade with the left hand to adjust it from up to down, left to right, front to back, so that the shoulder blade can go back to its normal position (Fig. 11-3-10).

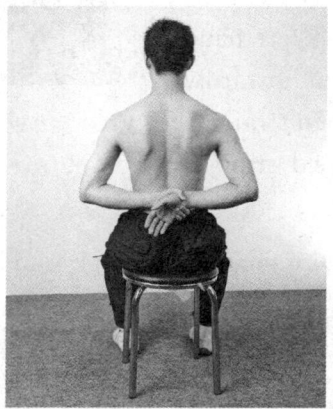
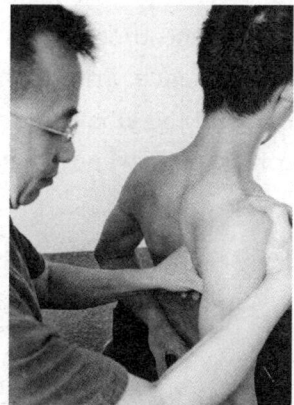

Fig. 11-3-9   Fig. 11-3-10

(The chiropractor) Adjust the glenohumeral joint as well as the under-horn of the shoulder blade to make the shoulder into a sinking position and fix the shoulder joint at the same time (Fig. 11-3-11).

(The patient) Droop the arms naturally down at the back and raise the right arm till the utmost and then relax the shoulder (Fig. 11-3-12). Turn the palm toward outside, and hang arm down the accordingly. (Fig. 11-3-13)

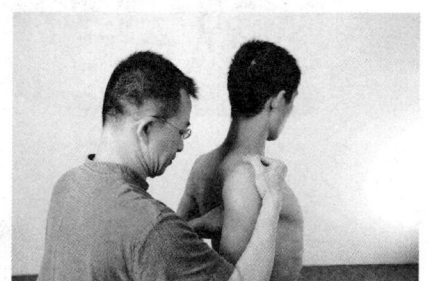

Fig. 11-3-11

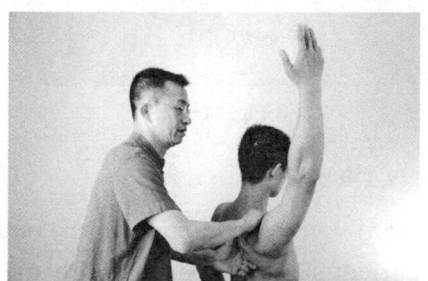
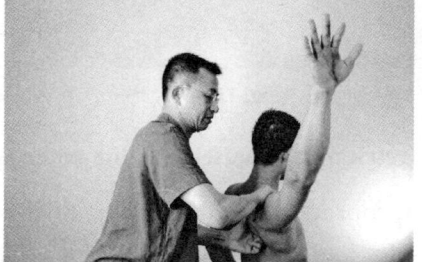

Fig. 11-3-12   Fig. 11-3-13

2.1.4 Elbow joint chiropractic

(1) Stretching the muscles of the inner side of elbow

The chiropractor stands before the patient. The patient with tendon node at the inner side of the right elbow and tenderness point sits on a bench, with the right elbow bent, and the palm facing up, the shoulder, elbow and wrist in relaxation.

(The chiropractor) Hold the elbow of the patient with the right hand and press the patient's Shaohai pressure point with his thumb, the left hand holding the wrist (Fig. 11-4-1). With the right hand fixed, use the thumb to press and turn the arm of the patient inwardly slightly. At the same time, turn the left hand inwardly so that the patient's arms turned inwardly with the palm down. Bend the elbow and then straighten it so that the arm is pulled and stretched straight (Fig. 11-4-2, Fig. 11-4-3).

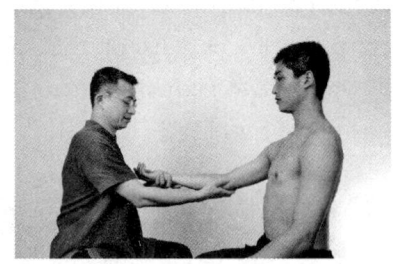

Fig. 11-4-1

Repeat the action several times or the vise versa (Fig. 11-4-4, Fig. 11-4-5).

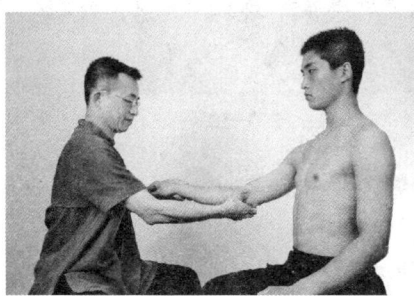

Fig. 11-4-2

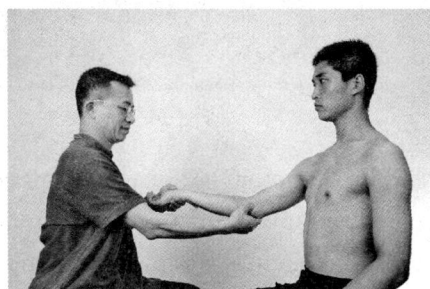

Fig. 11-4-3

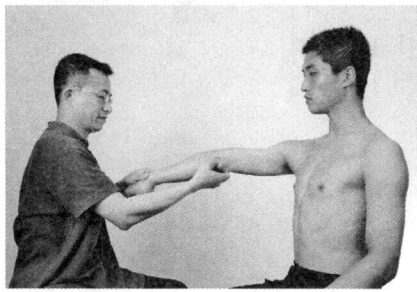

Fig. 11-4-4

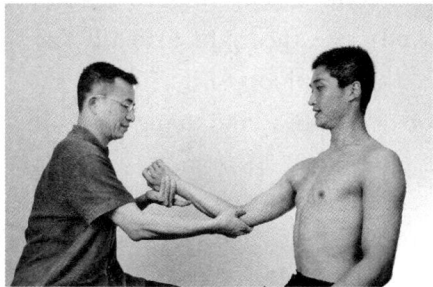

Fig. 11-4-5

(2) Stretching the muscles of the outer side of elbow

The chiropractor stands in front of the patient with tendon node on the outer side of elbow muscles and/or tenderness point. The patient sits on a bench, with the right elbow bent and palm upward; keep shoulder, elbow and wrist in relaxation.

(The chiropractor) Hold the elbow of the patient with the left hand and press the patient's Quchi pressure point with the thumb, the right hand holding the wrist (Fig. 11-4-6). With the left hand fixed, use the thumb to press Quchi and turn it inwardly slightly; at the same time, turn the right hand slightly inwardly, so that the arm of the patient can be turned outwardly with his palm of hand facing up. Bend the elbow and then straighten it, so that the arm of the patient can be pulled and stretched (Fig. 11-4-7, Fig. 11-4-8).

Repeat the action several times or the vise versa (Fig. 11-4-9, Fig. 11-4-10).

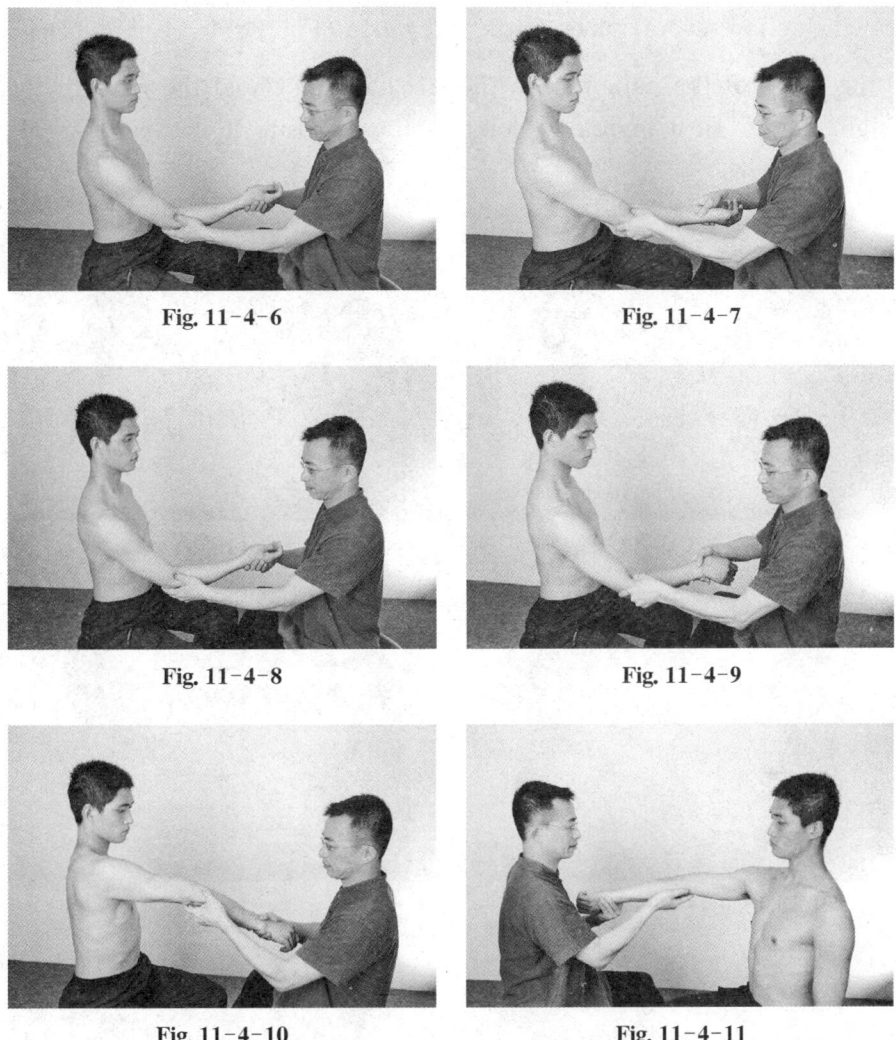

Fig. 11-4-6

Fig. 11-4-7

Fig. 11-4-8

Fig. 11-4-9

Fig. 11-4-10

Fig. 11-4-11

(3) Stretching the muscles behind the elbow

Stand in front of the patient with tendon node behind the elbow and/or tenderness point.

The patient sits on a bench, with the right elbow bent and palm upward; keep the shoulder, elbow and wrist in relaxation.

(The chiropractor) Hold the elbow withthe right hand, press the Tianjing pressure point or Qingleng pressure point behind the elbow, the left hand holding the wrist (Fig. 11-4-11).

With the right hand fixed, use the index finger and middle finger to press the aching point of the patient. Turn the left hand of the patient inwardly, the palm of the patient downward. Bend his elbow first and then straighten it. Pull the arm slightly and stretch it straight (Fig. 11-4-12, Fig. 11-4-13).

Repeat the action several times or the vise versa (Fig. 11-4-14, Fig. 11-4-15).

Hold the elbow of the patient with the left hand and hold the wrist of the patient with the right hand. Turn his elbow joint in the opposite direction (Fig. 11-4-16, Fig. 11-4-17).

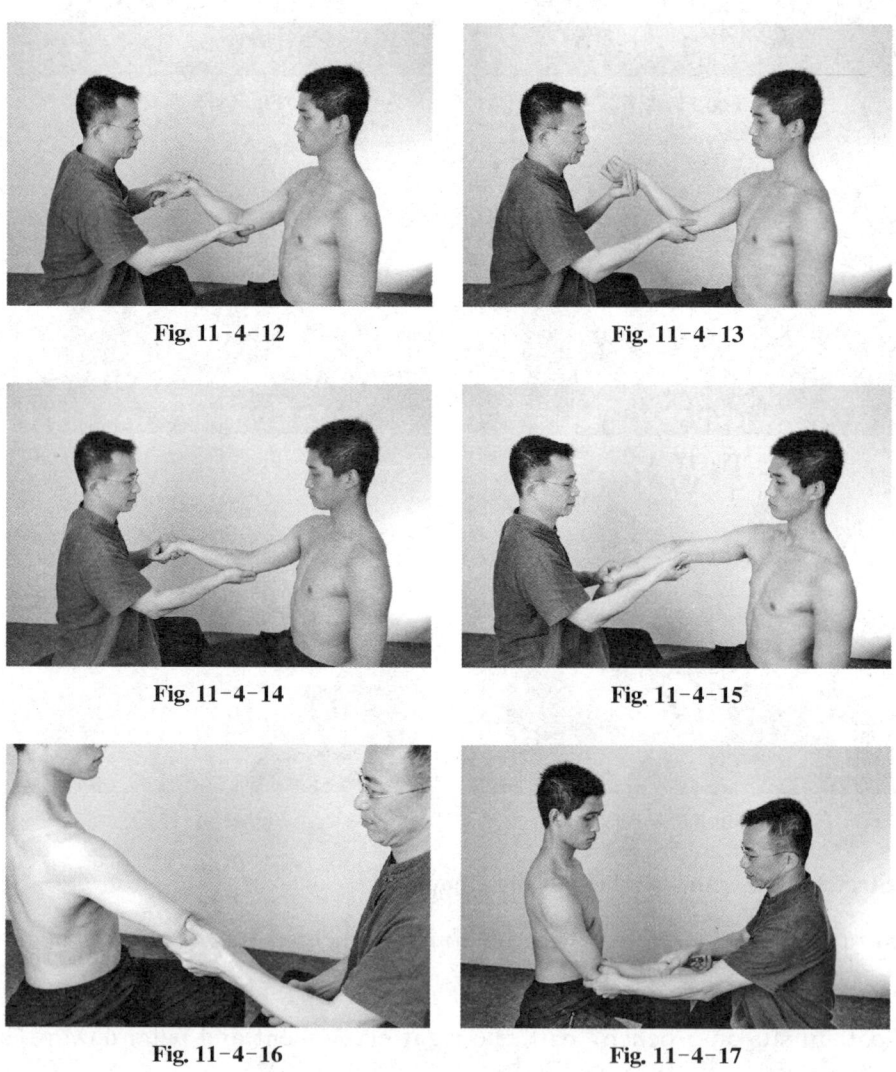

Fig. 11-4-12　　　　　　　　　Fig. 11-4-13

Fig. 11-4-14　　　　　　　　　Fig. 11-4-15

Fig. 11-4-16　　　　　　　　　Fig. 11-4-17

(4) Drooping, holding elbow and pausing

The patient with ached right elbow sits on a bench, the right elbow bent and palm of the hand facing up; keep the shoulder, elbow and wrist in drooping relaxation. The chiropractor stands in front of the patient, holding the elbow of the patient with the right hand, the left one holding the palm of the patient (Fig. 11-4-18).

(The chiropractor) Slightly turn the palm to make the arm move inwardly, the palm of the hand facing down. Hold the elbow and then pauses for a while (Fig. 11-4-19).

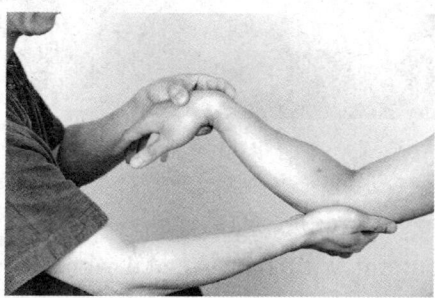

Fig. 11-4-18

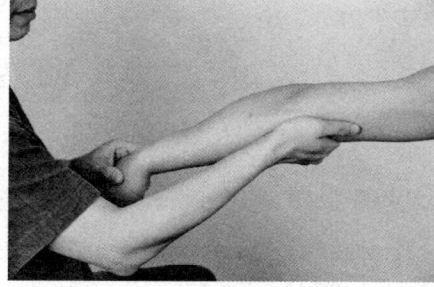

Fig. 11-4-19

Pressure points and indications

Shaohai [H73]: located at the sunken place between the inter side of the elbow strip and medial epicondyle of Humerus when bending elbow

Indications: forearm anesthesia and pain of soft tissue around elbow joint

Tianjing [SJ10]: located at the outer side of arm, 1cun of the top sinking place of elbow tip when bending elbow

Indications: headache, neck ache, damage of elbow joint or soft tissue of upper limbs, stiff neck

Qinglengyuan [SJ11]: located at the outer side of arm, 2cun of the top sinking place of elbow tip, that is, 1inch from Tianjing

Indications: inability to lift shoulder or arm because of the pain from them

2.1.5 Wrist joint chiropractic

(1) Pulling and turning

The chiropractor stands in front of the patient with the affected right wrist, who sits straight on the bench, his right elbow bent, the palm facing down, and the whole body in relaxation.

(The chiropractor) Use the index finger, ring finger and little finger to hold the Thenar (*Yuji* L10) and hypothenar (*Xiao Yuji*) of the patient respectively. Then use the index finger to hold the lower part of the patient wrist and press the upper part of the wrist with the thumbs of two hands (Fig. 11-5-1).

Pull the wrist and turn it (Fig. 11-5-2).

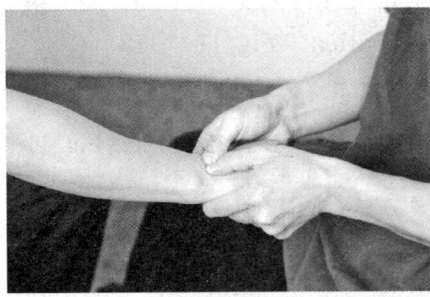
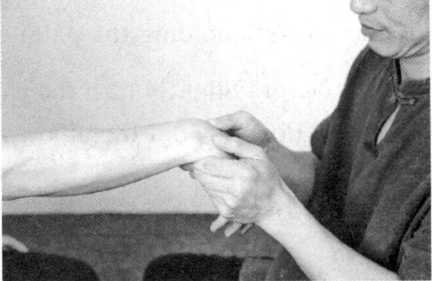

Fig. 11-5-1 Fig. 11-5-2

(2) Pulling wrist joint

The chiropractor stands in front of the patient with the affected right wrist, who sits straight on the bench, his right elbow bent, the palm facing down, the whole body in relaxation.

Clasp the wrist joint of the patient tightly and pull it outward and downward horizontally to make the upper joint of the wrist open (Fig. 11-5-3).

When keeping the upper joint of wrist open, continue to pull the wrist horizontally to make the lower joint open. Meanwhile press the protruding joint to restore it to the original place (Fig. 11-5-4).

Ask the patient to clench the fist immediately and then loosen the wrist to restore its original place (Fig. 11-5-5).

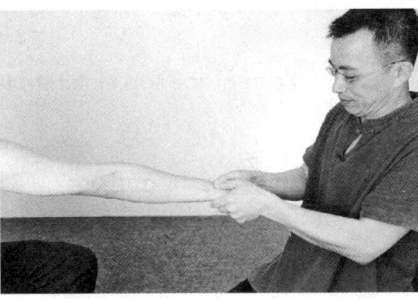
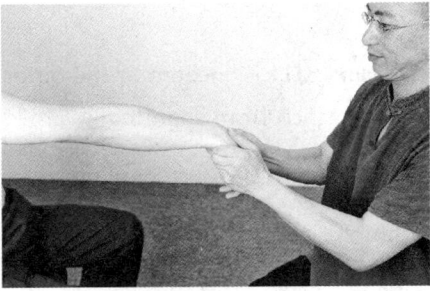

Fig. 11-5-3 Fig. 11-5-4

2.1.6 Relaxing the lower limb's back

Take the relaxing of the lower limb as an example. The chiropractor stands at the left side of the patient and the patient lies in bed on his back.

(1) With the bottom of the left or right palm, the chiropractor presses and kneads the part near the hip muscle group (Fig. 16-1-1).

(The chiropractor) Use the bottom of hands to press and knead the hamstrings (Fig. 11-6-2); use the two thumbs brought together or overlapped to press the hamstrings (Fig. 11-6-3); use one palm or two palms overlapped to press and knead hamstring (Fig. 11-6-4); open Hegu (Hukou) to place it at the back of thigh and move from greater trochanter of thighbone to the knee and snap the lateral thigh with thumb (Fig. 11-6-5).

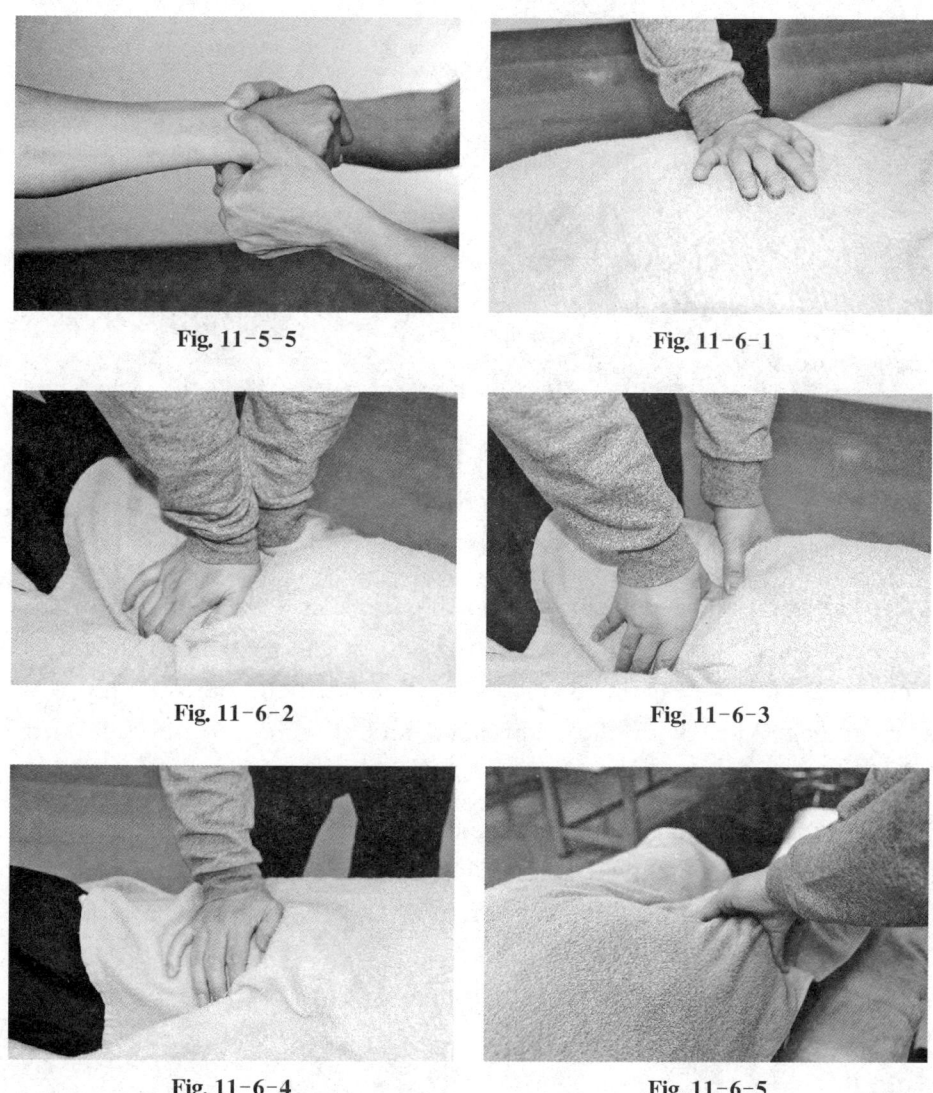

Fig. 11-5-5　　　　　　　　　Fig. 11-6-1

Fig. 11-6-2　　　　　　　　　Fig. 11-6-3

Fig. 11-6-4　　　　　　　　　Fig. 11-6-5

(2) Press and knead Weizhong pressure point and Chengshan pressure point on the crus with one thumb (Fig. 11-6-6). Grab and knead forcefully the rear thigh and crus muscle group till the chorda magna with two hands (Fig. 11-6-7). Keep pressing the lumbosacral portion with the left palm; use the right palm to push down the vertical axis of the lower limbs from the hip strip till chorda magna (Fig. 11-6-8). Keep pressing the lumbosacral portion with the left palm; use the right palm to push down the inner side of heel, the body weight onto the right hand (Fig. 11-6-9).

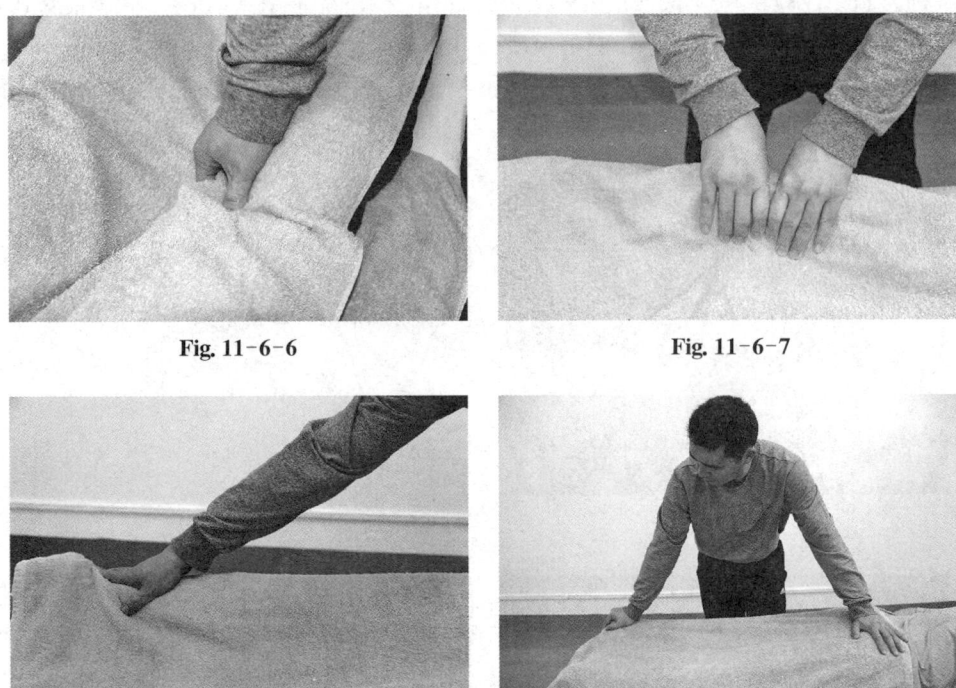

Fig. 11-6-6   Fig. 11-6-7

Fig. 11-6-8   Fig. 11-6-9

(3) Tap the back and outer side of the thigh and crus back and forth for several times with two hands. Use typothenar (*Xiao Yuji*) of the right hand to rub Yongquan pressure point of the sole (Fig. 11-6-11). Place the left hand onto the hip with force, hold the right bent knee with the right hand and stretch the hip backward several times (Fig. 11-6-12).

(4) Clasp the crus of the patient and bend it into the right angle and rub the crus at Sanyinjiao pressure point quickly. Use the right hand to hold the left foot, its knee being a right angle right now, and tap the sole of foot with the left clenched fist for several times (Fig. 11-6-14).

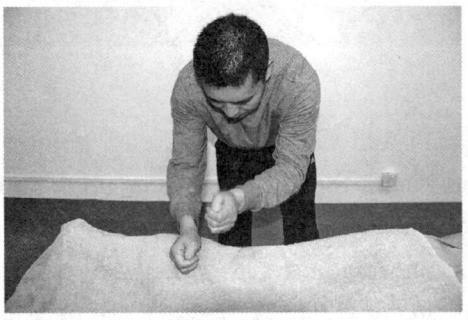 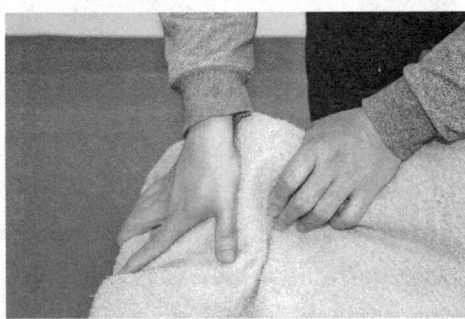

Fig. 11-6-10   Fig. 11-6-11

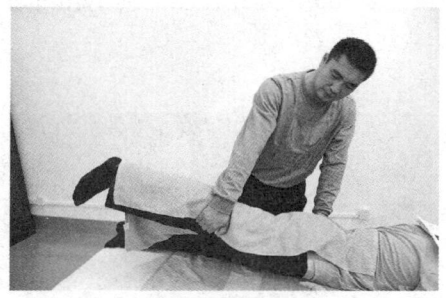

Fig. 11-6-12   Fig. 11-6-13

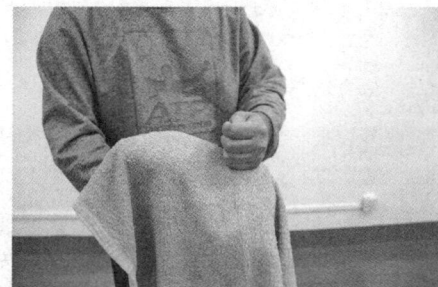

Fig. 11-6-14   Fig. 11-7-1

Pressure points and indications

Weizhong [BL40]: located at the center of Popliteal crease, the midpoint between Biceps femoris tendon and semitendinosus tendon

Indications: pain of waist and back, wilting and impediment of waist or lower limbs

Chengshan [BL57]: located in the middle of crus, the sharp-angled sunken place below musculus gastrocnemius when straightening the lower leg or raise heels

Indications: twitch of leg, anus disease

Yongquan: located at the sunken place of the front of sole, the one-third place of the line connecting heel and head of the seam of the second and third toes

Indications: pain of vertex, heat of sole center, acute gastroenteritis

2.1.7 Relaxing the front part of lower limb (E.g. the left limb)

(1) Facing the planta pedis of the patient, the chiropractor uses the thumb and index finger to knead the gap of metatarsal bones of each toe (Fig. 11-7-1) one by one.

Use the thumb to push the gap of metatarsal bones of the instep one by one (Fig. 11-7-2). Use thenar (*Yuji*) of the two hands to push the instep (Fig. 11-7-3). Hold the five toes of the patient with the left hand and pull them up and down (Fig. 11-7-4). Twist and rub each toe with force (Fig. 11-7-2). Hold the heel of the patient with the left hand, hold the sole with right hand, push and stretch the chorda magna of the patient (Fig. 11-7-5). Use the thumbs overlapped to knead Zusanli pressure point and Yanglingquan pressure point. Use the index finger to knead Sanyinjiao pressure point (Fig. 11-7-6).

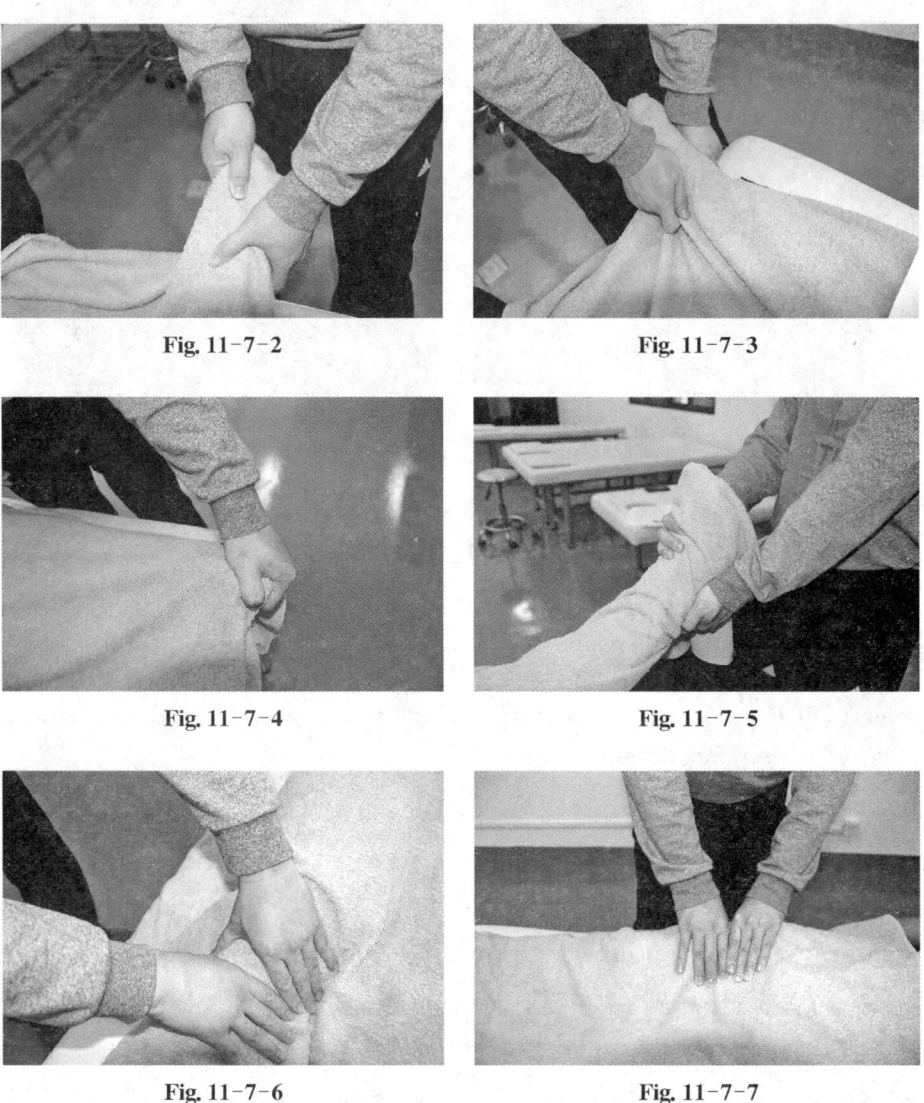

Fig. 11-7-2　　　　　　　　　Fig. 11-7-3

Fig. 11-7-4　　　　　　　　　Fig. 11-7-5

Fig. 11-7-6　　　　　　　　　Fig. 11-7-7

(2) With the bottom of palms facing together, push down the front of thigh up and down. Grab the quadriceps femoris and knead it (Fig. 11-7-7). Use the bottom of palms to knead the center of knee and push them down with the thumbs respectively. Bring the palm close to patella, turn the wrist to move the patella around slightly (Fig. 11-7-8). Use the middle finger hooked to knead Weizhong pressure point and Chengshan pressure point (Fig. 11-7-9). Hold the left ankle of the patient with the left hand and use the right hand to hold the left knee to bend knee and hip. With the hip joint as an axis, turn the knee and hip inward and outward several times horizontally (Fig. 11-7-10). With the knee joint as an axis, turn them several times vertically (Fig. 11-7-11) With the pa-

tient straightening his leg, the chiropractor holds the left hand of the patient with the left hand, use his right hand to hold the heel to pull and stretch the ankle first, and then turn it inward and outward slightly with the ankle joint as the axis (Fig. 11-7-12).

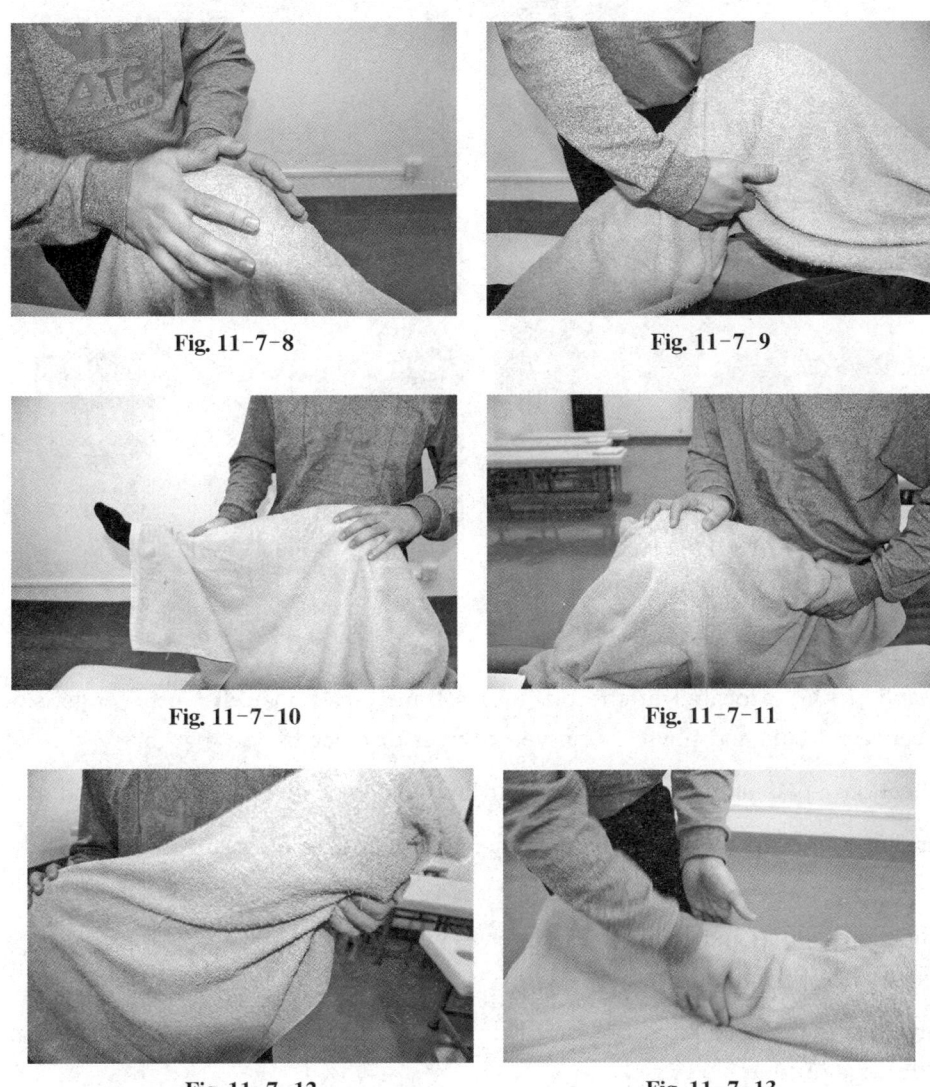

Fig. 11-7-8 Fig. 11-7-9

Fig. 11-7-10 Fig. 11-7-11

Fig. 11-7-12 Fig. 11-7-13

(3) Clamp the affected limb with two palms to rub the lower limb up and down for several times (Fig. 11-7-13). Hold the ankle of the patient with the left hand, place the right hand onto the knee, bend and stretch the lower limb several times (Fig. 11-7-14). With the left knee supporting the right heel of the patient forcefully, hold the left foot with his left hand, use the right hand to hold the left heel, and then pull and stretch down the ankle, knee, hip and muscle group with force (Fig. 11-7-15). Hold the left foot with the left hand, hold the left heel with the right hand to stretch the leg outward slightly and shake the lower limb up and down (Fig. 11-7-16).

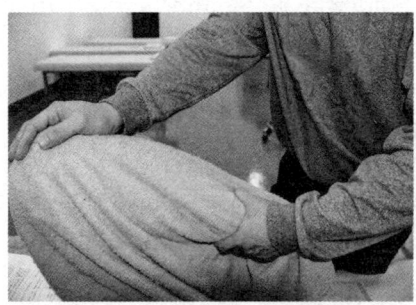

Fig. 11-7-14

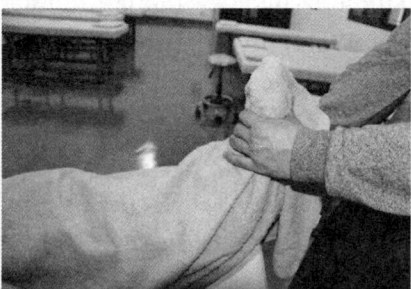

Fig. 11-7-15

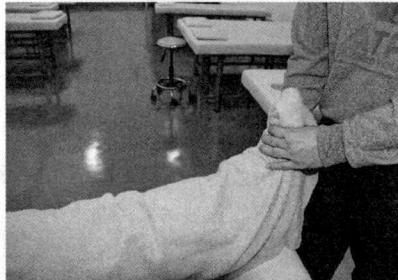

Fig. 11-7-16

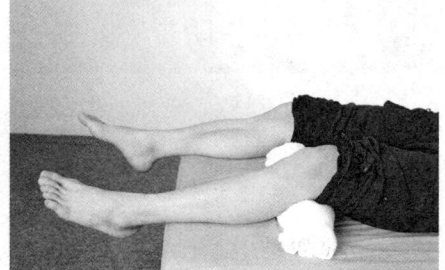

Fig. 11-8-1

Pressure points and indications

Zusanli [ST36]: located at the place of 4-transverse-finger distance, outer side of the knees, between fibula and tibia, 1-transverse-finger distance beside the tibia

Indications: pain and numbness of lower limbs, stomach trouble, fatigue and marasmus

Yanglingquan [GB34]: located at the outer side of crus, the sunken place before the bottom of capitula fibula

Indications: limbs and knee diseases such as wilting and impediment of lower limbs, swelling of knees etc.

Sanyinjiao[SP6]: located at the inter side of crus, 3cun above the inner ankle, behind the inner side edge of tibia

Indications: abdominal pain, abdominal distention, diarrhea, Dysmenorrhea, Irregular Menstruation, spermatorrhea, enuresis, insomnia, neurasthenia

2.1.8 Ankle joint chiropractic

(1) Holding and shaking ankle joint

The patient with the affected right ankle lies in the bed on his back, with the ankle off the bed. Put one pillow under the knee to let the knee slightly bend, so that the curs and foot are in a relaxing state (Fig. 11-8-1).

(The chiropractor) Hold the heel of the patient with the palm and press the ankle with the thumb; and hold the sole with the other hand (Fig. 11-8-2). Stretch it and turn it along the facies articularis malleoli with slight forces of two hands in balance (Fig. 11-8-3).

Note: first turn in rings the affected side of the ankle and then treat it (Fig. 11-8-4, Fig. 11-8-5).

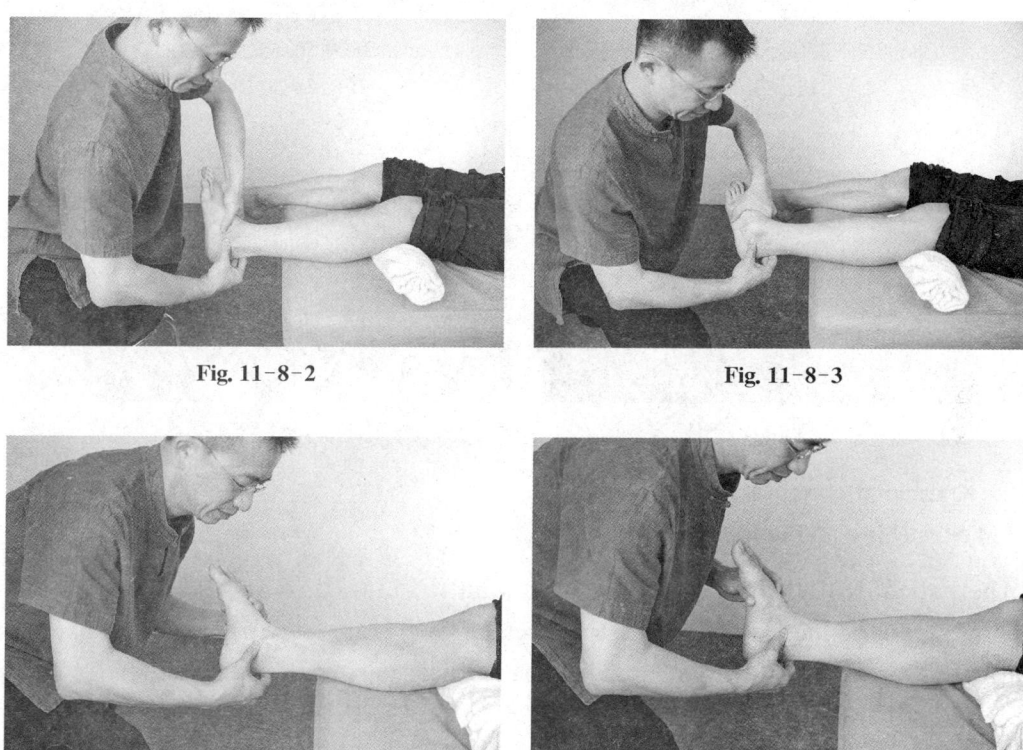

Fig. 11-8-2 Fig. 11-8-3

Fig. 11-8-4 Fig. 11-8-5

(2) Stretching ankle joint

The patient with the affected right ankle sits on a chair, with a support behind the knees or curs to make the legs relaxed. Or he can lie in the bed on his back. The chiropractor holds the affected heel of the patient with his left hand, and holds the sole of the affected foot with his right hand (Fig. 11-8-6).

(The chiropractor) Forcefully stretch and pull the ankle backward gradually with both hands to relax it. After the chiropractor shakes the ankle of the patient to make it relaxed, press the sole with the right hand to make the instep position of the foot stretch (Fig. 11-8-7). Pull the heel when the instep keeps stretched. At the same time bend the instep (Fig. 11-8-8). Finally loosen the force to return the instep to its original position.

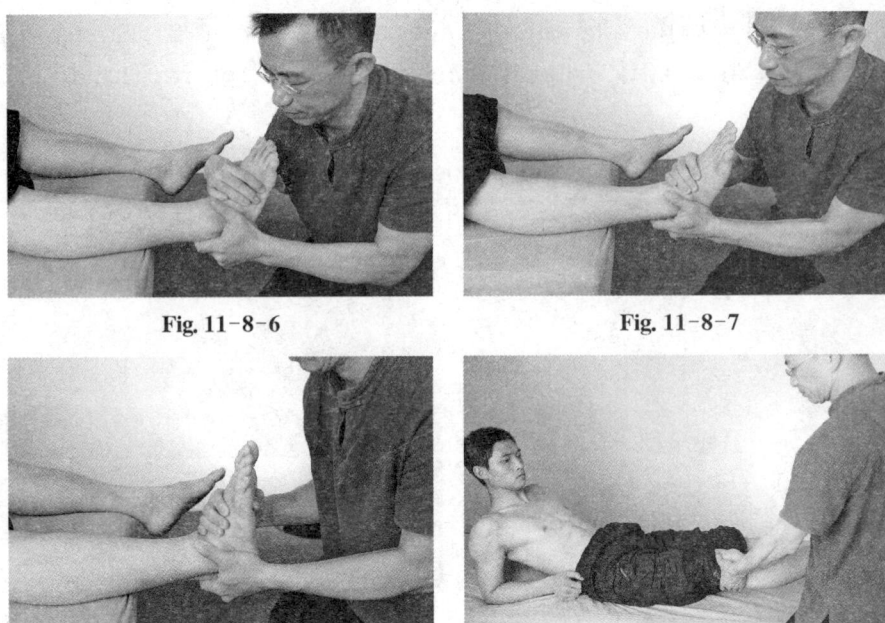

Fig. 11-8-6   Fig. 11-8-7

Fig. 11-8-8   Fig. 11-9-1

2.1.9 Knee joint chiropractic

(1) Stretching and holding

The patient with the affected right knee joint lies in the bed on his back and the chiropractor stands at the side of the affected leg. The chiropractor props up the patella of the affected leg with his left hand and holds the lower part of the curs of the affected leg with his right hand (Fig. 11-9-1).

Bend and stretch the knee joint to adjust the position of the patella. The adjustment includes:

Adjusting the patella upward:

If the patella of the affected leg is down, then the chiropractor adjusts it upward (Fig. 11-9-2): prop up the lower part of the patella with Hukou (Hegu) or thumb, stretch and pull the affected leg to make the knee bend and stretch. At the same time push the patella upward with Hugu or thumb to return it to the original position (Fig. 11-9-3).

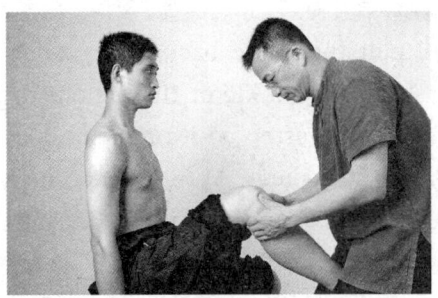

Fig. 11-9-2

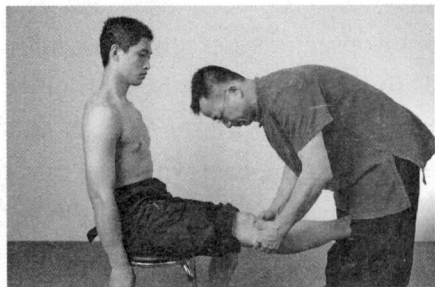

Fig. 11-9-3

Adjusting the patella downward:

If the patella of the affected leg is up, then the chiropractor adjusts it downward: prop up the upper part of the patella with the finger tip (Fig. 11-9-4) to stretch and pull the affected leg. At the same time push the patella downward with his finger tip to return it to the original position (Fig. 11-9-5).

Others: prop up the different parts of patella to adjust it on demand.

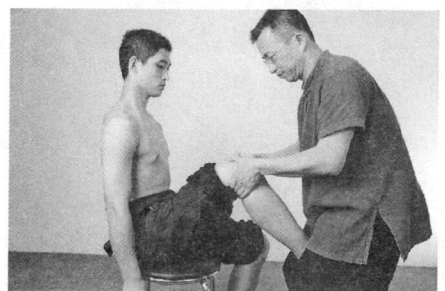 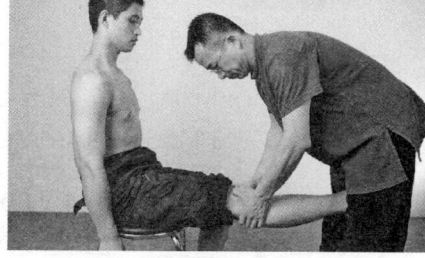

Fig. 11-9-4   Fig. 11-9-5

(2) Adjusting the upper part of fibula

The patient who has wrong with his fibula joint of the right knee, or has a moving upper part of the fibula head when pressing it, lies in bed on his back. And the chiropractor stands at the side of the affected foot of the patient.

(The chiropractor) Hold the affected foot with his left hand and place Hukou (Hegu) of his right hand on the knee of the affected leg (Fig. 11-9-6). Turn the ankle of the patient outward and press the upper part of the upper part of fibula head with the index finger and middle finger in order to fix it (Fig. 11-9-7). Stretch the right foot of the patient to make it straighten and bend for several times (Fig. 11-9-8).

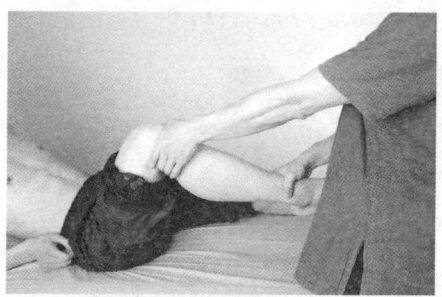 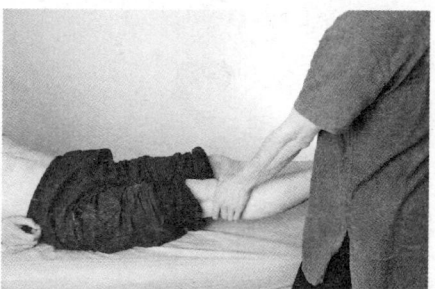

Fig. 11-9-6   Fig. 11-9-7

2.1.10 Hip joint chiropractic
(1) Turning and shaking

The patient who has something wrong with the right hip joint lie in bed on his back, and the chiropractor stands at the side of the patient's affected foot.

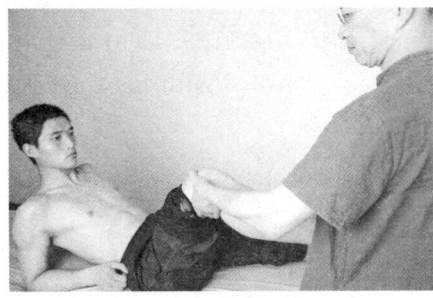 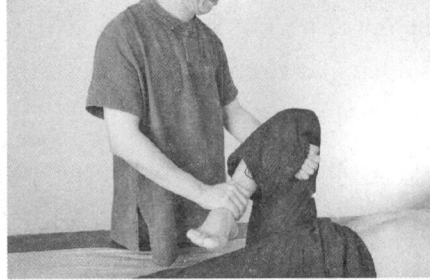

Fig. 11-9-8   Fig. 11-10-1

With the patient's right leg bent, the chiropractor holds the ankle of the affected leg with his right hand and places his left hand onto the knee.

Firstly, bend, straighten, withdraw inward and turn inward the hip joint to stretch the lateral muscle group in order for the caput femoris to leave the ilium (Fig. 11-10-1— Fig. 11-10-3). Then turn outward, stretch outward, straighten the joint to stretch the inside muscle group, so that the caput femoris can slide into the acetabulu (Fig. 11-10-4, Fig. 11-10-5). Repeat the movement several times to relax the soft tissue of the hip joint and thigh lateral muscle group.

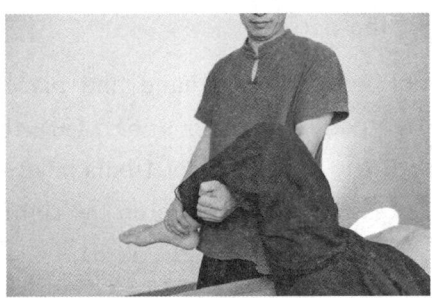 

Fig. 11-10-2   Fig. 11-10-3

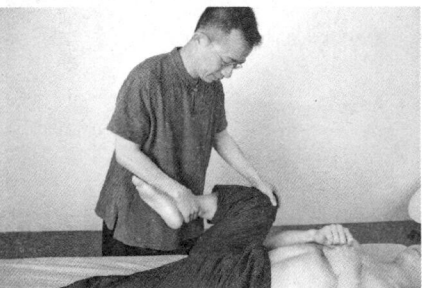 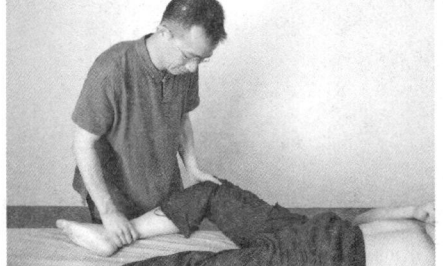

Fig. 11-10-4   Fig. 11-10-5

(2) Pressing and stretching

The patient who has something wrong with his right hip joint lies in bed on his back. And the chiropractor stands at the side of the patient's affected foot.

(The chiropractor) Turn the joint outward and stretch it outward without straightening and then place the ankle of the affected leg close onto the unaffected knee joint, near the thigh. Fix the unaffected hip bone with his right hand, press the affected knee with his left hand to stretch the medial vastus muscle, so that the caput femoris can slide into the acetabulum to return to its original position (Fig. 11-10-6).

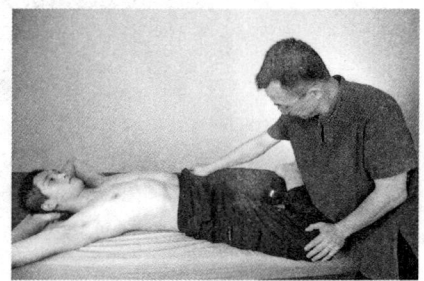

图 11-10-6 压伸手法

Or, in a slight rocking, press the knee joint and mdial vastus muscle repeatedly; meanwhile bend the hip to make the patient's affected ankle slide off the unaffected leg slowly. Gradually stretch the medial vastua muscle, so that the caput femoris slide into the acetablulum to return to its original position.

2.1.11 Trunk chiropractic

(1) Neck chiropractic

The patient lies on the back, while the chiropractor stands on the left.

Massaging the neck with thumbs: massage the muscles on the two sides and the ligamentum muchea with two thumbs through Fengchi, Jianjing, Fengfu, Dazhui repeatedly. First, massage the right side of neck with the right thumb, then the left side with the left thumb (Fig. 11-11-1).

Kneading the neck: knead the muscle group on two sides with 3 or 4 fingers of the right hand(Fig. 11-11-2).

Kneading the large tendon on two sides of the neck: knead the muscle fibers on two sides vertically with two thumbs by turns several times(Fig. 11-11-3).

Rubbing Fengchi and occipitalia: use the thumb and index finger of one hand or two thumbs to rub Fengchi pressure point, and then knead the occipitalias (Fig. 11-11-4).

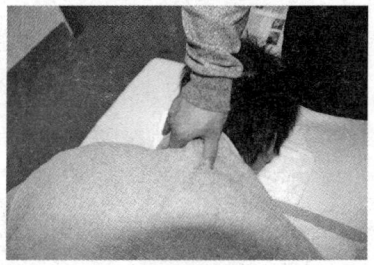 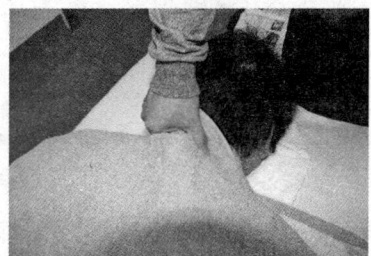

Fig. 11-11-1   Fig. 11-11-2

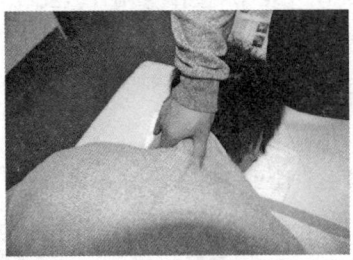
Fig. 11-11-3

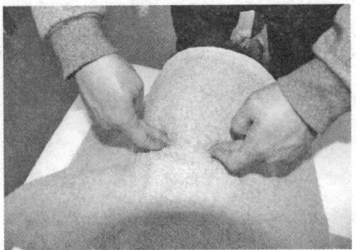
Fig. 11-11-4

Shoulders acupressure: press the 6 points of trapezius of supraspinous fossa from thoracic vertebra to the two sides with two thumbs (Fig. 11-11-5).

Kneading, rubbing and tapping Jianjing: knead trapezius of Jianjing on two sides with two hands (Fig. 11-11-6). Rub the Jianjing pressure points on two sides with two or three fingers of both hands (Fig. 11-11-7). Tap the upper shoulder blade and the muscles on two sides of the neck with two fists (Fig. 11-11-8).

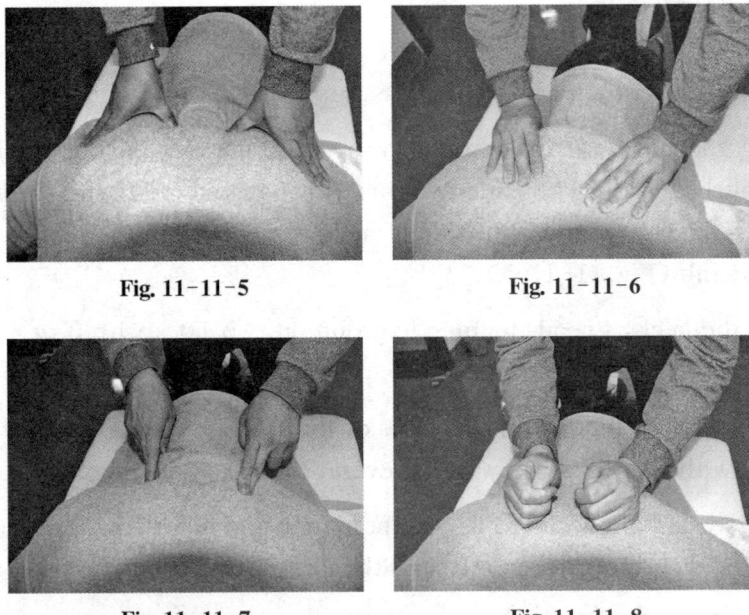

Fig. 11-11-5   Fig. 11-11-6

Fig. 11-11-7   Fig. 11-11-8

Pressure points and indications

Fengfu: 1cun up the mid-point of posterior hair line of the back neck, under the external occipital protuberance, in the sunken place between the two trapezius

Indications: headache, dizziness, stiff neck, stroke, epilepsy, sore throat, and aphonia

Dazhui: on the middle line of the back, in the sunken place below the spinous process of the seventh cervical vertebra

Indications: rigidity of nape and headache, pyreticosis, cough, asthma, shoulder muscle spasm, cervical spondylosis, stiff neck, cold, etc.

Fengchi [GB20]: on the back neck, parallel to Fengfu, in the sunken place between sternocleidomastoid and top of trapezius

Indications: stiff neck, scapulohumeral periarthritis, sequela of apoplexy, heel pain

(2) The lower back chiropractic

The patient is lying on the stomach while the chiropractor is standing on the left.

Pressing the shoulder, hip and spine: put the two palms on the upper back and ilium, and press them down outward simultaneously. Press the back and waist with the same strength to the two sides (Fig. 11-11-9). Press down the sacrum with the right hand and the upper spine with the left hand; press the spine several times to the two sides several times (Fig. 11-11-10).

Rubbing the waist with palm: put one hand on the other hand, press and rub the erectorspinae of spine together. Do it on the each side of the spine from up to down along the spine for several times (Fig. 11-11-11).

Rubbing Huatuo Jiaji (Ex-B2) and bladder meridian: rub Huatuo Jiaji (Ex-B2) and bladder meridian on the two sides of the spine with one or two thumbs. Do it from up to down at the 0.5cun away from spine (the middle line) first, then 1.5cun and then 3cun from spine (Fig. 11-11-12).

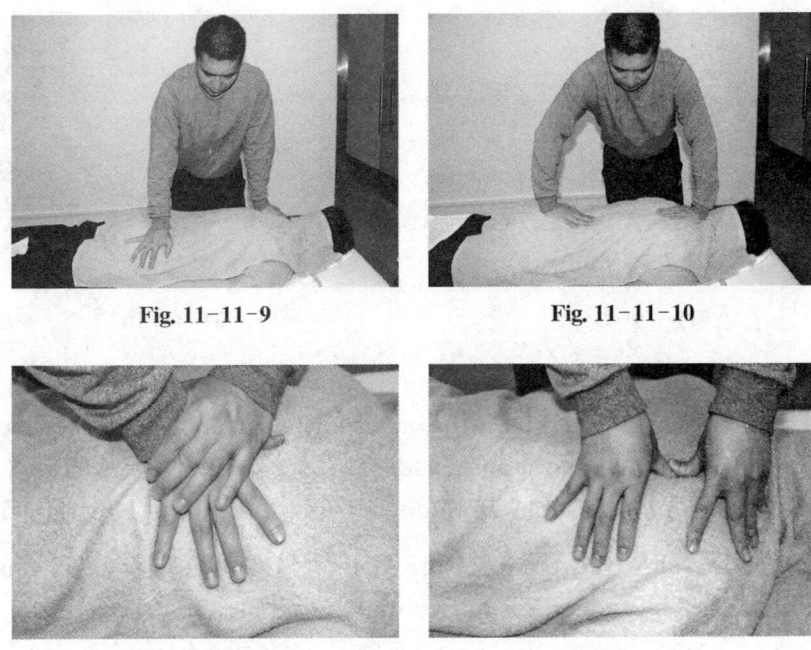

Fig. 11-11-9   Fig. 11-11-10

Fig. 11-11-11   Fig. 11-11-12

Pressing the waist with palm: put the bottom of palms together, and press the back and waist on the two sides along the spine from up to down (Fig. 11-11-13).

Pressing Huatuo Jiaji (Ex-B2) and bladder meridian with fingers: press Huatuo Jiaji (Ex-B2) and bladder meridian on the two sides of the spine with thumbs of two hands simultaneously. Do it from up to down on Jiaji (Ex-B2) first, then the first side line of meridian and then the second line of meridian (Fig. 11-11-14).

Pressing spine with palms: put one hand onto the other and press thoracic vertebra, lumbar vertebra and sacral vertebrae (Fig. 11-11-15).

Scratching Huatuo Jiaji pressure point (Ex-B2) and bladder meridian on the back: scratch Huatuo Jiaji point (Ex-B2) and bladder meridian on the back with thumbs, elbow tip, and etc. Do it from up to down on Jiaji (Ex-B2) first, followed by the first side line of meridian and the second line of meridian (Fig. 11-11-16).

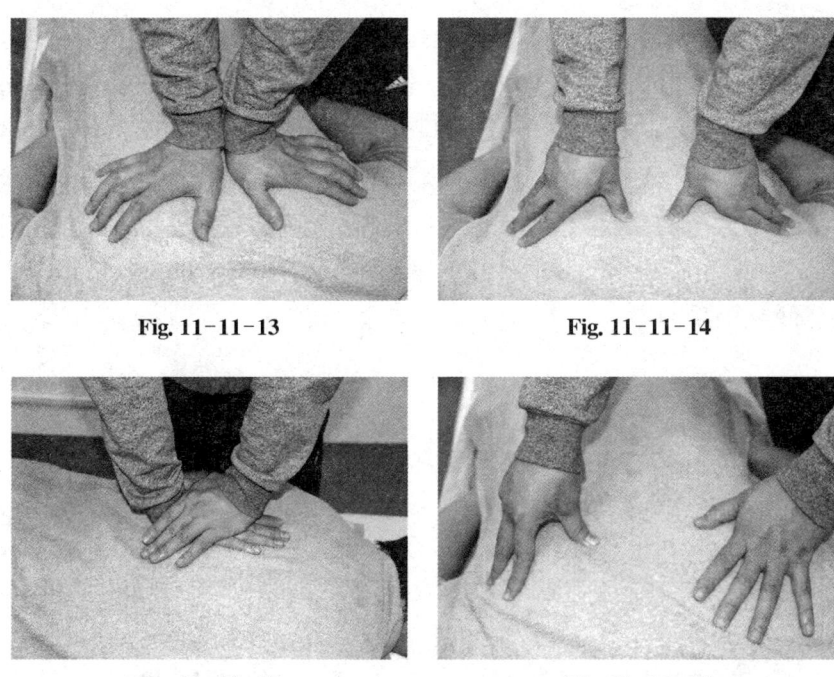

Fig. 11-11-13 Fig. 11-11-14

Fig. 11-11-15 Fig. 11-11-16

Pushing the lower back with palms and Jiaji pressure point (Ex-B2) with elbow: put one hand on the upper spine, and push the governor meridian and bladder meridian with the end of palm of another hand from up to down for several times (Fig. 11-11-17). Push Jiaji (Ex-B2) with elbow from up to down for several times (Fig. 11-11-18).

Rubbing the sacrum: rub the pressure points Mingmen (GV4), Yangguan, and Baliaozhu around the hip with palms horizontally (Fig. 11-11-19).

Knocking the back: change both hands into fists and knock the back up and down for several times (Fig. 11-11-20).

Patting the lower back with palms: pat the back up and down with two palms for several times(Fig. 11-11-21).

Rubbing the waist: grasp the two sides of waist with two hands and rub the waist up and down with force(Fig. 11-11-22).

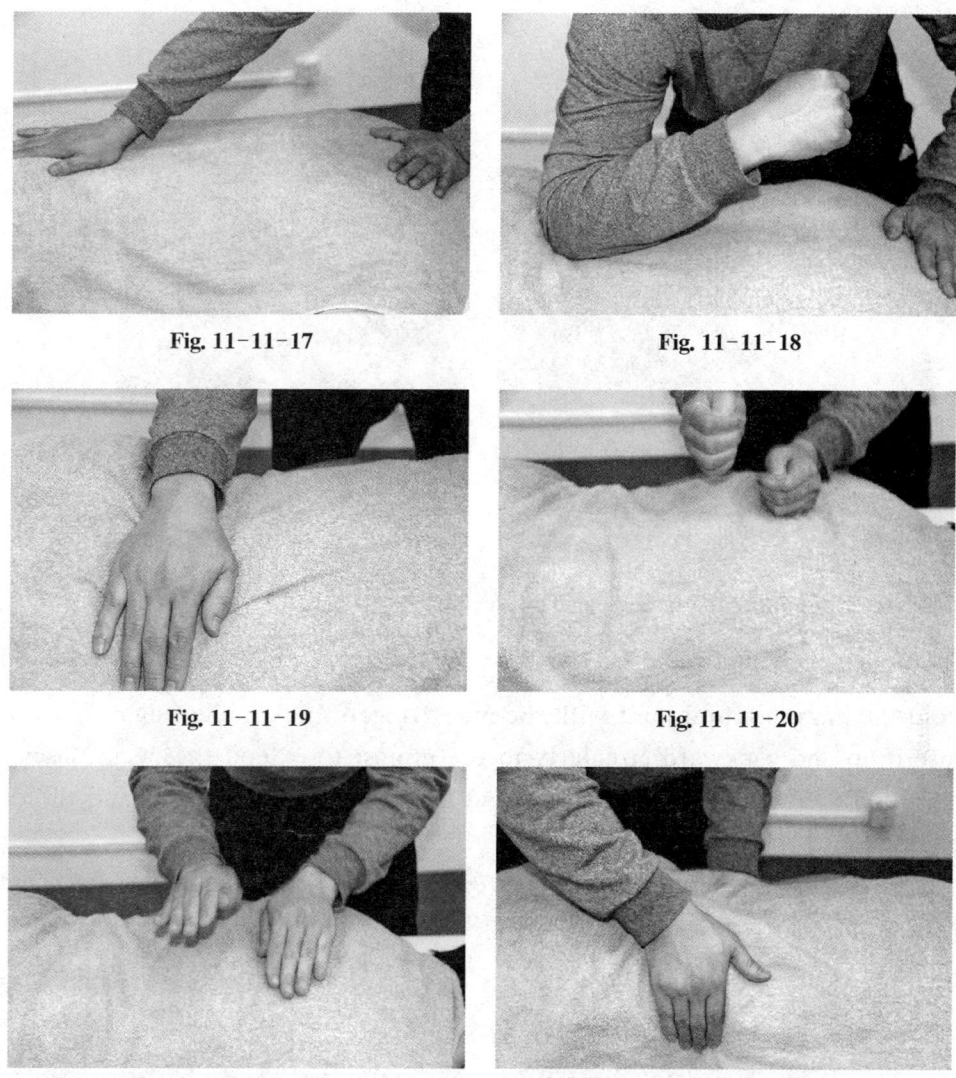

Fig. 11-11-17

Fig. 11-11-18

Fig. 11-11-19

Fig. 11-11-20

Fig. 11-11-21

Fig. 11-11-22

2.1.12 Neck chiropractic

(1) **Shaking the neck**

The patient is sitting on a bench, while the chiropractor is standing on his back with one hand on the back of head of the patient and the other supporting the lower jaw of the patient.

Move the patient's head clockwise and anticlockwise several times with two arms to help the neck relax. If the patient cannot move forward, stretch his head backward first and shake it(Fig. 11-12-1). Move his head to the forward position while shaking it. Afterwards, move the head forward and shake it (Fig. 11-12-2) and vise versa.

If the patient cannot move to the left, turn his head rightward first and shake it. Then turn his head leftward and shake and vise versa. Shake the head in four different directions.

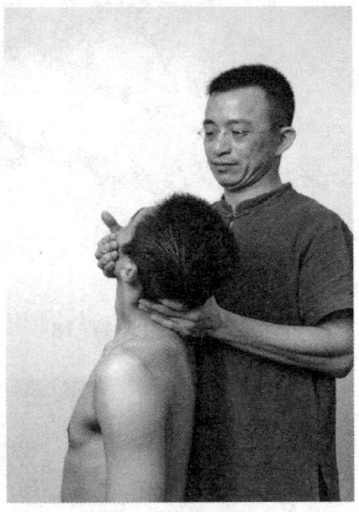
Fig. 11-12-1

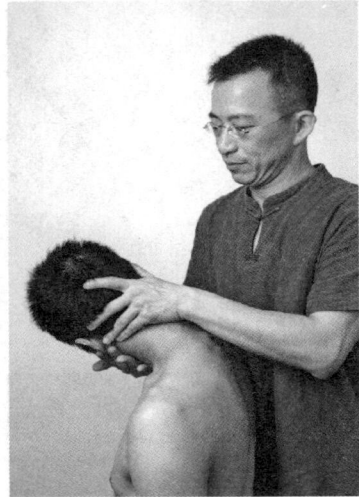
Fig. 11-12-2

(2) Stretching and raising the cervical vertebra

The patient is lying on the back, while the chiropractor is standing beside him.

Hold the intervertebral joint with the index fingers and middle fingers of two hands and raise it up and backward circularly to the utmost to extend the neck muscle group (Fig. 11-12-3). Twist the joint forward and backward for adjustment and the embolia of the joints.

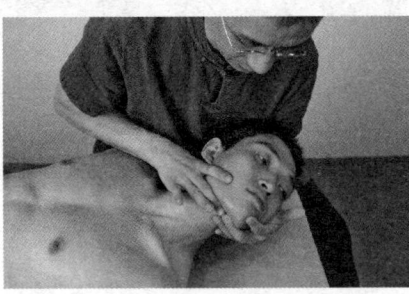
Fig. 11-12-3

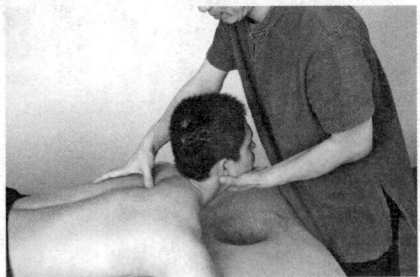
Fig. 11-13-1

2.1.13 Chest chiropractic

(1) Pressing the two sides of neck:

The patient who has the muscle group tension of upper thoracic and neck, or/and the derangement of the upper thoracic vertebra small joints is lying on the stomach, while the chiropractor is standing beside him.

Press the affected muscle nodule with the right hand and raise the patient's jaw with the left hand to the utmost (Fig. 11-13-1). Shake the patient's head to the right side with his left cheek on the bed when the patient breathes to relax. Please note that it is the cheek not the side of the head that attaches the bed (Fig. 11-13-2). Fix the left palm onto the right ear of the patient, press the affected muscle nodule with the right hand forcefully (Fig. 11-13-3). It is suggested to extend the healthy side first, then the affected side.

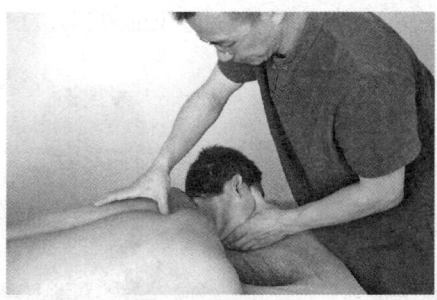
Fig. 11-13-2

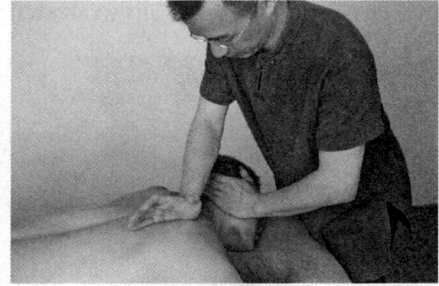
Fig. 11-13-3

(2) **Raising chest**

The patient with the derangement of the sternal rib small joints is sitting on the bed with two legs straight, holding the back of the neck with ten fingers crossed. The chiropractor is squatting at the back of the patient with one knee knelt (Fig. 11-13-4).

Stretch the two hands through the place between the patient's upper arms and forearms to hold his shoulder blade, then support the patient's back thoracic vertebra with the knelt knees of the chiropractor to let the patient lie on his thigh (Fig. 1-13-5); Wait till the patient exhales to relax, raise his chest with force to stretch the chest and adjust the sterna rib joints.

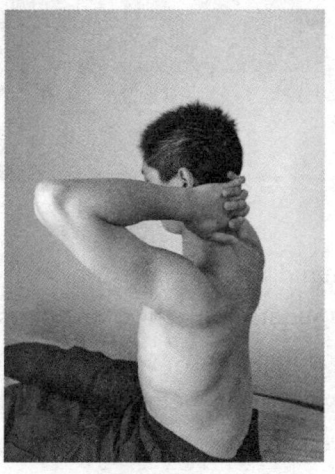
Fig. 11-13-4

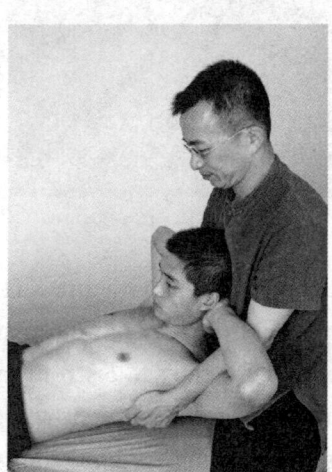
Fig. 11-13-5

2.1.14 Waist chiropractic

(1) Stretching waist

The patient with the affected left waist is lying on the back with his left leg bent and right leg straight. The chiropractor is standing on his right (Fig. 11-14-1).

The patient lies on the right side with his right hand outside the reduction bed.

(The chiropractor) Pull the patient's right hand with his left hand, press the patient's left leg with the right leg, fix the patient's left buttocks with the inner side of the right forearm and locate the right hand on the diseased side of the patient. Drag the patient's right hand, push the patient's left leg and fix the hip to stretch the diseased side of the waist (Fig. 11-14-2).

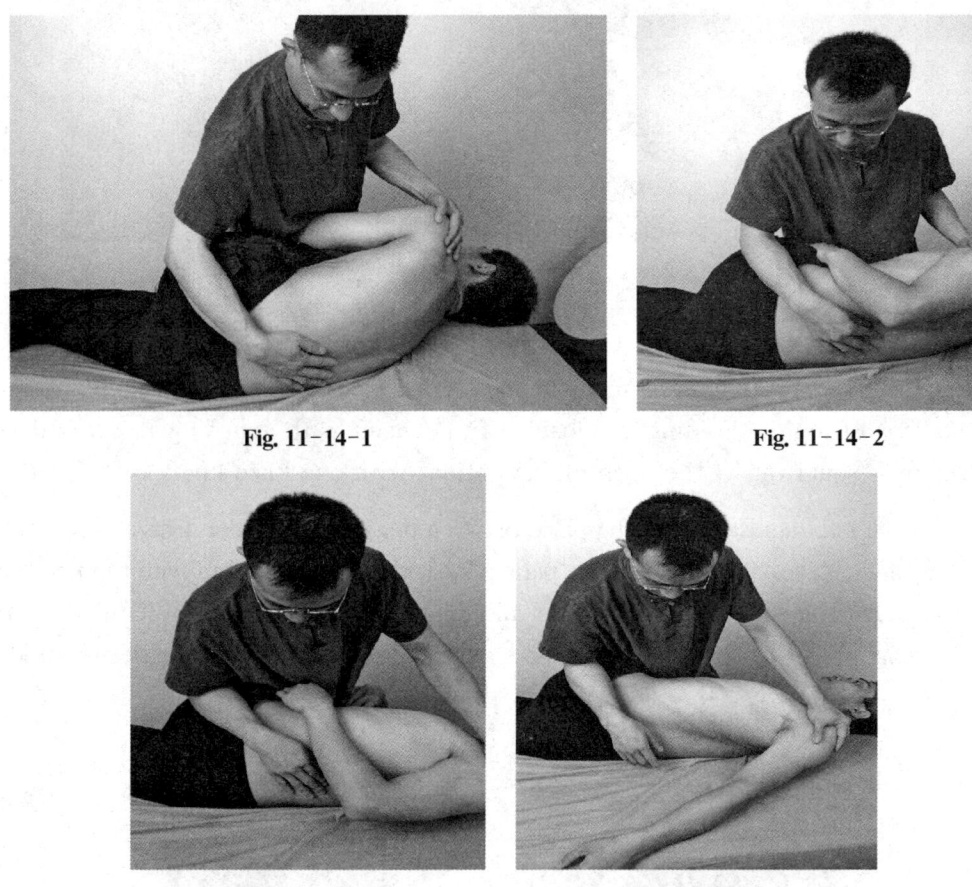

Fig. 11-14-1 Fig. 11-14-2

Fig. 11-14-3 Fig. 11-14-4

Fix the patient's shoulder with the left hand and the left hip with the inner side of the right forearm. Put the right palm on the junction of chest and waist (Fig. 11-14-3). Then shake the body with the same strength of two hands to relax the lumbar vertebra of the patient. Remove the right hand slowly away from the lumbar vertebra while shaking the body. During the shaking, extend the two sides of waist to the utmost by pushing the shoulder with the left hand, bending the buttocks with the forearm of the right hand

(Fig. 11-14-5). Guide the patient to exhale to relax and when the patient is relaxed, extend his waist in the opposite direction to stretch the muscle with two hands forcefully, thus to restore the lumbar vertebra to its original position (Fig. 11-14-6).

It is suggested to extend the healthy side first, then the diseased side.

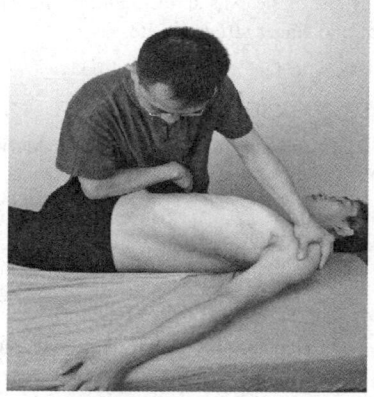

Fig. 11-14-5

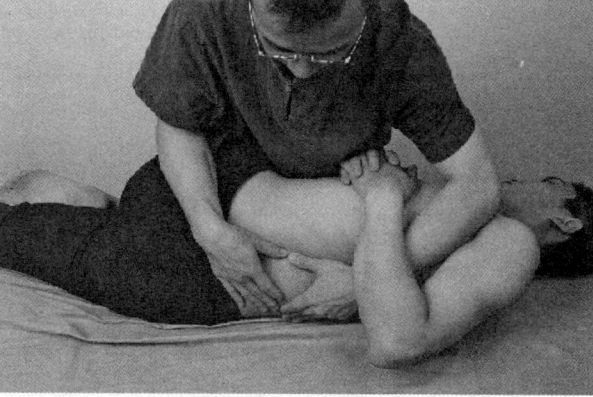

Fig. 11-14-6

(2) Stretching lumbar vertebra backward

The patient with the affected left waist is lying on the stomach with legs straight. The chiropractor is standing on his left side (the diseased side).

Fix the left side of the lumbar vertebra with the left palm. Hold and raise the right thigh from the inner side of the thigh with the right hand. Fix the left hand and bend the waist to the left with the right hand to adjust the lumbar vertebra (Fig. 11-14-7, 11-14-8)

It is suggested to treat the healthy side first, then the diseased side.

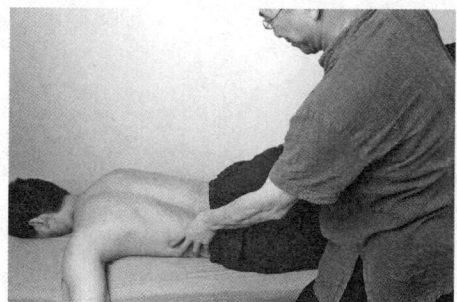

Fig. 11-14-7

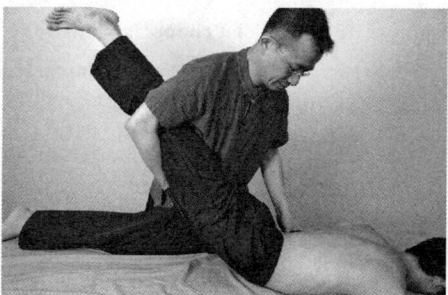

Fig. 11-14-8

2.1.15 The whole body chiropractic procedure

Relax the shoulder and upper limb (sitting position) →upper body chiropractic: adjust the shoulder, elbow and wrist (sitting) →relax the neck (lying on the stomach) → relax the lower back (lying on the stomach) →relax the bottom part of lower limbs (lying on the stomach) →relax the top part of lower limbs (lying on the back) →lower limbs chiropractic: adjust foot, knee and hip (lying on the back) →trunk chiropractic:

adjust chest, waist and neck (lying on the back)

2.2 Learning program

Category	Content
preparations	The preparations for learning wushu chriopractic needs the basic wushu techniques, the Health Qigong techniques, the knowledge about pressure points, and finger strength, etc. 1. The basic wushu techniques: the ability to exert the force, to feel and to control body 2. The Health Qigong techniques: the ability to feel the body and the ability to control 3. The knowledge about pressure points: the location of pressure points, the direction of Meridians and the position of muscles 4. Strength: finger strength, palm strength and gripping power

Learning schedule	1. Learning sequence
	(1) Learning basic skills, including massage, patting, shaking, waving and bending, etc.
	(2) Learning the location of pressure points, direction of meridians, the structure of body, such as Jianjing, Weizhong, bladder meridian, iliopsoas, femoral fascia, etc.
	(3) Learning the operational program of relaxing different parts of body, such as shoulder, upper limb, rear of the lower limb, top of the lower limb, etc.
	(4) Learning the chiropractic skills of different parts of body, including the skills of extending chest and arms, adjustment skills of high-low shoulders, the skills of pressing the two sides of chest, raising chest and adjusting it, etc.
	2. Teaching arrangement: this course contains 20-time learning, 3 periods each time, 45 minutes for each period.
	  1. Introduction to the chiropractic course
	  2. Basic relaxation techniques
	  3. Upper limb relaxation
	  4. Shoulder joint chiropractic
	  5. Elbow joint chiropractic
	  6. Wrist joint chiropractic
	  7. Practice of upper limb chiropractic
	  8. Lower limb relaxation
	  9. Ankle chiropractic
	  10. Knee chiropractic
	  11. Hip chiropractic
	  12. Practice of upper limb chiropractic
	  13. Trunk relaxation
	  14. Neck chiropractic
	  15. Chest chiropractic
	  16. Waist chiropractic
	  17. Practice of trunk chiropractic
	  18. Body relaxation and chiropractic
	  19. Practice ofbody relaxation and chiropractic
	  20. Evaluation

2.3 Technique experience

content	requirements
Technique requirements	1. The actions should be rhythmic. 2. The palm should cling to the skin. The strength should be used smoothly and the movement of the palm should be slow and even. The acting point should be fixed with the strength from light to strong. The movement should be slow. 3. Please note the correlation between the relaxation of shoulder, elbow and wrist, and the penetrating of the strength into them while patting. 4. Please note the correlation between the tightnessand looseness of body and the range & frequency while shaking. 5. Please note that shoulder should be sunk, elbow drooped, wrist hung, palm empty and fingers forceful when using the Pushing Manipulation with One-finger skill. 6. Rubbing should be quick and moving should be slow. 7. You should feel the springing when flipping the tendons without any friction on the skin. The pressure should be decided by the situation and tolerance of the patient. 8. The diseased position where it isn't covered by muscles is vulnerable and the strength used in these positions should be controlled. 9. The strength on popliteal fossa and the back of curs should be gentle. 10. The massage should avoid the sensitive part of the upper part of the inner side of thigh. 11. The movement of pressing the patella should be gentle and agile with the strength from light to strong. Violent strength should be avoided. Make the movement of patella gradually increasing. 12. The frequency of shaking the lower limbs should be a little lower than that of shaking the upper limb. The amplitude should be a little larger. 13. Bending movement should avoid violent strength. The main point of this skill is to relax the muscles and joints by waving, more extension and less twist. If the patient cannot bear the ache, the treatment should be stopped. 14. During the adjustment, force exertion should be short, clear-cut and strong. Otherwise you could only stretch the muscles, not open the joint space.
Regulations	1. Pushing manipulation: during the pushing, you should pay attention to the changes of the muscle strength to see if there are nodules. The strength should be equal and be able to press the tense muscle. 2. Grabbing manipulation: pay attention to the texture of diseased position to see if there are nodules with strips of muscle together. The strength should be in symmetry and the strips of muscle should be tightly pressed. 3. Feel the change of the strength caused by the change of the weight when rubbing. 4. Rolling Manipulation: feel the pressure when bending upper body forward and sinking shoulder and elbow. 5. Stretching Manipulation: feel the extension of the muscle and the openness of the joint space on diseased position. 6. Shaking and Bending Manipulation: feel the binding situation of the muscle when the joint is in different angles. Try to find the physiological limit of the patient's muscle and joint.

(continued)

content	requirements
Movement coordination	1. Pressing Manipulation: the pressing process should be coordinated with the breath of the patient with the gradually strong strength. Please pay attention to the change of the muscle tense on the diseased position and adjust the strength and position of massage. The strength should be pressed onto the tensed muscle. 2. Rubbing manipulation: the combination of pressing and rubbing, together with the coordination of the patient's breath is important. The rubbing point should be on the tensed muscle. 3. When rubbing the back with palm, you should make the patient's body move together with the palm, which is good to relax the body. 4. Keep the arm straight when pressing the back with fingers or palms. First, move the weight from fingers to the palms, and then move along. The first pressing should be light to help the patient get use to the strength and rhythm. 5. When rubbing the pressure point, make the patient feel the sore and swelling pain. When exerting force, do it with the strength from light to strong, then from strong to light. 6. The reduction skills have to be coordinated with the patient's breath. Only when the patient exhales out and relaxes the shoulder, back and waist, could the adjustment be done.
Sequences	1. The whole process should be as the following order to get the best effect: relaxation, adjustment, then relaxation again. 2. The order of relaxation should be shoulder, upper limb, neck, chest, waist, and then legs. 3. The order of chiropractic should be upper limb first, lower limbs and trunk.

3 Conclusion

1. Wushu chiropractic is the body adjustment done by wushu experts. It should be based on the wushu basic skills. The main method is the treatment by hand, combined with Health Qigong. It will help in body adjustment and the treatment of the body disorder.

2. The basic skills of wushu chiropractic include the wushu strength, movement control, feeling, etc. The chiropractor should learn the methods including muscular fasciae relaxation and joint adjustment, etc.; and understand the correlation between Qigong movements and body actions. They should also master the adjustment of imbalance of motor system, including shoulder, elbow, wrist, hip, knee, foot, neck, chest and waist, etc.

3. The basic skills in chiropractic are push, grab, press, rub, pat, shake, wave and bend. These skills are used in different parts of body adjustment in different sequences.

4. Learning wushu chiropractic needs to master the knowledge on pressure point and the body structure.

4 Extensive reading

1. Wushu chiropractic is based on the force exertion of wushu. The leaner have to

learn the force exertion skills from different Chinese fist plays such as Nanquan. For instant, the flexible use of the force exertion from waist, which is helpful to stretch the joints effectively in the short distance in the same angle, open the joints and extend the limited muscular fasciae.

2. The body posture of wushu chiropractic is the same as that in wushu. The learner should learn to adjust himself to the state of sinking shoulder and drooping elbow, relaxing waist and hip, raising head straight while lowering body weight, as he does in Taijiquan practice.

3. The target of wushu chiropractic is to adjust the body to the original and natural state. So the learner have to master the anatomy knowledge, be able to understand the body structure and function through wushu and Qigong practice and improve the awareness of the dynamic condition of the patient's body.

4. You could learn more about chiropractic or some massagist textbook (for the massagist documents), or read some materials about the body work and somatics after finishing this course.

5 Questions

(1) What are the relaxation skills in wushu chiropractic?

(2) What is the relaxation operational process of the upper limbs? How to relax the lower limbs and trunk?

(3) How do you do the chiropractic on shoulder joint, wrist joint, ankle joint and neck joint?

6 References

[1] Feldenkrais, M. Awareness Through Movement: Health Exercises for Personal Growh [M]. Taipei: Shimao Publish House, 1998.

[2] Feldenkrais, M. The Potent Self: A Guide to Spontaneity [M]. Taipei: Shimao Publish House, 1998.

[3] Knaster. M. Physical therapy Encyclopedia [M]. Taipei: Life Potential Publishing House, 1999.

[4] Marian Wolfe Dixon, Myofascial Massage [M]. Tianjin: Tianjin Science & Technology Translation & Publishing Corp, 2008.

[5] James. H. Cline, Dave. M. Pounds. Basic Clinic Therapy Massage: Integrating Anatomy and Treatment [M]. Tianjin: Tianjin Science & Technology Translation & Publishing Corp, 2006.

[6] Mary. B. Brown, Stiphen. J. Simenson. Introduction to Massage Therapy [M]. Tianjin: Tianjin

Science & Technology Translation & Publishing Corp, 2006.

[7] Li Zhiming. On Physical and Mind Chiropractic by Wushu [D]. Nanjing University of Traditional Chinese Medicine (Unpublished), 2009.

[8] Li Zhiming. Somatic Education Perspectives of Sun Lu-Tang's Chinese Martial Arts Study [M]. Taipei: Ahan Cultural Ltd, 2003.

[9] Zhou Xinwen, Zhou Zhemin. Massage Therapist (Intermediate) (the second version) [M]. Shanghai: Chinese Labor & Social Security Publishing House, 2009.

[10] Zhou Xinwen, Zhou Zhemin. Massage Therapist (Elementary) (the second version) [M]. Shanghai: Chinese Labor & Social Security Publishing House, 2010.

[11] Jin Hongzhu. Basics for Science of Chinese Massage [M]. Shanghai: Shanghai University of Traditional Chinese Medicine, 2000.

[12] Xiao Tianshi. Combined Issue of Authentic Muscle Change Classic and Unique Cope of Mind Clearance Classic [M]. Taipei: Free Press, 1992.

[13] Wang Zhen, Li Zhimin. Wushu Chiropractics [M]. Shanghai: Fudan University Publishing House, 2012.

Chapter Twelve

Nanshi

1 Introduction

Nanshi (Southern Lion Dance, the same as below) is a Lion Dance style originated from the southern China. Integrating music, dance, knitting, embroidery and painting, this dance style is played by two dancers to imitate the lion's airs and behaviors. The two main schools of this style are Fuoshan Lion Dance and Heshan Lion Dance.

The origin of Lion Dance

The lion didn't exist in ancient China. It came from the west Asia and the middle Asia through the Silk Road as a present from the foreign envoys. Since Zhang Qian went to Western Regions and built the international contacts for the Han Dynasty, it's the first time for the lion to get into China. The original lion dance is to simply imitate the lion with the Quizi music to express people's worship to this king of animal. The golden age for the Lion Dance in Central China is Tang Dynasty.

The development of Lion Dance

Lion Dance originated from people's daily life. In 1994, Dragon & Lion Dance was certificated as a sports competition by the former National Physical Culture and Sports Commission. In 1995, China Dragon & Lion Sport Association was established. In July, 1997, the Executive Committee Meeting and Congress Meeting of IDLDF were held in Malaysia, where the official decision to move the EC Secretariat to Beijing was made. In the IDLDF Congress meeting in Indonesia in December, 2006, IDLDF changed its name to International Dragon & Lion Sports Federation (IDLSF). Up to now, the number of associations in IDLSF has been up to 26 countries and regions. Also the continental unions were established in Asia, Europe and America.

2 Learning experience

2.1 Instructions

2.1.1 How to grip the lion

(1) Two-hand Gripping with the palms of hands facing up: Hold the connection

part of the lion's mouth on two sides of the lion's head with the Hukou (the part between the thumb and index finger, the same as below) of two hands, the palms of hands facing up and the rest four fingers under the lion's mouth (Fig. 12-1).

(2) Two-hand Gripping with the palms of hands facing down: Hold the connection part of the lion's mouth on two sides of the lion's head with the Hukou of two hands, the palms of two hands facing down. Hold the top of the mouth of the lion with the index finger and the other three under the mouth (Fig. 12-2).

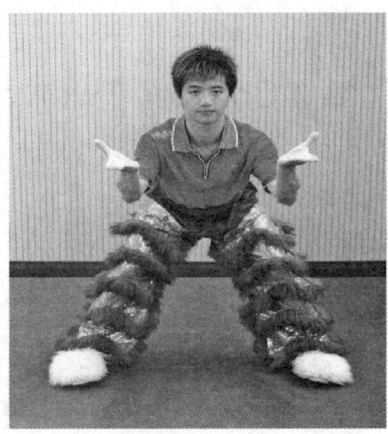

Fig. 12-1

(3) Single-hand Gripping: Grip the mid-part of the mouth connection with one hand, the palm of hand facing up or down and the thumb apart with the rest four (Fig. 12-3).

(4) Fore-and-back Gripping: Grip one end of the mouth connection with one hand, the palm of hand facing up; grip the cross frame inside the lion's head with another hand (Fig. 12-4).

(5) Single-hand Gripping with the palm of hand facing up: Hold the mid-part of the mouth connection with one hand, the palm of hand facing up and the thumb apart with the rest four (Fig. 12-5).

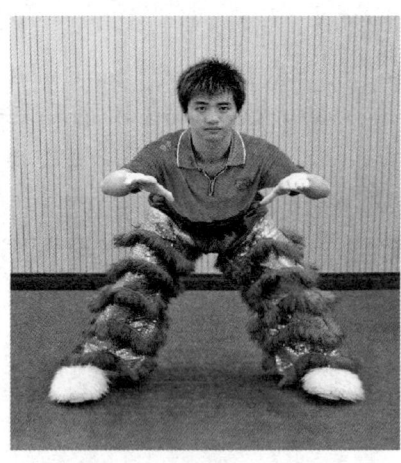 

Fig. 12-2 Fig. 12-3

2.1.2 Ready position

Keep the elbow, waist and knee bending (three bending positions) (Fig. 12-1).

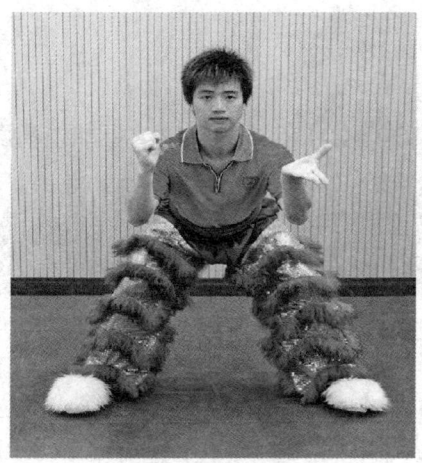

Fig. 12-4   Fig. 12-5

2.1.3 Standing stance

(1) Hand-lifting-up Standing (open stance, horse stance, bow stance, empty stance): Grip the pole inside the lion head with one hand and grip the mouth connection with the other hand, the palm of hand facing up. When the lion mouth is closed, lift the hands up to 45 degrees, the lion head separated from the body. Keep the mouth as high as the player's forehead. The player should use the strength of wrist to twist the head quickly and shortly (Fig. 12-6).

(2) Bending-forward Standing (open stance, horse stance, bow stance, empty stance and left-right Qilin stance, etc.): Hold the lion mouth connection using Two-hand Gripping with the palms of hands facing up or Two-hand Gripping with the palms of hands facing down and bring the back of hands close to the sponge protection cushion inside the lion head. Then hold the lion head with both arms as if holding a ball, and bend the body forward to about 40 degree (Fig. 12-7).

(3) Crouching Standing (open stance, horse stance, bow stance, horse stance on the knee, crouching stance, etc.): The two players stand in the crouching stance and move the head forward and backward in the leg direction (Fig. 12-8).

2.1.4 Footwork

(1) Horse Stance: Stand in horse stance with two legs apart to about three and a half feet wide. Bend two knees to 135 degrees with the body forward to around 40 degrees. Raise the head up with chest out (Fig. 12-9).

(2) Bow stance: Stand with one leg forward and the other backward. Bend the frond knee to 135 degrees and straighten the rear leg with the sole onto the ground. Incline the body forward to around 40 degrees and raise the head up with the chest out (Fig. 12-10).

Fig. 12-6　　　　　　　Fig. 12-7　　　　　　　Fig. 12-8

(3) Crouching stance: Stand with two legs apart and fully bend the supporting leg. Put the hip close to the supporting leg and straighten the front leg straight with the sole onto the ground. Incline the body forward to 40 degrees and raise the head up with the chest out (Fig. 12-11).

(4) Standing on one leg: Stand on one straight leg and bend the other leg to 90 degrees parallel to the waist. Incline the body forward to 40 degrees and raise head up with the chest out (Fig. 12-12).

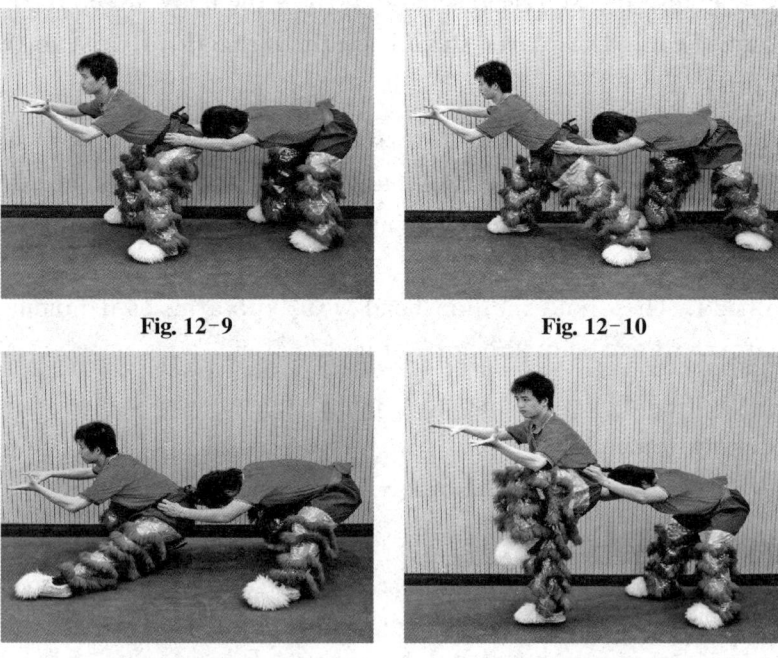

Fig. 12-9　　　　　　　Fig. 12-10

Fig. 12-11　　　　　　　Fig. 12-12

(5) Kneeling stance: Bend the frond leg and kneel to the ground. Stand with the rear leg bent 90 degrees onto the ground, incline the body forward to 40 degrees and raise the head up with the chest out (Fig. 12-13).

(6) Empty stance: Stand with two legs forward and backward apart. Bend the back supporting leg to 135 degrees and bring the front leg one-foot width in front of the rear leg with the knee bent to 135 degrees and the weight on the rear supporting leg. Incline the body forward to 40 degree and raise the head up with the chest out (Fig. 12-14).

(7) Qilin stance: Bend the frond leg onto the ground and stand with the rear leg bent 90 degrees. Incline the body forward to 40 degrees and raise the head up with the chest out (Fig. 12-15).

(8) Cross stance: Stand with two legs crossed. Bend the frond leg to about 50 degrees while straightening the rear leg with the tiptoes facing forward. Incline the body to 40 degrees and raise the head up with the chest out (Fig. 12-16).

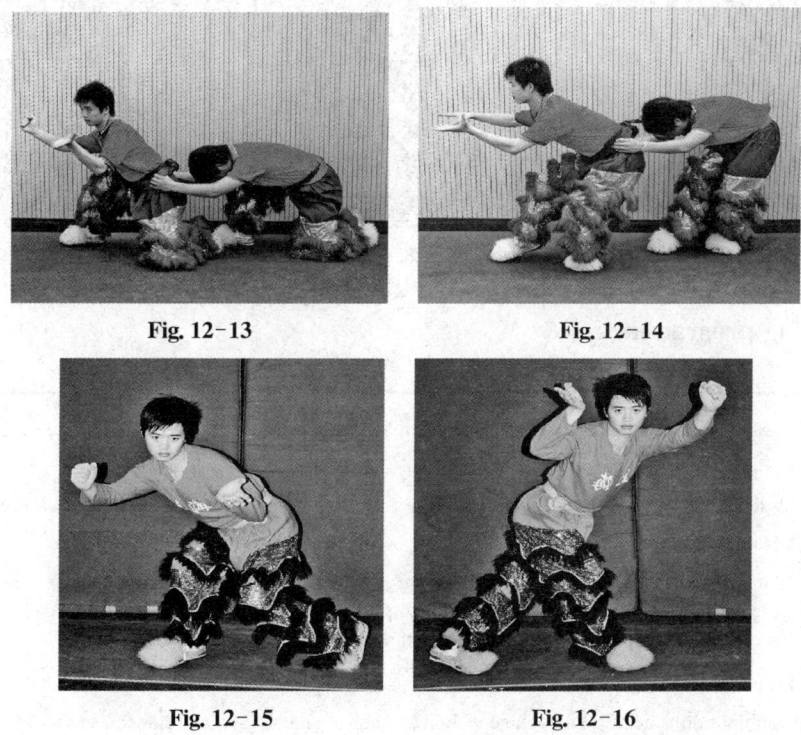

Fig. 12-13　　　　　　　　Fig. 12-14

Fig. 12-15　　　　　　　　Fig. 12-16

2.1.5　Movement coordination

(1) One leg coordination: The tail player grips the head player's belt and rises in a bow stance. The head player jumps up by one leg with the abdomen in and then land the leg to the connection of the tail player's hip joint and thigh with the sole turning outward. Raise the suspended leg up. The head player should raise his hands up and keep the trunk straight (Fig. 12-17).

(2) Two legs coordination: The head player jumps up to the connection of the tail player's hip joint and thigh with the abdomen in with the soles turning outward or inward and raise both hands up. The tail player should hold the head player by the belt in

a horse stance with the body straight (Fig. 12-18).

(3) The head coordination: The tail player rises up with both legs apart, holding the head player by the belt. The head player jumps up and drops onto the tail player's head with the suspended leg bent. The head player should lift up the hands with the trunk straight (Fig. 12-19).

Fig. 12-17　　　　　　　　　Fig. 12-18　　　　　　　　　Fig. 12-19

2.2　Learning programme

Items	Content
Preparation	**1. Basic skills** Flexibility of body; strength of arms, waist and legs; body coordination and the sense of rhythm **2. Basic footwork** salute stance, moving-twice stance, horse stance, bow stance, open-and-close stance, crouching stance, Qilin stance, kneeling stance, empty stance, independent stance, trotting stance, cross stance, leap stance, standing-on-one-leg stance, jump stance, etc.
Study schedule	**1. movement combination** Combination one: salute stance—horse stance—moving-twice stance—cross stance—crouching stance. Combination two: Qilin stance—leap stance—jump stance—empty stance. Combination three: independent stance—standing-on-one-leg stance—kneeling stance—trotting stance. Combination four: open-and-close stance—one leg coordination—two legs coordination—head coordination. **2. learning stages** Stage one: to learn the gripping methods, standing stance and footwork Stage two: to master the specific professional quality, coordinated movements, rhythm Stage three: to master the footwork route, performance skills

2.3 Technique experience

Content	Requirements
Movement standard	To keep the three bending positions, improve the movement quality and professional skills.
Coordination	The head and tail players should coordinate to keep the lion's body coherent. The coordination of stances, steps and the difficult movements should be coherent and accord with the lion's behavior.
The dance of lion	The lion's various behaviors and the moods should be fully imitated and followed by the players.

2.4 Cultural experience

- **The three different colors about lion head: black, red and yellow in Nanshi**

The three different colors represent the threeheroes' character in Peach Garden Oath—Liu Bei, Guan Yu and Zhang Fei. That's why they were named Liubei Lion, Guangong Lion and Zhangfei Lion. The dance of the Guangong Lion is bold and powerful, the Zhangfei Lion dance is rough and bellicose while the Liubei Lion dance is composed and imperatorial.

The music in Nanshi

The music is made up of drum, gong and cymbals. The drum makes"dong", gong makes "dang" while cymbals make "qiang".

The drum has three main playing styles named as three stars, five stars and seven stars. The sound of cymbals is summation tune. The gong works as rhythm control.

The three instruments work together to make different melody to control the changes of the rhythm and movement of the dance.

The lion's behaviors, expressions and difficult movements in Nanshi

The shapes and movements are presented by different gripping methods. Together with various stances, the integration of human and lion can fully be achieved.

The expressions of the lion are achieved by imitating its scare, doubt, tentative; and other movements like sleeping, waking, drunk, playing and watching are achieved via the mouth, eyes, ear or tail manipulation of the lion by the players.

The difficult movements means the difficult skills used during the performance, including throw, jump, body turning, roll, stand, waist twisting and stake standing, etc.

3 Conclusion

1. The basic skills and basic movements of Nanshi should be mastered.

2. The techniques in Nanshi is composed of lion-gripping, ready position, standing position, footwork as well as the coordination between the lion head and tail, etc.

3. Nanshi movement should present a lion's expressions and behaviors.

4 Extensive reading

1. After the mastery of all the skills, the players could start to create their own routine series of the movement, which should be close not only to a lion's form but to its spirit. The imitation should present the active spirit and the lion's power, violence, vigor and cleverness in its performance.

2. After the mastery of the basic skills and the routine series of "a waking lion jumping out of cave", the player should start to learn the combination with the music. The Nanshi music was made up of drum, gong and cymbals, in which, the drum is music score, gong is beat and cymbals are He (note). The first study part is the basic rhythm of the music, including "lei, zhen, ping, bu, san, kuai, qi", then the player could learn to dance with the music.

5 Questions

(1) What is the origin of Chinese Lion Dance and it's relationships with "the Silk Road"?

(2) What is the classification of Chinese Nanshi?

(3) What are the technique types for Nanshi?

(4) What are the musical instruments used in the drum music of Nanshi?

6 Reference books

[1] Yu Hanqiao. The status quo and development strategy of dragon and lion dance in China [D]. Wuhan Sport University, 2007, 3.

[2] International Dragon and Lion Dance Federation. The competition rules for international dragon and lion dance [M]. Beijing: People's Sport Press, 2008.

[3] Wei Zhiqiang. The dragon culture and movement in China [M]. Tianjin: Tianjin Ancient Works Publishing House. 2003.

[4] Huang Yisu. Dragon and lion dance and competition [M]. Changsha: Hunan Arts Publishing House. 1999.

[5] Chen Yaojia. The Southern Lion Dance [M]. Guangzhou: Guangdong Science and Technology Publishing House. 2007.